Panamá

Fourth Edition

Marc Rigole
Claude-Victor Langlois

Travel better, enjoy more

ULYSSES

Travel Guides

Offices

Canada: Ulysses Travel Guides, 4176 St. Denis Street, Montréal, Québec, H2W 2M5, ☎(514) 843-9447, ⇄(514) 843-9448, info@ulysses.ca, www.ulyssesguides.com

Europe: Les Guides de Voyage Ulysse SARL, 127 rue Amelot, 75011 Paris, France, ☎01 43 38 89 50, ⇄01 43 38 89 52, voyage@ulysse.ca, www.ulyssesguides.com

U.S.A.: Ulysses Travel Guides, 305 Madison Avenue, Suite 1166, New York, NY 10165, info@ulysses.ca, www.ulyssesguides.com

Distributors

U.S.A.: Hunter Publishing, 130 Campus Drive, Edison, NJ 08818, ☎800-255-0343, ⇄(732) 417-1744 or 0482, comments@hunterpublishing.com, www.hunterpublishing.com

Canada: Ulysses Travel Guides, 4176 St. Denis Street, Montréal, Québec, H2W 2M5, ☎(514) 843-9882, ext.2232, ⇄514-843-9448, info@ulysses.ca, www.ulyssesguides.com

Great Britain and Ireland: Roundhouse Publishing, Millstone, Limers Lane, Northam, North Devon, EX39 2RG, ☎1 202 66 54 32, ⇄1 202 66 62 19, roundhouse.group@ukgateway.net

Other countries: Ulysses Travel Guides, 4176 St. Denis Street, Montréal, Québec, H2W 2M5, ☎(514) 843-9882, ext.2232, ⇄514-843-9448, info@ulysses.ca, www.ulyssesguides.com

Canadian Cataloguing-in-Publication Data (see p 4)

Printed in Canada
ISBN 2-89464-431-0

It seems that if the world were to choose its capital,
the isthmus of Panamá would be appointed this illustrious destiny.

Simón Bolívar

Research and Writing
Marc Rigole
C.-Victor Langlois

Publisher
André Duchesne

Editor
Daniel Desjardins

English Editing
Jacqueline Grekin
Cindy Garayt

Production Assistance
Julie Brodeur
Amber Martin

Page Layout
Isabelle Lalonde

Computer Graphics
André Duchesne

Cartographer
Isabelle Lalonde

Artistic Director
Patrick Farei (Atoll)

Illustrations
Lorette Pierson
Marie-Annick Viatour
Stéphanie Kitembo

Photography
Cover Page
IPAT
Inside pages
IPAT

Acknowledgements: Special thanks to **Azmy J. Juárez Duarte**, **Héctor Jiménez Barsallo** and **Agadir G. Vasquez** for their contribution and tireless support.

We gratefully acknowledge the financial support of the Government of Canada through the Book Publishing Industry Development Program (BPIDP) for our publishing activities. We would also like to thank the government of Québec for its SODEC income tax program for book publication.

National Library of Canada Cataloguing-in-Publication

Main entry under title:

Panamá

(Ulysses travel guide)
Includes index.

ISSN 1493-3837
ISBN 2-89464-431-0

Panama – Guidebooks. I.Series.

F1563.5.R5413 917.28704'53 C00-300460-0

Symbols

≡	Air conditioning
bkfst incl.	Breakfast included
⊗	Fan
⇄	Fax number
⏲	Fitness centre
hw	Hot water
K	Kitchenette
≈	Pool
pb/sb	Both private and shared bathrooms*
sb	Shared bathroom*
ℝ	Refrigerator
ℜ	Restaurant
⌂	Sauna
#	Screen
❂	Spa
☎	Telephone number
tv	Television
	Ulysses's favourite

*Note that all establishments have private bathrooms unless otherwise indicated.

Attraction Classification

★	Interesting
★★	Worth a visit
★★★	Not to be missed

Hotel Classification

$	$25 or less
$$	$25 to $50
$$$	$51 to $90
$$$$	$91 to $150
$$$$$	more than $150

Unless otherwise indicated, the prices in the guide are for one standard room, double occupancy in high season.

Restaurant Classification

$	less than $8
$$	$9 to $15
$$$	$16 to $25
$$$$	$26 to $40
$$$$$	$40 or more

Unless otherwise indicated, the prices in the guide are for a three-course evening meal for one person, not including drinks and tip.

All prices in this guide are in US dollars.

Table of Contents

Table of Contents *(continued)*

List of Maps

Map Symbols

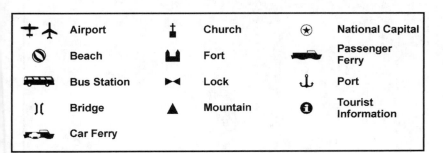

Airport	Church	National Capital
Beach	Fort	Passenger Ferry
Bus Station	Lock	Port
Bridge	Mountain	Tourist Information
Car Ferry		

Write to Us

The information contained in this guide was correct at press time. However, mistakes can slip in, omissions are always possible, places can disappear, etc. The authors and publisher hereby disclaim any liability for loss or damage resulting from omissions or errors.

We value your comments, corrections and suggestions, as they help us to keep each guide up to date. The best contributions will be rewarded with a free book from Ulysses Travel Guides. All you have to do is write us at the following address and indicate which title you would be interested in receiving.

Ulysses Travel Guides

4176 St. Denis Street
Montréal, Québec
Canada H2W 2M5

305 Madison Avenue
Suite 1166, New York
NY 10165

www.ulyssesguides.com
E-mail: ***text@ulysses.ca***

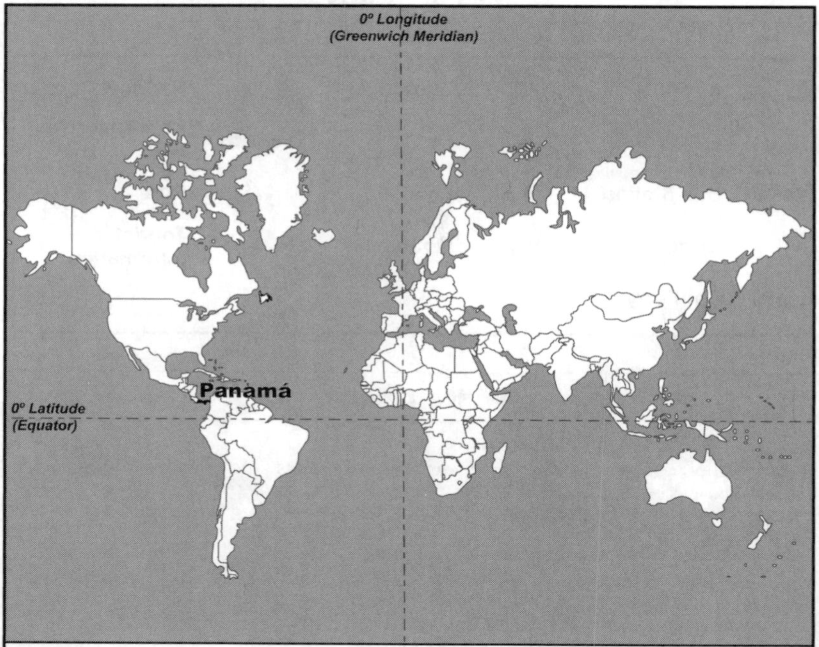

Where is Panamá?

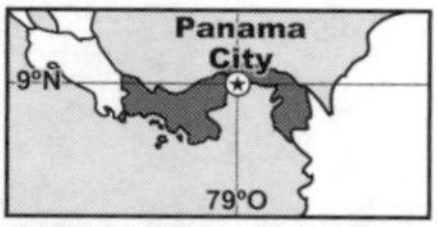

Panamá	
Capital:	Panama City
Language:	Spanish
Population:	3,000,000 inhab.
Currency:	Balboa
Area:	75,650 km²

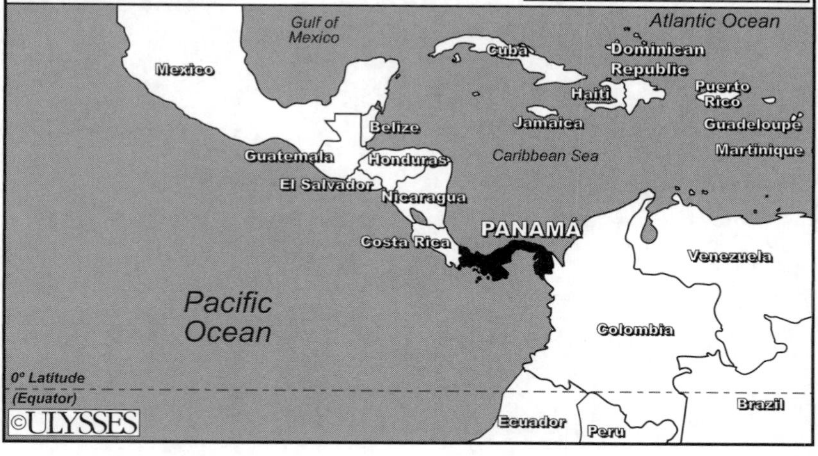

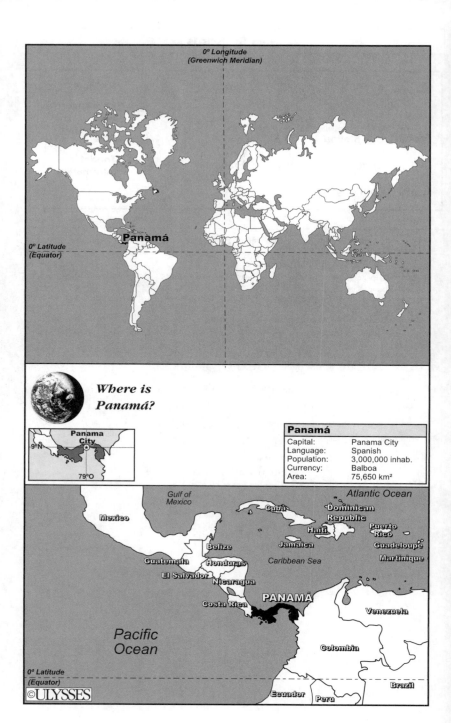

Portrait

Panamá, Central America's fourth-largest country, boasts a rich variety of landscapes within its 75,650km^2.

Bordered by Costa Rica to the west and Colombia to the east, Panamá forms a *S*-shaped bridge, extending 750km between the two Americas. Long and narrow (except for the Azuero peninsula), Panamá is bounded on either side by two of the world's great oceans, the Atlantic and the Pacific, and crossed by a mountain chain stretching almost its entire length. The highest peaks in this range are in the west, dominated by the 3,475m volcano, Barú. On the east side, the highest peak is Mount Tacarcuna, at 1,875m.

Geography

The Panamanian territory encompasses 2,866km of coastline and a great number of islands, scattered on either side of the isthmus. The two oceans are separated by only 51.4km at the country's narrowest point. With 153 rivers draining into the Atlantic and 325 into the Pacific, Panamá has an ample supply of fresh water as well.

From a geological standpoint, this part of the world is relatively new, Central America having been formed only three or four million years ago. The Cocos plate began its eastward shift some 20 million years ago, colliding with the Antilles plate and sliding partway underneath it, thus causing the temporary emergence of several islands. Much later—three to four million years ago—the movement of the plates became more pronounced, and new upheavals brought forth volcanoes, mountains and new land. This formed a "bridge" between the two continents, which had been separated until that time.

Though Panamá lies on the famous Pacific fire belt, it is still the safest of all Central American countries from a volcanic standpoint. Also, thanks to its geographic location, the isthmus is spared the terrible hurricanes that regularly ravage this part of the world.

Another great upheaval, although much more modest in scale and created by humans, was the construction of the Panamá Canal. This giant undertaking altered the face of the country significantly. When the canal was dug, and the Río Chagres was diverted, a large area was flooded. The result was the 425km^2

Lago Gatún; the mountain peaks left above water formed a number of artificial islands on which many animals took refuge (see p 125).

Flora and Fauna

Approximately three million years ago, the two American continents (North and South America) were connected by a narrow strip of land creating a land bridge or isthmus. As a result, this bridge has been crossed not only by humans, but also by the flora and fauna from both sub-continents. Thus, Panamá, with its varied climates and location between the two land masses, is a natural "biodome" with a diverse plant and animal life. Contrary to what one might believe, the original Panamanian forest is one of the largest in Central America, because the isthmus is sheltered from devastating hurricanes. While the vegetation varies enormously depending on the altitude and the richness of the soil, the country's flora can be roughly divided into two major types: equatorial and grassland. Along with these are all kinds of variations that have developed differently according to location and altitude.

The explorer Gonzalo Fernández de Oviedo y Valdés was one of the first Europeans to describe Panamá's fauna and flora, which are detailed in his writings from his voyage in 1513, entitled *Historia general y natural de las Indias*. However, the first truly scientific expedition to the tropics was organized by the Académie Royale Française des Sciences, from 1735 to 1744, and supervised by Charles Marie de la Condamine. Condamine's aides-de-camp left a substantial amount of written information on the natural riches of the isthmus. Much later, in the 19th century, the famous German scientist Alexander von Humboldt wrote a wealth of information about the tropics, gained through his many journeys.

Fauna

Because of its microclimates and geographical location on the Central American isthmus, Panamá has the greatest number of animal species in the world. Biodiversity, or the variety of plant or animal species, is measured by the number of species found in a particular area. Panamá is particularly renowned as a bird-watching paradise, with over 900 species of birds. Many different kinds of birds can be seen without having to travel very far.

Like the tourists seeking sun and sandy beaches, many birds migrate from North America to Panamá in the winter. These include swallows, buntings, thrushes, and warblers, among others.

Quetzal

Visitors will surely be amazed by the colours of the various species of toucans and parakeets. The saffron toucan and the majestic scarlet macaw are definitely among the world's most beautiful birds and are relatively easy to spot in certain areas of the country. The most ulustrious bird, however, is the quetzal. The quetzal is a rather large bird (up to 35cm) with a long emerald tail up to 60cm long. It lives in the tropical rain forests of the provinces of Chiriquí and Bocas del Toro. The best time for bird-watching is between January and May, during nesting season. At other times of the year, quetzals can also be seen in Parque Nacional La Amistad with the help of a good guide.

Curious travellers will have the opportunity more than anywhere else to see wildlife that is very much alive and very well adapted to its environment. In addition to the many bird species, this tiny corner of the planet is also home to some 15,000 kinds of butterflies, more than 200 mammals and reptiles, about 100 species of freshwater fish and amphibians, and countless insects. Many of these animals are indigenous to Panamá.

The animals visitors are most likely to see in Panamá are monkeys (white-faced capucin, howler and spider), sloths, agoutis, coatis, iguanas, lizards, toads, crocodiles and small brightly-coloured poisonous frogs. Mammals such as anteaters, tapirs and large felines (jaguars, pumas, ocelots) are harder to spot, but they sometimes leave their tracks behind. The country also has several kinds of snakes, including vipers and boas. Four of the eight types of marine turtles visit Panamá's beaches, where the females lay their eggs.

Common Symbols and Their Meaning

The turtle symbolizes fertility.

The lizard symbolizes prudence and speed.

The bird of prey symbolizes authority.

The puma and the jaguar symbolize pride, cunning, skill and strength.

Flora

According to a vegetation classification system devised by biologist L.H. Holdridge in 1947, there are some 116 life zones on earth. These observations are based on the different types of climates, temperature changes, precipitation, as well as seasonal changes. Due to Panamá's great diverse climatic conditions and very rugged terrain, the country has 12 life zones as well as eight transition zones.

Lagoons, marshes, grasslands, mangroves, plains, dry tropical forests, tropical humid forests and subalpine plains make up the Panamanian landscape, depending on the altitude and region. The country's high mountains have some of the lowest temperatures in Central America and their rivers flow into the Atlantic and Pacific oceans.

Although Panamá is a small country, it harbours 5% of all plant and animal species in the world. There are 10,000 species of plants (almost as many as in all of Europe), 1,000 species of trees as well as 1,200 species of orchids, including the national flower, **Espíritu Santo**, a white orchid.

While some plants produce poisons in order to protect themselves from herbivorous animals, others ensure their survival by producing particularly rich fruit which, when eaten and excreted by animals and insects, will spread the seeds far and wide.

The two main flowering seasons are at the beginning of the rainy season, from March to June, and at the end of the rainy season, September through October. Only the first one is essential for seed production.

An Exceptional Diversity

Biologists all over the world have long wondered why there is such a wide variety of flora and fauna in these regions. How is it that there are 10 or 15 times more species of trees in Central America than elsewhere? Why are there so many different types of animals, all with such widely divergent behaviour patterns and feeding habits? What could be the cause of such an explosion of life? Also, why is it that the same type of plant exists in several different regions, all far apart?

One possible answer might be the availability of protein in certain areas. Proteins are indispensable to every form of life. Made up of amino acids, they are found primarily in fruits, young leaves, shoots and seeds. Animals obtain amino acids by eating the shoots themselves or by eating other animals that have ingested them. In more temperate zones, where the change of seasons is pronounced, the arrival of spring heralds an awakening of nature, and a veritable explosion of young shoots yields an abundance of proteins.

The animals that depend on this type of food have adapted their way of life to the cycle. Birds migrate, and when mammals bear their young, an extraordinary abundance of food awaits the newborn. Protein production is all the greater because the seasons are short, and each plant must generate enough to ensure its own survival.

In tropical regions, however, things are different: the warm climate enables plants to develop year-round. Because of the heat and the difficulty of producing large quantities of proteins all year, species have had to find all sorts of ways to escape predators. This has led to two phenomena: diversity and disparity. Some plants have developed means of defence, like thorns, or the production of caustic substances. Others, of the same species, have spread into various regions and flower at different times to avoid being eaten all at once by voracious birds and mammals. These different means of defence have complicated the hunt for food, thus resulting in the same disparity and diversity among wildlife. The animals have had to specialize in their search for food, either by developing a specific morphology (a beak adapted to a particular food type), or by a specific type of behaviour that could be termed mutualism—a type of association between plant and animal. Some plants even go so far as to produce substances that are useful to certain insects, which in turn protect the plants against predators. This mutualism can also apply to the animal kingdom.

Tropical Dry Forest

The tropical dry forest is disappearing in Central America. Only about 2% of it is left, some in Panamá, more specifically in the central provinces.

Before the land was cleared, the Azuero Peninsula was made up of savannah. Now the land is covered by pastures, as well as cacti and other semi-arid vegetation. Deforestation has intensified the dry and rainy seasons, making the dry season, which runs from December to April, a desert-like climate where rainfall is almost non-existent. Some trees have even adapted to the lack of ground water by shedding their leaves.

The arrival of the rainy season brings relief and makes the desert bloom again. The grass becomes green, flowers burst with brilliant colours and the trees blossom with white, yellow, red and pink flowers.

The Tropical Rain Forest

The tropical rain forest is very diverse in Panamá, both on the Atlantic (Caribbean Sea) and the Pacific coasts, and even in the centre of the country. Like the Amazon, whose rain forests are better known, parts of Panamá receive at least 2,000mm of rain each year, sometimes as much as 6,000mm, especially in the provinces of Darién, Chiriquí and Bocas del Toro. Humidity is also very high, and the annual temperature fluctuates little from its average of approximately 24°C.

A constant supply of water is clearly essential to the survival of the tropical rain forest. In fact the tropical rain forest recycles 75% of its water through evaporation. Rain forest soils, for the part, are very thin and nutrient-poor. Nutrients are stored in living organisms it suck up plant and animal nutrients from the soil through their roots. Termites and mushrooms rapidly decompose dead vegetation making it available to trees.

Altitude also plays an important role in the rain forest's vegetal composition. The tropical rain forest starts at 1,000m in Panamá and vegetation gets sparser the higher the elevation. Between 1,000 and 3,000m, the forest is extremely dense, with mosses, lichens, lianas, vines, shrubs and trees whose canopy is shrouded in mist. Only vegetation that can adapt to the harsh climate grows above 3,000m, such as stunted shrubs. You can see this type of vegetation by climbing above the tree line in the high mountains of the Talamanca Cordillera, especially on the Barú volcano (3,475m).

Deforestation

Before the Spanish conquistadors set foot on its shores in the 16th century, Panamá was almost entirely made up of rich natural forests. Only small sections had been deforested by the Indigenous peoples, to grow corn and cassava, and other crops. When the Spanish colonized the country, they began clearing forested areas to make way for towns and later for crops, such as bananas and coffee, or for pastures.

Deforestation proceeded at a relatively moderate rate until the mid-20th century, when it took off at a drastic pace. Thus, it is extremely important to protect the existing forests and implement an efficient reforestation policy. If not, the deforestation of tropical rain forest will cause an ecological disaster and it will take decades, if not centuries before anything can grow again.

Deforestation has done more than just deface some of the most beautiful natural landscapes in Panamá. Soil erosion has actually created deserts in the central provinces. During the dry season, water for domestic and industrial consumption becomes scarcer. Some rivers dry up, endangering much of their flora and fauna. During the rainy season, floods cause the most extensive damage.

Environmental Conservation

The environmental movement sprang up in the United States and Europe in the 1960s, focusing attention on the importance of protecting natural resources including forests. These groups viewed the United States national park system as the basic model for conservation. However, since the population of tiny Panamá doubled within 20 years (1950-1970) and was distributed evenly throughout the country, farmers and breeders considered the forest conservation project as a threat to their prosperity. The challenge was to find a way to protest the forests while involving the local population and maintaining their livelihood. This is the notion of "sustainable development", economic development that does not occur at the expense of the natural environment and of the people who depend on it. For sustainable development to be successful, governments and environmental organizations must get more involved and set up programs to better educate the public about development.

Orchids

A Few Examples of Panamanian Flora and Fauna

Orchids: These flowers are known around the world for their beauty and their scent. There are more than 35,000 different species. While some spring directly from the soil, others are epiphytes, attaching themselves to other plants without taking their food; still others feed on decaying plant life. Orchids are part of the group Orchidaceae, which provide us, among other things, with vanilla flavouring.

Quetzals: This bird, part of the Trogonidae family has been called the most beautiful in the world. Birds of this group are unique in that they can remain motionless for up to an hour watching their prey which, after the slightest movement, is devoured. The average quetzal is 35cm long and its tail can reach a length of 60cm. The bird is of great symbolic cultural importance to indigeous peoples, and its feathers were once worn by high dignitaries. Its name is also associated with the pre-Columbian god of vegetation and regeneration, Quetzalcóatl. The god was represented by a serpent covered with quetzal feathers. The bird has bright green feathers on most of its body and vivid red ones on its stomach. Two very long tail feathers give it a striking elegance in flight. On its head is a small crest. Males have a yellow beak, females, a black one.

Although the quetzal is very popular, especially among ecotourism operators, many of which tout it as one of the country's major attractions, you will have difficulty spotting one in the wild, since they make their home in isolated areas between 1,200m and 3,000m above sea level in the humid tropical forests from the south of Mexico all the way to Panamá, where it is mostly found in the provinces of Chiriquí and Bocas del Toro. The best months to see it are from January to May, during nesting season. The rest of the year, it can be seen in Parque Nacional La Amistad with the help of a good guide.

The quetzal digs its nest in the trunk of a tree—generally a disceased tree whose wood is soft; the bird's beak is quite fragile and cannot penetrate hard wood. Then male and female build the nest and incubate the eggs together. When the male is sitting on the eggs, he tucks his long tail feathers behind his head and lets them hang out of the nest, so as not to damage them. Quetzal-watching entails an expedition into regions that are difficult to get to, and requires patience. It is therefore wise to go with an experienced guide.

Toucans: Next to the quetzal, the toucan is probably the most curious bird on the isthmus. There are some 40 species in the toucan family, known for their unique, colourful beaks, which grow to an impressive size (up to a third of the length of the bird's body) and appear massive and heavy, but are actually very light. The toucan's feathers are rather plain compared to its beak, whose striking colours apparently serve above all to frighten predators. Toucans are also reputated to be among the noisiest of birds. Observing them in the wild is not easy, since they often perch at the top of trees. They are very social, and you will often see them in small groups.

Hummingbirds: There are some 100 species of hummingbirds in Central America. Their feathers come in an infinite variety

Toucan

of colours. What distinguishes them most is their swiftness and agility: their wings can beat up to 79 times a second, allowing them to fly backwards. Their heart rate has been clocked at an incredible 273 beats per min!

Monkeys: Contrary to popular belief, there are not as many types of monkey in Central America as there are in Asia or Africa. In fact, there are only six types: the howler, the capuchin, the tamarin, the spider, the squirrel and the owl. They are distinguished from monkeys on other continents by several traits. Some species have a prehensile tail with which they can grasp trees, and all have broad noses, unlike the narrow noses of monkeys elsewhere in the world. There are also behavioural differences: they generally live in groups and in some races the males take care of educating the young. These patterns are peculiar to Central American monkeys.

The howler monkey is also called alouatta palliata. Alone or in a group, it can emit sounds that would frighten the most courageous person. The howl, which can carry very far, is intended to warn one group of the presence of another. It is also a means of communicating within the same group. When two groups meet, each tries to out-howl the other and frighten it away. This creates the impression of some ferocious battle between wild animals, but the confrontation is usually limited to lugubrious noise-making.

The howler monkey is one of the animal species being studied by the famous Smithsonian Tropical

Howler monkey

Research Institute on Isla Barro Colorado. Their research has revealed that the howler monkey has a very special kind of diet: about 50% of the monkeys' diet comes from at least 50 different kinds of plants, the other half composed of fruits and flowers. This may seem like a lot of food, but the monkeys population growth is very irregular and there can be food shortages some years. Further studies have revealed another factor essential for population growth: monkeys eat only the young leaves, which are richer in vitamins and contain fewer toxins than adult leaves but only grow at certain times of the year. Although the gestation period of howler monkeys usually coincides with the budding season, a variety of factors can delay the leaves from sprouting, causing an estimated 60% to 80% of young monkeys to die from malnutrition before the age of five.

Sloths: This strange-looking mammal moves extremely slowly, has long, curved claws, and hangs from branches, where it eats leaves and fruit. Strangely, its fur is covered with algae and butterfly larvae, which make for excellent camouflage. Once a week, the animal comes down from its tree to relieve itself. There are two species of sloth: one has two fingers, and the other three. Both are found mainly in the Darién forests and in isolated regions.

History

The PreColumbian Period

With the help of various objects unearthed during archaeological digs, it can be concluded that human life existed in Central America as far back as 12,000 (some say 20,000) BCE It is reasonable to assume that this can also be said for Panamá. The oldest traces of activity to be discovered in Panamá specifically are stone arrow tips dating back to 11,000 BCE Stone statues from before 2,000 BCE and small stone tables on which grain was ground (*metates*) have been found in the province of Chiriquí. Certain pieces of pottery date back to the same period. While there are no large monuments like those from other indigenous civilizations like the Mayas or the Aztecs, a number of handcrafted items tell us that the indigenous peoples of Panamá knew much about pottery and metalwork. The most oldest piece of ceramic work in Central America was discovered at the oldest-known site in Panamá, the village of Monagrillo in the province of Herrera. It dates back to 2,130 BCE The skill of the artisans is borne out in richly coloured pottery, whose handles are shaped like small animals such as frogs and lizards. Already, artisans were using a technique similar to what we call bisque. It would appear that most regions had their own style of pottery, and through various excavations it has been determined that this craft did not develop at the same rate everywhere. The provinces of Chiriquí, Veraguas and Coclé, for instance, were highly developed in comparison with Darién.

Iron and gold work were equally important, and in this, the indigenous peoples of the province of Coclé excelled. Their mastery of precious metalwork is evident in the magnificent specimens discovered on the archaeological site of Sitio Conte (near Natá). Among the many objects found here are numerous pieces of gold jewellery, sometimes representing animals or half-human figures. These *huacas* are on display at the Museo Antropológico Reina Torres de Araúz in Panama City (see p 82).

The use of semi-precious and precious stones, like emeralds, in ornaments tells us that countries like Colombia and Mexico

The Horn of Plenty

Not only did the indigenous peoples know a great deal about making pottery, they also had a vivid imagination. A lovely example of this is the horn of plenty. It rests on three hollow feet, with a small earthen marble in one of them. When the object is shaken, the marble makes a noise, creating the impression that the horn is full.

were already trading in such materials. Some of these items look exactly like gold, indicating that the indigenous people were also masters at the art of preparing and applying paint.

Unfortunately, we know very little about the many peoples who lived on the isthmus in pre-Columbian times. While the settlers may have taken great care in enumerating the precious things taken from the indigenous peoples, the writings of the time teach us very little about the way of life of these people. We know that in the early years of colonization most of the western territories of the country were controlled by two powerful groups, probably Guaymi tribes. The Azuero peninsula was ruled by a chief named Parita, and the land even farther to the west, by one named Urracá. Little is known about the customs of this period, largely because many of the tombs have been looted. Various excavations have, however, shed some light on the subject.

During the digs near Natá, graves containing 32 human skeletons were unearthed. When an important warrior chief died, he was buried not only with his household servants but also with his wife (or wives; he was allowed several). His possesions (pottery, gems, etc.) were buried with him. Research has taught us that during the funeral, which lasted several days, the dead chief's wives went down into the grave, sat down on a bench, and proceeded to get drunk on *chicha* (a fermented corn-based drink). After the ceremony, when the chief's body had been put into the grave along with his household servants and wives, the grave was filled with earth, and the chief's companions were buried alive. Customs varied according to the region and era. Some graves containing large urns full of human bones have been discovered, others containing only the personal belongings of the deceased. Sometimes the dead were burned. A great deal of mystery still surrounds the many tribes and the wide variety of sites they inhabited, all of which are still being studied.

The Colonial Period

Discovering the Isthmus

In 1500, Castilian Rodrigo Galván de Bastidas, accompanied by a young explorer named Vasco Núñez de Balboa, set sail for the New World from Cadiz, Spain in the hopes of discovering untold riches.

After sailing up the Venezuelan coast, they continued west past the Bay of Cartagena and the Gulf of Urabá (between Colombia and Venezuela) to Darién in present-day Panamá. After a brief stop there, they continued up the Panamanian coast until Nombre de Dios. From there, his ships in bad condition, Bastidas headed for nearby Hispañolia (today the Dominican Republic and Haiti) for some much-needed repairs. Thus, Bastidas was the first explorer to discover the Central American isthmus.

Later that year, another expedition, this one headed by Alonso de Ojeda and including cartographer Juan de la Costa and Amerigo Vespucci (see box "Amerigo Vespucci," in this chapter) explored Panamá's Caribbean coast before heading towards Hispañolia. Despite the discovery of these new lands, no permanent settlements were established. Towards the end of 1502, accompanied by his brother Dom Bartolomé,

Columbus explored the Honduran coast up to Portobelo Bay in Panamá. Columbus was warmly received by the indigenous people there and was showered with large quantities of jewellery and gold objects. This led Columbus to believe there was more gold in the area and he set sail for Hispaniola, where a ship awaited him to return to Spain. However, his plans fell awry when a sudden storm ran the ship aground on a sandbank at the mouth of present-day Río Belén. Trapped for some time, he decided to establish a permanent settlement there which he named Santa María la Antigua de Belén and entrusted to his brother before departing. Shortly after Columbus's departure, a chief named Quibián attacked the colonists and destroyed the village, forcing them to flee for their lives. Thus ended the first attempt at colonization.

Vasco Núñez de Balboa: An Exceptional Destiny

Little is known about the early life of Balboa. He was born between 1475 and 1477, probably in Badajoz (Jérez de Badajoz), Galicia (Spain). Of noble but poor origin, he was presumably the son of Don Nuño Arias de Balboa and a Badajozian woman. Young Vasco was apparently educated by Don Pedro Puertocarrero, nicknamed the "deaf seigneur" because of his hearing impairment. It was also at this time that Christopher Columbus set off from the neighbouring village of Palos de la Frontrera for the New World. Balboa, fed by these rumours of gold and riches, became passionate about finding a passage to the East, particularly India.

After having completed his apprenticeship as a knight under Puertocarrero, Balboa left for Seville where he worked for explorer Rodrigo de Bastidas. Towards the end of 1501, Balboa, along with Bastidas and cartographer Juan de la Cosa, set sail from the port of Cadiz hoping to reach the mysterious *tierra incógnita* that he had dreamed of for so long.

After stopping in the Canary Islands, Bastidas

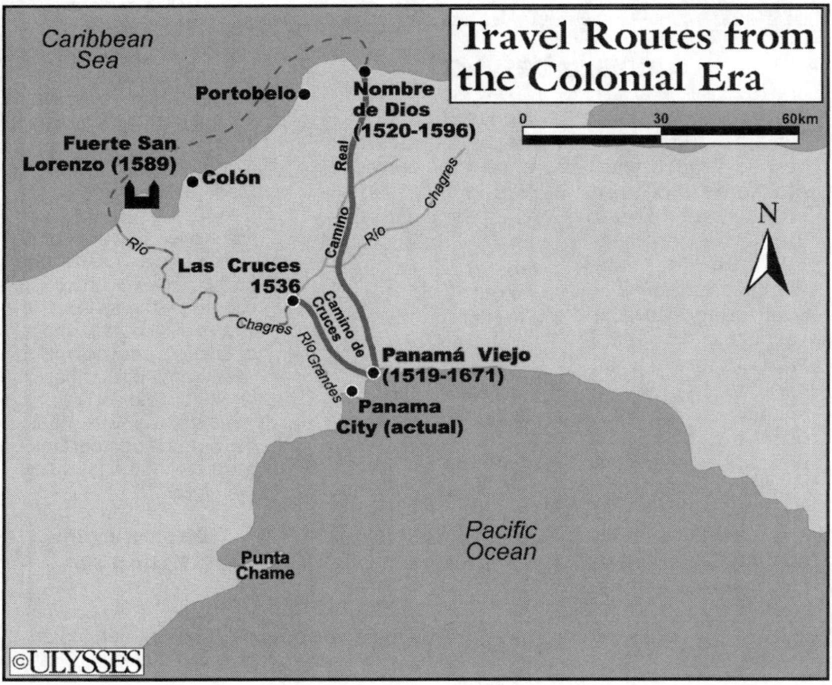

followed the route of Columbus's third voyage, passing Trinidad and Tobago, the Paria Peninsula and Isla Margarita off the Venezuelan coast. After crossing the Gulf of Maracaibo and the La Guajira Peninsula (the furthest west any explorer had ever gone before) they arrived in the Bay of Urabá, where they settled temporarily. It was during this voyage that Balboa met "Indians" for the first time. The Spanish traded the indigenous peoples' baubles (knives, tools, little bells, glass pearls, etc.) for what they believed to be pure gold but was actually only *guanín*, or an alloy of gold and copper. The indigenous peoples, according to Spanish accounts from this journey, feared the conquistadors' horses, because they had never seen any before.

After leaving the Bay of Urabá, Bastidas and Balboa briefly explored the coast of Darién, then sailed to the island of Hispaniola. Shipwrecked near Port-au-Prince, they finally reached Santo Domingo by an overland route.

Because of his involvement in the conquest of Hispaniola, its governor rewarded Balboa with slaves and land in which he founded a colony, Salvatierra de la Sabana.

In 1510, after several disastrous years as a farmer, Balboa secretly embarked on a ship bound for the Bay of Urabá. Finding nothing but an abandoned settlement, he headed further west, where he believed there was rich, fertile land. Soon after reaching a bay where they were greeted with hostility by the indigenous residents, the crew retaliated. Ignorant of local customs, the Spaniards tortured men who wore dresses. These men were supposed to supervise the work of the women, and tradition dictated that they wear long garments. The conquistadors believed them to be homosexuals instead, and punished them by burning them at the stake. The first settlement in Panamá, La Guardia, was founded after this tragedy.

The small village grew steadily because of the surrounding fertile soil and its location next to the mouth of a river, creating a natural port. In November 1510, Balboa had the village renamed Santa María la Antigua del Darién. The village's rapid growth led to a conflict of authority between Balboa Enciso. The governor named by the Spanish Courts. Taking advantage of Enciso's unpopularity in the colony, Balboa had him deported and took charge of the settlement. In 1511, Balboa became governor of the province of Darién.

Amerigo Vespucci

Born in Florence in 1454, Amerigo Vespucci sailed with Alonso de Ojeda on his first expedition to the New World in 1499. After four expeditions along the South American coast, Vespucci was named ***Piloto Mayor***, or chief explorer, by the Spanish crown. He used this title and his reputation in the Spanish court to pretend to be the first to discover the American continent. This is why cartographer Martin Waldseemüller of Lorraine published a map of the New World in 1507, in which he called the new continent ***Americi Terra***. In a way, Vespucci did discover America: unlike Columbus, who believed he had found the Far East, Vespucci realized that America was indeed a new continent. Although the mistake was later rectified, the American continent still bears Vespucci's name.

Discovering the Mar del Sur

In May 1511, Balboa set off with 200 men to conquer a land further west called Cueva, which the Indigenous peoples at Darién had told him was full of riches. Balboa took their chief, Careta, to help him find this land of riches, and in return promised to help overcome the chief's closest enemies, chiefs Ponca and Comogre. As dictated by local custom, the chief secured the deal by offering his tribe's women to Balboa's men, and his own daughter, Anayansi, to Balboa.

The whole village was then converted to Christianity and Careta baptised and renamed Fernado. With the help of their new allies, Babloa's troops succeeded in overcoming Ponca; then they continued further west to Chief Comogre's village where they were unexpectedly welcomed and given food and gold. After swearing allegiance to Balboa, the entire village was baptised and Comogre renamed Carlos. This conquest proved to be particularly fruitful, because it was here that Balboa was told for the first time about a vast stretch of water that lay beyond the mountains, possibly another ocean. The indefatigable Balboa pushed forward with his expeditions, but at the same time native hostility was building; the region's chiefs formed an alliance to chase away the great white chiefs and thus liberate the territory of Darién.

Once again, history turned bloody as Balboa ordered the chiefs killed and their villages burned as punishment for their participation in the plot. Finally, around 1513, two caravels arrived from Spain with long-awaited supplies, horses and settlers to increase the colony's population.

Vasco Núñez de Balboa decided to return to the Cueva region in August of 1513 to find the vast stretch of water, with the help of men provided by chief Careta. After a long jungle trek, they arrived in the village of Quareca on September 24 only to be greeted by a hail of arrows. Nevertheless, Balboa and his men managed to capture the village.

This time around, the victims were sacrificed to a hoard of ravenous dogs who devoured them before Balboa's steadfast gaze and the encouragement of his soldiers. The next day, the conquistadors continued on to Chief Porque's village and spotted the Pacific Ocean for the first time from the top of a nearby mountain.

What Balboa had actually seen was the Golfo de San Miguel. After resting in the seaside native vllage of Chape, 38-year old Balboa officially claimed the Mar de Sur in the name of the Spanish king and queen, Ferdinand and Juana, on September 29, 1513. Another aspiring explorer who was part of the expedition, Francisco Pizarro, had no idea of the great fate that awaited him, for it was he who would discover the Equator and Peru.

Shortly after claiming the territory, Balboa pursued his voyage along the coast as far as present-day Punta de San Lorenzo, where he once again sacked native villages and stole large quantities of their gold. Spurred on by rumours of even greater riches, he continued as far as the Las Perlas Archipelago. After landing on an island he baptised Isla Rica (present-day Isla del Rey) and gathering a large quantity of pearls, he decided to return to Santa María la Antigua in November 1513 and finally arrived there on January 19, 1514.

Arrival of Pedrarías and the Era of Plots

Merchant Pedro de Arbolancha arrived in Panamá at the end of January 1514 in search of new markets. Arbolancha informed Balboa that the court had named him the new governor of the Castilla d'Oro (the new name for the province of Darién). Balboa, hoping for a restitution of his authority, entrusted Arbolancha with a letter to the Spanish court claiming the discovery of the Mar del Sur in the name of the Spanish crown.

The Crown answered Balboa by sending a new governor, Pedro Arias de Ávila, also known as Pedrarías, to Darién on June 26, 1514. Pedrarias arrived with about 2,000 settlers; including bureaucrats, churchmen and workers, in addition to all kinds of supplies. Pedrarías had difficulty putting up with Balboa's governing of the colony right from the start. He blamed Balboa for the poor cramped conditions of the town: there were only 200 houses in Santa María la Antigua del Darién at the time, around which were clustered close to 1,500 indigenous people. Despite the presence of a church and hospital, Pedrarías was humiliated to be named governor of such a small colony. Although his initial reaction was to throw Balboa in jail, he changed his mind after the bishop warned him against it, citing Balboa's popularity.

Several months later, in December 1514, a new caravel arrived with a message from the court recognizing Balboa's merits (as discoverer of the Mar del Sur); the governor was instructed to consult Balboa for all important decisions. This assault on his authority made Balboa a sworn enemy in Pedrarías's eyes. Then followed a long period of intrigue and conflict during which Pedrarías plotted and schemed to get rid of his rival, even resorting to attempted murder.

Jealous of Balboa's treaties with the *Cacignes*, Pedrarías organized a series of punitive raids against the indigenous peoples, wiping out all previous efforts to bring peace to the region.In addition, he authorized their enslavement, citing disobedience to the Crown. Francisco Pizarro, who participated in these attacks, would put Pedraria's principles into practice during his conquest of Peru and Ecuador.

In March of 1515, the Spanish court decided to create two new provinces, Panamá and Coiba, and put Balboa in charge of them. Humiliated once again, Pedrarías secretly began pillaging the new territories before Balboa even arrived. Sensing a plot against him, Balboa sent messengers to Cuba for help. Hearing of this on his return, Pedrarías accused Balboa of treason and proceeded to arrest him. Then followed one of the most bizarre episodes of the whole Spanish Conquest.

Fearing an uprising from Balboa's supporters, the bishop once again warned Pedrarías against executing Balboa. Instead, the bishop suggested a marriage between the two rival families. His logic was that in one fell swoop, as a relative of the governor of the southern provinces, Pedrarías would have de facto access to their riches, in addition to the court's protection. So in August 1516, Pedrarías married off his daughter, Doña María Peñalosa, to Balboa. Shortly afterwards, the newlyweds set out for the new colonies of Panamá and Coiba, where Balboa founded the town of Aclá.

The indefatigable Balboa, with the help of his men, then started La Compañía de la Mar del Sur to finance a new expedition to on the Pacific Coast. It was the first example of capitalist colonization, once again highlighting Balboa's tremendous organizational skills. As soon as the funds were gathered, the expedition set off. After crossing the isthmus for the second time, Balboa continued on towards Isla del Rey and along the South Coast until present-day Bahía Piña before returning to Aclá.

The Assassination of Balboa

In 1518, King Ferdinand of Spain died, leaving the throne to Charles V, a native of Flanders. That same year King Charles sent a new governor, Don Lope de Sosa, to Santa María la Antigua del Darién. Afraid Sosa would blame him for bad management of the colony and violence against the local native communities, Pedrarías came up with a diabolic scheme to have his new son-in-law, Balboa, accused instead. With the judge's complicity and the false testimony of several witnesses, a trial was held and Balboa found guilty and thrown in jail in Aclá. Francisco Pizarro, who would go on to conquer Peru, was one of these witnesses, betraying his former friend. Aclá was chosen as the location for the trial because it was far from the major towns; the news of the sentence would not spread as quickly, thus avoiding riots.

Balboa was condemned to death on January 21, 1519 and beheaded at dawn the next day in Aclá's public square. He was 44 years old.

After Balboa

After Balboa's death, Pedrarías de Ávila continued exploring the Panamanian coast and discovered Isla Taboga, before founding the small town of Nuestra Señora de la Asunción de Panamá on the mainland. The town prospered, while the fortunes of Santa María la Antigua del Darién declined. The city of Panamá, for its part, obtained the title of "Ciudad Real" or (Royal City) in 1521 because of its ideal location and constant development. The rest of the colonial history, not only of Panamá but of the entire isthmus as well as South America, is marked by infighting between governors and nobles, each wanting to control the new territories and especially their riches.

By founding the city of Panamá, the Spanish set up the first European trading post on the Pacific Coast. Beginning in 1519, the celebrated Camino Real would occupy an important place in the development of the isthmus. This road linked the city of Panamá with Nombre de Dios and Portobelo, and for years was used to carry treasures (gold, silver, precious handicrafts) from the conquered colonies in Colombia and Peru. Around 1533, another road, the Camino de Cruces, was built along the Río Chagres. The Chagres was navigable at certain times of the year, and it too was used to carry merchandise. For a long time, these roads would provide the shortest access between the two oceans.

Later, as the Spanish pressed on in their search for new riches in the west, towns like Natá, Parita and Los Santos were founded. The newly acquired territory was first called Castilla del Oro, because of the gold mines in the province of Coclé. The gradual westward progress was not accomplished easily, however. The names of towns like Natá and Parita, bestowed in honour of two mighty native warriors, testify to the many battles fought with the indigenous peoples.

Once the colony was well established, Castilla del Oro flourished on the strength of trade and the transportation of goods. With the conquest of the Inca empire and its fabulous treasures, and the discovery of the Philippines by Magellan in 1521, the isthmus acquired a new strategic importance that ensured its continued development and growth up until the 18th century. By the 16th century, goods from Asia were already passing through Panamá on their way to Europe. At the administrative level, Spain attached Castilla del Oro to New Granada (now Colombia, Venezuela and Ecuador) in 1739.

The increase in riches passing through the isthmus attracted the attention of pirates and drew the envy of other powers. Acts of piracy multiplied. Even with fortifications at Portobelo and San Lorenzo, the Spanish were not able to defeat the pirates, and in 1746 Spain stopped shipping goods via the Camino Real, sending them around Cape Horn instead. This decision had a major impact on transportation, and trade went down.

In the 18th and 19th centuries, there were many civil wars in the region, provoked largely by nationalist sentiment. The economy turned sour, and the country was poised on the brink of bankruptcy. The decision was made to break with Spain, and Panamá declared its independence on November 28, 1821, following the example of New Granada, to which it decided to annex itself. The new political entity thus formed was called Gran Colombia, and consisted of present-day Peru, Venezuela, Bolivia, Ecuador, Panamá and, of course, Colombia.

Despite these troubled times, Panamá experienced true cultural growth in the 18th and 19th centuries. The first university was created in 1749. By this time the country had become a cultural centre, teeming with activity, where grand schemes for pan-American unity were debated. The fact that this

Simón Bolívar

General Simón Bolívar was born in Caracas, Venezuela, in 1783. He earned his place in history for becoming the first person to try to bring the countries of Latin America together as one nation. After long struggles against Spanish domination, he succeeded in liberating Venezuela, Colombia, Ecuador, Perú and Bolivia. Emboldened by his victories, he created the republic of Gran Colombia (encompassing the latter states) and became its president. Despite his military success and the first Pan American congress in Panamá, El Libertador ("The Liberator," as he became known after the liberation of Caracas) was unable to keep the countries together and died a desperate man in Santa Marta, Colombia, in 1830. He is venerated as a hero, and his name has been given to several places in Latin America.

country was chosen by **Simón Bolívar** to host the first Pan American Congress testifies to the activitism that reigned there.

After a long period of economic stagnation and even decline, Panamá, because of its geographical location, experienced a sort of second wind, which continued into the 20th century, thanks to the United States. The year 1848 marked the beginning of the California gold rush. The east-west roads across the U.S. were uncertain and difficult, so most of the pioneers opted for a sea voyage via Panamá. In order to speed up the westward migrations, the Americans, with the agreement of Colombia, to which Panamá was attached at the time, built a railway across the isthmus. The first train crossed the country in 1855 (see p 158). The development of the American west would prove a determining factor in the joint history of the two countries and would later lead to the digging of the canal.

Independent Panamá

While a number of revolutions took place against the centralist Colombian government well before successions, the history of independent Panamá really begins early in the 20th century, a few years before the Americans launched the second phase of canal building (see p 117). At this time, Bogotá's lack of interest in this remote province led to a feeling of frustration among the local elite, who felt far removed from the seat of power. During this time, the French, under the direction of Ferdinand de Lesseps, fresh from his triumphant realization of the Suez Canal, obtained Colombia's permission to build and manage a canal connecting the Pacific to the Atlantic.

Tropical diseases and financial troubles, however, got the better of the French project, which failed in 1889, nine years after work began. The Americans, meanwhile, were becoming increasingly anxious to see a navigable route joining the two oceans—as much to ensure the rapid development of the American west as for strategic reasons. They were unable to reach an agreement with Colombia, which was wary of the great power's appetite.

A combination of regional frustrations within Panamá and American impatience ultimately led to the independence of the isthmus. On November 3, 1903, a rebellion broke out. Secession was proclaimed, and a provisional military government installed. The following day, the declaration of independence was drawn up, and on November 6, the United States recognized the new state. American warships, supporting the Panamanian revolution, were anchored offshore, and while the Colombians did try to recover their territory, there was really nothing they could do. Very shortly afterwards, the new republic signed a treaty with its new ally, granting it the canal zone in return for military protection and financial compensation for the territory administered (see p 117).

In the wake of independence, a series of governments succeeded each other. At the political level, only a relatively small number of influential persons (large landowners, merchants, and soldiers) played an important role. With the construction and development of the canal came a noticeable change in the evolution of political thought in the country. One aspect of this change was the nationalistic attitude of the people, characterized by a contradictory feeling: on the one hand the people wanted total independence from the United States, while on the other they enjoyed the comfort and financial advantages that resulted from the presence of the American installations.

Important Dates in Panamá's Recent Political History

In 1936, the United States stopped guaranteeing Panamá's independence, thereby granting the country complete freedom in the defence of its territory. The annual $250,000 payment for use of the canal zone was increased to $430,000.

In 1955, certain aspects of the canal treaty, including provisions on financial compensation, were amended by the Eisenhower-Remón Treaty. From that time on, the U.S. would pay about two million dollars a year to rent the canal zone.

In the 1960s, a number of student demonstrations were held demanding Panamanian sovereignty over the canal zone. As a result, the Panamanian flag began to fly over the zone.

In 1964, diplomatic relations with the U.S. were broken off in the wake of violent riots, which caused some 20 deaths. The revolt broke out when the governor of the canal decided to pull down the Panamanian flag, and resulted in a promise by President Roberto Chiari to review the dispute over the 1903 treaty unconditionally and without restriction. The U.S. thus opened the door to a possible return to the zone under Panamanian sovereignty.

On October 11, 1968, President Arnulfo Arias Madrid was overthrown in a coup d'état (he himself had assumed power in a rather undemocratic manner). The political parties and the National Assembly were dissolved, and a government made up of a military junta and a civilian cabinet was installed. At the end of 1969, the members of the junta were replaced by civilians under General Omar Torrijos, who had instigated the coup and was also head of the National Guard. Torrijos's policies were both nationalistic and open to social reforms for the poorer classes, and he played a major part in the country's political history. His accomplishments included a review of the constitution in 1972, re-establishment of diplomatic relations with Cuba, membership in the movement of non-aligned nations, nationalization of energy and telecommunications, creation of state enterprises and many cooperatives, legislation promoting banking, and the list goes on. He was also the first to concern himself with The indigenous peoples and to grant them any benefits.

His most important accomplishment, however, came about in 1977, when the Torrijos-Carter agreement definitively marked the end of the treaty of 1903. Under the new agreement, the entire canal zone would be restored to the Panamanians, and all U.S. soldiers withdrawn from the region by 1999. Moreover, by 1979, Panamá would officially recover sovereignty over the canal zone.

In 1979, however, the U.S. Congress passed legislation reserving for itself the right to ensure protection of the canal, even after 1999, if its security is threatened. With the Torrijos-Carter agreement and all the measures he had undertaken for the country, the general enjoyed great popularity and became a veritable hero. Although he had come to power in a rather undemocratic manner, and despite a dramatic increase in the debt, it can truthfully be said that Torrijos catalyzed Panamá's development, allowing his country to assume an important place in the world.

In July 1981, General Omar Torrijos died in an airplane accident. The military influence he left on the political scene led to a constant struggle for political control between the military and the civilian camps—a cruel test for democracy.

In 1983, Manuel Antonio Noriega was appointed chief of the Panamanian Defence Forces, formerly the National Guard.

In May 1984, the old party, which had formed a coalition (the Democratic National Union), was elected to power, with the Democratic Alliance as the opposition. Although the election was contested by the opposition on the grounds that the Democratic National Union had been directly supported by the military, Nicolás Arditto Barletta was appointed President of the Republic.

In September 1985, the decapitated body of Hugo Spadafora was found near the Costa Rican border. Spadafora had been known for his less than flattering statements about the army, and especially about General Noriega. The military was suspected, and a little later, on the "advice" of Noriega, President N. A. Barletta was "asked to resign." He was succeeded by the first vice-president, Eric Delvalle.

In June 1986 the American press printed its first allegations that Noriega was involved in drug trafficking. Tension mounted between the general and the United States.

In June 1987, a former soldier who had been dismissed made statements to the effect that Noriega had been involved in the murder of Spadafora, had rigged the 1984 elections and was linked to drug trafficking. Riots broke out. The opposition mounted what was called a "civic crusade" to force the government and Noriega to resign. A state of emergency was called for ten days, followed by savage repression. All constitutional guarantees were suspended and the opposition press was outlawed.

In 1988 and 1989, tensions between Panamá and the U.S. continued to mount. Delvalle may still have been president, but it was mainly Noriega who controlled the situation. In the meantime, the U.S. Justice Department openly accused the General of international drug trafficking. In accordance with U.S. wishes, Delvalle asked for the general's resignation. In the wake of a failed coup d'état, however, Noriega appointed Manuel Solís Palma president. The dismissed president called upon the U.S. to boycott his country. Skillfully manipulating the nationalist trend, Noriega took an aggressive stance with the Americans, and stirred up anti-American sentiment. At the same time, he founded the Battalions of Dignity in 1988. According to Noriega, this group was created to protect the country against US invasion and to preserve the integrity of the Republic. In fact, it was used to suppress all forms of opposition and to keep civilians under his thumb.

In May 1989 came a final political upset: the opposition coalition (ADOC) and its head, Guillermo Endara, were elected to power on a platform which included, the demilitarization of politics. However, the election results were cancelled, and Noriega named his own candidate, Francisco Rodríguez, president. As a result, a number of countries followed the example of the United States and broke diplomatic relations with Panamá.

In October 1989, a bloody coup d'état was mounted by the army, but it failed. In the wake of incidents implicating Panamanian soldiers and members of the U.S. Army, by mid-December the National

Assembly declared a state of war with the United States. General Noriega was appointed head of state with full powers. This declaration provided the United States with an excellent excuse for an invasion: the Americans living in Panamá were now in danger.

Operation Just Cause

On December 20, 1989, 13,000 American troops invaded the country with the aim of deposing the dictator Noriega, capturing him, and placing him in the hands of U.S. justice. The 12,500 American soldiers already stationed in Panamá joined in the operation. Noriega took refuge in the Vatican embassy, surrendering, after two weeks of siege. He was then transferred to Miami for his trial. Guillermo Endara was reinstalled as the legally elected president of Panamá.

As for the number of victims of the intervention, each side had its own set of figures. Unlikely though it may seem, figures ranged from 400 dea (according to the U.S. Defence Department) to 7,000 dead and 25,000 homeless, a discrepancy that gave rise to much debate. Regardless of the number of victims, one thing remains certain: there was a breakdown in dialogue between two nations, providing more proof of the need for nations to communicate rather than fight.

While it is not our task to take a political stand on Operation Just Cause, we must still consider two points: first, the Noriega regime cared little for such concepts as democracy and human rights, and many people suffered because of this. Tension was such that in recent years it had become dangerous to make anything but positive remarks about the government, while anti-American talk was good form. Shortly before the intervention, there was a veritable climate of terror, and the Battalions of Dignity were infiltrating every level of society in an effort to better control them. People were arrested for such simple things as carrying a white handkerchief (symbol of the opposition) on their person or in a car. Members of the opposition were routinely physically assaulted. It can safely be said that a majority of Panamanians longed for a return to democracy, and that Noriega's fall was greeted with relief.

The second point to be considered is that there appears to be a real problem with regard to the relations between some Central American countries and the United States. Briefly, one important factor would seem to be respect for democracy. As long as democratic states continue to support countries that care little for democracy and human rights (Noriega was actually trained by the U.S. Secret Service and acted as an agent for a while) solely in the interest of economic and strategic influence, aggressive relations between states will continue to be a problem. In the long term, the wisest investment is to establish relations with truly democratic countries that respect human rights.

After Noriega

Immediately following the U.S. invasion, Panamá suffered a rude economic awakening. In 1987, a few years before Noriega's downfall, the United States imposed a boycott on Panamá, hoping to provoke the downfall of the regime. This boycott prohibited all American enterprises from dealing with Panamanian companies. This had an extremely negative impact on tourism, among other things. The Panamanian GNP fell 16% between 1987 and 1989, and the country went heavily into debt.

In 1990, an agreement with the United States brought banking secrecy to a halt; from then on, financial institutions could now be investigated with a view to better controlling movements of money and avoiding it being laundered by drug dealers. Then, to help the country get started again, the U.S. Congress approved humanitarian assistance; its example was then followed by the European Community and Japan. From 1990 to 1992, Panamá's GNP gradually returned to its pre-1987 levels. But even with the foreign aid, the government was forced to dismiss many civil servants and, in order to reduce the immense accumulated debt, to make major budget cuts. A number of strikes broke out. Disagreement within the coalition and allegations of presidential corruption did nothing to improve the government's position.

As a result of the major disorganization that followed the U.S. invasion, 1991 saw an increase in violence and crime. After the invasion, a number of members of former paramilitary groups set up under Noriega found themselves unstructured but still armed, and they took advantage of the reorganization of the forces of order to attack banks, businesses and other properties. The government dissolved the Fuerzas de Defensa Nacional and created the Fuerza Pública.

In 1992, the ruling coalition proposed a referendum asking for the people's agreement on various constitutional amendments, in particular, abolition of the army. The reply to this particular question was "No." Also, with the departure of the Christian Democratic Party from the ruling coalition, the government was once again in a minority position in the National Assembly. Despite the failure of the referendum, and despite all the social unrest that year, the ruling power did meet with some success in its fight against crime.

Despite the many political crises within the coalition, and after reshuffling his government, Guillermo Endara remained in power, but his popularity continued to decline. He persisted in carrying out a severe policy of economic renewal at the expense of certain social programs. This renewal did produce some results, as Panamá entered a period of sustained growth. Guillermo Endara's greatest achievement, however, was the reestablishment of security in the country. Nevertheless, in May of 1994, Ernesto Pérez Balldares, candidate of the Partido Revolucionario Democrático, was elected president with 33.2% voter turnout. The widow of former president Arnulfo Arias, in power in the 1940s and 1950s, came second, while singer Rubén Blades had to settle for third. His movement, Papá Egoró, did, however, succeed in getting six deputies , who approve government initiatives elected to parliament.

The party in power, the PRD, was largely made up of politicians who supported Noriega during the 1980s. The old guard was thus making a comeback, even though it had abandoned any vague militaristic impulses. In January 1995, a coup, apparently linked to certain factions of the army, was exposed before it was too late. Superior officers promptly disassociated themselves with such non-democratic acts by making statements to that effect in the daily newspapers.

In August 1998, thinking he would reap the benefits of four years of sustained growth, President Ernesto Pérez Balladares called a referendum that would have allowed him to run for another term (according to Panamanian law presidents can only hold office for one five year term). More than 60% of voters voted not to extend his presidency. In addition to his government's involvement in several corruption scandals, the people reproached the billionaire president's running of the country like a private company, with little regard for the "little people" and the widening gap between rich and poor.

The Year 2000

No fewer than 12 political parties were represented in the May 1999 elections (presidential, legislative and provincial). From these parties, three coalitions were formed: Nueva Nación (including the outgoing president's PRD party), Acción Opositora and Unión por Panamá. Although the Nueva Nación coalition wisely allied itself with celebrities such as singer Rubén Blades and presented the son of famous general Omar Torijos (see p 25) as a candidate for the presidency, this was not enough to sway the voters to once again vote for the PRD. The Unión por Panamá won the majority of votes, and Mireya Moscoso became president of the republic with a platform promising to pay more attention to social problems. In any case, the new president not only won a landslide victory but became the first woman president of a country with a macho culture.

Modern Panamá

The celebrations in 2000 that marked Panamá's full sovereignty over the Canal Zone were very colourful, and the milestone was commemorated with cultural events of all kinds throughout the country. Since then, Panamá has assumed complete control over the canal's administration with exemplary efficiency. Of course, the traffic along the canal provides significant revenue to the republic, so it is obviously in the government's interest to manage it efficiently.

Whatever happens, the presence of U.S. military bases on Panamanian soil will long continue to impact the current Panamanian political scene. The disastrous political situation in neighbouring Colombia and the persistent rumours of the infiltration of drug-trafficking militias via the Darién province are linked to this state of affairs. It is highly probable that the Panamanian state will continue to allow a minimal U.S. military presence in the region, especially since the presence of highly paid American soldiers generates an extra source of revenue.

Population

Although Panamá experienced very strong demographic growth between 1911 and 1998 (its population rose from 336,000 to 3,000,000), it is still quite scarcely populated, with 35 inhabitants per square kilometre.

As is the case in many other Latin American countries, Panamá's population is primarily young and urban. Panamá is unique, however, because of its great ethnic diversity. Aside from the native population (6%) and the descendants of the Spanish conquerors (10%), its population is made up of a good many descendants of the workers of various nationalities who participated in the construction of the canal.

While the great majority of Panamanians are of mixed origins (70%), there are also blacks of African descent. The black population is made up of two groups with distinct origins. The first group (mostly from Jamaica) came during the construction of the canal, and speak English primarily. The second group was brought here by force by the Spanish, to act as slaves in the early years of colonization. These are mainly Spanish-speaking. There is a high number of Mestizos, descendants of unions between the indigenous peoples and the conquerors. Finally there are many Chinese, Italians and other Europeans from Slavic or Germanic countries.

Kuna woman

The Indigenous Peoples

Contrary to the situation in neighbouring Costa Rica, Panamá's indigenous population constitutes a sizeable minority. It is estimated at some 200,000 people, most of whom live in the western and eastern parts of the country. Today, there are seven native groups in Panamá: the Ngobe and Bugle, also called the Guaymies, are the largest group; the Tule, also known as the Kuna, the Emberás and Wounaan called the Chocoes, and the Tlorio or Teribes. Finally, there is also a small Bri-Bri minority in the west of the country.

The Kunas and Chocoes have been allowed to administer their own territories, called *comarcas*, for many years now. Only defence and national security are still controlled by the Panamanian government. The Guaymies, on the other hand, have had a hard time getting their rights recognized. Despite the creation of the Reserva Tabasara in 1952, their lands have been exploited by farmers and mining companies.

After some dark years during which their traditions and social fabric started breaking down, the Guaymies started a long campaign for the recognition of their rights.

As a result, in 1965, following a national conference of all Ngobe-Bugle grand chiefs, the Guaymies Free Republic was created and a president named for the new territory. However, barely three days later, the Guaymies, under pressure from the army, were forced to give up their independence.

Despite the promise of a Ngobe-Bugle comarca, the Panamanian government has repeatedly broken its promises, taking advantage of the political and religious differences within the Ngobe communities that arose shortly after their independence was quashed. Things then quieted down in the Ngobe communities until 1991 when, during the festivities for the 500th anniversary of Christopher Columbus's landing, Ngobe chief David Binns painted some graffiti on the cathedral of Panamá stating "500 years of evangelization, enough!". The government responded by fining Binns B/. 100 for writing anti-Christian graffiti, thus demonstrating once again their ignorance of the whole native claims movement.

The same year, the Panamanian government secretly signed a contract with Texaco, which would have involved the expropriatation Guaymies lands, as well as Parque Internacional La Amistad and the Bastimentos marine park, thus violating the law on national parks. In 1992, the government granted the Cerro Colorado Mine Development Corporation (an Anglo-Panamanian venture) the rights to develop a copper mine on Ngobe territory. The government subsequently granted more land to foreign mining companies (mostly U.S. and Canadian) despite opposition from the Ngobe-Bugle delegation.

Fed up with the non-recognition of their rights, on November 25, 1996, six Ngobe and Bugle representatives, went on a hunger strike in the capital's anthropological museum. They demanded the annulment of past contracts with mining companies and a legal recognition of their lands. With public opinion in their favour as well as the support of various university groups, the government finally passed a law creating the Ngobe-Bugle comarca in January 1997. Although it was a first step, the land was small in comparison to what the Guaymies wanted. Of the 1.3 million ha claimed, the country's largest indigenous population has received only 700,000ha. In addition, because the development of natural resources within the *comarca* remains strictly under state control, large chunks of Guaymíe territory are still held by mining companies. As long as the government grants new mining exploration rights, the situation in the Ngobe-Bugle *comarca* will remain tense.

The Tlorios have made no official land claims up to now and the Bri-Bris are considered too small to be officially recognized as a native group; most of them live in Costa Rica. Now that the canal is under Panamanian control, it would be good to finally see ownership of native lands revert back to its original inhabitants.

The Guaymies and the Kunas belong to the Chibchan language family. Chibchan was the spoken language of the Chibcha tribes, whose influence extended from Nicaragua to Colombia and Ecuador, before the arrival of the Spaniards. The Chibchas are estimated to have numbered 500,000, and the largest group of them lived in the high valleys surrounding what is today the city of Bogotá, in Colombia. Their society was highly centralized and especially well organized. The Chocoes, for their part, belong to the Carib language group, which originated in Guyana and Brazil.

Panamá's indigenous peoples have a highly diversified culture. This is due to cultural blending caused by migrations, forced or otherwise. Several influences are felt, including those of the Mayas, Aztecs and even the Incas. The three main groups in the country are described briefly below.

The Ngobe-Bugle (Guaymies)

This is the largest native group in the country (population estimates range from 97,000 to 150,000); it is also the most integrated and the most assimilated. Until the Spaniards arrived, the Ngobe-Bugle lived primarily in the centre and the west of the country; particularly in the provinces of Veraguas, Herrera, Los Santos and Coclé. After the land was colonized, most moved to the provinces of Bocas del Toro and Chiriquí. A warlike people, the Guaymies apparently came from Colombia to settle in the central and western parts of the country. It is believed that before the Spaniards arrived they were divided into several nations, each with its own supreme chief (see also the section on the pre-Columbian period, p 17)

There are two main Guayami groups: those from the south, who live on the Pacific coast, and those from the north, who live in the mountains and shores along the Atlantic. The climates of these two regions differ greatly, and this seems to have had a considerable influence on each group's way of life and culture. Those of the north live in humid tropical forests and along the Caribbean shore; they are more isolated and their culture is said to be more "primitive."

Unlike their neighbours, those in the south, live in larger villages generally situated on hilltops. They chose this location, often to the detriment of their water supply, because they needed to have an excellent view of the surroundings. They had once been warriors, and found it important to be able to watch the enemy from afar. Since they lived in drier and less wooded areas, they became adept farmers. Today, they often work on a seasonal basis on the plantations in the area, or in the mines that have sprung up on their land over recent years. The women make dresses and jewellery for sale in the villages and along the Interamericana.

At the social level, the Guaymies are now monogamous, though this was not always the case. The women wear long dresses of two colours often blue and red or green and orange, and decorated mainly at the bottom and on the collar. Sleeves are generally short. Sometimes the women wear large necklaces (see illustration) made of tiny beads of different colours. Both dresses and collars have geometric patterns, mostly triangles.

Among important rituals is the coming of age ceremony for males called "La Clarida." A group gathers in the forest near a source of water and a mountain. Then, a priest-healer or *sukia* teaches the males chants and sacred prayers. Today, however, the capitalist way of life has driven many men away from the reserves, and this has led to many social changes in the Guaymíe community. Tribal customs are disappearing along with the influence of the *sukias*. Only time will tell if land-claim efforts will in their turn be followed by attempts to preserve traditions.

The Kunas (Tule)

The Kunas are generally shorter and more thickset than the Guaymies. They emigrated a number of centuries ago from Colombia. Some 500 to 1,000 of them live in Darién, but the biggest

Mola

group (50,000-60,000) settled in the San Blas islands. Long before colonization, they also occupied the central part of the country.

The word *Kuna* means "the people" and is applied primarily to those living on the continent; those on the islands call themselves San Blas. Although contacts with pirates profoundly influenced both groups, because of their isolation in the jungle, the continental Kunas have maintained a more "primitive" lifestyle. The principal activities of the San Blas Kunas are fishing and farming, and the women make the famous *molas* (see box "The Mola," Comarca de San Blas.)

The Emberás and the Wounaan (The Chocoes)

The Chocoes of Panamá, unlike their Colombian neighbours who mixed with the local black populations, were opposed to all assimilation and withdrew into the forest of Darién. They have separated into two distinct groups: the Emberás who number 14,000; and the Wounaan, totalling about 3,000 people. Unlike the Kunas and the Guaymies, the Chocoes do not live in a community, but live in an isolated manner, usually along rivers. They appear to have neither leaders nor political or economic structures, and live mainly in families. Their principal activities are fishing, hunting and farming. Little is known about their origins, though they appear to have come from neighbouring Colombia. Of all the indigenous peoples in Panamá (some would say in the world), these are the most "primitive" and the most isolated. This can be explained by their environment (the Darién rain forest) and by the fact that they avoid all contact with other groups.

Politics

Panamá is a presidential republic. Its constitution was adopted in 1983 following a referendum, and provides for legislative power represented by a unicameral (one chamber) legislative assembly. Executive power is vested in the president of the republic, who is assisted by two vice-presidents. Both presidential and legislative elections are held every five years.

In 1989, the Fuerza de Defensa Nacional (formerly the Guardia Nacional), which represented the military power, was abolished and replaced by the Fuerza Pública.

Commanding officers serve a two-year term. This "public force" also acts as a police force. The courts and the districts are governed by a supreme court, while the president of the republic appoints a governor for each province.

At the administrative level, the country consists of nine provinces, divided into districts and consisting of municipalities. Each province has its own cultural and geographical peculiarities. The province of San Blas, for instance, is an autonomous territory, or *comarca*. Among other features, it contains a large group of islands, and the villages are inhabited and administered exclusively by the Kunas. The province of Chiriquí is inhabited both by Guaymies and by people of Spanish, German and Slavic descent. Both in its countryside and in its climate, it is reminiscent of Switzerland! The inhabitants are very proud of their regions; each province has its own capital; when someone talks about "the capital," he or she means the capital of the province. The population is unequally distributed, and the provinces of Panamá and Colón alone account for more than half the country's population. Nombre de Dios and Natá are among the oldest cities, dating back to the colonial period.

Economy

From an economic standpoint, revenue from the canal still plays an important role. Many people are employed in the Zona Libre in Colón and in the administration of the canal.

Another major source of revenue is in the west of the country: the pipeline carrying oil from one ocean to the other and running from Puerto Armuelles to Chiriquí Grande. Yet another source of revenue related to petroleum is the oil tankers. A great many ships fly the Panamanian flag, so the country has a good-sized merchant fleet, although the original Panamanian fleet is not all that large. Farming and fishing have also developed significantly and become major activities. The main crops are corn and rice, and the country exports fruits, sugar, coffee, cocoa and shrimp. Its principal clients are the United States, Costa Rica, Germany and the European Community.

Panamá is one of the most indebted countries in the world, with respect to its GDP. Its debt, as well as its GDP, is $6 billion. Over the last few years, Panamá has managed to reduced its deficit substantially and in 1995, a portion of the interest and capital it owed to international creditors was cancelled.

Nevertheless, the country is still undergoing significant economic growth (close to 2% since 1994), and does not suffer from inflation, which hovers around 1.8% per year.

The recent decision made to partially or totally privatize certain public companies has brought in significant foreign investment and in some cases has allowed the quality and competitiveness of services to be improved. In addition to the total privatization of the phone company, a large part of the country's electricity is presently provided by Hydro Québec International. The Québec giant, in partnership with the Fonds de Solidarité des Travailleurs du Québec, owns 50.1% of the shares of the Fortuna hydroelectric generating station in the west of the country, and provides 40% of Panamá's electricity.

The government has created certain incentives to develop the country's tourism industry. A law was passed, for example, which exempts investors from paying taxes on their tourist-related ventures. With the transition of the canal to Panamá, a committee called the Autoridad de la Región Interoceánica was also set up to oversee an ambitious real-estate development project for the canal zone. Land that used to house American military bases has been put up for sale and is expected to fetch $30 billion, or five times the total national debt! Architect Frank Gehry, famous for his design of the Guggenheim Museum in Bilbao, Spain, has been put in charge of the project.

The government hopes to attract the foreign capital necessary to realize the country's enormous potential as a tourist destination.

Panamá's unemployment rate remains high, at 12.8%. The development of tourism, an industry that employs a large workforce, should help lower that rate. On the whole, Panamá is in an enviable position compared to its neighbours: it has the highest GNP per capita, the strongest growth and the lowest inflation rate of all Central American countries.

Society

Panamá has 3,000,000 inhabitants (1998), most of them Roman Catholics. There are also Protestant and Jewish minorities. There is a social security system and the state pays old age and disability pensions. While the number of physicians stands at a little more than 1 per 100 inhabitants, the child mortality rate remains at 25 per 1,000 (versus 7 per 1,000 in Canada, and 9 in the United States). Education is compulsory from age 6 to age 15, and about 93% of the children go to elementary school. Only

28% of the population continues to higher studies and 11.9% still cannot read. The country has three universities, one of them private.

Panamá ranks among the three top Central American countries for standard of living, life expectancy and general quality of life. Still, there is a great difference between the people who work for the canal and the rest of the population. With high unemployment, and a sizeable public debt, the workers in the zone are considered spoiled children.

The major challenge facing the country is the reduction of the country's enormous foreign debt.

Panamanians and Tourism

From the point of view of tourism, the country has suffered enormously since the dark days of the Noriega regime. The number of visitors (mostly Americans) was relatively high beforehand, but plummeted afterward. Since 1992 however, there has been some recovery. While there are a number of tourist facilities in place, these are more frequently adapted to Panamanian families. A number of initiatives are developing, and these have the support of the government. There are also various programs aimed at attracting foreign investors (see p 33).

The variety and beauty of the countryside, the exceptional bio diversity and the endless beaches make Panamá an ideal destination. Some people maintain that Panamá is just a big American base whose culture has become largely Americanized, and that there is no room left for anything but anglicization and a Coca-Cola lifestyle. This is simply not true. The country has a real culture of its own, steeped in colonial history. The Spanish language, furthermore, is very much alive here.

While some remain bitter toward the Americans (especially after the 1989 invasion), the general attitude is a mixture of malaise combined with gratitude toward the invaders: malaise by reason of legitimate pride and a feeling for their country's independence, gratitude for being liberated from a terrible dictatorship. In any case, Panamanians are generally pleasant, courteous and good-humoured. Regardless of the problem you may be facing, ask someone for help and invariably, with a smile, will come the answer "*Si, como no*?" ("Yes, of course!"). Panamanians also enjoy celebrating and having fun; there is music almost everywhere.

Arts

The first forms of artistic development in Panamá date back to the pre-Columbian period, with the large-scale production of ceramics and jewellery in the central provinces and in Chiriquí. This was the period of Coclé culture (see p 17). From the colonial conquest until the birth of the republic, artistic activities were limited to religious demonstrations and feasts (like Corpus Christi), and the erection of religious buildings. The same applied to painting and sculpture. Many folkloric ceremonies developed as well, some of them a mixture of pagan and Catholic rituals. Native cultures exerted their influence on these customs, mixing with those brought from Spain.

Literature

With the exception of the works of writer Victor de la Guardia and poet Darío Herrera, there was no intense literary movement until the birth of the republic as an independent country. A number of poets and writers appeared in the 20th century: Ricardo Míro, José María Núñez and Rogelio Sinán are just a few examples. A number of works of realism were produced, mostly influenced by the many sociopolitical upheavals that had a profound impact on Panamanian literature. Two fine Panamanian writers are Joaquím Beleño, whose book *Luna Verde* describes workers in the canal zone, and the poet Amelia Denis de Icaza.

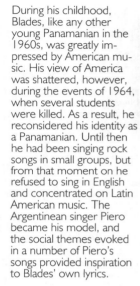

Music and Dance

Panamanian folk dancing has a long and rich past. Originally brought by the settlers, it assimilated various elements from inside and outside the country as it spread among the regions. Slaves from Africa and, much later, workers from the Caribbean, also contributed much to local folklore. The dance called *Congo*, performed mainly on the coast of Colón, reflects a strong African influence. Panamá's most celebrated dances are still, however, the *tamborito* (the national dance), the *mejorana*, and the *punto*, during which the female dancers wear the *pollera* (see box "La Pollera," in The Central Provinces and the Azuero Peninsula).

Music too has been enriched by a long tradition and developed very rapidly in Panamá; a national symphony orchestra was created in 1941. The most celebrated Panamanian composer of the 20th century was Alberto Galimany (1889-1973). Popular, contemporary Panamanian music is in many respects highly distinctive and quite different from that of the neighbouring countries. In addition to the omnipresent accordion, characteristic shouts called *saloma* very often punctuate the songs, imparting a pleasant, pastoral style. Among popular singers are Victorio Vergara, Alfredo Escudero, Dorindo Cardenas and Sony and Sandra Sandoval. Besides all of these, one performer, known around the world and praised in Panamá, stands out: Rubén Blades.

Rubén Blades

Rubén Blades was born in Panamá City, the second of five children. He grew up surrounded by artists and musicians, with a father who played bongo, and a mother, the daughter of a Cuban and an American, who sang with one of the greatest Cuban lyricists, Ernesto Lecuona. Blades was brought up mostly by his feminist grandmother, a painter and author; one can imagine how much she influenced a young Blades.

Female dancer dressed with the traditionnal pollera

During his childhood, Blades, like any other young Panamanian in the 1960s, was greatly impressed by American music. His view of America was shattered, however, during the events of 1964, when several students were killed. As a result, he reconsidered his identity as a Panamanian. Until then he had been singing rock songs in small groups, but from that moment on he refused to sing in English and concentrated on Latin American music. The Argentinean singer Piero became his model, and the social themes evoked in a number of Piero's songs provided inspiration to Blades' own lyrics.

The Torrijos coup d'état occurred while Blades was enrolled in law at the University of Panamá, and brought him to another turning point in his life. The military authorities closed the university, and Blades decided to accept an offer he had received some years back from a group of New York musicians; in 1969 he emigrated to the United States. At this time *salsa music* was very much in fashion, and Blades joined the very popular artist Rodríguez. He made a record with Rodríguez, but it failed to bring him the recognition he sought. His future in the United States looked uncertain, and since the University of Panamá had reopened, he went back to finish his law studies. After two years with the Central Bank, however, Blades realized that he could never abandon music, so he returned to the United States.

In New York he became very popular, but at the same time he began looking for something more. He was tired of music that carried no message—he wanted songs that were more personal, a salsa that was more committed. He found this depth with Willie Colón, and their album *Siembra*, for which Blades had written most of the songs, became an immediate success.

Around 1982, after many other successes, Blades and Colón went their separate ways. Blades formed a group called "Seis del Solar," and in 1984 the group's album, *Buscando América*, was released in two languages: Spanish and, for the first time, English. It was an immediate hit. On this album, Blades sings of the difficulty of living under corrupt and tyrannical regimes. One of the songs is dedicated to Cardinal Romero of El Salvador; another, *Decisiones*, was banned in Panamá. Despite the ban, the song was still heard everywhere, even on city buses, and when Blades appeared for a concert, he was an immediate success.

After helping produce the film *Crossover Dreams* and taking a break for a law degree from Harvard, Blades returned to music. In 1985 he and Linda Ronstadt released a new album, *Escenas*. A voracious reader, Rubén Blades was an admirer of Colombian novelist Gabriel García Márquez and became one of his friends. The writer's influence was felt in the album *Agua de luna*, which is directly based on Márquez's writings. By 1989 he had formed a new group, "Son del Solar", and released a new album, *Antecedente*. This was followed in 1991 by *Caminando*.

While Rubén Blades is an accomplished singer and musician, he is also appreciated, though less known, as an actor, and has appeared in such films as *Milagro Beanfield War* and *Critical*.

He travels regularly to Los Angeles, and in 1990 he was given his greatest role, in *Dead Man Out*, filmed in Québec, Canada, for which he won a prize as best actor. To date, Rubén Blades has taken part in 13 films.

As someone constantly in search of new ways and a more just and more democratic society, Blades was shaken by the tragic events in Panamá. Pleased at Noriega's departure but crushed by the American invasion, Blades is now ready to take a more active part in his country's political life. As a candidate in the May 1994 elections, Blades came in third, while six members of his party were elected to parliament.

Practical Information

Most regions in Panamá can be explored without much difficulty, though visiting certain places, such as Darién, will require prior arrangements.

Whatever your destination, planning ahead is always a good idea. This section is intended to help you organize your visit to Panamá by providing general information and practical advice on local customs.

Entrance Formalities

Before leaving home, be sure you have the official documents that will allow you to enter and leave Panamá. Take good care of these documents; keep them with you wherever you travel in the country.

To enter Panamá, travellers, of all nationalities, must have a passport, valid for at least six months after entering the country, and either a "tourist card" or visa, valid for the length of their stay.

Citizens of the European Community (with the exception of Sweden), as well as Swiss and Costa Rican nationals, do not require a visa or a tourist card, only a valid passport. Canadian and American citizens, as well as citizens of most Western European countries, must have a tourist card or a visa in addition to their passport. As a general rule, a tourist card will be issued by your travel agency upon purchasing your airline ticket. If not, the card can be obtained at customs upon entering the country, for a cost of about B/.6; a card is valid for 30 days. You must keep the card throughout your travels as it must be returned to customs upon departure. A two-month extension on your tourist card can be obtained by simple request at the airport's immigration office.

When entering the country overland from Costa Rica or Colombia, you must present the same card or a visa and a return plane ticket. In some cases, proof of sufficient funds for the duration of your stay may be required. Though the tourist card is available as a rule from the main border crossings, it is strongly advised to purchase a visa ahead of time to avoid any problems. They sometimes run out of these cards at borders. Visitors entering the country by car will also need official authorization to drive in the country. This authorization is given at border crossings after the registration for the car and car insurance have been verified. Travellers wishing to visit Colombia or Costa Rica during their stay must follow certain formalities and are advised to check with those countries' consulates.

It is a good idea to photocopy the important pages of your passport and to write down your passport number. This will make it easier to replace this document should it be lost or stolen (do the same with all official documents, such as your driver's license and tourist card). In the event that you lose an important piece of identification, contact your country's embassy or consulate (see addresses below) to have a new one issued.

As events and policies evolve rapidly, it is a good idea to make sure the formalities described above still apply before leaving on your trip.

Travellers wishing to stay longer than 90 days can renew their tourist card for another 90 days at the Departamento de Inmigración y Naturalización in Panama City (see address below). In addition to two passport-sized identification photos, you will need to present a ticket out of the country and a short letter in Spanish explaining why you want to extend your stay. You may also be asked to prove that you have sufficient funds to support yourself on a longer visit. In addition, it is important to get an exit permit (permiso de salida) when you do decide to leave. They can be obtained at the Ministerio de Hacienda y Tesoro by asking for a *paz y salvo*.

Departamento de Inmigración y Naturalización
at the corner of Calle 29 and Avenida 2a Sur (Cuba)
☎225-8925 or 227-1448
☎227-1175 or 227-1209

Ministerio de Hacienda y Tesoro
Calle 36 y 35 between Avenida Perú and Cuba
☎227-4879 or 227-3033
⇄227-2357

In order to avoid delay, it is preferable that you ask the Panamanian consulate in your home country for an extended visa **before** your departure.

Departure Tax

Everyone leaving Panamá must pay a departure tax of B/.20. The payment (to be made in cash—credit cards are not accepted) is made when reserving seats for your return flight.

Embassies and Consulates

Embassies and consulates representing your home country can provide valuable assistance in the event of health emergencies, legal problems or the death of a travel companion. However, visitors are responsible for any costs incurred as a result of services provided by these official bodies. If there is no representation in Panamá, then the closest consulate or embassy is given below

Canada
World Trade Center
Galería Comercial, Piso 1
Calle 53E, Marbella
☎(507) 264-9731
☎(507) 264-7115
⇄(507) 263-8083

Denmark
Via Cincuentenario 28A
Esquina Calle 50
San Francisco
☎(507) 270-0944
⇄(507) 270-0874

Germany
Calle 53E
Urbanizacion Marbella
Edificio World Trade Centre
No.20
☎(507) 263-7733
⇄(507) 223-6664

Great Britain
Swiss Tower
(Apartads 889) Zona 1
Panama City
☎(507) 269-0866
⇄(507) 223-0730

Netherlands
Consulado Tower Plaza
1er Piso
Calles 50 y Beatriz M. Cabal
Panama City
☎/⇄(507) 264-7257

Sweden
Av. Balboa y Aquilino de la Guardian
Edificio Galerias Balboa
Primer Alto Local 18
☎(507) 264-3748
⇄(507) 264-6358

United States
Calle13 and Avenida Balboa
Panama City
☎/⇄ (507) 207-7000

Panamanian Consulates and Embassies Abroad

While consulates can sometimes provide general travel information, their main function is to issue official documents (visas, immigration papers etc.). When possible, contact a Panamanian tourist office for additional information.

Canada
Embassy of Panamá
130 Albert St.
Suite 300
Ottawa, Ontario
K1P 5G4
☎***(613) 236-7177***
⇄***(613) 236-5775***

Consulate General of Panamá
1425 Boul. René-Levesque Ouest
Suite 504
Montréal, Québec, H3G 1T7
☎***(514) 874-1929***
⇄***(514) 874-1947***

Denmark
c/o Advokaterne
Amaliegade No. 42
1256 Copenhagen k.
☎***33 11 33 99***
⇄***33 32 46 25***

Germany
Joachim-Karnatz 45
3. OG
Berlin-Tiergarten 10557
☎***226-05-811***
⇄***226-05-812***

Great Britain
40 Hertford St
48 Park Street
London W1Y 7TG
☎***7-493-4646***
⇄***7-493-4333***

Sweden
Ostermalmsgaten 34
2 tr 114
32 Estocolmo
Sweden
☎***66 26 535***
⇄***66 30 407***

United States
2862 McGill Terrace N.W.
Washington D.C. 20008
☎***(202) 483-1407***
⇄***(202) 483-8416***

Consulates
24 Guenway Plaza, Ste. 1307
Houston, TX 77046
☎***(713) 622-4451***
⇄***(713) 622-4468***

1212 Avenue of the Americas
6th floor
New York, NY 10036
☎***(212) 840-2450***
⇄***(212) 840-2469***

2801 Ponce de Leon Blvd
Suite 1050
Coral Gardes, FL 33134
☎***(305) 447-3700***
⇄***(305) 447-4142***

1324 World Trade Centre No.2
Canal St
New Orleans LA 70130
☎***(504)525-3458***
⇄***(504)524-8960***

Tourist Information

IPAT (Panamanian Tourist Institute)

Offices of the Panamanian Tourist Institute (IPAT) are found only in Panamá and the United States. However, Panamanian consulates and embassies in many countries can usually provide information and a small selection of brochures. The IPAT offices found throughout Panamá are there to answer questions and help visitors explore the country. Unfortunately, the documentation they have on hand is limited and dated.

The addresses and telephone numbers of IPAT regional offices can be found in the "Practical Information" section of each chapter. There is also an office at the international airport to assist visitors on arrival.

International Airport
8am to midnight
near the customs offices
☎***238-4356***
☎***238-4102***

Publications

A publication entitled *Focus Panamá* is available free of charge in many hotels and restaurants in the capital. The magazine describes Panama City's nightlife and cultural activities, and provides short descriptions of interesting activities that take place elsewhere in the country. It is available in English and Spanish.

One small English -language publication provides information on the latest in theatre, tourism and dining out. ***The Panama News*** *(thepanamanews.com)* is available for free in most hotels and restaurants.

The best place to get detailed maps of the country is from the **Instituto Geográfico Nacional Tommy Guardia**, located across from the University of Panamá (take the pedestrian walkway over Vía

Some Interesting Web Sites

www.ipat.gob.pa
Official site of the Panamanian Tourist Office

www.pa
The country's most complete site, but also the slowest!

www.sinfo.net
Panamá City's official site

www.pancanal.com
Official Canal Commission site

www.trainweb.org/panama
Site of Panamá's only railway

www.boyds.org/recipes.htm
Astonishing religious site with many Panamanian recipes

thepanamanews.com
Web site of a small English-language weekly newspaper devoted to news in the fields of entertainment, tourism and gastronomy.

paginasamarillas.com/pagamanet/panama/home.aspx
Web site providing access to Panama's yellow pages.

copaair.com
National Panamanian airline's official Web site.

www.tacaregional.com/aeroperlas/index.html
For domestic flights, be sure to check out the Aeroperlas airline's Web site.

anam.gob.pa/portada.htm
An interesting Web site on all you ever wanted to know about Panama's national parks.

Simón Bolívar). Unfortunately, the maps are not up to date and the staff is not very helpful. Maps of the country, including excellent ones published by the ITMB at a scale of 1:800,000, are also available in many travel bookstores in Europe and North America.

Instituto Geográfico Nacional Tommy Guardia
Calle 57 Oeste
(Melchor Lasso de la Vega) y
Avenida 6A Norte
Apartado 5267
Panama City 5
☎ ***236-1844***

Getting There

By Plane

From Canada

At present there are no direct flights between Canada and Panamá. However, indirect flights, with a stopover in the United States, are offered by Delta Airlines, Continental Airlines and Air Canada. The best deal seems to be with Continental, which has an arrangement with Copa (the national airline of Panamá). This deal is sold as a single ticket which means that in the event of a delay, the passenger is guaranteed a hotel and a restaurant meal. Chartered flights are also offered during the winter from Montreal and Toronto.

Other air travel possibilities include travelling though Mexico and most countries in Central America and the Caribbean.

From Europe

Most airlines flying to Panamá from Europe make stop overs in the United States or in one of several Latin American countries. Depending on the point of departure, several combinations are possible.

The following two airlines offer direct flights to Panamá:

Iberia: three flights a week out of Madrid.

KLM: two flights a week out of Amsterdam.

As the fares can vary substantially depending on the season and the "fare wars" waged between competing airlines, it is a good idea to shop around.

From the USA

Panamá's national airline, **Copa**, has daily flights from Miami. Certain American airlines such as **Continental**, **Northwest** and **America West Airlines**, have made arrangements with Copa to provide several connections between the United States and Panamá. A number of possibilities exist for flying out of Mexico and most countries in Central America and the Caribbean.

By Car

From Costa Rica

Two regions of Panamá are accessible from Costa Rica: the province of Bocas del Toro and the province of Chiriquí, along the Interamericana highway to Paso Canoa, the border town in the province of Chiriquí. The latter option is the most convenient for those travelling by car or bus. Remember that the Costa Rican border crossings are only open from 8am to 11pm.

Also remember that no matter how you enter the country, certain formalities apply (see p 37). There is a time difference between Costa Rica and Panamá, so remember to put your watch ahead an hour when you cross the border into Panamá.

By Bus

From Costa Rica

Two companies provide service from the capital of Costa Rica to Panama City: **Tica Bus** and **Panaline**.

The trip lasts about 16hrs and costs B/.25, whatever the company. Given the high demand, reservations are highly recommended. Also, be sure to bring your passport as it will be requested when you purchase your ticket. Below are the addresses and phone numbers of both companies in the two respective capitals.

From Panama City

Buses depart from the **Terminal Nacional de Transporte** *(☎314-6171 or 314-6167)*, located on Calle Curundú, right near the M. A. Gelabert airport.

Tica Bus
departs at 11am
☎314-6385 or 262-2084
⇄314-6387

Panaline
departs at 12:30pm
☎227-8648 or 227-1133
⇄227-8647

From San José

All departures are made from downtown San José, at the Terminal-Costado Norte de la Iglesia La Soledad

Practical Information

Tica Bus
departures at 10am
☎221-8954
⇌223-89758
ticabus.com

Panaline
departures at 2pm
☎255-1205

Another possibility is to take a Tracopa bus from San José to David; from David you can change buses and travel on to Panama City (this is the more time-consuming of the two bus routes).

The buses cross the border at Paso Canoa, a town with a number of banks and other services. Note that the border sometimes closes for a while in the middle of the day and at night.

TRACOPA
corner of Avenida 18
and Calle 14
San José
☎775-0585

From Colombia

It is impossible to travel by bus from Colombia to Panamá. While there are a few rudimentary paths in northern Colombia that wind toward the border, and plans have been made to extend the Interamericana highway, the thick jungle in the province of Darién in southern Panamá acts as a barrier between the countries. The trip is technically possible on foot but very risky, so it is best left to well-equipped and experienced travellers who know the region. Insects, including disease-carrying mosquitoes, poisonous snakes and drug dealers are just a few of the dangers likely to be encountered along the way. In addition, passing through some native villages in the area requires authorization from village chiefs, and lodging facilities in the region are non-existent or very basic. In short, road travel between Colombia and Panamá is not recommended (unless big risks and adventure are a priority).

Airports

Besides Tocumen International Airport, there are a number of smaller airports scattered around the country. International flights into Panamá touch down at the Tocumen airport. The Albrook military airport has recently been converted to handle domestic flights.

Tocumen International Airport

The Tocumen International Airport is a relatively modern facility with most of the services expected of a major airport.

Along with a number of duty-free shops and international car rental agencies, the airport also has a cafeteria and a bar. The national tourist information bureau, IPAT, has an office in the airport open from 8am to midnight.

For arrival and departure information:
☎238-4322

If you wish to visit several countries in Central and South America, use **Latin AirFlex**, sold by the **Taca** company (taca.com). This program allows you to travel on one of Central America's four airlines, namely Lacsa, Nica, Aviateca and Taca. A minimum of four destinations must be selected. For more information:

In Canada
Grupo Taca
1235 Bay Street, Suite 600,
Toronto, Ontario
☎416-968-2222

In the U.K.
Flighthhouse, Fernhill Rd.
Horley, Surrey
☎(44-870) 608 0737
☎(44) 8702 410-340

From Tocumen International to Panama City by car, (see p 70).

In the area around the airport there are all kinds of people offering their services or selling different merchandise. If you decide to buy something, don't open your window too wide when paying. It is safer to drive from the airport during the day.

Domestic Flights

Domestic flights have recently been transferred to Albrook, the former military airport, which is larger and better-equipped than the airport at Punta Paitilla. Four companies currently offer regular flights within Panamá: Aeroparlas, Mapiex-Aero, Aviatur and Ansa. They have offices at the new airport, which is also called Aeropuerto Marcos Gelabert.

For all general information:
☎315-0400 or 315-1622

Mapiex-Aero
Aeropuerto de Albrook
☎315-0888
mapiexaero.com
Mapiex-Aero has regular flights to David, Bocas del Toro, Changuinola and Colón from the capital.

Aeroperlas
Aeropuerto de Albrook
☎315-7500
www.aeroperlas.com
www.tacaregional.com/aeroperlas/index.html
Aeroperlas is Panamá's largest domestic airline and flies to numerous destinations from Panama City including Isla Contadora, Colón, Chitre, David, Bocas del Toro, Changuinola, Garachiné, Sambú, La Palma, Bahía Piña, El Real, Jacqué and several islands of the Comarca de San Blas.

Aviatur
Aeropuerto Albrook
☎315-0311 or 315-0309
www.panamareservation.com/index.htm
Aviatur offers flights to La Palma, Jacqué, Bahía Piña, Sambú, Garachiné as well as to San Miguel and Isla Contadora and some islands in the Comarca de San Blas. Note, however, that several of these flights are only offered seasonally.

Ansa
Aeropuerto Albrook
☎315-7521
The Ansa airline mainly serves the Comarca de San Blas.

Finding Your Way Around

By Car

The Interamericana

The Interamericana highway crosses nearly the full length of the country, from the border of Costa Rica to the village of Yaviza. However, not all sections of the road are paved. The stretch of highway leading out of the capital toward the border of Costa Rica is in excellent condition and wider. Heading east from the capital, the highway is paved only as far as the village of Chepo. From here to just beyond the village of Metetí, the road is paved in places but is more often covered with gravel. Beyond the village of Yaviza, the road becomes little more than a jungle track. The long-discussed plans to extend the Interamericana highway have not yet been carried out. The project has been put on hold because of the enormous price tag involved and the potential social and environmental problems involved.

Although the speed limit on the Interamericana is 90 km/h, a more realistic average speed is about 60 km/h. Travel slows down considerably in the many villages and larger towns along the route and at major intersections. The speed limit is lowered to 40 km/h along these sections. There are police officers keeping an eye out for driving violations at many of the bigger intersections. The only place where the speed limit is as high as 100 km/h is on the section of highway between La Chorrera and Panama City, as well as on the newer toll highways surrounding the capital (Corredor Norte and Corredor Sur) or en route to Colón.

Secondary Roads

As a result of uneven road conditions in certain parts of Panamá, reaching some destinations requires the use of a four-wheel-drive vehicle. A description of conditions will be given for most of the roads mentioned in this guide.

In the Capital

See p 70.

Driving in Villages

Remember to reduce driving speed to 40 km/h when passing through villages. It is not unusual for village children to play in or along the road; it often seems that villagers see the road as their own.

Drivers should also keep a look out for a host of animals, including chickens, cats, dogs, horses and donkeys, that often wander onto the road.

Additional Information for Drivers

As most roads in Panamá do not have street lights, make sure to plan road trips so as not to end up driving at dusk. Panamá is near the equator; darkness falls in this part of the world at about 6:30pm in January and 7pm in July. It can be very difficult to see signs for hotels (they are often not lit)after dark.

At highway intersections and on busy city streets, drivers stuck in traffic are often approached by individuals offering to wash their car windows. Even if turned down, they may clean the windshield regardless, hoping the driver will give in and pay them something. Keep in mind, that for many of them this is their only way of making ends meet and so they may get angry if their services are refused. By agreeing to have your windows washed, and parting with a few coins in return, you will be doing a good turn and making the best of the situation. Be careful, however (particularly in Colón and Panama City) not to open your window more than a few inches. An appropriate payment is B/.0.25. Drivers may also be asked if they want their cars watched. Pay about B/.0.25 for this service. While this may seem a strange service, it will reduce the likelihood of theft. As a general rule, however, never leave anything valuable in your car.

Taxis

Taxis can be found just about anywhere and are probably the safest way to get around. The cars do not have meters; fares are based on which urban area you are travelling to and from. You will have to negotiate the cost of the ride, and it is a good idea to agree on a price before getting in. Taxi drivers are not tipped.

In addition to many personal taxis, there are also collective taxis which offer the advantage of shared costs (even if destinations vary somewhat). Collective taxis travel within and between cities.

Buses

A number of bus companies have routes between the country's larger cities. Long-distance buses are better equipped and more comfortable than city buses, but they do stop frequently. Buses on express runs are faster and hardly stop at all. As some destinations are very popular, it is a good idea to reserve bus tickets in advance. In the countryside, travellers can flag down buses along the road and pay the driver. In Panama City, buses depart from the new **Terminal Nacional de Transporte** *(☎314-6171 or 314-6167)*, located on Calle Curundú, right near the M. A. Gelabert airport.

The locations of the various bus stations can be found in the "Practical Information" section of each chapter.

The following are several typical one-way fares from Panama City on regular long-distance buses (they are subject to change).

Colón: B/.2.20
Santiago: B/.6
David: B/.11 (Express B/.15)
Chitré: B/.6
Punta Chame: B/.2.25
El Valle: B/.1.50

Other destinations:

Colón to Portobelo: B/.2
David to Boquete: B/.1.50
David to Almirante: B/.10
David to Cerro Punta: B/.3

Hitchhiking

For safety reasons we suggest that you avoid hitchhiking.

Trains

With the exception of two small private railway lines in Bocas del Toro province, which are used for freight, the only existing line is the one following the canal from Balboa to Colón.

For more information, see p 224.

Renting a Car

Renting a car in Panamá is relatively easy to do. Most

Table of distances (km)

Via the shortest route

	Boquete	Cerro Punta	Chitré	Colón	David	Divisa	El Valle	Las Tablas	Panama City	Paso Canoa	Penonomé	Portobelo	Santiago	Volcán
Boquete														
Cerro Punta	114													
Chitré	306	350												
Colón	549	593	326											
David	35	79	271	514										
Divisa	263	307	43	289	228									
El Valle	408	452	182	200	373	145								
Las Tablas	338	382	32	358	303	75	214							
Panama City	473	517	250	76	438	213	124	282						
Paso Canoa	88	73	324	567	53	281	426	356	491					
Penonomé	327	371	101	225	289	64	81	133	149	345				
Portobelo	572	616	349	43	537	312	223	381	99	590	248			
Santiago	277	271	79	325	192	36	181	111	249	245	100	348		
Volcán	92	22	328	571	57	285	430	360	495	62	346	594	249	
Yavisa	757	801	534	360	722	497	408	566	284	775	433	383	533	779

Example: The distance between Ciudad de Panamá and Santiago is 249km.

of the major car rental agencies have offices in the bigger towns. If you have reserved a car, make sure to bring the rental reservation document, which should indicate the rate to be paid. Sometimes, rental agents in Panamá will make up excuses in an attempt to increase the price previously agreed to. If you have your contract and are being asked to pay more than was earlier stipulated, threaten (politely) to go elsewhere or to contact the company's head office.

Be patient, smile, and tell yourself that bargaining is part of a complete travel experience. Expect to pay an average of B/.330 a week (with unlimited mileage) for a small air-conditioned car. You will also be charged a 5% tax, a B/.8 daily insurance charge and a B/.500 deposit in case of accident. A credit card can be used to cover the latter. Choose a car that is in good condition and preferably new. Some agencies offer lower prices, but generally their cars are older and in worse condition. Before signing a rental contract, make sure that the conditions of payment are clearly laid out. You must be at least 23 years old to rent a car. A valid driver's license from any country is accepted in Panamá. Cars drive on the right side of the road.

Following are the telephone numbers of some car rental agencies in the capital:

Avis
☎*236-0133*

Hertz
☎*260-8123*
⇄*263-6903*

Thrifty
☎*264-2613*

Alamo
☎*265-3786*

National Car Rental
☎*265-2222*

Dollar Rent a Car
☎*270-0355*

Road Accidents

When driving through small towns, beware of the livestock that sometimes wanders onto the road. Chickens in particular seem fatally attracted to the front bumpers of moving cars. If you should accidently kill an animal, head to the nearest police station rather than deal directly with villagers who may become aggressive. In the case of a more serious road accident, contact the police and phone your car rental agency as soon as possible.

Highway Police

Police officers are posted at various spots along the Interamericana. They have the right to pull over anyone who commits an infraction or just to inspect their papers. If you are charged with committing a traffic violation, make sure you are given a document stipulating the nature of the infraction. All fines are to be paid at the Autoridad del Tránsito y Transporte Terrestre (ATTT) office in the town in which the offence took place. You'll find the address of various ATTTs on the back of the ticket, or the officer can direct you to the nearest one. We have also provided the address of an ATTT branch in downtown Panama City for your convenience.

Although a very rare occurrence, unscrupulous police officers may ask for immediate payment of the fine in order to pocket the money themselves. In such a case, we advise you to calmly but firmly ask the officer for his or her name and badge number, which should indicate to the officer that you are not taken in by this illegal transaction. Should the officer still insist on being paid directly, we advise you to acquiesce but request a receipt in due form signed by the officer in question. Although some will advise you to negotiate with the officer (which is often the case) in order to halve the amount of the fine, be forewarned that doing so will make it more difficult to file a complaint later on.

Parking tickets, on the other hand, are paid at city hall. Here too, the appropriate address is indicated on the back of the ticket.

Panamanian police officers are generally obliging and will come to your assistance if you run into problems on the road. Remember that it is always best to be patient and amiable, a smile always

A Few Streets with Multiple Names

Many city streets in Panamá, particularly those in Panamá City, have several names. For example, the same street can be known as both "Calle 49 Este" and "Calle Aquilino de la Guardia." Here are some examples:

Avenida Simón Bolivar	Transístmica
Avenida 1a Sur	Perú
Avenida 2a Sur	Cuba
Avenida 3a Sur	Justo Arosemena
Avenida 4a Sur	Nicanor de Obarrio or Calle 50
Avenida Ecuador	Calle Brasilia
Calle 48 Este	Uruguay
Calle 49 Este	Aquilino de la Guardia
Calle 49 A Oeste	Veneto
Calle 50 Este	Ricardo Arias
Avenida 2a A Norte	Eusebio A. Morales
Avenida 1a A Norte	Calle D
Avenida Ricardo J. Alfaro	Tumba Muerto

These are just a few of the many examples. Perhaps the most complicated example of all is Avenida Nicanor de Obarrio, also known as Avenida 4a Sur and, more commonly, Calle 50! To complicate matters even further, some people designate a lower or higher number, depending on their direction, to streets running parallel to well-known numbered streets. As such, Avenida 4a A Sur is suddenly nicknamed Calle 49 since it is located south of the famed Calle 50. As the latter intersects with Calle 49 Este, it is simply a matter of distinguishing the real 49 from the imposter. A challenging riddle to look forward to! In the capital, the avenues (avenidas) usually run parallel to the coast, whereas streets (calles) run perpendicular. Sometimes, even local inhabitants do not know the exact names of all the streets. It is therefore easier to ask directions to a specific building (such as a church or monument) or well-known store near the street you are looking for.

being appreciated in Panamá. Moreover, speaking Spanish is, of course, an undeniable asset.

Autoridad del Tránsito y Transporte Terrestre
Avenida Juan Díaz
at the Mercado Artesanal, behind the Reina Torres de Araúz museum

Gasoline

There are gas stations all along the Interamericana highway. It is still a good idea to fill up before heading too far as gas stations can be hard to find off the highway. The price of gas in Panamá is fairly low by European standards, but a bit higher than in the United States. Expect to pay about B/.0.60 a litre. Some gas stations do not accept credit cards; this is more often the case outside big cities, so make sure to travel with sufficient cash.

Insurance

Cancellation

This type of insurance is usually offered by travel agents and is purchased along with airline tickets or holiday package deals. Cancellation insurance ensures that the cost of an airline ticket or package deal will be refunded in the event that a trip must be cancelled as a result of illness or death. This can be useful, but one should weigh the likelihood of such an event against the cost of the insurance.

Theft

Most residential insurance policies cover a percentage of personal belongings against theft if they are stolen outside the country. To file an insurance claim for a theft incurred while on holiday, you will need a police report from the country you are visiting. If you have a residential insurance policy, you may already be sufficiently protected. If you plan to travel with valuable objects, check your policy or consult with an insurance agent.

Health Insurance

This is the most useful kind of insurance for travellers, and should be purchased before departure. Recommended is a comprehensive health insurance policy that provides a level of coverage sufficient to pay for hospitalization, nursing care and doctor's fees—keep in mind that health care costs are rising quickly everywhere. The policy should also have a repatriation clause in case the required care is not available where you become ill. As patients are sometimes asked to pay for medical services immediately, find out what provisions your policy makes in this event. If you have to pay for health care in cash, make sure to keep all documents related to the transaction so that you can present them to your insurance company later for a refund. To avoid any problems during your vacation, always keep proof of your insurance policy on you.

Climate

Panamá has a tropical climate characterized by two seasons: the dry and the rainy, or green, season. Depending on the region and the altitude, there are many possible variations, resulting in many different microclimates within the country. The Caribbean coast gets plentiful rain all year long, while the dry season on the Pacific side is more pronounced. On the Azuero Peninsula, the climate is extremely arid during the dry season, and several weeks can go by with no rain at all. At the other extreme, it can rain for two days out of three during the wet season in the mountains!

The rainy season is from May to November. Panamánians call this season *invierno* (winter), not to be confused with the cold and snow of North American or European winters. Indeed, the rainy season is generally referred to as the "green season" because of the explosive growth of greenery at this time of year. In fact, many repeat visitors prefer to come during this season because of the incredible greenery, lack of tourists and lower prices. The dry season (*verano*, meaning summer) is from December to April; March and April are generally the hottest months.

Temperatures are relatively constant in Panamá, and variations are linked to altitude. Temperatures on the coasts regularly climb to more than 35°C. The higher the altitude, the colder the temperature, which falls about 1°C for every 150m of elevation. For the past few years, the climate has been irregular and unpredictable. But as Panamá is a small country with many climates, there is always somewhere that is comfortable! Those who do not like the heat and humidity would be more comfortable staying in the El Valle, Boquete, Volcán or Cerro Azul regions, where the temperature is almost always cool and pleasant.

Health

Illnesses

Panamá is a wonderful country to explore, however, travellers should protect themselves against a number of health risks associated with the region. In addition to diseases found throughout the world, including AIDS and various venereal diseases, a number of illnesses specifically related to Panamá's hot, humid climate pose a less familiar threat. Malaria, yellow fever, hepatitis A, typhoid and occasionally cholera are all present in most Central and South American countries, though the risk of contamination varies according to location. Other health problems travellers risk encountering include diphtheria, tetanus and polio.

Please note that this section is intended to provide general information. Since recommendations can change, see your doctor (or visit a traveller's clinic) before leaving for more complete advice on protecting yourself) against the health risks mentioned here. It is much easier and convenient to take precautions—such as getting vaccinations and bringing along medication—than to deal with what may be a serious illness with long-term effects.

Malaria

Malaria is caused by a parasite in the blood transmitted by anopheles mosquitoes; it cannot be passed from one person to another.

The symptoms of malaria include high fever, chills, extreme fatigue and headaches as well as stomach and muscle aches. There are several forms of malaria, including one serious type caused by *P. falciparum*. The disease usually takes hold while travellers are still on holiday or up to 12 weeks following return; in some cases, the symptoms will recur months later.

While most people recover from malaria, it is important to take all possible precautions against the disease. A doctor can prescribe anti-malarial medication to be taken before and after your trip (various types exist, depending on the destination, length of trip, age, etc.). Since the parasite that causes malaria is constantly evolving, anti-malarial medication is not foolproof. As much as possible, travellers should avoid getting bitten by mosquitoes (see p 50).

Diphtheria and Tetanus

These two illnesses, against which most people are vaccinated during their childhood, can have serious consequences. Before leaving, check that your vaccinations are valid; you may need a booster shot. Diphtheria is a bacterial infection that is transmitted by nose and throat secretions or by skin lesions on an infected person. Symptoms include sore throat, high fever, general aches and pains and occasionally skin infections. Tetanus is caused by a bacteria that enters the body through an open wound that comes in contact with contaminated dust or rusty metal.

Yellow Fever

Like malaria, yellow fever is transmitted by infected mosquitos. The symptoms usually appear three to six days after infection, do not last long and their intensity can vary; they include headaches, a very high fever, vomiting, sore back, and a slight yellowing of the skin. An effective vaccination against yellow fever, best taken before departure, is available; consult your physician. Once again, the vaccine is not 100% effective, so it is important to avoid getting bitten by mosquitoes (see p 50).

Hepatitis A

This infection is generally transmitted by ingesting food or water that has been contaminated by fecal matter. The symptoms include fever, yellowing of skin, loss of appetite and fatigue, and these can appear between 15 and 50 days after infection. An effective vaccination, given by injection, is available. Besides the recommended vaccine, good hygiene is important. Wash your hands before every meal and ensure that the food and preparation area are clean.

Hepatits B

Hepatitis B, like hepatitis A, affects the liver, but is transmitted through direct contact with bodily fluids. The symptoms are flu-like, and similar to those of hepatitis A. A vaccination exists but must be administered over an extended period of time, so be sure to check with your doctor several weeks in advance.

Typhoid Fever

This illness is caused by ingesting food that has come in contact (direct or not) with an infected person's stool. Common symptoms include high fever, loss of appetite, headaches, constipation and occasionally diarrhoea, or red spots on the skin. These symptoms will appear one to three weeks after infection. Besides good hygiene, there is a typhoid vaccination, which must be administered in two or three doses to be most effective. Once again, check with your doctor.

Additional Health Care Advice

Bodies of fresh water are frequently contaminated by the bacteria that causes schistosomiasis. This illness, caused by a worm-like parasite that enters the body and attacks the liver and nervous system, is difficult to treat. Swimming in fresh water should thus be avoided.

Strict controls on blood quality have been put into place by the health care systems in most countries. However, in the unlikely event that you require an emergency blood transfusion, make sure (if possible) that such measures have in fact been taken. Also, remember as well to use condoms during all sexual encounters.

The health problems that most often plague travellers are usually related to poorly treated water containing bacteria. In most of the bigger hotels, this danger has been almost completely eliminated. Still, in certain high risk areas (especially along the Atlantic coast and in Darién), it is a good idea to drink only bottled water. When buying bottled water, make sure the bottle is properly sealed. Ice cubes should be avoided, as the cold does not destroy the bacteria. In addition, fresh fruits and vegetables that have been washed (especially those that are not peeled before being eaten) can also pose a health risk. Make sure that the vegetables you eat are well-cooked and peel all your fruit.

If you do get diarrhoea, several steps should be followed to treat it. First, try to soothe your stomach by avoiding solids; instead, drink carbonated beverages, bottled water, or weak tea or coffee (avoid milk) until you recover. As the resulting dehydration can be dangerous, drinking sufficient quantities of liquid is crucial. To remedy severe dehydration, a solution containing a litre of water, two or three teaspoons of salt and one teaspoon of sugar will help re-establish the body's fluid balance. Pharmacies also sell ready-made preparations to help cure dehydration. Finally, gradually reintroduce solids to your system by eating easily digestible foods. Medication, such as Imodium or Pepto-Bismol, can help control intestinal discomfort. If more serious symptoms develop (high fever, bloody stool), see a doctor.

Remember that consuming too much alcohol, particularly when accompanied by prolonged exposure to the sun, can cause severe dehydration and lead to health problems. Sunstroke is a common affliction among travellers—protect yourself with a hat and sunglasses.

Medication

Some types of medication require a prescription and can be very expensive in Panamá; in some areas they may not be available at all. Bring along whatever prescription drugs and other potentially expensive medication you may need. It is also useful to have a small first-aid kit containing adhesive bandages, disinfectant, aspirin and antihistamines.

Mosquitoes and Other Insects

A nuisance common to many countries, mosquitoes are no strangers to Panamá. They are particularly numerous during the rainy season. Protect yourself with a good insect repellent. Repellents with DEET are the most effective. The concentration of DEET varies from one product to the next; the higher the concentration, the longer the protection.

Because of potential health hazards associated with

the extended use of products containing DEET at concentrations above 30%, these products are not recommended. A product with a 30% DEET content will provide adults adequate protection for 6.5 hours. Children should not be exposed to DEET at concentrations above 10%. Products containing a combination of DEET and sunscreen are not recommended because of their contrary application instructions: DEET should be applied sparingly, while sunscreen should be applied liberally and often. Instead, use two separate products. If you do so, however, note that applying DEET on top of sunscreen will reduce the effectiveness of the sunscreen by about 30%. Additional protection, in the form of clothing and a wide-brimmed hat, therefore becomes even more important.

To further reduce the possibility of getting bitten, do not wear perfume or bright colours. Sundown is an especially active time for insects. When walking in wooded areas, cover your legs and ankles well. Insect coils can help provide a better night's sleep. Before bed, apply insect repellent to your skin and to the headboard and baseboard of your bed. If possible, get an air-conditioned room, or bring a mosquito net.

Lastly, since it is impossible to completely avoid contact with mosquitoes, bring along a cream to soothe the bites you will invariably get.

Dangerous Wildlife

A graphic description of the snakes, scorpions, spiders and other creatures native to Panamá could be enough to put off potential travellers. However, keep in mind that their presence varies according to region—they are almost non-existent in cities—and that a number of simple precautions can be taken to avoid problems:

Shake out your clothes in the morning.

Shake out your shoes before putting them on.

Move your bed away from the wall by an inch or two.

Do not leave food out that could attract insects or animals.

Take the necessary precautions against mosquitoes.

Snakes

Among a country's rich and diverse fauna, there are bound to be some species that are less congenial than others. Accordingly, Panamá is home to several kinds of snakes, some of which are poisonous. There is no need to get too alarmed, as you are unlikely to cross paths with one during your visit. Nevertheless, it is important to keep your eyes open and watch where you step. In the forest, look around before you lean against something or sit down somewhere. When hiking, be careful as you part the foliage that sometimes hangs across the path, and check the shores as well as the surface of the water if you go swimming in a river. Some people think they are faster than snakes and tease, or poke them to see if they can make them move; needless to say, this is not a good idea! The presence of snakes should not prevent you from exploring everything that Panamá has to offer. Like most wild animals, snakes avoid contact with humans as much as possible.

Other Animals

People are sometimes tempted to pick up the coloured frogs seen throughout Central America. Avoid this. Though not all frogs in Panamá are poisonous, many do secrete a toxic substance that protects them from predators. Avoid touching any frogs and you will avoid potential problems.

The Sun

Exposure to the sun, as pleasant as it can be, can also cause a few problems—some of them serious. In recent years there has been a higher incidence of skin cancer around the world. A good sun screen is invaluable, but be aware that most dermatologists recommend buying a brand name sun screen with a minimum SPF of 15 for adults and 25 for children. To be fully effective, the cream must be applied at least 30 min before exposure to the sun and should be re-applied regularly while outside. Avoid staying in the sun for too long, especially the first few days, as it may take a little while to get used to the sun's strength. A hat and proper sunglasses will also help protect you from the sun. The longer you stay out in the sun, the higher the risk of getting sunstroke, so be careful.

The Sea

The long sandy beaches along both coasts of Panamá are among the country's most beautiful attractions; many are completely undeveloped and have no facilities.

For the sake of safety and enjoyment, beach-goers should keep the following suggestions in mind:

Choose a beach where other people are swimming—busy beaches are generally safer ones. This is a particularly good idea if you are on your own, as it means there will be someone around if you need help. A number of areas have strong undercurrents that can pull swimmers under the surface or out to sea.

If you are intent on swimming alone off empty beaches, make sure these places are safe for swimming. Certain stretches of coastline on the Pacific side are heavily frequented by sharks.

Find out about the jellyfish situation where you are. They have cycles of abundance and are present close to shore at certain times of the day.

Wear sandals or shoes rather than walking barefoot over rocks or coral. Be careful of insects at the beach as well, as some can cause painful stings.
In general, avoid venturing too far out from deserted beaches, which are deserted for a reason, probably because they are more dangerous.

Follow the example of the local inhabitants and, so as not to offend, do not sunbathe or swim in the nude (or topless).

Jet Lag and Motion Sickness

The discomfort of jet lag is inevitable. Some tricks might help lessen it, but remember that the best way to get through it is to give your body time to adapt. You can even start adjusting to your new time gradually before your departure and on the airplane. Eat well and drink a lot of water. You are strongly advised to force yourself to switch to the new time as soon as you arrive. Stay awake if is morning and go to sleep if it is evening. This way your body will become adjusted more quickly.

To minimize the discomfort of motion sickness, avoid the jolts as much as possible and keep your eyes on the horizon (for example, sit in the middle of a boat or in the front of a car or a bus). Eat small, light meals, both before leaving and during the journey. There are accessories and medications that can help reduce symptoms such as nausea. Some friendly advice: try to relax and think about something else!

Packing Checklist

Insect repellent (indispensable if travelling outside Panama City)

Insect coils

Sun block (cream)

Sink stopper

Sunglasses

Hat

Umbrella

Hiking boots

Binoculars

Light wind-breaker

Compass (for hikers)

Plastic sandals for shower and beach

First-Aid Kit

A small first-aid kit can prove useful, and should be carefully prepared before leaving home. Bring along sufficient amounts of any medications you take regularly, as well as a valid prescription. Also bring along the prescription for your glasses or contact lenses. Your kit should also include:

- adhesive bandages
- a disinfectant
- an analgesic
- antihistamines
- tablets for upset stomach or motion sickness

Don't forget to include your contact lens solution, and an extra pair of glasses, if applicable.

Packing

As the temperature in Panamá varies according to altitude and season, the type of clothes to bring depends on when and where you plan to go. In general, loose-fitting cotton clothing is best in low-lying areas. Wear shoes rather than sandals when exploring cities, as they will protect you from cuts that could get infected.

During the rainy season, and in tropical forests, it is useful to have a light windbreaker. In areas of higher elevation, where the nights can be quite cool, a sweater will come in handy. Bring walking shoes or boots that cover the ankle if you plan to explore the countryside (see p 51). Do not forget to bring along a cheap pair of plastic sandals to wear in the shower and at the beach. Certain restaurants and clubs (particularly those in cities) have a dress code—pack a few appropriate items.

Safety and Security

While Panamá has a reputation as a place where theft is common, it is important to put the facts in context. To the majority of Panamanians, your possessions (particularly things like cameras, leather suitcases and jewellery) represent a great deal of money. Theft is much more common in cities because of the high rate of poverty. Rural areas are generally safer. A degree of caution can help avoid problems. For example, do not wear too much jewellery, keep your electronic equipment in a nondescript shoulder bag, and avoid revealing the contents of your wallet when making a purchase. A money belt can be useful for hiding money, traveller's cheques and passports. And if your bags should happen to be stolen, you will at least have the money and documents necessary to get by. Remember that the less attention you draw to yourself, the less chance you have of being robbed.

Avoid bringing anything of value with you to the beach. However, if you do, keep a close eye on it. Most hotels have a safe where you can leave your valuables.

When driving in Panamanian cities, particularly Colón and Panama City, keep your doors locked. It is recommended that you park your car in a guarded lot or in an open area. Wherever you end up parking, don't leave anything valuable in the car and leave the glove compartment open.

One last piece of advice: never leave your bag in the checkroom of a major store, particularly in the capital. Even in the presence of a guard, you risk never seeing it again!

Money and Banking

Currency

The official currency of Panamá is the Balboa. The Balboa is kept on par with

Exchange Rates*

B/.1	= $1.33 CAN	$1 CAN	= B/.0.75
B/.1	= $1 US	$1 US	= B/.1
B/.1	= £0.60	£1	= B/.1.68
B/.1	= 0.87 € (euro)	1 € (euro)	= B/.1.15
B/.1	= 6.47 DKK	1 DKK	= B/.0.15

*Samples only—rates fluctuate

Panamanian Currency and the US Dollar

Panamá's balboa has been worth exactly $1US since 1934. Panamá no longer prints bank notes; bills in circulation are US dollars. Coins are the only currency still minted in Panamá, making the medio-balboa (worth $0.50) a fun souvenir. American coins are accepted everywhere.

When a small country decides to adopt the currency of another, larger country, it essentially abandons money as a tool to influence its economy. It can no longer diminish the value of its currency to stimulate exports, or increase it to control inflation. It has been proven, however, that countries with small money supplies cannot use this tool to their advantage and that a small floating supply is easy prey to speculators. A few fortunes in Hong Kong, New York or London easily could lower a small money supply by 10%. Therefore, Panamá has probably made a wise choice since its small money supply, relative to its two million inhabitants, would have been an easy prey for speculation.

the US dollar: 1 balboa = 1 US dollar. The national bank does not print bank notes. As a result, the paper money currently in use in Panamá is American (it is best to travel with American currency – including traveller's cheques). American and Panamanian coins are both used. The balboa is divided into 100 *centésimos*. There are coins *medio-balbo* (B/.0.50), *cuarto de balboa* (B/.0.25), *décimo de balboa* (B/.0.10) and cinco centésimos *de balboa* (B/.0.05). This last coin is sometimes called a real, and you may be asked for cinco real for something that costs B/.025.

Some establishments will not accept $100 and $50 bills because of the circulation of counterfeit money. Make $20 bills the largest denomination you carry.

Banks

Banks are open from 8am to 1pm. Try to avoid banks on Fridays, as this is the day many businesses do their banking. There are banks in all of the moderate and mid-size towns. Most will exchange a number of currencies, though fewer will exchange traveller's cheques.

Traveller's Cheques

It is always best to keep most of your money in traveller's cheques in U.S. dollars. A small commission (usually USD$0.10 per cheque) is sometimes charged in banks.

Traveller's cheques in US currency are accepted in some hotels, restaurants and stores.

Credit Cards

Credit cards, particularly Visa and MasterCard, are accepted by many businesses. Do not rely on credit cards alone, however, as many places, especially in the countryside, will refuse them. Always carry some cash.

Telecommunications

Mail

There are post offices, or ***Correos y telégrafos***, in every sizeable town, distinguished by a blue-and- yellow sign. In the capital, some hotels also sell stamps and provide mail service for guests. Post cards to North America cost B/.025 and to Europe B/.045.

Telephone and Faxes

Panamá's country code is ***507***; there are no area codes. To call Panamá, first dial the number for international calls (e.g. 00 from Europe and 011 from Canada and the United States), followed by 507 then the seven-digit Panamánian number.

To call abroad from Panamá, dial 00, followed by the country code of the country you are dialling, then the area code (if applicable) and finally your party's number.

For example, to call ***Great Britain***, dial 00-44, followed by the area code (London 171/181) and your party's number.

For ***Canada*** and the ***United States***, dial 00-1, the area code, then your party's number. Canada Direct ☎***0 800 019 0119*** will connect you directly to an operator in Canada for free. However, if you are calling from a public telephone, you must still use a calling card or insert change in order to get a line. International telephone calls can be made from post offices and from most large hotels.

If you want to send a fax to Panamá and the fax and telephone numbers are the same, you will usually have to call first to check that the fax machine is turned on.

Newspapers

The most widely distributed newspapers are *La Prensa*, *El* Siglo, *El Panamá América* and *Crítica*.

Press

www.elsiglo.com

www.sinfo.net/prensa/home.htm

www.eluniversal-pma.com

www.epasa.com/El_Panama_America/today/index.html

www.epasa.com/critica/hoy/critica.html

Accommodations

Many visitors to Panamá find that staying in air-conditioned rooms is necessary for maintaining a minimum level of comfort (nights in Panamá can be extremely hot and sticky). At the very least, be sure that the rooms you rent have good mosquito netting. In some hotels, the price of a room includes breakfast. Ask about this before registering.

As in many countries, a wide range of accommodation possibilities is available in Panamá. Not surprisingly, the cheapest places—those costing less than B/.25 a night—are also the least comfortable (they usually do not have air-conditioning, mosquito netting or private bathrooms). A 10% tax is added to the price of hotel rooms. It is often possible to negotiate a 10% to 20% reduction in the price of a hotel room. However, this may be more difficult to do on weekends, Panamanian national holidays and during vacation periods. With the competition between hotels in Panama City, it is often possible to negotiate a reduction of as much as 25% off the price of a room. In the beach resorts, hotels can give reductions up to 40% during low season. The bigger hotels usually accept credit cards, while smaller establishments often do not.

The school year in Panamá runs from March to December. At present, the country's tourist infrastructure is primarily geared toward meeting the demands of Panamanian holiday-makers, who flock to the country's most popular sites between December and March; visitors from outside the country are advised to make reservations during this period.

The Ulysses Boat

The Ulysses boat pictogram appears next to our favourite accommodations. While every establishment recommended in this guide was included because of its high quality and/or uniqueness, as well as its high value, every once in a while we come across an establishment that absolutely wows us. These, our favourite establishments, are awarded a Ulysses boat. You'll find boats in all price categories: next to exclusive, high-price establishments, as well as budget ones. Regardless of the price, each of these establishments offers the most for your money. Look for them first!

Accommodation Rates and Taxes

Five price categories are used in the descriptions of the hotels and other types of lodgings mentioned in this guide (see below). The prices listed are for double rooms and do not include taxes. In most cases, a 10% tax will be added to the price of a room.

Unless otherwise indicated, prices in the guidebook refer to US dollars.

$	$25 or less
$$	$25 to $50
$$$	$51 to $90
$$$$	$91 to $150
$$$$$	more than $150

Hotels

While the range of comfort and services offered by hotels in Panamá can vary greatly, most of the places mentioned in this guide have at least a small bathroom and airconditioning. The low budget hotels (*with nightly rates between B/.25 and B/.50*) provide a basic level of comfort but can be quite pleasant. Moderately priced hotels (*B/.50 to B/.150*) offer a level of comfort visitors may be used to from hotels back home. They often have a bar, restaurant and pool.

Hotels in both categories are often family run and are good places to meet Panamanians. More expensive hotels (*more than B/.150 per night*) offer a range of services and a level of comfort typical of major international hotel chains and are often located in the best tourist spots.

Apart-Hotels

Apart-hotels offer a full range of services plus rooms equipped with fully functional kitchenettes (pots, pans and dishes included). This type of accommodation is most often found in larger towns (there are many in Panama City). Visitors planning on longer stays can save on meal costs by staying at these places. Room rates tend to be lower for longer stays (though you may have to bargain).

Cabañas

Cabañas are small huts or cabins that are usually located on or near the beach. Some are extremely basic and do not even come with mosquito netting, while others have air-conditioning and kitchenettes. Less expensive *cabañas* often have several beds in one room. On national holidays and during vacation periods, people from all over Panamá descend on the beaches. During these periods accommodation can be hard to come by (if you have not made reservations) but there is much more activity day and night. For a more peaceful stay, try to get a *cabaña* set well away from the others on the beach, as they are often poorly soundproofed.

Motels

Motels tend to be a bit less expensive than medium-priced hotels, but are correspondingly less comfortable. Despite a few drawbacks (less attractive locations, poor soundproofing), motels can be useful to travellers in a hurry, as they are often conveniently located next to major roads and highways (though they sometimes turn out to be brothels). The more expensive

The colonial homes in the neighbourhood of Casco Viejo will charm one and all.
– courtesy of IPAT

A true national symbol, the *pollera* is the pride of Panamanian women.
– courtesy of IPAT

Panamá is also the Caribbean. *– courtesy of IPAT*

The province of Bocas del Toro: for unique atmosphere! *– courtesy of IPAT*

Menu Glossary

Breakfast *(el desayuno)*

Frutos	fruit
Huevo	egg
Jamón	ham
Jugo	juice
Leche	milk
Marmelada	jam
Naranja	orange
Pan	bread
Piña	pineapple
Plátano	banana
Queso	cheese
Tocino	bacon
Tortilla	flat corn bread

Lunch and supper *(el almuerzo y la cena)*

Agua	water
Ajo	garlic
Arroz	rice
Bistec	roast beef
Camaroncitos	small shrimp
Camarones	shrimp
Carne	meat
Carne al carbon	meat cooked on a charcoal grill
Cerdo	pork
Cerveza	beer
Chuleta	pork chop
Conejo	rabbit
Empanadas	vegetable or meat-filled pastry
Ensalada	salad
Filete	escalope
Hongos	mushrooms
Langosta	scampi
Mariscos	seafood
Papas fritas	fried potatoes
Patacones	fried plantains
Pescado	fish
Pollo	chicken
Pollo asado	grilled chicken
Postre	dessert
Sopa	soup
Verdura	vegetables
Vino	wine

motels have a pool and restaurant.

Cottages

In the western part of the country, most often in mountainous areas in the province of Chiriquí, small cottages are available for rent. These fully equipped little houses are often rented to families. This is a recommended form of accommodation for visitors interested in exploring nature and enjoying the cooler mountain air. Usually, cottages can only be rented for stays of at least several days, if not weeks.

Camping

The country's very hot nights and many insects do not make this a very attractive activity. Camping in Panamá can also be unsafe because of the abundance of insects and animals.

Restaurants

Restaurants in the country's bigger cities reflect Panamá's cultural diversity by offering a wide range of cuisines. Whether you prefer Italian, French, Chinese or, of course, Panamanian cooking, you will find what you are looking for. In the countryside, the choice is much smaller and is often restricted to Panamanian food. With the heat and the big portions, it is often difficult to eat three meals a day.

The Ulysses Boat

The Ulysses boat pictogram appears next to our favourite restaurants. For more information, see p 56.

Prices, Taxes and Tips

The prices mentioned in the restaurant sections of this guide generally refer to a meal for one person, including appetizer, main course and dessert. Drinks (wine, beer, etc.) and tip are not included, but taxes are. A 10% tip is standard in bars and restaurants. Check your bill carefully, as the tip is sometimes included automatically.

$	less than $8
$$	$9 to $15
$$$	$16 to $25
$$$$	$26 to $40
$$$$$	$40 or more

Panamanian Cuisine

Panamanian food is delicious and not too spicy. Corn, in all its forms, has a very prominent place. However, the cuisine in general is not particularly varied. Cooking is done mainly in oil. Certain dishes, especially *pollo, ceviche, patacones, corvina, camarones*, as well as corn prepared in a variety of ways, are sometimes the only things available.

While a large variety of fruits are grown in the country, restaurants serve very little fresh fruit. For example, it is very rare to be offered fresh fruit for breakfast. The best place to buy fruit is at outdoor markets and at stands along major roads.

Drinks

Horas Felizes (Happy Hour)

At certain times of the day in Panama City, usually between 4pm and 7pm, bars offer reduced prices on drinks. Like happy hour in many other countries, during these periods you can either buy two drinks for the price of one or pay a reduced price for a single drink.

Beer

Beer is the most popular alcoholic drink in Panamá. Most beer in Panamá is light, has a fairly low alcohol content (between 3% and 3.8%), and of good quality. The most popular brands include *Panamá, Cristal, Atlas* and *Balboa*.

Wine

Wine is not very popular in Panamá and there is little in the way of local production. The French wines sometimes sold in restaurants are often very expensive. We recommend the more affordable (and usually very good) Chilean wines instead. Expect to pay between B/.15 and B/.20 a bottle.

Panamanian Dishes Not to Be Missed

Bollo: A corn-based dish that can be prepared with various ingredients (chicken, vegetables, beef, etc.) and served in corn husks.

Camaroncitos: Small shrimp (fish, seafood and shellfish dishes are very good in Panamá).

Carimañola: Pastry stuffed with manioc and meat or fish, mixed with egg.

Carne de Res: Beef from Bollo Chiricano cows (beef is a specialty of the southwestern regions).

Ceviche: Raw fish, usually corvina, in lemon juice and coriander.

Chicharrones: Pork rinds (an acquired taste).

Corvina: White fish common to the Pacific.

Empanadas: Pastry (often made of corn flour) filled with meat or vegetables.

Patacones: Fried plantain slices.

Platanos en tentación: Dessert consisting of very ripe plantains slowly cooked in cane sugar.

Ropa Vieja: Ground hamburger seasoned with onions, green peppers and even cassava.

Sancocho: Soup with chicken, cassava, onions, oregano, coriander and even corn.

Sopa Borracha: Moist rum cake with prunes and raisins.

Sopa de Gloria: Moist milk cake with sugar and nuts.

Tamales: Cornmeal mixed with chicken or pork with spices wrapped in a banana leaf—a delicacy.

Spirits

The most popular type of distilled liquor in Panamá is Seco, a sugarcane-based rum. The brand Capita Vieja is also very popular.

Chicha

This refreshing drink is made of milk and fruit juice. While it is generally a good idea to avoid milk products in Panamá, Chicha is usually safe to drink in the northern regions of the province of Chiriquí. The drink comes in a variety of flavours.

Identity and Culture Shock

Another Culture

Culture Shock

You're going to visit a new country, get acquainted with different people, taste new flavours, smell unfamiliar scents, see surprising things—in short, discover a culture that is not your own. You'll gain a great deal form this encounter, but it may also shake you up more than you'd think. Culture shock can strike anyone, anywhere... even, sometimes, not so far from home!

All the more reason, if you go to a foreign country, to be on the alert for the symptoms of culture shock. Faced with the different ways of doing things in the new culture, your usual reference points may prove of little use to you. The language may be unfamiliar to you, beliefs may strike you as impenetrable, customs incomprehensible, people unapproachable... and some things might seem unacceptable from the outset. Don't panic—we humans are very adaptable!

Remember that cultural diversity is a treasure! Instead of searching for your usual touchstones, put yourself in the shoes of the people around you and try to understand their way of life. When you stay courteous, unassuming and sensitive, people can be extremely helpful. Respect is the simple key to improving many situations.

Remember that it isn't a question of simply tolerating what seems odd to you. Respect means much more than that. Who knows, trying to understand the whys and wherefores of different facets of a culture might well become one of the things you enjoy most about travel.

Laws and Customs Abroad

It isn't necessary to memorize the legal code of the country you're going to visit. However, be aware that you are subject to the laws of the land you are in, even though you are not a citizen of that country. Never assume that because something is permissible by law at home, it is automatically legal elsewhere. Also, never forget to take cultural differences into account. Certain gestures or attitudes that seem trivial to you can get you in trouble in other countries. Staying sensitive to the customs of your hosts is the best strategy for avoiding problems.

The Responsible Traveller

The adventure of travelling will probably be an enriching experience for you. But will it be the same for your hosts? The question of whether or not tourism is good for a host country is controversial. On one hand, tourism brings many advantages, such as economic development, the promotion and rejuvenation of a culture and intercultural exchange; on the other hand, tourism can have negative impacts: an increase in crime, deepening of inequalities, environmental destruction, etc. But one thing is for sure: your journey will have an impact on your destination.

This is rather obvious when we speak of the environment. You should be as respectful of the environment of your host country as you would be at home. We hear it often enough: we all live on the same planet! But when it comes to social, cultural and even economic aspects, it can be more difficult to evaluate the impact of our travels. Be aware of the reality around you, and ask yourself what the repercussions will be before acting. Remember that you may make an impression that is much different than the one you wish to give.

Regardless of the type of travelling we choose, it is up to each and every one of us to develop a social conscience and to assume responsibility for our actions in a foreign country. Common sense, respect, altruism, and a hint of modesty are useful tools that will go a long way.

Travelling with Children

Travelling with children, however young they may be, can be a pleasant experience. A few precautions and ample preparations are the keys to a fun trip.

There are numerous activities, tours and diversions for the whole family to enjoy in Panamá.

In Hotels

Many hotels are well equipped for children, and there is usually no extra fee for travelling with an infant. Many hotels and bed and breakfasts have cribs; ask for one when reserving your room. You may have to pay extra for children, however, but the supplement is generally low.

If you have evening plans, your hotel may be able to provide you with a list of trustworthy babysitters.

Car Rentals

Most car rental agencies rent car seats for children. They are usually not very expensive. Ask for one when making your reservation.

The Sun

Needless to say, a child's skin requires strong protection against the sun; in fact, it is preferable not to expose toddlers to its harsh rays. Before going to the beach, remember to apply sunscreen (SPF 25 for children, 35 for infants). If you think your child will spend a long time under the sun, you should consider purchasing a sunscreen with SPF 60.

Children of all ages should wear a hat that provides good coverage for the head throughout the day.

Swimming

Children usually get quite excited about playing in the waves and can do so for hours on end. However, parents must be very careful and watch them constantly; accidents can happen in a matter of seconds. Ideally, an adult should accompany children into the water, especially the younger ones, and stand farther out in the water so that the kids can play between the beach and the supervising adult. This way, he or she can quickly intervene in case of an emergency.

For infants and toddlers, some diapers are especially designed for swimming, such as "Little Swimmers" by Huggies. These are quite useful when having fun in the water!

Ecotourism

Agencies Specializing in Ecotourism

Canada

Voyages Delta
475 Avenue du Président-Kennedy, Montréal, QC, H3A 1J7
☎(514) 322-6500

In Panamá

Ancón Expeditions
Calle Elvira Méndez
Edificio El Dorado
☎269-9414 or 269-9415
⇄264-3713
www.anconexpeditions.com

Starlite Travel
Ave. Roosevelt et Heights L-639, Balboa
in front of the canal administration building and next to McDonalds
Apdo 6-6200, El Dorado
☎232-6423 or 232-6401
⇄232-6448

Iguana Tours
Vía. Porras, facing Parque Omar
☎226-8738 or 226-1667
⇄226-4736
www.nvmundo.com/iguanatours/

Aventuras Panamá
Apdo 9869, Panamá 4
☎260-0044 or 236-5814
⇄260-7535
www.aventuraspanama.com

Pesantez Tours
Plaza Balboa, Oficina 2
Apdo 55-0716, Punta Paitilla
☎263-7577 or 263-8771
⇄263-7860
www.pesantez-tours.com

Gamboa Tours
Holiday Inn, Planta Baja, Suite 8, Av. Manuel E. Batista
☎269-3176 or 269-3391
⇄269-1500

PEX (Panama Explorer Club)
Edificío El Virrey, Planta Baja
Vía Italia, Punta Paitilla
☎215-2330
⇄215-2331
www.pexclub.com

Miscellaneous

Women Travellers

Women travelling alone should not encounter any problems. Panamá is one of the rare Latin American countries to have elected a woman as president of the republic (Mireya Moscoso). Of course, a certain level of caution should be exercised, but for the most part, people are friendly and not aggressive. Generally, men are respectful of women. Some men will show a tendency toward macho behaviour, and this includes making unwanted verbal advances or comments. However, this is not usually done in a threatening manner. You may be more likely to be left alone if you dress conservatively in this Catholic country.

Gay and Lesbian Life

Despite the relatively important role women play in Panamanian society, the situation for gays and lesbians is about the same as in other Latin American countries. Although there are a few gay bars in the capital (see p 113), gays and lesbians are still repressed to a certain extent. Machismo, the ideology of male superiority, remains alive and well, and its insistence upon maintaining rigid sex-based stereotypical roles is responsible more than anything else for the repression of gays and lesbians and the attempt to keep women in their traditional roles.

At press time, a new Panamanian gay magazine, *Verzatil Magazine*, was available in most of Panama City's gay establishments. The fact that this is the very first publication of its kind devoted entirely to the gay community is proof positive that attitudes toward sexual minorities are improving in Panamá. Another positive sign of change is the recently launched *www.chebimel.com* Web site, which provides a great deal of information on the capital's gay community.

Electricity

Electrical appliances run on an alternating current of 110 volts (60 cycles), just as in North America. European travellers will need both a converter and an adapter with two parallel flat pins for any appliances they plan to bring along.

Smokers

There are no restrictions on smoking in Panamá, and cigarettes are very cheap.

Holidays

All banks and businesses close their doors on holidays and the country seems to function in slow-motion. Make sure you do not get caught needing to change money or buy last minute souvenirs on one of these days.

January 1
New Year's Day

January 9
Martyrs' Day

May 1
May Day

October 12
Hispanic Day (Dia de la Raza; arrival of Columbus)

November 3
Independence Day (separation from Colombia)

November 10
Declaration of Independence Day

November 28
Independence Day (separation from Spain)

December 8
Mother's Day

Shifting
Good Friday

Panamá's famous carnival celebrations are particularly spectacular in the Azuero peninsula. They always take place from the Saturday to the Tuesday preceding Ash Wednesday.

Easter is also a time for celebration in various cities throughout the country.

Time Zones

Panamá is in the Eastern Standard Time Zone. This means that when North America is not on daylight savings, there is no time difference with the East Coast, and it is three hours ahead of the West Coast. Panamá is six or seven hours behind continental Europe, depending on the time of year.

Weights and Measures

Officially, Panamá uses the metric system.

Outdoors

A wealth of highly varied natural attractions awaits the visitor to Panamá; these can be discovered through the various outings recommended in the "Outdoor Activities" section of each chapter.

During your stay you will certainly have the opportunity to try various sports, which will allow you to get better acquainted with the country's rich environment. This chapter provides an overview of the major parks and activities and places at which they can be enjoyed.

National Parks

Panamá may have fewer national parks than Costa Rica, but the great variety of plant and animal life in Panamá is extraordinary. Panamá's tropical forest has remained intact and virtually untouched, thanks to the absence of violent hurricanes. The variety of flora harboured within will delight travellers interested in botany.

Despite this extraordinary stroke of luck, major ecological problems seem to be looming in the future. Like many other countries in the region, Panamá must come to grips with the problem of deforestation, the result of an aggressive expansion of agriculture. These fertile regions have attracted many peasants, who have harshly cleared the land, leading to serious erosion problems. Among the hardest hit is the province of Chiriquí, especially the region around the Volcán Barú. This problem has made Panamanians strongly aware of ecological concerns, and a number of nature preservation societies have been founded.

In addition to creating national parks and various protected zones, the Panamanian government has also established two environmental research organizations: ANAM (Autoridad Nacional del Ambiente) and IDIAP (Instituto de Investigación Agropecuaria de Panamá). ANAM is responsible for managing the national parks and protecting the environment, while IDIAP takes care of agricultural matters. Unfortunately, the government greatly reduced its spending on environmental protection after the economic crisis. The crisis even forced the government to lease protected lands for profit. Therefore, tourist facilities in the parks are not as developed as in Canada, the U.S. or even Costa Rica. Information centres, accommodation, picnic areas and hiking trails vary enormously from one park to another, and are unfortunately non-existent in many cases.

Roads to the parks are often unpaved and require a four-wheel-drive vehicle. However, realizing the success of ecotourism in neighbouring Costa Rica, the Panamanian government is trying to improve the parks to draw more visitors. Nevertheless, here as everywhere else, government bureaucracy isn't budging much and it will probably take several years for significant improvements to be seen. However, because of the ongoing withdrawal of American military forces and the large loss of U.S. capital, the Panamanian government will have to act more quickly. The government has made some efforts, though, such as setting up the Autoridad de la Región Interoceánica, to carry out a general development plan for the canal zone. This plan involves the sale of numerous lots bordering the canal as well as the issuing of tax breaks to attract investors to the former zone.

Overdevelopment of the canal is also a concern, especially for environmental organizations. In the future, the Panamanian government will hopefully do even more to protect the country's rich heritage.

Today, there are 13 national parks, one of which is managed jointly with Costa Rica. One metropolitan park and 27 other zones have also been given special status and are classified under such names as reserve, refuge, recreational zone and recreational park. The majority of these zones are fully or partially protected and make up 22% of the isthmus. A list of the main parks is provided in the boxed text in this chapter. For further information, refer to the "Parks" section in the chapter on each province.

An ANAM permit is required to visit or camp in a national park. Although permits can be obtained at certain park entrances, it is more practical to get one beforehand in the capital (see address below). ANAM regional offices are not always open when you get there and are sometimes far from the park you wish to visit. Park entrance fees vary between B/.3 et B/.10 per park.

National Parks

1. Parque Nacional Cerro Hoya
2. Parque Nacional y Reserva Biológica Altos de Campana (see p 138)
3. Parque Nacional Soberanía (see p 125)
4. Parque Nacional Chagres (see p 126)
5. Parque Nacional Coiba
6. Parque Nacional del Darién (see p 254)
7. Parque Nacional Volcan Barú (see p 208)
8. Parque Nacional Camino de Cruces (see p 125)
9. Parque Nacional Portobelo
10. Parque Nacional Marino Isla Bastimentos (see p 229)
11. Parque Nacional Sarigua (see p 185)
12. Parque Nacional General de División Omar Torijos Herrera
13. Parque Nacional Marino Golfo de Chiriquí
14. Parque Internacional La Amistad (see p 207)

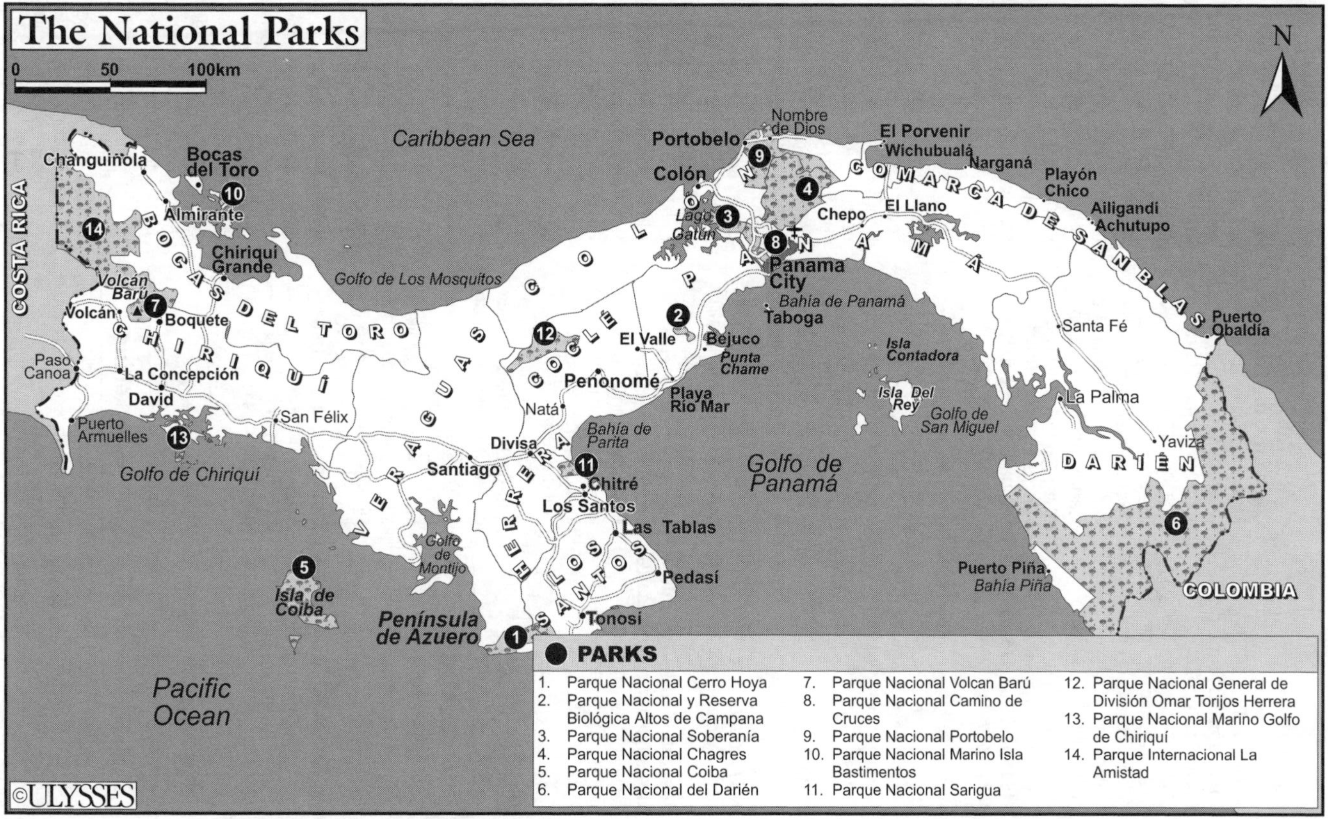
The National Parks
0
50
100km
N
Caribbean Sea
Pacific Ocean
Golfo de Panamá
Golfo de Chiriquí
Golfo de Los Mosquitos
Bahía de Panamá
Bahía de Parita
Golfo de San Miguel
Golfo de Montijo
Bahía Piña
COSTA RICA
COLOMBIA
BOCAS DEL TORO
CHIRIQUÍ
VERAGUAS
COCLÉ
COLÓN
PANAMÁ
HERRERA
LOS SANTOS
DARIÉN
COMARCA DE SAN BLAS
Changuinola
Bocas del Toro
Almirante
Chiriqui Grande
Volcán Barú
Volcán
Boquete
Paso Canoa
La Concepción
David
Puerto Armuelles
San Félix
Santiago
Divisa
Natá
Penonomé
El Valle
Playa Río Mar
Bejuco
Punta Chame
Taboga
Panama City
Colón
Lago Gatún
Portobelo
Nombre de Dios
El Porvenir
Wichubualá
Narganá
Playón Chico
Ailigandí
Achutupo
Puerto Obaldía
Chepo
El Llano
Santa Fé
La Palma
Yaviza
Puerto Piña
Isla Contadora
Isla Del Rey
Chitré
Los Santos
Las Tablas
Pedasí
Tonosí
Península de Azuero
Isla de Coiba
PARKS
1. Parque Nacional Cerro Hoya
2. Parque Nacional y Reserva Biológica Altos de Campana
3. Parque Nacional Soberanía
4. Parque Nacional Chagres
5. Parque Nacional Coiba
6. Parque Nacional del Darién
7. Parque Nacional Volcan Barú
8. Parque Nacional Camino de Cruces
9. Parque Nacional Portobelo
10. Parque Nacional Marino Isla Bastimentos
11. Parque Nacional Sarigua
12. Parque Nacional General de División Omar Torijos Herrera
13. Parque Nacional Marino Golfo de Chiriquí
14. Parque Internacional La Amistad
©ULYSSES

For information:

ANAM (INRENARE)
Dirección Nacional de Areas Protegidas
Calle Curundú also called Vía La Amistad and Avenida Ascañio Villalaz (in front of the bus station)
Edificio 804, Apdo C
Zona 0543, Balboa
Corrigimiento de Ancón
☎315-0855 or 315-0990
www.anam.gob.pa

Among the environmental organizations working in Panamá, the following two are particularly well reputed.

ANCÓN
Quarry Heights
Balboa, 41
☎314-0060
www.ancon.org

Instituto Smithsonian de Investigaciones Tropicales
Avenida Roosevelt nº 401
Edificio Tivoli, Ancón
☎227-6022

Outdoor Activities

Swimming

Naturally, swimming is a popular activity in Panamá—after all, people come here to enjoy the sea and the sun.

Furthermore, many resorts have been built along the country's most beautiful beaches, such as those on **Isla Taboga, Isla Contadora, the Islas San Blas** and in the region west of PanamaCity, which includes **Costa Blanca**. The beaches on either side of the country have their own characteristics. The water on the Atlantic, or Caribbean, side is clearer, making it easier to spot interesting fish. However, this part of the country also gets more rain and is more humid. The Pacific coast has a greater number of beaches with fine sand and has drier weather, but the water is less clear. Since the country is much longer than it is wide, it has countless islands and beaches, most of which remain completely undeveloped. Visitors seeking solitude will have no trouble finding kilometres of deserted beach in the provinces of **Los Santos** and **Chiriquí**. On the other hand, those looking for lively activity will be delighted with the beaches in the districts of **San Carlos**, **Costa Blanca** or **Isla Taboga**, which are crowded with Panamanian families on weekends. Finally, if you would like to swim in waters ideal for observing fish and have a taste for adventure, you can head out to **Isla de Colón** and **Isla Bastimentos** in the province of Bocas del Toro.

Snorkelling

This sport requires little equipment—flippers, a mask and a snorkel, all of which are easy to rent in Panamá for just a few dollars. Anyone can snorkel, and no courses are required. It's a very pleasant way to explore the sea bottom in this wonderful part of the world. Snorkellers should note that the water on the Atlantic coast is clearer than that on the Pacific coast, although with the many islands on either side of the isthmus, the sport is just as accessible on either coast. Some beaches are skirted by superb coral reefs that add to the beauty of the underwater scenery. It is preferable to snorkel in bays and quiet waters, and a degree of caution should be taken. Among the more beautiful places are the **Islas San Blas**, **Isla de Colón** and **Isla Bastimentos** (at Bocas del Toro), **Isla Grande** (in the province of **Colón**) and **Isla Contadora** in the **Las Perlas** archipelago.

Scuba Diving

Scuba diving is more complicated than snorkelling and requires some training and experience. Before diving, you must attend courses and obtain a certificate. A few tourist centres provide these courses (see below). For coastline diving, the Atlantic is your better option. The water there is clearer and the marine wildlife especially abundant. In addition, the tides are not as high, making the water safer for divers. Places like **Bocas del Toro**, the **San Blas islands** and **Isla**

Grande are famous for the sport. Diving along the Pacific coast is not recommended because of tidal variations, which can be as much as six or seven metres in a day. The sport can, however, be practised near the great many islands along the coast.

In artificial **Lago Gatún**, divers have an extraordinary chance to explore a silent world, where some of the most unusual wildlife can be seen. Long ago, tropical forests grew here, and the sight of submerged villages only enhances the impression of having discovered some lost world. Some cities along the lake (like **Gamboa**, **Escobal** and **La Arenosa**) provide various services for this activity.

Whether you are planning to rent or buy equipment, or for information on diving guides or diving instruction, various stores in downtown Panama City can help you out (see p 76).

Surfing and Windsurfing

Equipment for surfing and windsurfing, like that for diving, can be rented in the capital (see p 76) or from various seaside hotels. Beginner windsurfers will particularly enjoy the beaches at **El Palmar** and **Río Mar**, scarcely half an hour's drive from the capital. Those who want a little more excitement should look for windier bays. In the province of **Los Santos, the high waves at Playa Venado**, make it one of the country's best spots for windsurfing. Unfortunately, there are few services there, and the beach is isolated.

Deep-Sea Fishing

The more luxurious hotels in the **Las Perlas archipelago** and the **Gulf of San Miquel** often organize deep-sea fishing expeditions, although you need not be a guest at one of these hotels to take part. This is a fine opportunity to sail about and enjoy the open sea, while learning about the various species of fish native to the Pacific. Equipment and advice are available on board, and an outing usually lasts half a day.

Hiking

Hiking is the best way to discover Panamá's parks, reserves and untamed wilderness. Because the country is relatively small and covered by rugged terrain, mountain hikes are particularly spectacular. In the province of Chiriquí, you can climb 3,474m to the top of **Volcán Barú**—quite an invigorating hike! Some parks have rainforest trails that are more widely accessible, including the historic **camino de cruzes** (see p 125), a trail formerly used by the Spaniards. This trail is difficult to hike on, not because it is steep but because of the heat and humidity, which can sometimes be suffocating. Unfortunately, marked trails on the isthmus are hard to find, so it is best to contact one of the environmental protection organizations (see p 66) or one of the many ecotourism agencies for information. The addresses and telephone numbers of some of these companies can be found in the "Practical Information" chapter (see p 61). Various outings are also described in the "Outdoor Activities" section of each chapter. Finally, before setting out on a hike in one of the country's numerous parks, keep in mind that a permit is required to visit them (see p 66).

Cycling

Panamá's road system includes everything from two-lane main highways with no shoulders, to small secondary roads riddled with potholes — certainly not a cyclist's dream. Cycling may be a very pleasant way of getting about, but it is fairly dangerous on these roads, especially on the Interamericana, where large trucks, not always well-maintained, travel at dangerous speeds. There are also the perpetually warm daytime temperatures and lack of shade to contend with, and few roads are lit at night. Nevertheless, outside the major urban centres, cycling can be extremely pleasant— but watch out for speeding cars.

Horseback Riding

For some Panamanians, especially those in the remote countryside, riding is more than just a sport; in the province of **Los Santos** and in the whole **Azuero peninsula**, it is still an important means of transportation. In fact, there are more horses than there are cars! Riding is a pleasant form of relaxation, and a good way to discover certain parts of Panamá. However, follow the same advice provided for nature hikes: consult an agency.

Rafting

Although Panamá is not well-known for rafting, it offers some rivers that are ideal for it. Among the best-known are **Río Chagres** (see p 127), which runs into the gigantic artificial **Lake Alajuela** (less than one hour from the capital), as well as the **Río Chiriquí** (see p 211) in the more mountainous and temperate province of Chiriquí. The latter is one of the few rivers where rafting can be enjoyed year-round as a result of its partially controlled flow. However, the level of difficulty on these two rivers changes according to the time of year. The best months for rafting are from September to December.

Golf

A popular pastime in Europe and North America, golf is becoming increasingly popular in Panamá. Despite the construction of a new course on **Isla Contadora** and a few private courses in the former canal zone, the only professional course accessible for tourists is **Playa Coronado**, barely an hour from the capital (see p 144).

Bird-watching

With 900 bird species, Panamá is without a doubt one of the best places in the world for bird watching. People come from all over the world to see the famous quetzal (Guatemala's national emblem), which can be seen in the **Parque Internacional La Amistad** (part of which is in Costa Rica). Other good places for bird watching are **Parque Nacional Soberanía** (known for its excellent observation platform) (see p 125), and the large **Parque Nacional del Darién**, which still harbours the harpy eagle (Panamá's national emblem), one of the world's most powerful raptors. Hiring a naturalist guide will maximize your chances of seeing the greatest number of bird species. The forest is so dense that it can be extremely difficult for the untrained eye to spot certain birds. The Audubon Society, internationally renowned for its research on birds, regularly organizes hikes led by biologists at quite affordable prices. For more information:

Sociedad Audubon de Panamá
Calle 74 Este (close to the Parque Recreativo)
Carrasquilla, Apdo 2026
Balboa
☎***224-9371***
⇄***224-4740***
www.orbi.net/audubon
www.panamaaudubon.org

Harpy eagle

Panama City

The province of Panamá is the most populated on the isthmus, with 1.2-million inhabitants, some 800,000 of whom live in and around Panama City (Ciudad de Panamá), the country's capital. The Canal Zone slices through the province (and neighbouring Colón), bringing with it huge quantities of merchandise.

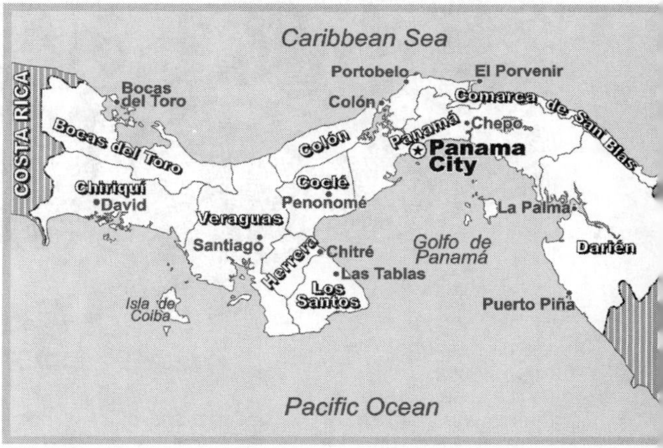

The province has much to recommend it to visitors, including the canal itself, and the beautiful countryside it crosses, attractive islands and beaches nearby as well as Panama City, with its colonial buildings. The present chapter is devoted solely to Panama City. The Canal Zone and the islands and beaches in the Bahía de Panamá (Gulf of Panamá) are covered in the two following chapters.

Whatever the point of your visit to Panamá, put aside at least a few days to explore the many splendours of this city. You will not be disappointed.

History

Panama City was founded on two separate occasions and in two different places. Its history begins in 1519, when Pedrarias Dávila founded the small village of Nuestra Señora de la Asunción de Panamá in a bay where today lie the ruins of Panamá Viejo. This modest settlement developed slowly at first, its main activities including fishing and the mining of small quantities of gold in the west of the territory. Later on, the discovery of the fabulous riches of the Inca Empire and the quarrying of a major silver mine in Potosí, Peru ensured the expansion of the *ciudad*. The opening of trails linking Panama City to both Nombre de Dios and the Fuerte San Lorenzo on the Atlantic coast made the isthmus a crucial transit point for goods being shipped between the two oceans. Because of its strategic location, Panama City gained the status of the first European commercial trading post on the Pacific coast; the city was designated a *Ciudad Real* as early as 1521. The busy overland trade route through which precious merchandise was conveyed soon made the city prosperous and, as early as the mid-17th century, it attracted the attention of both the colonial powers

Panamá Viejo

and pirates, who regarded it as a choice prey. Thus in 1671, the city was stormed by Welsh pirate Henry Morgan, who bled the capital dry and left it in ruins (see "Panamá Viejo," see p 86).

Under the orders of Governor Fernando de Córdoba, a second city was established a few kilometres west in 1673. It did not, however, grow at the same pace as Panamá Viejo. Construction was slow, and the city was damaged by numerous fires. The largest of these took place in 1737 and 1756, sending many buildings up in smoke, including the former Convento de Santo Domingo. The city's development was further hindered by Spain's decision to stop transporting goods across the isthmus once again, and by New Granada's declaration of independence. It was not until a rail link was established between Colón and Panamá (1855) and work was begun on the canal (1880) that the city finally began to thrive.

Modern-day Panama City boasts a wide variety of architecture. These different styles reflect two distinct periods: the colonial era, from which several lovely buildings still exist in Casco Viejo; and the period coinciding with the opening of the railway between Colón and Panamá, and the opening of the canal. Accordingly, buildings similar to those found in Europe, and more specifically, in France, began to appear, soon followed by the newer styles popular in the United States in the 1900s. Thus, Neoclassical, Art Nouveau and Art Deco buildings now stand side by side in Casco Viejo, the old city, and bear witness to its rich past. In the 1940s, development in the capital was concentrated mainly in the suburbs, and the large residences in the heart of the old city were gradually abandoned. Many were then divided into small apartments for low-income families, resulting in a deterioration of their facade and interior. At the end of the 1970s, however, the public began to show a certain interest in preserving the city's historic buildings. Since then, many restoration projects have been carried out, a number of which are still in progress. The great challenge facing authorities in the future will be to continue this urban renewal while protecting the fragile social fabric of the neighbourhoods.

Finding Your Way Around

By Car

From the Airport

The quickest way into the city is to take the **Corredor Sud** *(B/.2.40)*, a 22km-long highway, recently built at a cost of millions of dollars by a Mexican consortium, which continues to operate it. It runs directly from the international airport to Avenida Balboa, to the

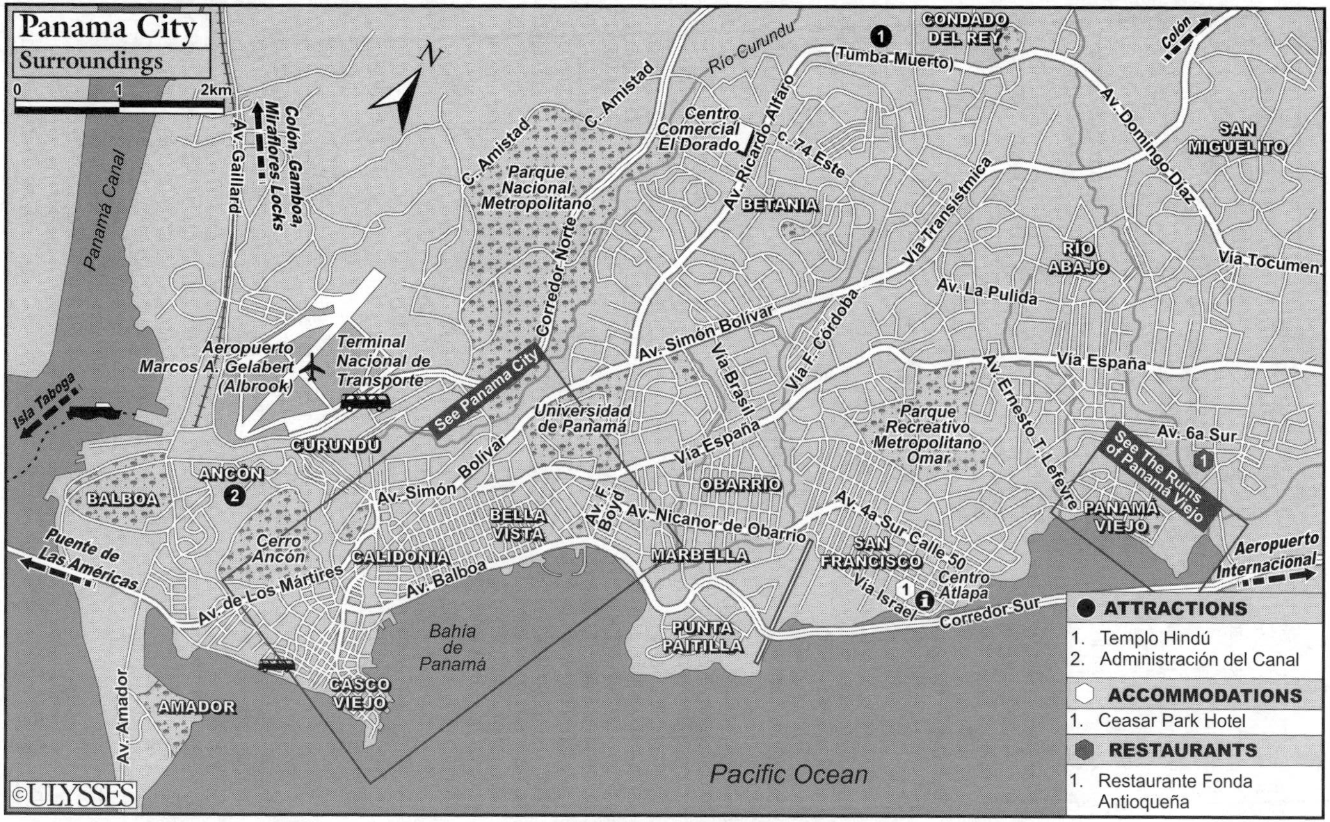

Panama City
Surroundings
0
1
2km
Colón, Gamboa, Miraflores Locks
Av. Gaillard
Panamá Canal
Isla Taboga
Aeropuerto Marcos A. Gelabert (Albrook)
Terminal Nacional de Transporte
CURUNDÚ
ANCÓN
BALBOA
Puente de Las Américas
Cerro Ancón
AMADOR
Av. Amador
Av. de Los Mártires
CALIDONIA
Av. Balboa
Bahía de Panamá
CASCO VIEJO
C. Amistad
Parque Nacional Metropolitano
Corredor Norte
See Panama City
Universidad de Panamá
Av. Simón Bolívar
BELLA VISTA
Río Curundu
Centro Comercial El Dorado
Av. Ricardo Alfaro
c. 74 Este
BETANIA
(Tumba Muerto)
CONDADO DEL REY
Colón
Av. Domingo Díaz
SAN MIGUELITO
Vía Transístmica
RÍO ABAJO
Vía Tocumen
Av. La Pulida
Vía Brasil
Vía F. Córdoba
Vía España
OBARRIO
Av. F. Boyd
Av. Nicanor de Obarrio
MARBELLA
PUNTA PAITILLA
Parque Recreativo Metropolitano Omar
Av. Ernesto T. Lefevre
Av. 6a Sur
See The Ruins of Panamá Viejo
PANAMÁ VIEJO
Av. 4a Sur Calle 50
SAN FRANCISCO
Vía Israel
Centro Atlapa
Corredor Sur
Aeropuerto Internacional
Pacific Ocean
©ULYSSES
ATTRACTIONS
1. Templo Hindú
2. Administración del Canal
ACCOMMODATIONS
1. Ceasar Park Hotel
RESTAURANTS
1. Restaurante Fonda Antioqueña

great dismay of environmentalists who claim it causes major pollution and defiles the bay.

Unfortunately, the thoroughfare runs right past the historic site of Panamá Viejo across a viaduct that overhangs the bay all the way to Punta Paitilla! Say goodbye to lovely photos of the ruins against the backdrop of the bay.

Driving in Panama City

The traffic in Panama City is often heavy, but finding your way around town is not particularly difficult. Here are a few hints for getting around the city.

On certain days, several major downtown arteries become one-way streets. For example, the Las Americas bridge becomes one way at certain points during the weekend to facilitate getting in or out of town. On weekdays, some of the main roads leading into town from the east also become one-way.

Be careful because the direction of certain roads is not always clearly indicated with signs.

In order to ease traffic in the capital, major work has been underway for several years now to complete two major highways, known as **Corredor Sud** and **Corredor Norte**. The latter, located north of the city, now allows drivers to reach the city of Colón without having to go through the capital's city centre. Not surprisingly, taking the highway will cost you the modest sum of B/.1.50.

To Islas Naos, Perico and Flamenco

From Avenida de los Mártires, take Avenida Amador, which will take you to the peninsula of the same name and onto the islands via the Calzada de Amador, a guarded spit of land.

To Panamá Viejo

Take Punta Paitilla—bound Avenida Balboa, which becomes Avenida 6a Sur or Vía Israël after the small viaduct that overhangs the Monumento a Las Madres roundabout. This road, which becomes Avenida Cincuentenario after the Atlapa Convention Centre, goes all the way to the ruins.

To Cerro Azul

To get to Cerro Azul take the road to the airport first. Just before the airport, turn left at the Riande Aeropuerto hotel and take the main road for 6.5km until you get to an intersection with Supermercado Xtra on the right. Turn left at this intersection and drive 1.8km until you see a sign on your left indicating the road to Cerro Azul. Take this road for 15km until you reach a gate and a sign indicating Portón Las Nubes. Turn left again and follow the main road until the summit.

By Bus

Note: the following schedules and rates are provided for reference only and are subject to change.

From the Airport to Downtown

There is a bus going between the airport and downtown every 30min. Though this is the least expensive way of getting downtown, it makes for a long trip; it takes at least an hour, two if there's traffic downtown. On the other hand, given that the bus station is far from the airport and that the place is not the safest in town, visitors are strongly advised to take a taxi to get downtown. The downtown bus stop is in the **Terminal Nacional de Transporte** *(☎314-6171 or 314-6167)*, located on Calle Curundú, near the M. A. Gelabert airport. As this bus station is located outside the city centre, in a somewhat remote area, it is safest to take a taxi there. Fare: B/.0.35.

In the City

Panama City does not have a government-run public bus company; several small companies service different parts of the city. The buses tend to be old and drivers sometimes show a disregard for the safety of pedestrians. Buses are always crowded, especially on weekends. Stops are frequent, so this is not the best mode of transportation if you are in a hurry. It is best to travel on buses with as little

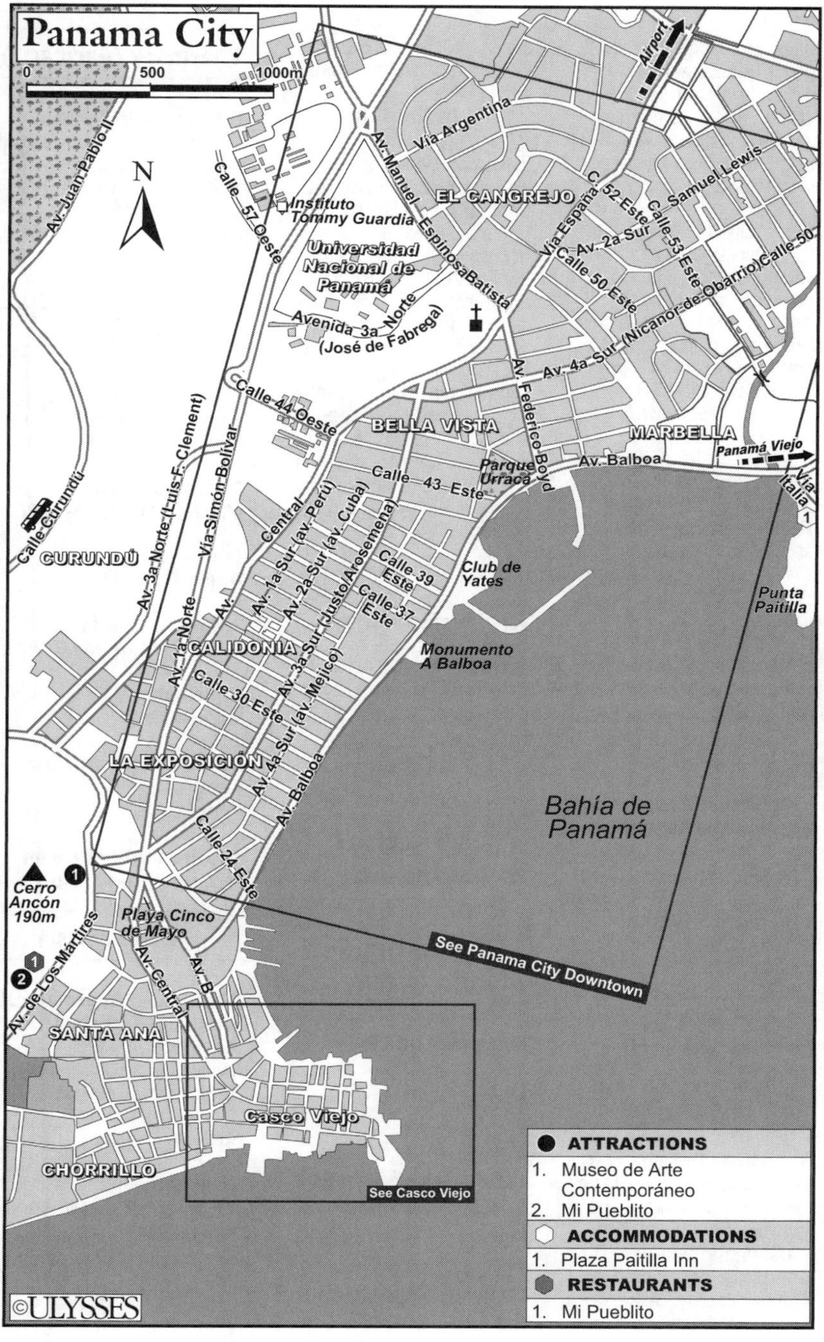

Panama City
0
500
1000m
N
Av. Juan Pablo II
Calle 57 Oeste
Instituto Tommy Guardia
Universidad Nacional de Panamá
Avenida 3a Norte (José de Fabrega)
Vía Argentina
Av. Manuel Espinosa Batista
EL CANGREJO
Vía España
C. 52 Este
Calle 53 Este
C. Samuel Lewis
Av. 2a Sur
Calle 50 Este
Av. 4a Sur (Nicanor de Obarrio)
Calle 50
Airport
Av. Federico Boyd
Calle 44 Oeste
BELLA VISTA
MARBELLA
Panamá Viejo
Av. Balboa
Parque Urraca
Calle 43 Este
Vía Italia
Calle Curundú
CURUNDÚ
Av. 3a Norte (Luis F. Clement)
Vía Simón Bolívar
Av. Central
Av. 1a Sur (av. Perú)
Av. 2a Sur (av. Cuba)
Av. 3a Sur (Justo Arosemena)
Calle 39 Este
Calle 37 Este
Club de Yates
Punta Paitilla
Av. 1a Norte
CALIDONIA
Monumento A Balboa
Calle 30 Este
Av. 4a Sur (av. Mejico)
LA EXPOSICIÓN
Av. Balboa
Bahía de Panamá
Calle 24 Este
Cerro Ancón 190m
Playa Cinco de Mayo
Av. de Los Mártires
Av. Central
Av. B
See Panama City Downtown
SANTA ANA
Casco Viejo
CHORRILLO
See Casco Viejo
ATTRACTIONS
1. Museo de Arte Contemporáneo
2. Mi Pueblito
ACCOMMODATIONS
1. Plaza Paitilla Inn
RESTAURANTS
1. Mi Pueblito
©ULYSSES

baggage as possible; theft, pick-pocketing, usually, is not uncommon, so be careful. Despite these inconveniences, bus travel is cheap and can be a good way to meet people.

Generally, buses keep to the main streets of the city, such as Avenida Central, Avenida 3a Sur (Justo Arosemena), or other less busy streets in shopping and hotel areas. To get off, you'll have to yell (buses are noisy) "*la parada*".

The terminus for inner-city travel, **Panamá Viejo**, **Amador** and **Isla Naos**, **Perico** and **Flamenco** is located on Plaza 5 de Mayo, on Avenida Central. Although destinations are indicated on the windshields, they are not always visible. Most trips within the city centre cost B/.0.15. To catch a bus from anywhere other than the terminus, ask someone to point out the closest bus stop, because they are seldom indicated.

For safety reasons, travellers heading to **Mi Pueblito** (see p 84) or **Parque Metropolitano** are advised to take a taxi.

By Taxi

From the Airport to Downtown

Taxis from the airport to downtown cost B/.20 per person or if you are sharing the taxi with other passengers, between B/.8 and B/.12 depending on the number of passengers. In the latter case, make sure to tell the driver that you are sharing the taxi.

In the City

Taxis can be found just about anywhere and are probably the safest way to get around town. The cars do not have meters. In Panama City, taxis work by zone instead of with meters. Sharing a cab ride with another person costs B/.1.25 to B/.4 each for trips within the city centre. You will have to negotiate the cost of the ride, and it is a good idea to agree on a price before getting in. Taxi drivers are normally not tipped.

There are also collective taxis which offer the advantage of shared costs (even if destinations vary somewhat). Collective taxis travel in and between cities.

Practical Information

Post Office *(Correos y Telégrafos)*

Some post offices:

La Exposicíon
Avenida Balboa and Calle 30 Este

Calidonia
Calle 33 Este and Avenida Central

El Cangrejo
Vía España facing Calle 51B Este

Pharmacy (*Farmacia*)

The **Farmacia Arrocha** (Aquilino Guardia, south of Vía España) or the pharmacy in the **Supermercado Rey** (Vía España) can help you deal with those little scrapes, scratches and pains.

Theatre

For information on various Spanish-language productions:

Teatro Nacional
☎***262-3525 or 225-4951***

Teatro en Círculo
☎***261-5375***

Teatro La Cúpula
☎***223-7516 or 264-1989***

Teatro Aba
☎***260-6316***

For information on English-language performances:

Theatre Guild of Ancón
☎***264-4271 or 272-6786***

Cybercafés

Cibercentro Internet@cafe
Edificio Sun Tower Mall
Second floor, Suite 32
Avenida Ricardo J. Alfaro or Avenida Tumba Muerto

Stratos
Vía Argentina
Edificio Don Julio
Bella Vista, El Cangrejo district
☎***264-5956***

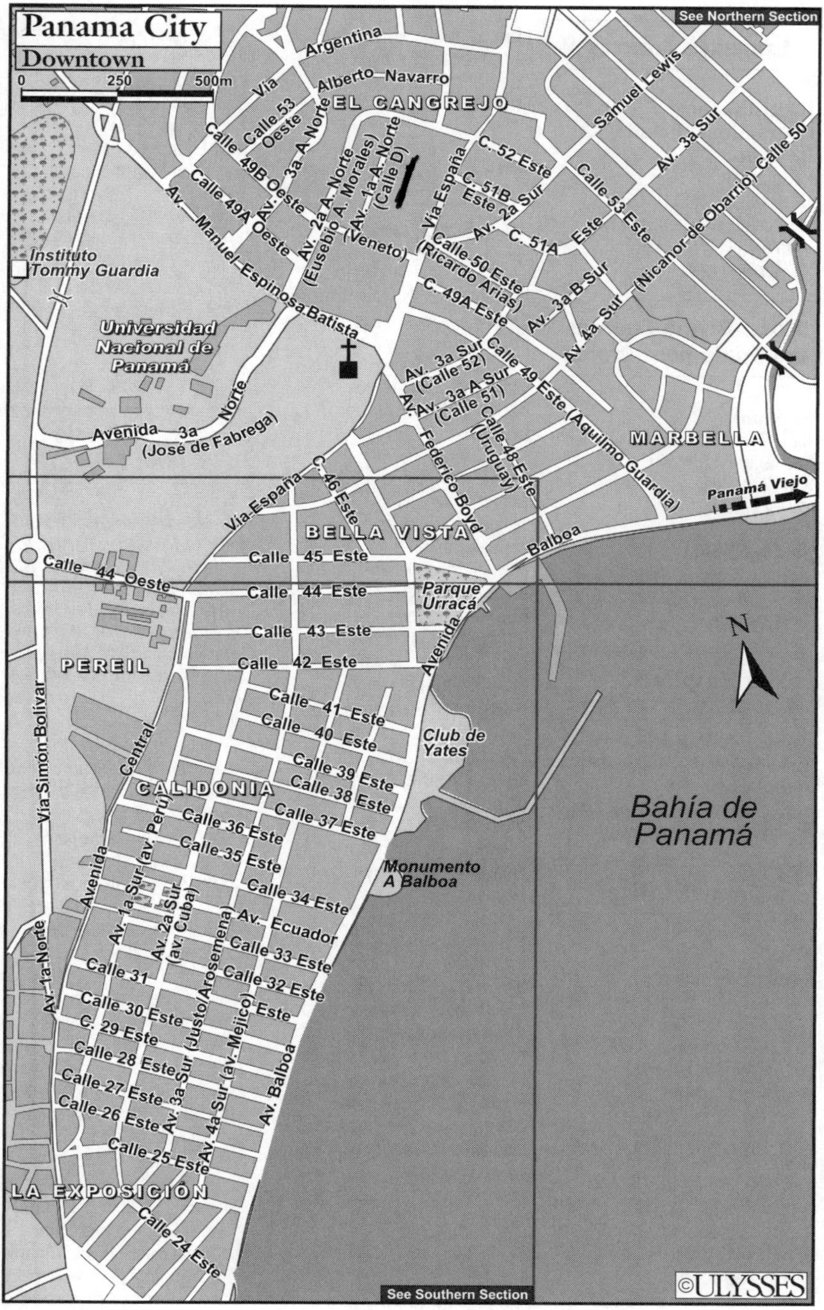
Panama City
Downtown
0
250
500m
See Northern Section
See Southern Section
Vía Argentina
Alberto Navarro
EL CANGREJO
Calle 53 Oeste
Calle 49B Oeste
Calle 49A Oeste
Av. 3a A Norte
Av. 2a A Norte (Eusebio A. Morales)
Av. 1a A Norte (Calle D)
(Veneto)
Vía España
C. 52 Este
C. 51B Este
Av. 2a Sur
C. 51A Este
Samuel Lewis
Av. 3a Sur
Calle 53 Este
Calle 50 (Nicanor de Obarrio)
Calle 50 Este (Ricardo Arias)
C. 49A Este
Av. 3a B Sur
Av. 4a Sur
Instituto Tommy Guardia
Av. Manuel Espinosa Batista
Universidad Nacional de Panamá
Avenida 3a Norte (José de Fabrega)
Av. 3a Sur (Calle 52)
Av. 3a A Sur (Calle 51)
Calle 49 Este (Aquilino Guardia)
Calle 48 Este (Uruguay)
Av. Federico Boyd
MARBELLA
Panamá Viejo
Vía España
C. 46 Este
BELLA VISTA
Balboa
Calle 45 Este
Calle 44 Oeste
Calle 44 Este
Parque Urracá
Calle 43 Este
Calle 42 Este
Avenida
PEREIL
Calle 41 Este
Calle 40 Este
Club de Yates
Vía Simón Bolívar
Central
CALIDONIA
Calle 39 Este
Calle 38 Este
Calle 37 Este
Calle 36 Este
Calle 35 Este
Bahía de Panamá
Monumento A Balboa
N
Avenida
Av. 1a Sur (av. Perú)
Av. 2a Sur (av. Cuba)
Calle 34 Este
Av. Ecuador
Calle 33 Este
Calle 32 Este
Este
Av. 1a Norte
Calle 31
Calle 30 Este
C. 29 Este
Calle 28 Este
Calle 27 Este
Calle 26 Este
Av. 3a Sur (Justo Arosemena)
Av. 4a Sur (av. Mejico)
Av. Balboa
Calle 25 Este
LA EXPOSICIÓN
Calle 24 Este
©ULYSSES

Language Courses

ILERI-Language & International Relations Institute
Amistad Avenue
Altos del Chase, El Dorado
Casa G-42, Vía La Amistad
Apdo 6-6331
☎/⇌260-4424

Scuba-Diving Courses and Equipment Rental

Neptuno
Calle 73, n°12 (between Vía Porras and Calle 50)
San Francisco
☎/⇌226-2020

Scubapanamá
Avenida 6C Norte, Calle 62A
☎261-3841
⇌261-9586

Hospitals

Clínica de Paitilla
at Avenida Balboa and Calle 53
Marbella
☎265-8800 or 269-0655
☎265-8888 (emergencies)

Tourist Office

IPAT
Ciudad de Panamá
Centro de Convenciones ATLAPA
Avenida 6a Sur (Vía Israel)
☎226-7000 or 226-7614
From North America
☎800-231-0568
The entrance to the ATLAPA building faces the road. Ask the guard at the reception desk to show you where the IPAT office is, because it is hard to find. Furthermore, be prepared to do some fancy footwork to obtain information. Most brochures available on site are outdated, contain many ads and are therefore of little use.

Exploring

Panama City's most important historic area is San Felipe, commonly known as Casco Viejo (the old city). This is the site of most of the city's colonial buildings.

The lively Avenida Central, parts of which are reserved for pedestrians only, is a good base for touring; from here the area can be explored fully in a day. There are other interesting buildings in parts of Bella Vista and Calidonia. To help you make the most of your time in the city, we have included descriptions of several interesting sights and suggested a walking tour of Casco Viejo. Nevertheless, before heading off to explore this fascinating city, take note that with regard to your personal safety, be careful in the Casco Viejo area, and in the Santa Ana and Calidonia neighbourhoods. To avoid drawing attention to yourself, wear little or no jewellery and keep your camera and any other valuables hidden. Be on your guard in crowds, as pick-pockets may be on the prowl. Stay away from Chorrillo, in the southwest part of the city.

Furthermore, do not walk around after dark in Casco Viejo, Santa Ana and Calidonia unless you absolutely have to. The safest neighbourhoods at night are Bella Vista, El Cangrejo, Campo Alegre and Marbella, which have many pleasant bars and restaurants. Keep to the major well-lit streets when getting around after sundown. Taxis are very cheap here, so do like most Panamanians, and take one.

★★★

Casco Viejo (San Felipe)

To fully appreciate the old part of Panama City and its beautiful monuments, we recommend starting off by taking in a bit of bustling Avenida Central, starting from Playa 5 de Mayo, in the Santa Ana neighbourhood.

Transformed into an attractive pedestrian street, **Avenida Central** is a long commercial artery crowded with Panamanians, thus offering a wonderful, kaleidoscopic view of the capital's residents. Trees have been planted all along the avenue, and you can relax on any of a number of benches. As you walk down the street, the music streaming out of the stores will plunge you right into the lively Latin American ambiance. Although the appearance of most storefronts has been marred by placards and neon lights, some are still worth a second look. For example, the building on the first corner on the right side of the street is graced with a

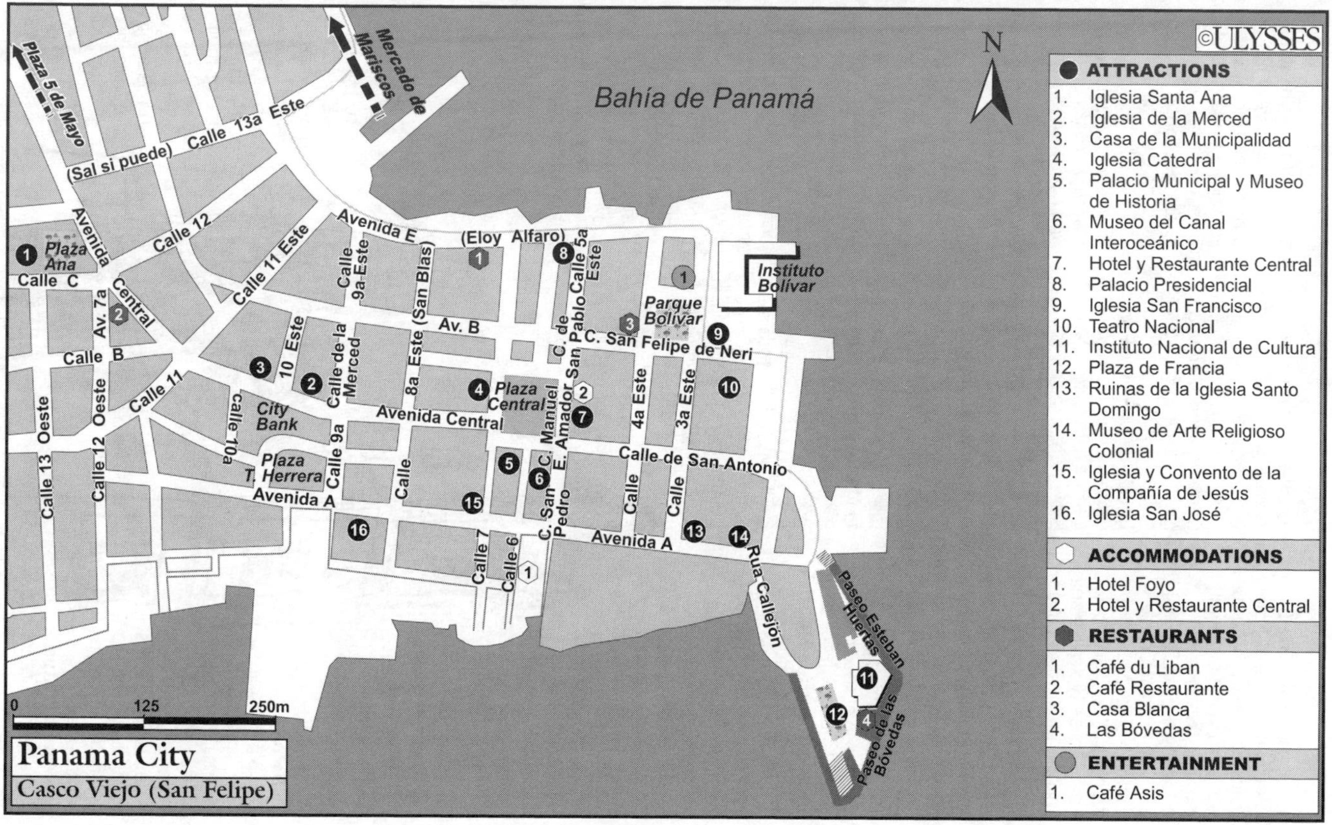

©ULYSSES
Bahía de Panamá
N
Plaza 5 de Mayo
Mercado de Mariscos
Calle 13a Este
(Sal si puede)
Avenida E
(Eloy Alfaro)
Calle 12
Avenida Central
Plaza Ana
Calle C
Av. 7a
Calle 11 Este
Calle 9a-Este
8a Este (San Blas)
Calle 5a Este
Instituto Bolívar
Parque Bolívar
C. San Felipe de Neri
Av. B
Calle B
10 Este
Calle de la Merced
C. de San Pablo
Calle 11
Plaza Central
City Bank
calle 10a
Avenida Central
Calle 13 Oeste
Calle 12 Oeste
C. Manuel E. Amador
4a Este
3a Este
Plaza T. Herrera
Calle 9a
Calle de San Antonio
Avenida A
C. San Pedro
Calle 7
Calle 6
Rua Callejón
Paseo Esteban Huertas
Paseo de las Bóvedas
0
125
250m
Panama City
Casco Viejo (San Felipe)
ATTRACTIONS
1. Iglesia Santa Ana
2. Iglesia de la Merced
3. Casa de la Municipalidad
4. Iglesia Catedral
5. Palacio Municipal y Museo de Historia
6. Museo del Canal Interoceánico
7. Hotel y Restaurante Central
8. Palacio Presidencial
9. Iglesia San Francisco
10. Teatro Nacional
11. Instituto Nacional de Cultura
12. Plaza de Francia
13. Ruinas de la Iglesia Santo Domingo
14. Museo de Arte Religioso Colonial
15. Iglesia y Convento de la Compañía de Jesús
16. Iglesia San José
ACCOMMODATIONS
1. Hotel Foyo
2. Hotel y Restaurante Central
RESTAURANTS
1. Café du Liban
2. Café Restaurante
3. Casa Blanca
4. Las Bóvedas
ENTERTAINMENT
1. Café Asis

lovely **Moorish-style facade** with wrought-iron balconies. Also, make sure not to miss the beautiful ceramic **frescoes ★** adorning the facade of the unusual building beside the Banco Nacional, farther along on the right. They cover three typically Panamanian themes: the Spanish discovery of Panamá, the construction of the canal and the operation of the locks. Finally, the most recent addition to Avenida Central, which is so much more interesting than all its shops would indicate, is the house at the corner of Calle 13a Este. Its blue **facade, featuring Moorish elements** and adorned with small, wrought-iron balconies, seems tailor-made for this tiny pedestrian street, nicknamed "*Sal si puede*" (Leave if you can). It is so narrow and so full of shops that passers-by do indeed seem to have a hard time moving about.

You can start your tour of the historic centre by stopping at Plaza Ana, the square at the end of the pedestrian street.

Many Panamanians gather in **Plaza Ana**, a pretty, verdant little square to discuss all sorts of topics, generally related to politics. The place is always full of life. Here, you will find the charming facade of **Iglesia Santa Ana**. Although the interior of the church has been completely renovated, certain parts of its walls date back to the 17th century.

Continue along Avenida Central to Calle 10 Este.

Iglesia de la Merced ★ *(at the corner of Avenida Central and Calle 10 Este)* is of interest mainly for its very pretty baroque facade, which dates back to 1680. The interior of the church was entirely renovated after a fire and is not particulary interesting.

Just opposite, the **Casa de la Municipalidad** *(at the corner of Avenida Central and Calle 10 Este)*, once the home of an affluent family, has a lovely classical facade, which has been beautifully restored. An underground passage once connected the building to the cathedral and the city's former fortifications.

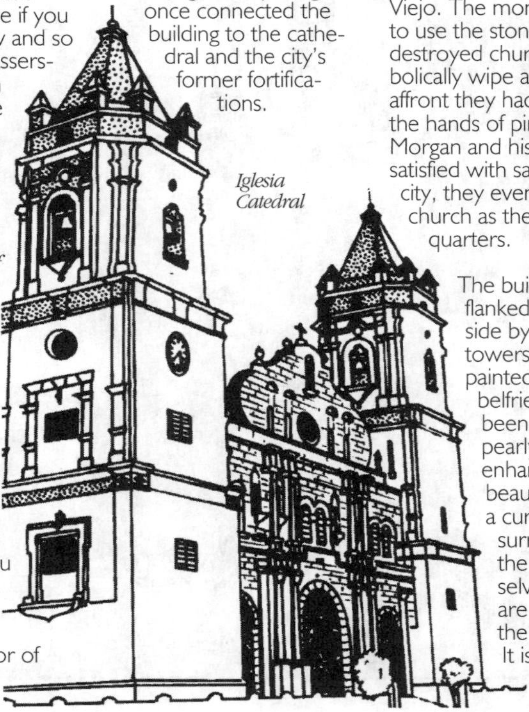

Iglesia Catedral

The Art Deco **City Bank** building, located on the other side of the street, is yet another example of the great variety of architectural styles found on Avenida Central.

Continue along Avenida Central to Plaza Central, also known as Plaza de la Independencia, where you will find a number of interesting buildings.

Erected between 1688 and 1796, the **Iglesia Catedral ★★★** *(Plaza de la Independencia/ Plaza Central)* is one of the city's architectural showpieces. Its most notable feature is its facade, whose central portion was built with stones from the former church of the Convento de la Merced in Panamá Viejo. The monks decided to use the stones of the destroyed church to symbolically wipe away the affront they had suffered at the hands of pirate Henry Morgan and his men. Not satisfied with sacking the city, they even used the church as their headquarters.

The building is flanked on either side by pyramidal towers, which are painted white. The belfries have been inlaid with pearly shells to enhance their beauty. There is a curious legend surrounding the bells themselves, which are also from the old church. It is said that when they were being made in Toledo (Spain), Isabella of Portugal, who was passing through the city, threw her ring into the molten metal. Because of this, supposedly, the bells have a distinctive sound. The airy interior of the cathedral features a few lovely stained-glass windows, which could use some fixing up. You will also find a few paintings from the Seville school.

Erected on the same site as the former municipal building in which the Panamanian isthmus's declaration of independence was signed in 1821, and again in 1903, the **Palacio Municipal y el Museo de Historia de Panamá** *(B/.1; Mon - Fri 9am to 3:30pm; Plaza de la Independencia/ Plaza Central and Calle 7a Oeste, ☎228-6231)* now houses a museum of Panamanian history. Located on the third floor, this museum covers the history of the Panamanian isthmus from the colonial era, through independence and the birth of the republic, and up until the Torrijos-Carter agreements of 1977. Unfortunately, little background information is provided in most of the rooms. The building itself is neoclassical in style, reflecting a distinct Italian influence.

Right next door, the **Museo del Canal Interoceánico de Panamá** ★★★ *(B/.2; Tue-Sun 9:30am to 5pm; Palacio Municipal, Plaza de la Independencia or Plaza Central, between Calles 5a Oeste and 6a Oeste, ☎211-1649 or 211-1650, www.sinfo.net/pcmuseum)* is one of the most interesting museums in the capital. Before heading inside, however, take the time to admire the building's beautiful proportions. Erected in 1875 in an architectural style that reveals its French influence, the building is steeped in history.

After housing the aptly named Grand Hotel for 16 years, it was sold to the Compagnie Universelle du Canal Interocéanique, which used it as its headquarters throughout the French period of the construction of the Panamá Canal. After the dismal French failure under the aegis of Ferdinand de Lesseps, the U.S. took over the construction of the canal in 1904 and purchased the building for its administrative offices. The Panamanian government acquired it in 1910 and housed various administrative services under its roof until very recently, when it was converted into a museum, thus reviving its historic link to the canal.

The museum offers a chronological view of the country's history. The museum's exhibits include the outstanding *La Ruta-El Agua-La Gente*, which chronicles Panamá's development and its historic role as an interoceanic route from the pre-Colombian era to the 20th century.

A particularly informative section is devoted to the building of the Panamá Railroad, which preceded the construction of the Canal. One learns that in 1889, no fewer than 1.2-million people crossed the isthmus by train, a number all the more surprising because, at the time, a first-class ticket cost as much as B/.25 *(B/.10 in second class)*! The section devoted to the canal itself, also very instructive, highlights the French and American construction periods. The quality and originality of its presentation make this exhibit an absolute must. Explanations are provided in both Spanish and English.

Hotel y Restaurante Central *(Plaza de la Independencia/Plaza Central and Calle Manuel E. Amador)* a rundown hotel, is worth visiting for its architecture, typical of houses built in the Caribbean in the colonial era. It has a large indoor patio, where you can admire an elegant wooden staircase leading to the upper floors. The lovely three-storey galleries give the place an airy look despite its imposing structure. Once known as the most luxurious hotel in town, it was frequented by key players in the construction of the canal.

If you are fond of Art Deco architecture, before leaving Plaza Central, make sure to take a look at the white building known as **Casa Al Ansa** located on the northeast corner of the square. Although its modern-looking windows detract somewhat from its overall appearance, this building is an example of Art Deco architecture in its purest form. Admire the sizeable entrance and the vertical lines on either side leading up to a balcony.

Continue your tour by walking away from the post office along Calle 5 Este/de San Pablo, then take Avenida E/Eloy Alfaro, to the waterfront.

If the national guard lets you, head to the front of the **Palacio Presidencial ★** *(Avenida E/Eloy Alfaro, corner Caller 5 Este)*. As the name suggests, this is the official residence of the president of the republic. The building, which has characteristics typical of Andalusian architecture, dates from 1673 and was restored in 1922. It originally served as the home of the governor. The central courtyard, Moorish in design, contains a small fountain around which herons preen. The birds have long been a fixture in the building; indeed, the palace is also known as Palacio de las Garzas (Heron Palace). The interior is unfortunately not accessible to the public, unless of course you are invited by the president himself!

Nearby, on the same street, several upper- class houses that date from the early 20th century have been restored particularly successfully. One of them is home to the famous singer Rubén Blades.

Double back toward Plaza Central, and take Calle San Felipe de Neri/Avenida B, located to your left. This street will lead you straight to Parque Bolívar.

The **Belfry Iglesia San Francisco ★★** *(opposite Parque Bolívar)*, a charming white church offers a 360° view of the city (to visit the bell tower, inquire at the office behind the church, to the right). The interior is fairly austere overall, but features a pretty choir decorated with a large, gilded mosaic. Originally erected in 1673, the Iglesia San Francisco was twice destroyed by fire, in 1737 and in 1761, and then rebuilt in 1766. In those years, it was one of the largest churches in Panamá.

From the belfry, you can gaze off into the distance at the ships awaiting their turn to enter the canal. The sheer number of vessels of such impressive sizes is a good indication of the importance of the canal on an international level.

Other interesting views include the Paseo de Las Bóvedas and Plaza de Francia, the ruins of Santo Domingo church and its arch (*Arco Chato*), the Cathedral square, Iglesia Catedral, Puente de las Américas, Cerro Ancón and Punta Paitilla. This is a great place to get a feel for the layout of the city and to take photographs.

As you leave the church, be sure to check out the former convent next door, which once housed a high school known as the Instituto Bolívar. You can admire its beautiful Salamanca-style facade, admirably restored and adorned with lovely pastel colours, as well as its carved-wood portal. At the time of our visit, it was slated to welcome the Foreign Affairs minister. If you obtain permission to enter, be sure to visit its large main courtyard, where you can see coats of arms representing the various republics that participated in the 1826 conference, which took place right here under the aegis of Simón Bolívar.

Many of the grand houses bordering Parque Bolívar, such as the former Colombia hotel, have recently been or are currently being restored. The current focus on the city's colonial history promises to make Casco Viejo the next "*Cartagena*" of Panamá.

The **Teatro Nacional ★★★** *(ask the security guard for access into the theatre; Calle 3a Este, beside the Iglesia San Francisco; since half of the building is used by the Ministry of Justice, the entrance to the theatre is located opposite the bay, ☎262-3525 or 225-4951)* was built between 1903 and 1908. Its interior bears a strange resemblance to La Scala in Milan — not surprisingly, since both buildings were designed by the same architect, Ruggieri. The celebrations marking the opening of the theatre were attended by Sarah Bernhardt. The garnet-red and gold interior, with its small, suspended balconies (make sure to take a look at the centre, or presidential, balcony, adorned with the national coat of arms) will send you off into a reverie. The crystal chandelier, imported from France, is also striking. The painting on the vault was executed by Roberto Lewis in 1907; it glorifies Panamanian patriotism and features the national colours. During the renovations carried out in the 1970s, Roberto Lewis's own son was in charge of restoring the painting. The richly furnished foyer, for its part, reveals a clear French influence. Concerts are presented in the theatre from May to October.

Continue the walking tour by turning left on Calle San Antonio. Shortly after the street curves to the right, take the small staircase to the left. These stairs lead to Paseo de la Bóvedas.

The **Paseo de las Bóvedas ★★** is a charming rampart-walk overlooking the walls built to protect the city. From here, you can enjoy a stunning view of the sea, with the ships waiting to enter the canal off in the distance. The Paseo de las Bóvedas is extremely romantic, and is frequented by large numbers of Panamanian couples; indeed, it seems to be the place of choice for lovers.

Continue walking along the ramparts until you reach the Plaza de Francia, located below.

Plaza de Francia ★★★ Is a lovely square with an old-fashioned charm about it. An obelisk topped by a proud French cockerel, erected in honour of the French workers and engineers involved in digging the canal, stands at the end closest to the sea.

Behind the monument is a semicircular gallery, below which the history of the construction of the canal is engraved right into the walls. Another monument, erected in memory of Carlos Finley, the celebrated Cuban who discovered the cause of yellow fever, stands in the centre of the square. Various military buildings were once located here. All that remain today, however, are the dungeons used to confine prisoners, which now house a private art gallery and an excellent restaurant called **Las Bóvedas** (see p 99).

Right next door, the imposing **Courthouse**, which is crowned with a bizarre dome, now houses the **Instituto Nacional de Cultura** *(Mon-Fri 10am to 4pm)*. Temporary exhibits featuring works by Panamanian artists are housed on the main floor.

Also facing onto the square is the lovely colonial residence that serves as the French Embassy, and a little further, on the left, another newly renovated upper class home, which testifies to the current revitalisa- tion of the district.

Those who are passing through the *Ciudad* on July 14 should make sure to drop by, as the French embassy organizes a big outdoor party here every year, complete with atmosphere and fireworks.

Take Rua Callejón, located to the left of the French embassy, then turn left to head back up Avenida A.

The **Ruinas de la Iglesia Santo Domingo ★★★** *(Avenida A and Calle 3a Oeste/San Francisco)* are the ruins of an old monastery and adjoining chapel built by the Dominicans in 1678. What remains of the church facade makes it clear that it was once an impressive building. This delightfully peaceful sight features an incredibly wide arch, known as Arco Chato. Built entirely of brick and mortar, with no internal reinforcements, it has stood here for centuries, miraculously seeming to defy gravity. This feat attracted the attention of those in favour of building the canal in Panamá, who viewed it as irrefutable proof that the country was ideal for the project, being subject to minimal seismic activity. To visit the grounds, ask the caretaker of the religious art museum to let you in.

Museo de Arte Religioso Colonial ★★ *(B/.0.75; Tue - Sat 8am to 4pm, Sun 1pm to 5pm; Avenida A and Calle 3a Oeste/San Francisco)*, a little museum, set up inside a church right alongside the ruins of the Iglesia Santo Domingo, exhibits sacred paintings and sculptures from various parts of the country, dating from the 16th, 17th, 18th and 19th centuries.

There is also a lovely collection of metal-work. The most impressive piece on display is the remarkably beautiful 18th century altar from the former chapel of the monastery, which is covered with gold leaf. Actually, you will notice that colonial art is almost exclusively baroque. This is probably because the baroque style is particularly expressive, and thus well-suited to depicting scenes with an educational content. The church used this type of art to spread its moral doctrine and establish its power. Humility, devotion and sacrifice, three signs of submission, were the watchwords in those years.

Nearby, on the same street, you will find the ruins of the **Iglesia y Convento de la Compañia de Jesús** *(Avenida A and Calle 7a Oeste/Santos Jorge)*. Founded in 1749, this was once home to the largest Jesuit community in Panamá. A university was even established here in 1767. The buildings were destroyed by fire around 1781, but since then the ruins have remained more or less intact.

Erected in 1671, the **Iglesia San José ★★★** *(Avenida A and Calle 8/de San Blas)* has a rather modest exterior, and is interesting mainly for its beautiful Altar de Oro. This magnificent gold altar, which originally graced the former church of the same name in Panamá Viejo, dates from the 17th century, and is one of the few treasures to have survived the destruction of the old city. According to legend, the Recollect friars saved it from the pirates by painting it black, thus concealing its true value. In any case, even though the altar is still covered with gold, it is most striking for its style. Essentially baroque, it includes a number of unusual elements relating to native culture in the colonial era (exotic fruit, physical traits). The altar forms an extremely harmonious whole, and is perhaps Panamá's most prestigious sacred object from the colonial era.

To end your tour of the old city, take Calle 9/de la Merced to Avenida Central to the Santa Ana district.

★

Santa Ana

The **Museo Antropológico Reina Torres de Araúz ★★★** *(B/.1; Mon to Fri 9am to 4pm; Plaza 5 de Mayo, ☎262-8338 or 212-3089)* occupies an imposing former railway station erected in 1913. This is the most important anthropological museum in the country due to the quantity of objects on display, as well as the quality of these pieces. Although many treasures were destroyed by grave robbers, and others have been dispersed to museums around the world, a number of remarkable pre-Columbian pieces can be found here. A leisurely tour of the museum's galleries rooms reveals a great deal about Panamá's past. You are sure to spend at least one hour discovering how the isthmus has evolved over the centuries. In addition to some lovely pottery and sculptures, an interesting collection of *Huacas* (pre-Colombian jewellery) is exhibited.

La Exposición

The **Museo de Ciencias Naturales** *(B/.1; Tue - Sat 9am to 3:30pm; Calle 30 Este and Avenida Cuba; ☎225-0645)*, a natural science museum, exhibits a selection of stuffed mammals, reptiles and birds along with an interesting section on geology that contains a number of fossils. With the exception of a pamphlet sold at the entrance, the museum provides little information on the exhibits.

The small **Museo Afro-Antillano** *(B/.1; Tue-Sat 8:30am to 3:30pm; Avenida 3a Sur/Justo Arosemena near Calle 24 Este; ☎262-5348 or 262-1668)* contains various objects related to the Afro-Caribbean community at the time of the construction of the Panamá Canal.

Calidonia

Erected in honour of Balboa, the freshly repainted **Monumento Vasco Nuñez de Balboa ★** *(Avenida Balboa)* is a statue of a globe held up by four individuals of different races. Above them, Balboa points his sword toward the Pacific, which he "discovered" in 1513. A visit to the site can also include a walk along the promenade by the bay, from which there are beautiful views of Casco Viejo and Punta Paitilla.

West of the monument, the stroll becomes all the more pleasant as the sidewalk that skirts the sea

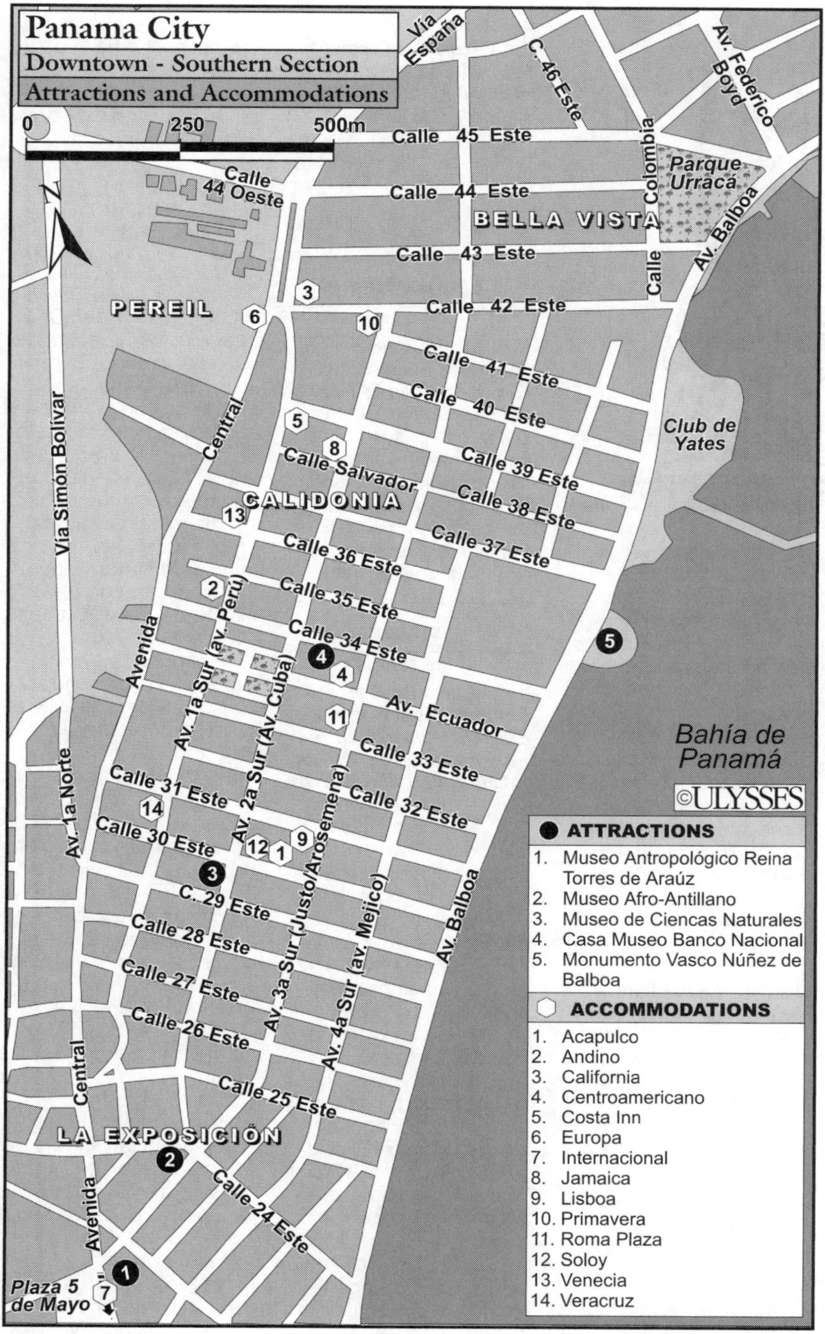

Panama City
Downtown - Southern Section
Attractions and Accommodations
0
250
500m
Vía España
C. 46 Este
Av. Federico Boyd
Calle 45 Este
Calle 44 Oeste
Calle 44 Este
Calle Colombia
Parque Urraca
BELLA VISTA
Calle 43 Este
Av. Balboa
PEREIL
Calle 42 Este
Calle 41 Este
Calle 40 Este
Club de Yates
Central
Vía Simón Bolívar
Calle Salvador
Calle 39 Este
CALIDONIA
Calle 38 Este
Calle 37 Este
Calle 36 Este
Calle 35 Este
Calle 34 Este
Avenida
Av. 1a Sur (av. Perú)
Av. 2a Sur (Av. Cuba)
Av. Ecuador
Bahía de Panamá
Calle 33 Este
Calle 32 Este
Calle 31 Este
Calle 30 Este
Av. 1a Norte
Av. 3a Sur (Justo/Arosemena)
Av. 4a Sur (av. Mejico)
C. 29 Este
Calle 28 Este
Calle 27 Este
Calle 26 Este
Calle 25 Este
Calle 24 Este
Central
Avenida
LA EXPOSICIÓN
Plaza 5 de Mayo
©ULYSSES
ATTRACTIONS
1. Museo Antropológico Reina Torres de Araúz
2. Museo Afro-Antillano
3. Museo de Ciencas Naturales
4. Casa Museo Banco Nacional
5. Monumento Vasco Núñez de Balboa
ACCOMMODATIONS
1. Acapulco
2. Andino
3. California
4. Centroamericano
5. Costa Inn
6. Europa
7. Internacional
8. Jamaica
9. Lisboa
10. Primavera
11. Roma Plaza
12. Soloy
13. Venecia
14. Veracruz

Monumento Vasco Nuñez de Balboa

wall was recently refurbished. Amusing little mosaics with thalassic designs now adorn the low wall bordering it, and benches and new lighting have been provided. All that is needed now is an effort to reduce the non-stop traffic on this lovely avenue. Indeed, Avenida Balboa has become a veritable highway, as motorists speed along, unimpeded by traffic lights (or police controls). Crossing the avenue at certain times of day is a challenge!

Casa Museo del Banco Nacional de Panamá *(Mon-Sat 8am to 12:30pm and 1:30pm to 4pm, Calle 34 and Avenida Cuba; ☎225-0640)* houses an exhibition of coins and stamps in a lovely upper-class home.

La Cresta

It is worth taking a few moments to admire the neo-Gothic architecture of the **Iglesia del Carmen** *(corner of Vía España and Avenida Manuel Espinosa Batista)*. The interior is airy and harmoniously proportioned, but otherwise of little interest.

★

Campo Alegre

Built in 1949, the **Santuario Nacional ★** *(corner of Calle 53 Este and Avenida 2a Sur/Samuel Lewis)* merits a visit. The church has an interesting facade fashioned out of travertine marble, which makes it look much older than it really is. There is not much to see inside.

Ancón

The **Museo de Arte Contemporáneo ★** *(B/.1; Tue-Sun 9am to 5pm, Sat 9am to noon; Avenida de los Mártires and Calle San Blas in the Ancón area; ☎262-8012 or 262-3380, macpanama.org)* is a very interesting museum with a collection of more than 450 works by artists from Panamá and other Latin American countries. The pieces include paintings, sculptures and drawings, most of which were donated to the museum. A few of the paintings should not be missed, particularly *Los Satiros* by Humberto Ivaldi (1909-1947), and *The Unseen Eye is Watching You* and *Salutacíon al Pajaro Sagrado* by Guillermo Trujillo. Travelling exhibits by well-known artists from around the world are presented on the ground floor. The museum also has a boutique that sells interesting and inexpensive (*B/.10*) T-shirts and works by local artists.

Located in the Cerro Ancón area, **Mi Pueblito ★★★** *(Tue-Sat 10am to 11pm, Sun 10am to 10pm; Avenida de los Martires between Calle Julio A. Sosa and Calle J. De la Ossa; ☎228-7178)* is a life-sized re-creation of small rural villages that can still be found in Panamá today. Panamá's three main ethnic groups are represented here, each in a space set up to reflect their culture in the most realistic manner possible. For example, the **Mi Pueblito** section, which represents the colonial culture, features a typical central square, surrounded by a small church, a barber shop, a grocery store and a set of traditional houses like those still seen today on the Azuero peninsula. Also on site is a small museum devoted to the traditional dress (*pollera*) and a pleasant restaurant (see p 109). Finally, folk evenings featuring music and dancing are organized here every Thursday and Friday from 7pm *(reservations recommended, ☎228-2124, 228-7178 or 228-7714)*. This section should not be missed.

Nearby, the **Pueblito Afro-Antillano** follows the same concept, encompassing a church as well as shops and dwellings typical of people of West Indian ancestry, most of whom came to Panamá during the construction of the Canal. This display is particularly colourful and

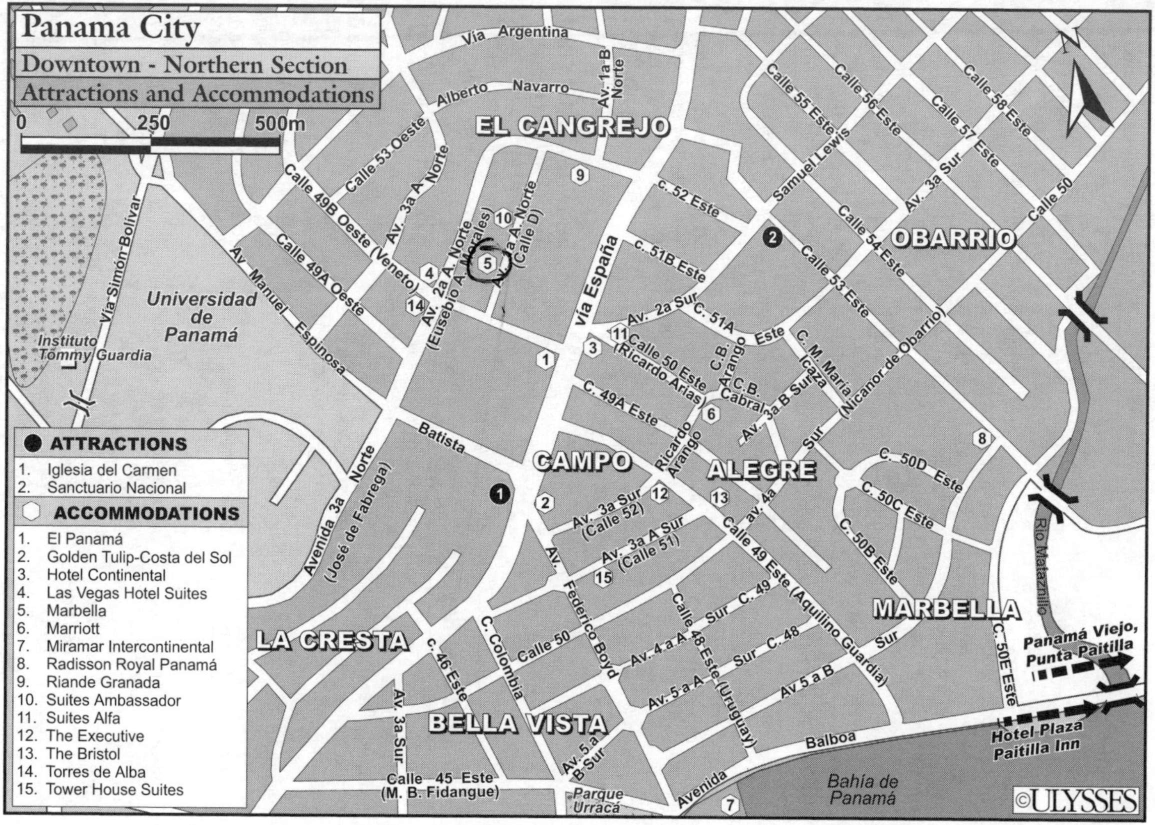
Panama City
Downtown - Northern Section
Attractions and Accommodations
0
250
500m
ATTRACTIONS
1. Iglesia del Carmen
2. Sanctuario Nacional
ACCOMMODATIONS
1. El Panamá
2. Golden Tulip-Costa del Sol
3. Hotel Continental
4. Las Vegas Hotel Suites
5. Marbella
6. Marriott
7. Miramar Intercontinental
8. Radisson Royal Panamá
9. Riande Granada
10. Suites Ambassador
11. Suites Alfa
12. The Executive
13. The Bristol
14. Torres de Alba
15. Tower House Suites
EL CANGREJO
OBARRIO
CAMPO
ALEGRE
MARBELLA
LA CRESTA
BELLA VISTA
Universidad de Panamá
Instituto Tommy Guardia
Bahía de Panamá
Vía Argentina
Alberto Navarro
Av. 1a B Norte
Calle 53 Oeste
Av. 3a A Norte
Calle 49B Oeste (Veneto)
Calle 49A Oeste
Av. Manuel Espinosa
Vía Simón Bolívar
Av. 2a A. Norte (Eusebio A. Morales)
Av. 1a A. Norte (Calle D)
Vía España
c. 52 Este
c. 51B Este
Av. 2a Sur
C. 51A Este
Calle 50 Este (Ricardo Arias)
C.B. Arango
C.B. Cabral
C. 49A Este
Av. 3a B Sur
C. M. María Icaza
(Nicanor de Obarrio)
Samuel Lewis
Calle 55 Este
Calle 56 Este
Calle 57 Este
Calle 58 Este
Av. 3a Sur
Calle 54 Este
Calle 53 Este
Calle 50
Batista
Ricardo Arango
Av. 3a Sur (Calle 52)
Av. 3a A Sur (Calle 51)
Calle 49 Este (Aquilino Guardia)
av. 4a Sur
C. 50D Este
C. 50C Este
C. 50B Este
Avenida 3a Norte (José de Fabrega)
Av. Federico Boyd
C. Colombia
Calle 50
c. 46 Este
Av. 3a Sur
Calle 45 Este (M. B. Fidangue)
Av. 4 a A Sur C. 49
Calle 48 Este (Uruguay)
Av. 5 a A Sur C. 48
Av 5 a B
Av. 5 a B Sur
Parque Urracá
Avenida Balboa
C. 50E Este
Río Mataznillo
Panamá Viejo, Punta Paitilla
Hotel Plaza Paitilla Inn
©ULYSSES

remarkably similar to a small Caribbean village.

A little farther still is the **Pueblito Indígena**, which features various traditional dwellings of indigenous peoples, namely those of the Kuna, Guaymi (or Ngobe-Bugle) and Choco peoples. While the latter are set up in a jungle-like environment, those of the Kunas make up a veritable little village, similar to those that still exist on the San Blas Islands. The "village" is staffed by actual Kunas.

Every shop on site carries the handicrafts of each culture represented, though the prices are higher than elsewhere. This place is a must for those with little time to spare while in Panamá, as it offers a quick introduction to the country's ethnic wealth.

Condado del Rey

Visiting an East Indian temple in Panamá? Not only is it possible, it is recommended, particularly for those who appreciate millennial Asia and its fascinating religions. Those who wish to pay their respects to Shiva, Ganesh or Vishnu should visit the **Templo Hindú** ★ *(free admission; Ave. Ricardo Arias, or Tumba Muerto, at Calle 12C Norte, on the left-hand side when heading toward the USMA)*, where, besides a smiling reception, an interesting view of the *Ciudad* awaits.

★★★

Panamá Viejo

Panamá Viejo (Old Panamá) which covers several kilometres is so called because it is the site of the first city in Panamá. Historically speaking, it is interesting to note that around the 1600s, when the city's population was about 4,000, only 850 people of Spanish origin were considered residents. The rest of the population consisted of slaves, mostly from Africa. These individuals were later sent to the Caribbean islands and the colonies to the south. Furthermore, although the city was strategically located, making it a required point of passage between the mother country and the new colonies to the south (Peru and Ecuador), its population grew very slowly. According to some, this was due to the many vast swamps nearby, which fostered the development of numerous illnesses, and also to the lure of gold, which had been discovered in other regions.

The park-like setting of the site, complete with descriptions, is like an open-air museum. The site was listed as a national monument by the Panamanian government back in 1976 and, since 1995, has been administered by the Patronato Viejo foundation, which ensures its protection and carries out excavations.

Before setting off to explore this wonderful historical park, be sure to visit the **Museo de Panamá Viejo** ★★ *(B/.1.50; Mon-Sun 8:30am to 4:30pm; Ave. Cincuentenario, opposite Plaza Mayor and the ruins of the Catedral, ☎224-2155, www.panamaviejo.org)*, where, in addition to various artifacts unearthed during excavations, there is a magnificent model of the city as it was in 1671, which helps visitors decipher the ruins on display. Small temporary exhibits are also presented here on a regular basis. Be sure to check out their excellent Spanish-language Web site, which features a very detailed description of the ruins. Below are some of the most interesting ruins (from west to east):

Fuerte la Navidad (The Fort of Nativity) was erected in 1658 to protect the entrance to the city. Fifty men were permanently stationed here, with six canons at their disposal.

Located just before the above fort, the **Puente del Matadero**, built in the 17th century, still spans the Río Algorroboa. It was constructed to make it easier to transport goods from the port to the city centre.

In 1552, the Mercedarian friars (a Catalan order originally instituted to ransom Christians imprisoned by the Moors) settled here and built a monastery and later a church facing the Gulf. These structures, called **Iglesía y Convento La Merced**, were amongst the very few to be spared from Morgan's wholesale destruction of

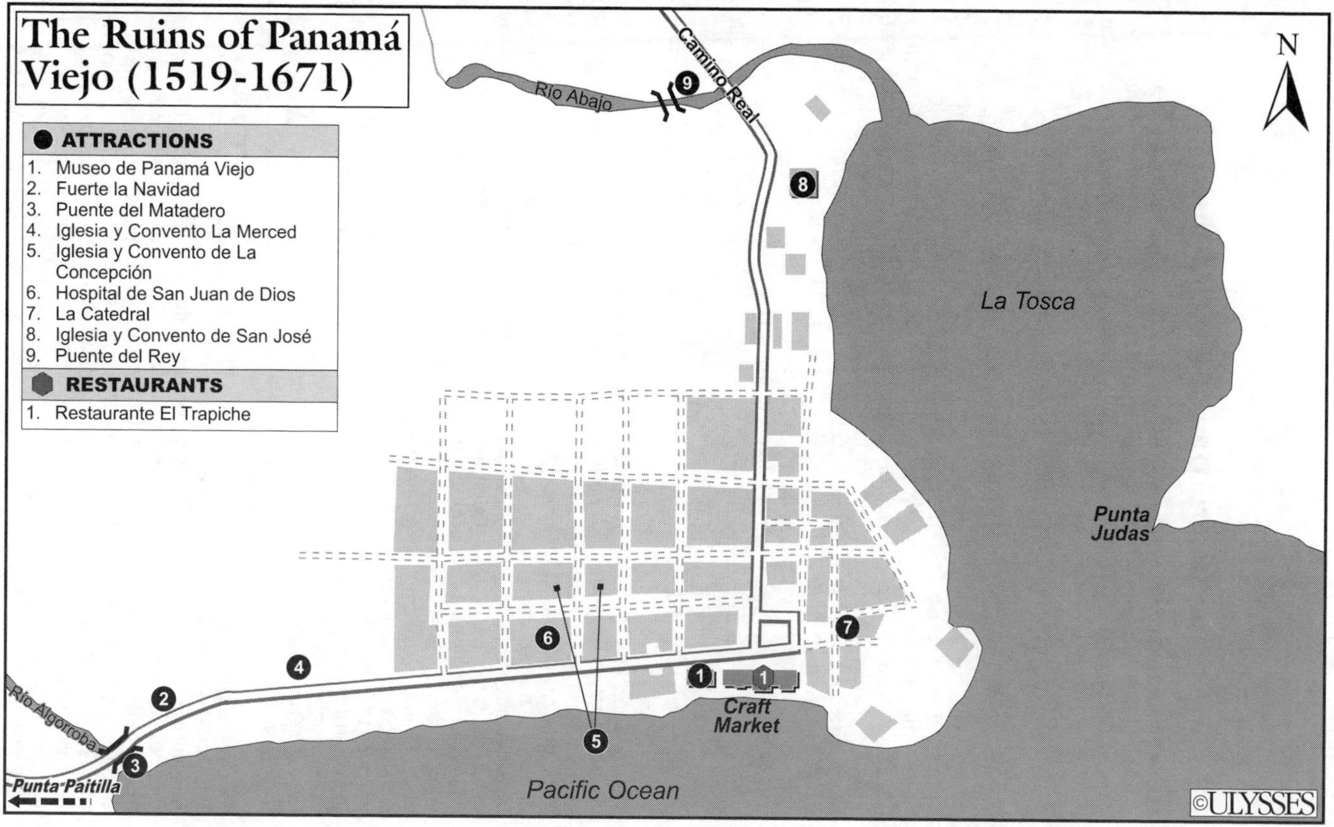
The Ruins of Panamá Viejo (1519-1671)
ATTRACTIONS
1. Museo de Panamá Viejo
2. Fuerte la Navidad
3. Puente del Matadero
4. Iglesia y Convento La Merced
5. Iglesia y Convento de La Concepción
6. Hospital de San Juan de Dios
7. La Catedral
8. Iglesia y Convento de San José
9. Puente del Rey
RESTAURANTS
1. Restaurante El Trapiche
N
Río Abajo
Camino Real
La Tosca
Punta Judas
Craft Market
Río Algorroba
Punta Paitilla
Pacific Ocean
©ULYSSES

The Destruction of Panamá Viejo

In February 1671, pirate Henry Morgan sailed up the Río Chagres from the Fuerte San Lorenzo (see p 162) with a fleet of ships and an army of over a thousand, with the aim of plundering Panamá City. After several days of rough sailing, the pirates reached the city gates, where they settled to regain their strength. Determined to defend the capital, then-governor D. Guzman, leading nearly 2,000 soldiers, resolved to head off the predator. Although they markedly outnumbered the pirates, the Spanish retreated after several hours of hard-fought battle, leaving the city to the invaders. According to certain historians, this defeat can be explained by the fact that Guzman's garrison was then largely made up of slaves, who obviously had little motivation to defend a power that had subjugated them. Morgan seized the undefended capital and committed abominable acts of pillaging, murder, rape and desecration. Devastated, Panamá Viejo was then ultimately destroyed by a rash of fires, leaving behind only ruins to impress visitors.

the city. Soon after the city's devastation however, the monks chose to settle in the new city of Panamá, dismantling the church facade in order to build that of the cathedral, which can still be seen on Plaza de laIndependencia. Unfortunately, the remains do not give a very good idea of the scale of the original buildings, particularly since Avenida Cincuentenario awkwardly bisects the existing ruins.

The impressive ruins of **Iglesía y Convento de La Concepción**, along with those of the bell tower from the old cathedral, are among the best-preserved on site. The other ruins here are those of the temple built by the very prosperous Conception order of nuns.

Hospital de San Juan Dios is the site of handsome ruins of the city hospital which date from 1620.

Begun in late 1619, **La Catedral** took six years to complete. Rather than facing the central square, as was the custom at the time, the church was built alongside the square and faced the sea. The ruins of the enormous clock tower suggest how impressive the original building must have been.

The well-preserved ruins of **Iglesia y Convento de San José** are located just north of the main site. The famous altar that now stands in the San José church in Casco Viejo originally came from this building. Along with the Iglesia la Merced, this is one of the few in the city not destroyed by Morgan's fire.

Near the ruins of the San José convent, the **Puente del Rey**, built in 1617, was vital to the city since it connected it to the famous road known as Camino Real, which led to Portobelo, on the Caribbean Coast.

★

Cerro Azul

The climb to Cerro Azul is a lovely excursion and a great way to escape from the sometimes stifling heat of the capital without straying too far from the city. Those with a car can benefit not only from cooler temperatures (20 to 24°C), but also see flora similar to that found in most of the country's major national parks, all just a short ride away. It is a wonderful opportunity to observe a great diversity of flora and photograph beautiful panoramas.

Keep in mind, however, that the higher the altitude, the more the climate changes, and rather quickly too. Grey and rainy skies are commonly encountered at a high altitude in certain times of the year, even when blue skies and a blazing sun illuminate the plains below. Several tourism agencies in the capital offer guide services, taking those who wish to explore the flora and fauna in greater depth off the beaten track. Those who choose not to will still find this little jaunt very peasant, particularly for the good restaurant along the way (see p 110).

Parks

★

Parque Natural Metropolitano

The **Parque Natural Metropolitano** *(B/.1, every day 8am to 5pm, entrance located on Avenida Juan Pablo II, near Calle de la Amistad, ☎232-5552, www.sinfo.net/pnmetrop)* is one of few nature parks in a very urbanized area. Lush tropical rain forest covers 192 of the park's 265ha. This large park is only 15min from downtown, and is inhabited by **monkeys**, **iguanas**, **exotic birds** and **sloths**.

For a map or additional information on the park's plant and animal life, head to the welcome centre near the parking lot. A guide service is also available to the public. If you are interested in observing the wildlife, it is best to get here early in the morning, when the animals come out to look for food.

Punta Culebra

On Isla Naos, more specifically on Punta Culebra, the Smithsonian Institute has opened an educational and well laid-out interpretation centre: the **Centro de Exhibiciones Marinas** ★★★ *(B/.1, Tue-Fri 1pm to 5pm, Sat and Sun 10am to 6pm, Calzada Amador, ☎227-4918 or 227-6022)*, which is devoted to the understanding and preservation of the thalassic environment. Explanatory signs on a trail skirting the island's headland introduce visitors to various aspects of marine life, from the formation of different kinds of sand and coastal vegetation, such as mangrove swamps, to the animals encountered here (birds, crustaceans, mollusks,

An Abundance of Fish

There are several legends about the origin of the word Panamá. According to one, the site upon which the city was founded was full of trees bearing an edible fruit (resembling the chestnut), whose indigenous name was "panamá". Another, put forth by the Kunas, explains that the word comes from the Kuna phrase "pa na ma", or "panamai", meaning "way overthere." This was often the response to the Spaniards' insistent questions about where the indigenous had found the gold with which they adorned themselves. While some people claim that the word actually means "abundance of butterflies," others say it signifies "abundance of fish." To this day, no historian has been able to determine the exact origin of the word. However, the "abundance of fish" theory has earned official status and seems to have been unanimously adopted by the Panamanian people.

etc.). The site also has quite a history! Visitors may be surprised to learn that several cannons were set up on Naos as well as on its sister islands (Perico and Flamenco) during World War II in order to protect the canal. Among them was a huge cannon that could be moved to the mouth of the canal along the 6km-long causeway! Two small museums devoted to marine life are also an integral part of the site.

Farther on, the trail leads to the heart of a small dry forest where, here too, visitors are provided with ample information about the flora and fauna. With a little luck, **sloths** or **iguanas** can be spotted. The entire Centro de Exhibiciones Marinas can easily be explored in a morning or an afternoon, and a visit can be topped off with a pleasant meal at one of the restaurants on the island (see p 109) or a swim at one of its beaches.

Beaches

Isla Naos, Isla Perico and Isla Flamenco

These islands are located off the Amador peninsula and are connected to the mainland by a long spit of land called Calzada Amador, though visitors are not allowed on Isla Flamenco. While the beaches on the other two islands are not very clean, the area is worth a visit for the lovely views and the more interesting attraction, Le Centro de Exhibiciones Marinas (see above), located within a small park. The narrow stretch of land connecting the islands and the mainland is bordered by palm trees and a number of benches, and is an ideal place to go for a bicycle ride or a morning jog. If you like lively places, head to La Playita on Isla Naos, where a great family atmosphere is guaranteed on weekends.

Outdoor Activities

Hiking

Parque Natural Metropolitano

This vast 265ha park is one of the few nature reserves within city limits. Four trails are accessible here, including the 1,000m-long Sendero La Cienaguita and Sendero del Mono Tití (named after the Tití monkeys who live in the park), which are linked together and thus allow visitors to enjoy a strenuous hike.

For the more adventurous, the Mono Tití trail leads to the park's summit, Cerro Cedro, at about 140m in altitude. At the lookout on top there is a beautiful view of the Bahia de Panamá , the Panamá Canal and the gulf islands in the distance. Less adventurous types can take the Los Momótides and Los Caobos trails, both of which are easier. While a guide can provide information on the plants and animals along the trails, they can be tackled alone with the help of a leaflet published in both English and Spanish.

Accommodations

Casco Viejo

Although Casco Viejo is extremely charming, and the efforts made by authorities to revitalize the area are admirable, the historic centre of town still has no middle-range or luxury hotels to speak of. All you will find here are a few boarding-houses and outdated places offering only the most basic level of comfort. Furthermore, the neighbourhood is not safe after nightfall, and it is highly inadvisable to wander about here. Those staying in Casco Viejo should either get there before dark or take a taxi. Despite these inconveniences, we have listed below a few of the most inexpensive places to stay in the capital.

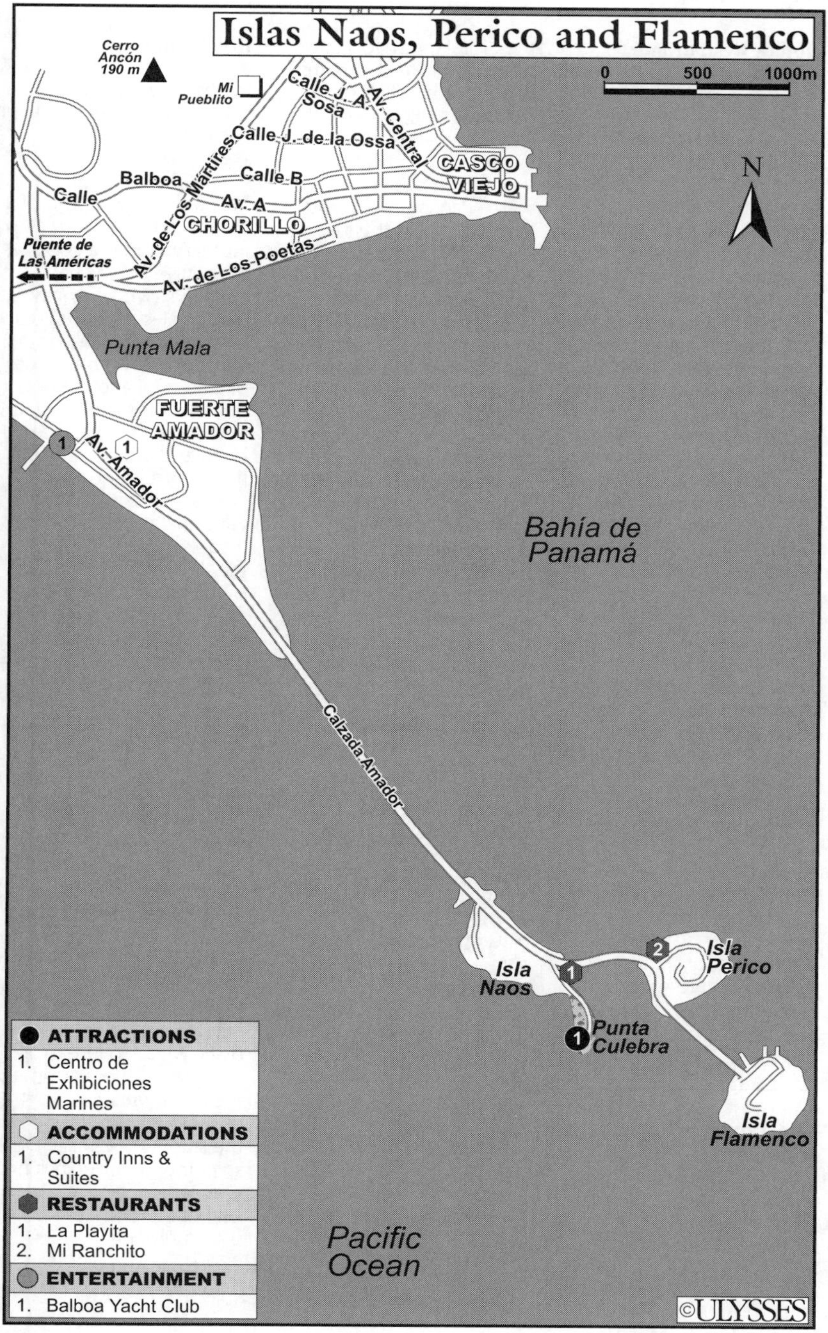
Islas Naos, Perico and Flamenco
Cerro Ancón 190 m
Mi Pueblito
Calle J. A. Sosa
Av. Central
Calle J. de la Ossa
CASCO VIEJO
Calle B
Balboa
Calle
Av. de Los Mártires
Av. A
CHORILLO
Puente de Las Américas
Av. de Los Poetas
Punta Mala
FUERTE AMADOR
Av. Amador
Bahía de Panamá
Calzada Amador
Isla Naos
Isla Perico
Punta Culebra
Isla Flamenco
Pacific Ocean
0 500 1000m
N
ATTRACTIONS
1. Centro de Exhibiciones Marines
ACCOMMODATIONS
1. Country Inns & Suites
RESTAURANTS
1. La Playita
2. Mi Ranchito
ENTERTAINMENT
1. Balboa Yacht Club
©ULYSSES

Hotel y Restaurante Central
$
sb/pb, ⊗
Avenida Central and Calle 5 Este, on Plaza de la Independencia/Plaza Central
This hotel, where the engineers working on the canal used to stay, still has a certain charm about it. Its wide patio, three-storey galleries and large wooden staircase all bear witness to its glorious past. The rooms, separated from one another by simple wooden panels, are very basic, however. Those at the front of the building are the most pleasant, as they are connected to a small balcony with a view of the Central Sqaure.

Foyo
$
sb/pb, ⊗
Calle 6a Oeste, near Ave. A
☎262-8023
Among the budget hotels in town, Hotel Foyo is a good choice. Its 39 high-ceilinged rooms are equipped with fans, which do not always work, however. Though clean, the place offers only rudimentary comfort. Foyo is nonetheless a decent alternative for those who do not wish to spend more than B/.10 per night.

Santa Ana

Hotel Internacional
$-$$
pb, hw, ≡, *tv,* ℜ
Plaza 5 de Mayo, Apartado 2751, Balboa
☎262-4933 or 262-4948
⇄262-9760
A few steps away from the Museo Antropo-lógico Reina Torres de Aráuz, the Hotel Internacional offers comfortable rooms, which are hardly luxurious but nevertheless decently decorated. There is a rooftop bar and patio, where you can enjoy the warm Panamanian nights. Another plus is the free shuttle service to the beach at Isla Naos (see p 90), where a variety of services are available, including a bar, a restaurant, chaise longues and pedalboat and parasol rentals. The hotel's only drawback is its proximity to the congested Plaza 5 de Mayo and equally busy Avenida Central, which make for a rather noisy atmosphere. Also, it is safer to get about by taxi after dark. In spite of these inconveniences, this hotel is a good choice for travellers on a limited budget.

La Exposición

This bustling area is not very safe after dark, so it is best to get about by taxi.

Hotel Acapulco
$
pb, hw, ≡, ⊗, ℜ, *tv*
Calle 30 Este, between Avenida Cuba and Avenida Perú
☎225-3832
Located near busy Avenida 3a Sur, Hotel Acapulco rents out simply decorated, reasonably comfortable rooms at attractive rates.

Hotel Andino
$
pb, hw, ≡, *K, tv*
Calle 35 Este, west of Ave. 1a Sur or Ave. Perú
☎225-1162
⇄227-7249
Located at the far end of a somewhat run-down alley, Hotel Andino is a good alternative for budget travellers, who can stay here for less than B/.20 a night. Although the long corridors resemble those of a hospital and the decor of the rooms is old-fashioned, overall the place is clean and decent. Each of the rooms is equipped with a small kitchen area with sink, refrigerator and a cooking burner, so guests can prepare their own meals. Though the area surrounding the hotel is not very attractive, this is compensated by the staff's warm, smiling welcome.

Lisboa
$
pb, hw, ≡, *tv*
Ave. 2a Sur or Cuba, between Calles 30 Este and 31 Este
☎227-5916 or 227-5917
⇄227-5919
Occupying a new building, the Lisboa hotel has modern, comfortable rooms whose cleanliness seems to be one of the staff's main concerns. Fortunately, lovely dark-hued rustic wooden furniture provides a little warmth to the somewhat cold surroundings made sterile by the stark white walls. Despite the rather uninviting welcome, the Lisboa is one of the district's better establishments.

Gran Hotel Soloy
$$
pb, hw, ≡, ℝ, ≈, ℜ
Avenida Perú and Calle 30 Este, Apdo 3385, Panamá 4
☎227-1133
⇄227-0884
hgsoloy@pan.gbm.net
Gran Hotel Soloy has 200 comfortable, spacious rooms decorated in an unoriginal style that borders on kitsch. In addition to its casino, the hotel has two bars, a nightclub, a roof top with a panoramic view and a 24-hour restaurant. The prices are reasonable as well. The only drawback is that it is not safe to walk around in this area after dark.

Veracruz
$$
pb, hw, ≡, ℜ, *tv*
Avenida Perú and Calle 30 Este, Apartado 4944, Zona 5
☎227-3022
⇄227-3789
A modern building with Spanish touches, this hotel has comfortable rooms decorated in a conventional modern style. It is conveniently located near the old city. However, although the neighbourhood is quite pleasant during the day, it is best to be cautious here at night.

Roma Plaza
$$-$$$
pb, hw, ≡, ℜ, ≈, *tv*
corner of Avenida 3A Sur/Justo Arosemena and Calle 33 Este
☎227-3844
⇄227-3711
The Roma is a large hotel (160 rooms) that offers the kind of comfort expected of a luxury establishment, including a bar and a nightclub. The rooms are comfortable and the service is friendly (though the decor is not great). Be careful in this area at night.

Calidonia

Residencial Primavera
$
pb, hw, ⊗
Avenida Cuba, near Calle 42 Este
☎225-1195
Although the rooms here are very basic, this place has the advantage of being located in a relatively safe area, not far from the residential neighbourhood of Bella Vista.

Hotel Venecia
$
pb, hw, ≡, *tv,* ℜ
Avenida. Perú, between Calles 36 and 37
☎227-7881
⇄227-5642
hvenecia@usa.net
On the upper floors of a new building with neocolonial-inspired balconies, Hotel Venecia offers one of the best quality-to-price ratios in the capital. The long, tiled and somewhat cold-looking corridor leads to charming little rooms that are tastefully decorated.

Ask to see several rooms before renting one, as some have particularly elegant colonial-style furnishings. Unfortunately, none offers a truly interesting view. Also, a swimming pool would be a welcome addition. On the other hand, for as little as B/.20 a room per night, there is hardly cause to complain. The staff is welcoming and the place is kept spotlessly clean.

Hotel Centroamericano
$-$$
pb, hw, ≡, ℜ, *tv*
Avenida Ecuador and 3a, near Justo Arosemena
☎227-4555
⇄225-2505
This reasonably comfortable hotel has 61 well-kept rooms, decorated in a conventional manner. It is located near a small park and numerous restaurants. Although this area is quite pleasant during the day, it is not the safest of place after dark, so visitors are advised to be cautious. Nevertheless, this hotel offers good value for your money.

Residencial Jamaica
$-$$
pb, hw, ≡, *tv*
Avenida Cuba, between Calle 38 Este and 39 Este
☎225-9870 or 225-9840
Residencial Jamaica is a modern colonial-style villa with comfortable, well-decorated rooms. The hotel's attractive woodwork and wrought iron styling bring to mind classical Spanish design. Though rooms can also be rented by the hour, this hotel is worth considering.

Costa Inn
$$-$$$
pb, hw, ℜ, ≡, *tv,* ≈, ⊙, ⌂
corner of Avenida Perú and Calle 39 Este
☎227-1522 or 225-6700
⇄225-1281
costainn@panama.phoenix.net
The Costa Inn is a modern 130-room hotel with a number of services. The rooms are comfortable, and the decor is modern but unexceptional. The pool and fitness centre are rather small for a hotel of this size.

Bella Vista

California
$$
pb, hw, ℜ, ≡, tv
corner of Avenida Central and Calle 43 Este, Apdo 61-93, Zona 5
☎263-7736
⇌264-6144
www.hotel-california.ws
Located in a fairly safe neighbourhood, not far from Bella Vista, this hotel has 60 modestly decorated but quite comfortable rooms. The staff is friendly and the owner is from Madrid. The rooms are old-fashioned but a good value. The only drawback is that the building faces onto noisy Vía España, so ask for a room at the back, preferably on one of the upper floors, for a more pleasant view. The hotel also has a cafeteria/restaurant.

Hotel Europa
$$$
pb, hw, ≡, ≈, ℜ, tv
Avenida Central, opposite Calle 42 Este, Apdo 7511, Panama 5
☎263-6369 or 263-6911
⇌263-6749
Located on noisy Vía España, Hotel Europa has about a 100 comfortable, but rather unattractively decorated rooms. There is also a conference room, a restaurant, bar and kitschy reception area. Friendly service.

Miramar Intercontinental
$$$$$
pb, hw, tv, ≡, ≈, ℜ, ⊙, ✪
Ave. Balboa, Apdo 7336, Panamá 5
☎214-1000
⇌223-4891
www.panama-city.panama.intercontinental.com
One of the newest major additions to the capital's hotel scene, the Miramar Intercontinental is housed in one of the two huge twin towers recently erected between busy Avenida Balboa and the bay.

The lack of urban planning is obvious here, and the ill-considered development of skyscrapers that once seemed to be confined to Punta Paitilla and the Marbella district now seems to be spreading to the downtown area. The Miramar Intercontinental is thus the only hotel in the capital to offer a direct view of the Gulf of Panamá. Despite its choice location, most of the rooms lack balconies, and guests must be content with observing the islands of Naos, Perico and Flamenco, as well as the many ships waiting to enter the canal, through enormous but inoperable windows.

The building offers 206 guest rooms and 13 suites, all of which are tastefully decorated, and come with a clock radio, a mini bar, an in-room safe, and a very quiet air conditioner. The sinks are separate from the toilet in the fully marbled bathrooms, which are stocked with all the amenities of a first-class hotel. Of course, numerous services and facilities are available to clients, including several restaurants, a bar with panoramic view, a spa, various shops, a tennis court as well as a fitness centre.

Also, among the establishment's most important assets is its very large swimming pool (the largest of any hotel in the capital), complete with a spacious patio which looks out on the gulf and the yachts in the marina. Unfortunately, despite the hotel's ideal location and irrefutable level of comfort, the guest rooms are not soundproof and the restaurant offers is overpriced and amateurish service.

Campo Alegre

Aparthotel Suites Alfa
$$$
pb, hw, ≡, tv, K, ℝ
Calle 50 Este/Ricardo Arias, near Vía España
☎263-4022
⇌223-0724
suitesalfa@pty.com
The four-story Aparthotel Suites Alfa has 65 comfortable rooms with modern furnishings and kitchenettes. The place is somewhat depressing, however, for several reasons: there is no view, the rooms are somewhat stark with tinted windows, and the decor is unoriginal. In contrast with the austerity of the premises, however, the staff is not only efficient, but also very friendly.

Tower House Suites
$$$ bkfst incl
pb, hw, ≡, *tv, K,* ≈
Avenida 3a A Sur (also called Avenida Frederico Boyd). Apdo 55-0309, Pta. Patilla
☎269-2244
⇄269-2869
The Tower House Suites rents out 40 nondescript modern suites, each equipped with a kitchenette. The rooms are comfortable and quiet.

Golden Tulip Hotel
$$$$
pb, hw, ≡, ≈, ℜ, ℝ, *K,* ⏲, ⌂, *tv*
corner of Avenida Federico Boyd and Avenida 3a Sur/Ricardo Arango, (also known as Calle 52), near Vía España. Apdo 8572, Panamá 5
☎206-3333
⇄206-3336
www.costadelsol-pma.com
The Golden Tulip offers beautiful, comfortable little apartments with all the modern conveniences and a tasteful, modern decor. On the roof, which offers a particularly interesting view of the church and Iglesia Del Carmen, you'll find a small swimming pool surrounded by a garden, and a bar-restaurant. In the evening, you can drink in a magical nightime view of Panama City from this patio. There is also a tenniscourt on the roof.

The Executive
$$$$ bkfst incl
pb, hw, ≡, ℜ, *tv,* ≈, ℝ
corner of Avenida 3a Sur and Calle 49 Este/Aquilino de la Guardia, near Avenido Ricardo Arango, Apdo 5370, Panamá 5
☎265-8011 or 264-3989
⇄269-1944
This big building contains 96 comfortable, well-kept rooms with classic, tasteful decor in warm colours. Also, most of the rooms have a small balcony and all have a fridge and coffee maker. The cafeteria is open around the clock.

Hotel Continental
$$$$
pb, hw, ≡, ≈, ℜ, *tv*
Calle 50 Este/Ricardo Arias, corner of Vía España. Apdo 8475, Panamá 7
☎263-9999 or 265-5114
⇄269-4559 or 265-6380
www.hotelsriande.com
Larger than its little brother (the Riande Granada), the Hotel Continental is also more luxurious and more expensive. A 200-room complex, it offers all the services you could dream of — a conference room, a casino, a bar, a nightclub, a 24-hour cafeteria, restaurants, as well as a small swimming pool. The decor is quite attractive, and most of the rooms have a balcony. Ask for a room on the pool side as they are nicer and offer a better view. This hotel is popular with business people.

The Bristol
$$$$$
pb, hw, ≡, ⏲, ℜ, *tv*
Avenida. Aquilino de la Guardia or Calle 49 Este, Apdo 810-542, Zona 10
☎265-7844
☎888-767-3963 (U.S.A.)
⇄265-7829
www.thebristol.com
Located among the many skyscrapers sprouting up in the Campo Alegre district, The Bristol is absolutely charming. Although modern, the exterior of the building is adorned with French-style windows with decorative fittings and pastel hues, giving it a touch of refinement. The interior is classically decorated with elegant furnishings and intricate woodwork that give it a distinguished look. The guest rooms themselves, each unique and opulent, boast a comfortable sofa, a small desk with a telephone, a fax machine, Internet access and a CD player. To top it all off, luxurious fabrics, attractive curios and fresh orchids add to the almost aristocratic surroundings. Moreover, each of the fully marbled bathrooms comes with either a shower with glass doors or a bath with many complimentary bath oils. Newspapers, fruit, mineral water, coffee and tea are also offered daily. The only drawback is that there is no swimming pool, always pleasant in the tropics.

Panamá Marriott
$$$$$
pb, hw, ≡, ≈, ℜ, ⏲, ⌂
at Calle 52 and Calle 50 Este or Ricardo Arias
☎210-9100
☎800-228-9290 US and Canada
⇄210-9110
www.marriotthotels.com/PTYPA
Open since January 1999, the Panamá Marriott Hotel, part of the giant hotel chain, is the new kid on the block in the business district. Though it constitutes yet another mammoth building in a city already teeming with skyscrapers, its architects have succeeded in giving the building a certain cachet evoking the Roaring Twenties. The interior is an entirely different story, however, with its very classical and opulent decor characteristic of this hotel chain.

As might be expected, guests will find everything they could possibly wish for. The same holds true for the spacious guest rooms, each equipped with a coffee maker, alarm clock, mini bar, iron and in-room safe, will make guests feel right at home. Several rooms are reserved for non-smokers, and the major English-language dailies are delivered to your door every morning. In short, nothing but the best, for those with a high limit on their credit card, of course.

El Cangrejo

Aparthotel Las Vegas Hotel Suites
$$
pb, hw, ≡, ⊗, ℝ, *K*
Avenida 2a Norte/Eusebio A. Morales, Apartado D, Balboa,corner of Calle 49B West.
☎269-0722
⇄223-0047
www.hotelvegas.com

Located in the pleasant neighbourhood of El Cangrejo, the Aparthotel Las Vegas has a brand new lobby and about 100 studios, each equipped with a little kitchenette, and several suites with washing machines. Although decent enough, the furnishings are plain and somewhat outmoded. Furthermore, the air conditioners, in wall units, are noisy.

Despite these drawbacks, this place offers an acceptable level of comfort, and ensures the safety of its guests. Moreover, renovations are presently under way, and a number of units have already been completely overhauled; ask for one of these. The hotel is also conveniently located in the heart of a pleasant neighbourhood, near many excellent restaurants and stores. TV addicts will be delighted to learn that they can pick up as many as 33 channels. International news is broadcasted in English on ICN. A good deal.

Hotel Marbella
$$
pb, hw, ≡, *tv*
Ave. 1a A Norte or Calle D
☎263-2220
⇄263-3622

Located on a quiet street near the Aparthotel Suites Ambassador and Vía España, the small Hotel Marbella will mainly suit those looking for a quiet place right downtown. The rooms are clean and comfortable but the decor, as well as the space, are minimalist. Nevertheless, the price is right.

Aparthotel Torres de Alba
$$$-$$$$
pb, hw, ≡, *tv,* ℝ, *K,* ≈, ⊙
Avenida 2a Norte/Eusebio A. Morales and Calle 49b Oeste/Veneto;
Apdo 10213 Zona 4
☎267-7770
⇄269-3924
www.torresdealba.com.pa

Built in 1994, Aparthotel Torres de Alba rents out modern, spacious studios with kitchenettes equipped with range hoods, microwaves, washers and dryers. The studios are tastefully decorated mostly in marble, which also adorns the bathrooms.

Aparthotel Suites Ambassador
$$$$ bkfst incl.
pb, hw, ≡, ≈, *tv,* ℝ, *K*
Avenida 1a A Norte/Calle D, Apdo 5364, Zona 5
☎263-7274
⇄264-7872

This 40-unit modern hotel is located in a pleasant, quiet area near numerous shops and restaurants. The studios and apartments are modern and nondescript. A small rooftop swimming pool adds to the pleasure of staying at this pleasant, but somewhat expensive place.

El Panamá
$$$$
pb, hw, ≡, *tv,* ℜ, ≈, ⊙, ⌂
Vía España and Calle 49b Oeste, Apdo 1753, Panamá 1
☎269-5000 or 269-5421
⇄269-5990 or 223-6080

Hotel El Panamá is set back slightly from the road, and is therfore not easily reached on foot. This huge complex, equipped with 340 units, offers all of the extras one would expect from a hotel in this category including: bars, restaurants (including one open 24 hours a day), a casino, luxury boutiques, a nightclub and a fitness centre. Guests also have access to a large swimming pool surrounded by a garden. The main building has spacious, tastefully decorated rooms, and a split-level side wing is surrounded by a pretty garden with a bar and a swimming pool. Although this part of the complex is a veritable tropical oasis, the rooms here are much smaller and plainly decorated. This area is also much noisier, and does not offer much privacy, since the rooms face each other. Three rooms are reserved for travellers with disabilities.

Riande Granada
$$$$
pb, hw, ≡, ℝ, ≈, ℜ, *tv*
Avenida 2A Norte/Eusebio A. Morales, near Avenida 1a A Norte/Calle D
☎264-4900 or 269-1068
⇄263-7197
www.hotelsriande.com
Part of a chain of hotels, the Riande Granada has 177 great rooms, which are simpler and less luxurious than those of its counterpart in Bella Vista, the Hotel Continental (see p 95), but nevertheless offer all the necessary comforts. In addition to a casino, a bar and a 24-hour restaurant, there is a large swimming pool surrounded by an attractive garden. Furthermore, the place is not only less expensive than the Riande Continental Ciudad, but is also located on a quieter street.

Marbella

Radisson Royal Panamá Hotel
$$$$$
pb, hw, tv, ≡, ≈, ℜ, ⊘
Calle 53 Este, at Ave. 5a B Sur, Apdo 8-320239
☎265-3636
☎800-333-3333 (U.S.A.)
⇄265-3550
www.radisson.com/panamacity.pa
In the heart of the chic Marbella district, right next to the World Trade Centre the Radisson Royal Panamá Hotel is not particularly attractive at first sight. Once inside the tower, however, guests will be delighted to find a pleasant, beautifully appointed lobby graced with a harmonious blend of glass, marble and woodwork. Conversely, the guest room decor is somewhat disappointing, as the functional furniture shows a distinct lack of originality. The rooms are nevertheless comfortable and come with all the amenities required by business people (Internet access, modem hookup and in-room safe). The swimming pool and fitness centre are unfortunately rather modest.

Punta Paitilla

Hotel Plaza Paitilla Inn
$$$$ bkfst incl.
pb, hw, ≡, *tv,* ℝ ≈, ℜ
Vía Italia, Punta Paitilla, Apdo 1807, Panamá 1
☎269-1122 or 269-1069
⇄223-1470 or 263-6998
Cylindrical in shape and resembling a large, modern guard tower, this hotel has several things going for it. The rooms are large, particularly well soundproofed and have large French doors leading out onto small balconies, some of which have unobstructed views of the gulf and the city centre. Each room also comes with an alarm clock, a table and chairs as well as a refrigerator that is far more practical than the standard mini bar. Unfortunately, the rooms do not have safes and the antiquated air-conditioners are noisy.

Noteworthy among the hotel's other assets is the spacious swimming pool with patio. Although the large on-site restaurant is worth mentioning and has an engaging staff, prices are too high and furthermore, the large glass doors surrounding it do not provide an interesting view and the old-fashioned decor needs to be refurbished. Despite these drawbacks, the hotel remains a good choice for its quality service and location.

San Francisco

Caesar Park Hotel
$$$$
pb, hw, ≡, ≈, ℜ, *tv,* ⊘, △, ℝ
Vía Israel and Calle 77, San Francisco, Westin Hotels & Resorts, Apartado 6-4248, El Dorado, Panamá 6A
☎270-0477
⇄226-0116 or 226-4262
Canada and U.S.
☎800-937-8461
www.caesarpark.com
This big, modern hotel, located near the Atlapa convention centre, has 400 fully equipped and tastefully furnished rooms. Non-smoking rooms are also available. In addition to a wide range of facilities, including tennis courts, a casino and a nightclub, there are four restaurants on the premises, one of which is open 24 hours a day (Las Hamacas). A number of luxury shops and galleries can also be found here. The hotel does have a few drawbacks, however. First, it is located far from the downtown area, which makes it somewhat tedious to get about. Also, its unique swimming pool seems very small for such a large hotel complex. Lastly, the

international atmosphere could almost be termed sterile, making a stay here rather uninteresting, except for those attending conventions at the Atlapa centre.

Calzada Amador

Country Inns & Suites
$$$$
pb, hw, ≡, ≈, *tv,* ⊘
Amador Blvd. y Pelicano Av.
☎***211-4500***
☎***800-456-4000 (U.S.A. and Canada)***
⇄***211-4501***
www.countryinns.com/panamacanalpan
www.panamacanalcountry.com
Although located outside the city centre, this lovely hotel's 98 rooms and suites offer an exceptional view of the canal and the famous Puente de las Américas. Moreover, given the proximity of the Calzada Amador pier (see p 90), guests can combine pleasant bike rides (onsite bike rental) or walks to the islands of Naos and Perico with the pleasures of swimming at the nearby beaches. Each of the rooms is tastefully decorated and features a balcony. A view of the canal and a swimming pool with whirlpool bath round out the amenities. Finally, lest we forget sports enthusiasts, also on site is a tennis court surrounded by lovely gardens.

Cerro Azul

Cabañas 4X4
$$$-$$$$
Vía Principal de Cerro Azul
☎***680-3076 or 686-3693***
Those in search of a total retreat in the heart of the wilderness will enjoy the Cabañas 4X4. This establishment is comprised of four wooden cabins as well as five *bohios* (native-style huts) surrounded by lush tropical vegetation and only accessible by all-terrain vehicle. The rustic cabins' interior layout consists of a simple kitchen with all the necessary cooking utilities, a shower room, one or more bedrooms and a living room.

Rates vary from B/.80 to B/.145, depending on the size of the cabin *(for 2 to 8 people)*. As for the *bohios* *($$)*, they are simple, basic one-room cabins on stilts with beds for four people. The "main floor" of the *bohios*, with an outdoor table and benches, serves as a dining area. The kitchen and showers are communal. Remember to bring insect repellent, as the mosquitos are particularly attentive here!

Hostal Casa de Campo
$$$$ bkfst incl
pb, hw, tv, ≈, ℜ, ⌂
Ave. Los Cúmulos, 3-G Las Nubes
☎***297-0067 or 270-0018***
⇄***226-0336***
www.panamacasadecampo.com
In a completely different style, Hostal Casa de Campo has several comfortable rooms in two buildings on a 4ha estate, where several interpretive trails have been marked out. The rooms in the main building, a grand villa, are very tastefully decorated with magnificent antiques. Each room has a unique style, and lovely antiques make them even more charming. The same holds true for the common areas, where paintings, carpets and chandeliers bring to mind the Old World.

Unfortunately, the rooms in the new section, though comfortable, lack charm and are not tastefully decorated. So is the area around the pool, where the bizarre Greek-style columns look somewhat out of place. Different health packages are offered here, ranging from the "eco-stay" (including lodging, meals and fauna- and flora-observation hikes) and the "anti-stress workshop" (including lodging, meals, massages, sauna and many other treatments) to the "anti-aging workshop" (including meals and lodging as well as massages and revitalizing treatments). In addition to the pool, there is also a rather small outdoor sauna and whirlpool. For those seeking adventure, the establishment organizes several expeditions, including a hike to the top of Cerro Azul, a visit to a Kuna reserve and a kayak trip down the river.

Near the International Airport

Continental Riande Aeropuerto
$$$
pb, hw, tv, ≡, ≈, ℜ
Vía Aeropuerto Carretera Interamericana, Apdo 6-999, El Dorado
☎290-3333
☎800-742-6331 (U.S.A and Canada)
⇄290-3017
www.hotelsriande.com
Situated near Tocumen International Airport, the Continental Riande Aeropuerto is primarily suited for a stopover in Panamá. The rooms are located in a two-storey *U*-shaped building that surrounds a garden and a pleasant swimming pool. Though the hotel looks more like a motel, the rooms are comfortable, if somewhat lacking in intimacy. Guests can have a game of tennis or volleyball while awaiting their flight.

Restaurants

Casco Viejo

Restaurante Las Bóvedas
$$$
Mon-Sun 7pm to 11pm
Plaza de Francia
☎228-8058 or 228-8068
Adjoining pretty Plaza de Francia, inside some of the city's 18th century fortifications (see p 81), Restaurante Las Bóvedas serves quality French cuisine in an extremely attractive setting. Be careful as there is no sign on the restaurant, which is located on the west side of the plaza. In a lovely vaulted room, away from the heat, you can savour a fish or meat dish served with a thick sauce and baby vegetables. For those who prefer to be out in the sun, there is a small patio where you can quench your thirst. Live jazz music from Thursday to Saturday, starting at 9pm. Friendly service.

Café du Liban
$$$
Mon-Sun noon to 3pm and 7pm to midnight
Avenida E or Eloy Alfaro
Casco Viejo
☎212-1582
Located a stone's throw from the presidential palace, this restaurant is worth the trip both for its pleasant view of the Golfo de Panamá and its good food. Upstairs, the patio (limited seating) will delight those who enjoy the open air and want to feel the gulf breeze on their faces. Diners can partake of the great classics of Lebanese cuisine, such as baba gannouj, hummus, taboule, falafel and many other dishes besides. On Thursdays, Fridays and Saturdays, a belly-dancing show is offered from 9pm to midnight. Good value.

Casablanca
$$$$
Mon-Sat from 7pm
Parque Bolívar
Casco Viejo
☎262-7507
Set on charming Bolívar square—within the former, colonial-style Colombia hotel, now fully renovated and converted into luxury apartments—this small Casablanca restaurant is worth a visit. In a modern setting, diners can choose one of many dishes on the menu. Unfortunately, the international-style cuisine offered here hardly does justice to the pompous names that designate the dishes. Young, middle-class Panamanians frequent this popular meeting place with sure-fire ambiance. A great place for those who like to see and be seen. Belly-dancing shows are featured on Fridays and Saturdays.

Santa Ana

Café Restaurante
$
7:30am to midnight
at Calle 12 and Ave. Central
Café Restaurante is probably the best of the least expensive. Located on a street corner, just steps from busy Avenida Central, this crowded establishment is very popular with locals who come here to eat for a reasonable price. The daily menu costs as little as B/.3, including soup, a main course and coffee (alcoholic beverages not available), which you can eat while seated in lovely leather chairs. More than a good deal, a true wonder!

La Exposicíon

Mi Salud
$
Mon-Sat 7am to 6pm
Calle 31, near Avenida 4a Sur/Mejico
Located in a simple little house, this restaurant

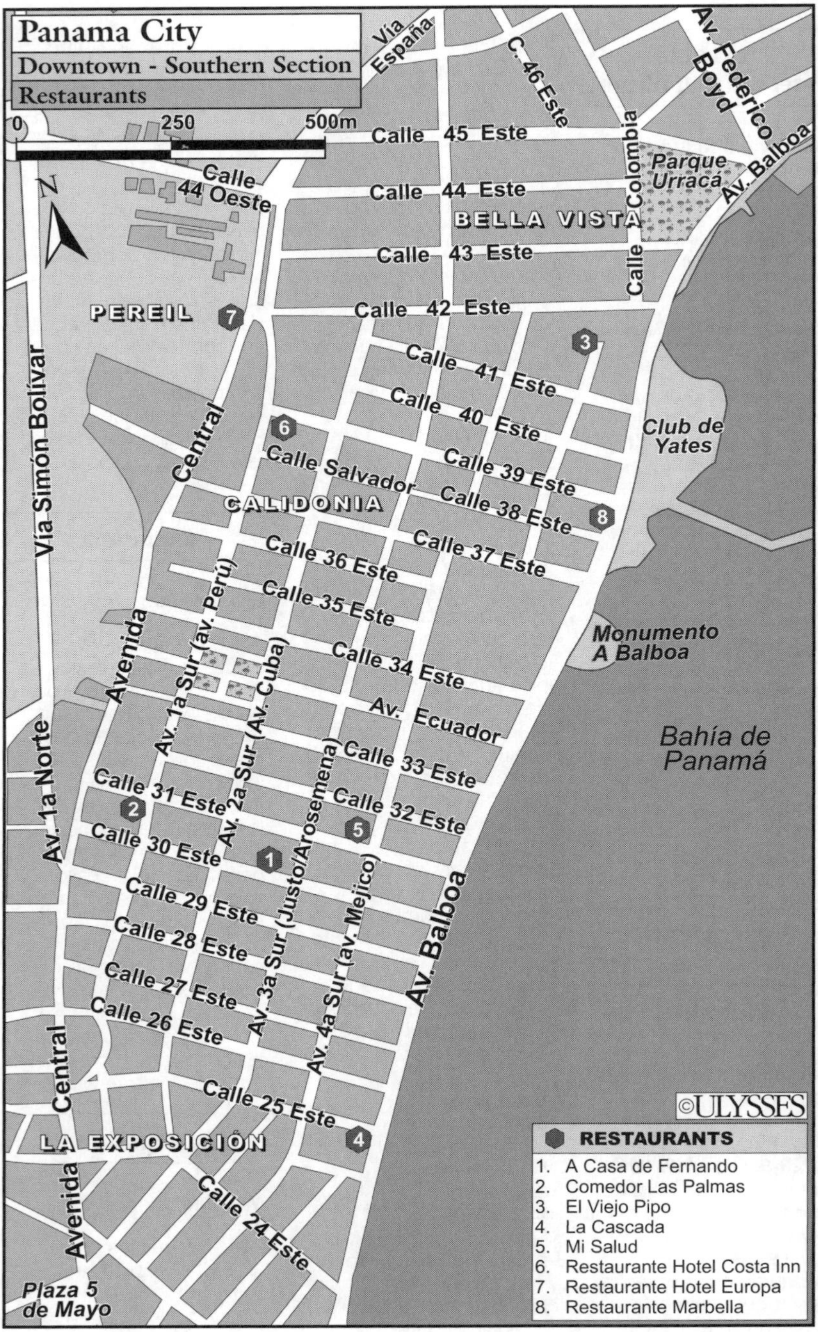

Panama City
Downtown - Southern Section
Restaurants
0
250
500m
N
Vía España
C. 46 Este
Av. Federico Boyd
Av. Balboa
Calle 45 Este
Calle Colombia
Parque Urracá
Calle 44 Oeste
Calle 44 Este
BELLA VISTA
Calle 43 Este
PEREIL
Calle 42 Este
Calle 41 Este
Calle 40 Este
Club de Yates
Vía Simón Bolívar
Central
Calle Salvador
Calle 39 Este
Calle 38 Este
CALIDONIA
Calle 37 Este
Calle 36 Este
Calle 35 Este
Monumento A Balboa
Avenida
Av. 1a Sur (av. Perú)
Av. 2a Sur (Av. Cuba)
Calle 34 Este
Av. Ecuador
Bahía de Panamá
Av. 1a Norte
Av. 3a Sur (Justo/Arosemena)
Calle 33 Este
Calle 31 Este
Calle 32 Este
Calle 30 Este
Av. 4a Sur (av. Mejico)
Calle 29 Este
Calle 28 Este
Av. Balboa
Calle 27 Este
Calle 26 Este
Central
Calle 25 Este
©ULYSSES
LA EXPOSICIÓN
Avenida
Calle 24 Este
Plaza 5 de Mayo
RESTAURANTS
1. A Casa de Fernando
2. Comedor Las Palmas
3. El Viejo Pipo
4. La Cascada
5. Mi Salud
6. Restaurante Hotel Costa Inn
7. Restaurante Hotel Europa
8. Restaurante Marbella

offers a small selection of vegetarian dishes in a rather non-descript dining room. The decor is accentuated by arches, and livened up by bright, colourful tablecloths. One the few vegetarian restaurants in the capital.

A la Casa de Fernando
$$
Calle 30 Este, between Ave. 3a Sur or Justo Arosemena and Ave. 2a Sur or Cuba
☎225-2378
In a rustic Portuguese-style setting, A la Casa de Fernando offers patrons *sancocho de Gallina* for B/.1.75, *sopa de mariscos* for B/.2.75, *cazuela de mariscos* for B/.11.25 or *pargo rojo* for B/.9. A real bargain! Also featured on the menu are *calamares, camarones, langostinas* and *pulpos* in all its forms and with a variety of sauces at very reasonable prices. The best place in the district, with Panamanian music to boot!

Comedor Las Palmas
$$
noon to midnight
at Ave. Perú and Calle 30 Este, on the main floor of the Veracruz hotel
In a simple and somewhat impersonal setting, Comedor Las Palmas offers very simple *corvina*, chicken and spaghetti dishes. Its long opening hours are especially convenient.

La Cascada
$$$
Mon-Thu 4:30pm to 11pm, Fri and Sat 3pm to 11:30pm, Sun 11am to 11pm
Avenida Balboa and Calle 2
☎262-9963
The truly unusual restaurant La Cascada merits a short visit, if only to see its amusing decor. Guests dine near a series of pools and little fountains adorned with a number of fake swordfish. All the water comes from an artificial waterfall that looks like the real thing! As if the decor was not kitschy enough already, coloured Chinese lanterns have been put up all over the place, creating a carnival-like atmosphere. The menu is equally peculiar, made up of 16 pages of jokes and games referring to the food, which consists mainly of seafood and grilled meats. There is another branch of this restaurant in El Cangrejo (see p 106). Finally, La Cascada is also unusual in that its staff is made up exclusively of young Panamanian women.

Calidonia

El Viejo Pipo
$$$
Tue-Sun noon to 3pm and 6pm to 11pm
Calle 42 Este, near Avenida Balboa; on the right as you head toward the avenue
☎225-7924
Located within a little villa surrounded by greenery, the Italian restaurant El Viejo Pipo has a pretty decor, whose wooden shutters, earth-coloured floor tiles and quaint little tablecloths evoke all the charm of Italy.

The menu features a refreshing *insalata de Mozzarella*; curiously enough, the chef prepares it without the traditional tomatoes. As for the main course, naturally a choice of pasta dishes is offered, as well as a delicious *corvina a la gorgonzola*, served with broccoli. What a treat! The clientele consists mainly of business people, and proper dress is expected. The only drawback is the slow service. After all, though, who cares about a little lost time when the food is so delectable? Friendly, cheerful staff.

Restaurante Hotel Costa Inn
$$$
corner of Avenida Perú and Calle 39 Este
☎227-1522 or 225-6700
This cafeteria-restaurant is most notable for its quality breakfasts, including an excellent fruit salad — a rarity in the capital. During the rest of the day, predictable international cuisine is served. The restaurant has a bright dining room with a view of the neighbourhood's greenery and is open 24 hours. Prices are on the high side.

Restaurante Hotel Europa
$$$
Avenida Central, near Calle 42 Este, facing the Bella Vista theatre
☎263-6369
Located in the hotel of the same name, this restaurant serves generous portions of several types of cuisine: Panamanian, Italian and French, all of which is good. The modern decor

is a little cold, but the friendly service more than compensates.

Marbella
$$$$
11am to 11pm
Avenida Balboa, between Calle 38 and 39 Este
☎225-9065
Occupying a chalet, Marbella will delight fish and seafood lovers. The chef prepares *corvina* and *gambas* in all sorts of sauces, as well as excellent paellas. The decor is adequate, but somewhat dull.

Bella Vista

Palacio Rey-Kung
$$
Vía España, near Calle 46
☎269-0956
The Palacio Rey-Kung is an attractive, if over-priced, Chinese restaurant. The fare is made up of slightly expensive, but classic, Chinese dishes. Wine from B/.14 to B/.18.

Café Balear
$$$$
Mon-Sat noon to 3pm and 7pm to 11pm
17 Calle Colombia, between Ave. 4a A Sur and Ave. 5a B Sur
☎269-2415
Frequented mainly by business people, the lovely family-run restaurant Café Balear serves typical Spanish cuisine complimented by a few more exotic dishes, such as the *dorado* with mushrooms and port or sweet-and-sour *corvina* with coconut and tomatoes. A tapas menu is also offered for B/.24, as is an extensive wine list (*from B/.17*). Though the food is of good quality and well presented, desserts are rather inconsistent. For example, while the *biscocho con almendra* is excellent, the chocolate cake is particularly disappointing. The decor is quite formal, despite a few plants and scores of paintings by Panamanian artists, including one by contemporary artist Antonio Alvarado.

Campo Alegre

Niko's Café
$
Calle 51b Este/Eg. Ortega, just south of Vía España
This self-service cafeteria is a good place for a light, inexpensive meal. Besides serving a large selection of dishes like shrimp, cutlets, crayfish and *corvina*, pitas, gyros and sandwiches to go. For breakfast, you can enjoy an omelette, corn tortillas or croissants stuffed with meat, for as little as B/.2.50. Simple, tasty food in modest but comfortable surroundings, reminiscent of Manolo's (see p 105). Cappuccino and expresso is available. The place also has a large patio. Very popular with the locals.

Café Jimmy
$
Avenida 2a Sur/Samuel Lewis, south of Vía España, near the Riande Continental hotel; attention motorists: there are no signs to warn you, but this is a one-way street!
In the same price category, but with a less elaborate menu, self-service Café Jimmy also offers light, simple meals in an equally simple decor. Local clientele. Patio.

Mireya
$
Mon-Sat 6am to 8pm
corner of Calle 50 Este/Ricardo Arias and Avenida 3a/Ricardo Arango
☎260-5169
Located in a pleasant and relatively quite neighbourhood, Mireya is a vegetarian restaurant that serves good, light dishes, perfect for breakfast or lunch. It has a pretty patio adorned with wrought-iron furniture and all sorts of plants, where you can sample dishes like *torrejas de maiz nuevo*, *changa de maiz con queso* and *empanadas de maiz con queso*. Various fruits are also available. Soy coffee and herbal tea are offered instead of regular coffee. Although the menu is fairly limited, this is a pleasant place to enjoy a healthy meal. Give it a try!

Costa Azul
$$
7am to 11pm
Calle 50 Este/Ricardo Arias, left side of the street on the way to Vía España
☎269-0409
Panamanian cuisine and sandwiches in a simple but comfortable setting. Small but pretty patio. Draft beer at B/.0.75.

Costa Del Sol
$$
Avenida Federico Boyd and Avenida 3a Sur/Ricardo Arango/Calle 52, near Vía España
☎206-3333
The Costa del Sol restaurant, located on the roof of the hotel of the same name, is worth visiting for its panoramic view encompassing the beautiful Iglesia del Carmen. Happy hour is between 5pm and

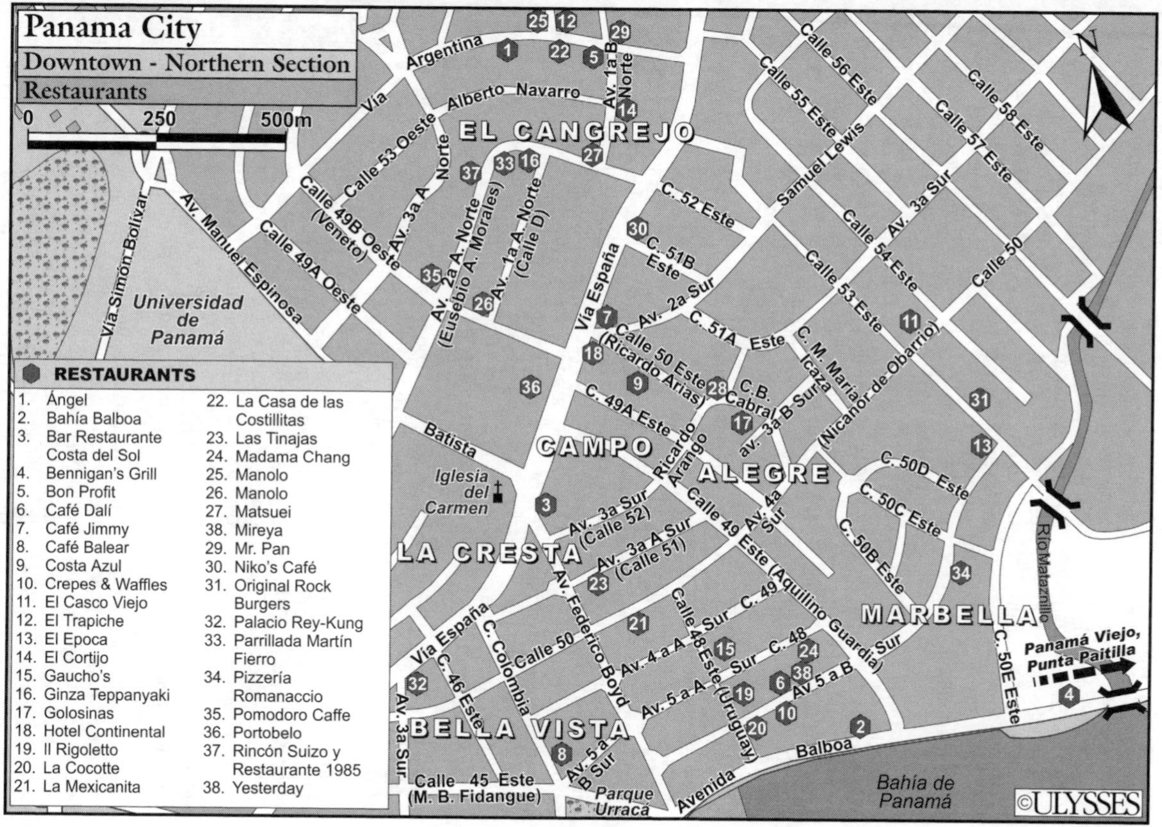
Panama City
Downtown - Northern Section
Restaurants
0
250
500m
RESTAURANTS
1. Ángel
2. Bahía Balboa
3. Bar Restaurante Costa del Sol
4. Bennigan's Grill
5. Bon Profit
6. Café Dalí
7. Café Jimmy
8. Café Balear
9. Costa Azul
10. Crepes & Waffles
11. El Casco Viejo
12. El Trapiche
13. El Epoca
14. El Cortijo
15. Gaucho's
16. Ginza Teppanyaki
17. Golosinas
18. Hotel Continental
19. Il Rigoletto
20. La Cocotte
21. La Mexicanita
22. La Casa de las Costillitas
23. Las Tinajas
24. Madama Chang
25. Manolo
26. Manolo
27. Matsuei
38. Mireya
29. Mr. Pan
30. Niko's Café
31. Original Rock Burgers
32. Palacio Rey-Kung
33. Parrillada Martín Fierro
34. Pizzería Romanaccio
35. Pomodoro Caffe
36. Portobelo
37. Rincón Suizo y Restaurante 1985
38. Yesterday
EL CANGREJO
CAMPO ALEGRE
LA CRESTA
MARBELLA
BELLA VISTA
Universidad de Panamá
Iglesia del Carmen
Bahía de Panamá
Río Mataznillo
Panamá Viejo, Punta Paitilla
Parque Urracá
Vía Simón Bolívar
Av. Manuel Espinosa
Vía Argentina
Alberto Navarro
Av. 1a B Norte
Calle 53 Oeste
Av. 3a A Norte
Calle 49B Oeste (Veneto)
Calle 49A Oeste
Av. 2a A. Norte (Eusebio A. Morales)
Av. 1a A. Norte (Calle D)
Vía España
Batista
Calle 56 Este
Calle 55 Este
Samuel Lewis
Calle 58 Este
Calle 57 Este
Av. 3a Sur
Calle 54 Este
Calle 50
Calle 53 Este
C. 52 Este
C. 51B Este
Av. 2a Sur
C. 51A Este
C. M. María Icaza
(Nicanor de Obarrio)
Calle 50 Este (Ricardo Arias)
C. B. Cabral
av. 3a B Sur
C. 49A Este
Ricardo Arango
Av. 4a Sur
Calle 49 Este (Aquilino Guardia)
C. 50D Este
C. 50C Este
C. 50B Este
C. 50E Este
Av. 3a Sur (Calle 52)
Av. 3a A Sur (Calle 51)
Av. Federico Boyd
Calle 48 Este (Uruguay)
C. 49
Av. 4 a A Sur
C. 48
Av. 5 a A Sur
Av. 5 a B
Vía España
C. Colombia
Calle 50
C. 46 Este
Av. 3a Sur
Av. 5 a B Sur
Calle 45 Este (M. B. Fidangue)
Avenida Balboa
Sur
©ULYSSES

7pm—a good time to try delicious cocktails including *banana coladas*, and *sunsets* (made with a lot of rum). The restaurant serves traditional fish (grilled *corvina*) and chicken dishes. The hanging garden is a beautiful addition to the decor.

Hotel Continental
$$$
Calle 50 Este or Ricardo Arias, near Ave. España
☎263-9999
The restaurant of the Riande Continental Ciudad hotel has nothing special to offer, but is worth the trip nonetheless for its good, typically Panamanian breakfast. Called *desayuno Montuño*, this hearty breakfast is composed of *yuka, platano* and a *bollo de maiz*, cheese and an omelet. Its patio with swimming pool and an assortment of green plants provides a pleasant little oasis in the heart of the city.

Golosinas
$$$$
Mon-Sat
Calle Beatriz M. de Cabal/Ricardo Arias, near Avenida 3a B Sur
☎269-6237 or 269-2028
Golosinas, which has a new location on a pleasant street, serves fine, innovative international and Panamanian cuisine. The dishes are served with excellent vegetables, and the presentation is simply beautiful. Although the building is new, the decorators skilfully succeeded in concealing its concrete structure. The decor is post-modern, and pastel colours soften the harsh, cold look of the walls, which are adorned with a few contemporary paintings. Business people and consulate employees make up the lunchtime clientele. The restaurant seems to be suffering from its own success lately as the quality and speed of service has declined.

Las Tinajas
$$$$
Mon-Sat
22 Avenida 3a Sur/Calle 51, near Avenida Frederico Boyd
☎263-7890
Las Tinajas is a restaurant in a Spanish-style villa that offers an excellent variation on traditional Panamanian cuisine. *Lengua fria con alcaparras* (beef tongue with capers), *guacho de marisco* (a shellfish dish) and *pastel de yucca* (a soufflé with yucca, corn, chicken and peppers) are a few of the delicious specialities. The desserts are equally good and include coconut flan and *sopa borracha* (a rum, plum, and raisin cake). The prices are reasonable for the level of quality, the careful preparation and the pleasant service. The decor is attractive and features objects from various regions throughout the country and from various time periods, including the pre-Columbian and colonial periods. Every Tuesday, Thursday, Friday and Saturday, starting at 9pm, the restaurant showcases traditional Panamanian dancing (the dancers wear the beautiful *pollera*). The restaurant also has an overpriced souvenir shop.

El Casco Viejo
$$$$
Mon-Fri noon to 3pm and 6pm to 11pm, Sat 7pm to 11pm
Avenida 4a Sur/Nicanor de Obarrio, also known as Calle 50, near Calle 53 Este
☎223-3306 or 223-3316
Once located in Casco Viejo, the Restaurante Caseo Viejo now occupies a large villa with a garden patio. As far as the interior design is concerned, the dining room is tastefully decorated in classic French style, and the tables are set in the traditional French manner.

The main attraction here, however, is the excellent, innovative cuisine prepared by the friendly chef, Pascal Finet. His Breton origins should already give you an idea of the quality of the food. The menu includes smoked duck salad, tomato tartare on a bed of spinach, crayfish on a bed of leeks and *corvina* with crayfish mousse and champagne. Talk about a treat! To perfectly accompany your meal, you can choose a bottle of Chilean wine from the restaurant's excellent and affordable selection. The Sauvignon blanc is particularly good. Finally, top off your meal—undoubtedly the best you will have in Panamá—with a *marquise de chocolat* with strawberry coulis. There is only one little snag: although the trilingual menu lists a wide choice of dishes, few of these actually seem to be available. Good value.

Rincón Suizo y Restaurante 1985
$$$$$
Mon-Fri 11am to 3pm and 6pm to 10pm, Sat and Sun 11am to 3pm and 5:30pm to 11pm
Avenida 2a Norte/Calle Eusebio A. Morales
☎263-8541 or 263-8310
Rincón Suizo y Restaurante 1985 is actually two very good restaurants in one. The first offers French cuisine in luxurious surroundings and has an elaborate menu; expect to pay B/.15 to B/.30 per dish. The second restaurant is simpler in design and is reminiscent of a Swiss chalet. The menu is equally imaginative, with cucumber salad, *quenelle* of *corvina* mousse with basil sauce, and for dessert, the famous *sachertorte* (chocolate cake flavoured with passion fruit) and chocolate crêpes. By choosing carefully, you can eat for B/.25 per person. There is a good selection of wines; the service is impeccable and the decor attractive.

Ángel
$$$$$
noon to 11 pm
68 Vía Argentina facing Parque Andres Bello
☎263-6411
☎263-6868
For a quiet evening or business dinner in a comfortable, refined setting, head to Ángel, where you will be served delicious Spanish cuisine and seafood specialties by a courteous staff. The high-ceilinged dining room is exceptionally elegant. The ambiance calls for formal dress.

El Cangrejo

Mr. Pan
$
Mon-Sat 7am to 8pm
Vía Argentina, near Vía España, on the right-hand side when heading toward the university
The little Mr. Pan bakery is just the place for early risers who like simple breakfasts. Brioches and coffee can be enjoyed at one of the few tables here, as can various very affordable sandwiches and ice creams at lunch time.

Manolo
$
Calle 49B Oeste-Veneto and Ave. 1a A Norte or Calle D
Those who like lively places should have breakfast at Manolo. From the street-corner patio, patrons where they can take in the endless comings and goings of passers-by in this bustling neighbourhood. Be sure to try the excellent fruit plate along with an egg dish. Breakfast is a good deal here as the generous portions are easily enough for two! You can also enjoy typical Panamanian fare, or the pizza for B/.5 or some tasty spaghetti for as little as B/.4.50. The coffee, moreover, is excellent, and both espresso and cappuccino are available. The only weak point is the slow service.

Manolo
$
Vía Argentina and Ave. 2a B Norte
Not to be confused with the restaurant of the same name above, this Manolo is also a pleasant and reasonably place for breakfast. Also situated on a street corner, its patio is smaller but just as pleasant, particularly since Vía Argentina is greener and quieter. Typical Panamanian food, pizzas, pastas and many other dishes are offered.

Caffe Pomodoro
$$
noon to 11pm
Calle 49B Oeste or Veneto, near Ave. 2A Norte or Eusebio A. Morales, next to Aparthotel Las Vegas
☎269-5936
Despite its somewhat kitschy exterior, Caffe Pomodoro is a delightful place. In a small room decorated by a few frescos and plants, patrons can sample good and very affordable Italian cuisine. The extensive menu features a wide selection of pasta *(spaghetti dishes from B/.5.95)*, fish (*corvina* or salmon) and meat dishes. For more intimate dining away from the noise of the street, sit out back on the patio surrounded by greenery.

El Trapiche
$$
7am to 10:30pm
10 Vía Argentina, corner of Avenida 2a B Norte
☎269-4353
This restaurant is notable mainly for its charming patio, which is covered with a tile roof and adorned with rustic wooden furniture. You can enjoy a variety of typical Panamanian dishes here, such as the *guacho de mariscos* (seafood platter). This is also a pleasant spot to have a drink and nibble on some yucca chips, *patacones* or an appetizer

of *surtido de Picadas* (assorted finger-foods) for only B/.1.50. Very popular with Panamanians.

Parrillada Martin Fierro
$$
Avenida 2a Norte/Calle Eusebio A. Morales
☎264-1927
This is an Argentinean restaurant in a Spanish-style house. It specializes not only in grilled meats, but also in seafood and fish. Most meat dishes come with the salad bar. The decor is simple, service friendly and the food reasonably priced.

Bon Profit
$$
Tue-Sat noon to 3pm and 6pm to 11pm
5 Vía Argentina, just before Avenida 1a B Norte
☎263-9667
For classic Spanish cuisine, Bon Profit is a pleasant place with an elegant little dining room. It's a little somber but you can admire the old photographs of the city adorning the walls. Their tiny patio (two tables) allows you to watch the bustle of the city while enjoying a cold drink. Make sure to take advantage of the lunch special (*Mon - Fri 11am to 3pm*), which includes the dish of the day and dessert for only B/.6.50—a bargain!

La Casa de las Costillitas
$$$
Tue-Thu 4:30pm to 11pm, Fri and Sat 3pm to 11:30pm, Sun 1pm to 10pm
Vía Argentina, just before Avenida 1a B Norte
☎269-6670
On the other side of Bon Profit is La Casa de las Costillitas, a branch of the

1. Cayenne Pepper
2. *Mirasol colorado*
3. Small Cayenne Pepper
4. Dwarf Cayenne Pepper
5. *Pequin*
6. *Hontaka*
7. *Ancho*
8. *Güero*
9. *Mulato*

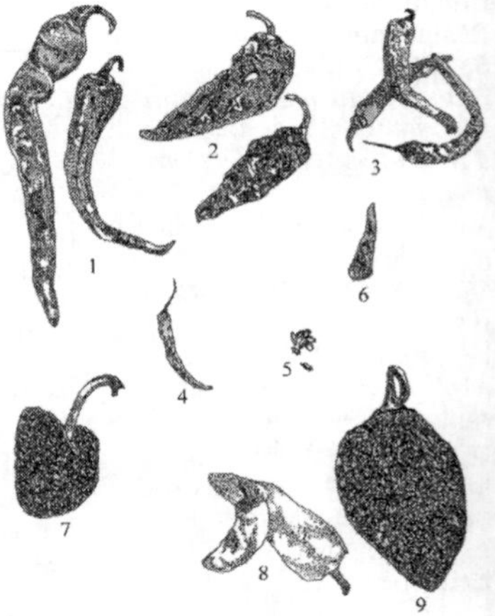

restaurant La Cascada (see p 101) with a similar menu based on a large selection of grilled meat dishes. Fish and seafood are also served. Although the decor is just as "colourful" as that of the main restaurant, La Casa de las Costillitas is located in more attractive surroundings on verdant Vía Argentina, in a pleasant part of town.

Matsuei
$$$
Mon-Sat noon to 11:30pm, Sun 6pm to 11:30pm
12-A Avenida 2a Norte/Eusebio A. Morales, opposite the Riande Granada hotel
☎264-9562
This Japanese restaurant serves the famous *Bento* boxes, as well as a few other typical dishes. Besides the *Obento Matsuei*, essentially a mixture of raw fish and seafood, the *Obento Sushi* is worth trying for the chicken sushi with nuts. The food is excellent and served in generous portions; one Bento box is easily enough for two people. Though the decor may be less sophisticated than Ginza's (in El Cangrejo), the room at the back is nonetheless decorated in typical Japanese fashion. Although the quality and freshness of the fish are exemplary, it is generally better to avoid raw fish in the tropics.

Restaurante Ginza Teppanyaki
$$$
noon to 3pm and 6pm to 10pm
corner of Avenida 1a A Norte/Calle D and Avenida 2A Norte/Eusebio A. Morales
☎269-1389
Restaurante Ginza Teppanyaki is an authentic Japanese restaurant complete with *teppanyaki* tables. The decor is elegant, but a bit austere. Excellent vegetarian dishes starting at B/.12 are also available. Proper dress required.

El Cortijo
$$$$
Mon - Sat noon to 3pm and 6:30pm to 11pm
Avenida la B Norte, near Calle 53 Oeste/Alberto Navarro
☎269-6386
If you appreciate a sophisticated decor, make sure to try El Cortijo, where you can savour classic international cuisine in the most elegant of settings. A pleasant surprise and ideal for a business lunch. Proper dress required.

Portobelo
$$$$
Vía España and Calle 49b Oeste
☎269-5000
Situated inside the El Panamá hotel, Portobelo serves French and Panamanian cuisine, including excellent *langostinos bahia piñas*, in a somewhat flashy setting. There is a seafood buffet on Fridays and Monday to Friday afternoons you can listen to some light piano music while enjoying a coffee. The prices are a bit high, but impeccable service is guaranteed. Proper dress required.

Marbella

La Mexicanita
$
11am to 11pm
Ave. 4a Sur or Nicanor de Obarrio, between Calles Uruguay and Aquilino de la Guardia
☎213-8952
La Mexicanita serves tacos, enchiladas and quesadillas at unbeatable prices. The decor, however, is simple to a fault and without any real charm.

Originl Rock Burgers
$
every day 11am to 11:30pm
Calle 53 Este and Avenida José de la Cruz Herrera
Craving an old-fashioned hamburger? Head to super-trendy Original Rock Burgers, where you can grab a tasty snack.

Pizzeria Romanaccio
$$
every day noon to 3pm and 5pm to 11pm
Calle 50c Este
☎264-9482
Pizzeria Romanaccio serves huge pizza and pasta dishes. If you have room for dessert, try the tiramisu. The portions are gigantic! The decor is attractive but a bit cold. Distinguished clientele. The lovely covered terrasse allows you to enjoy the beautiful weather out of the sun's reach.

Crepes & Waffles
$$
noon to 11pm
22 Ave. 5a B Sur or Calle 47, between Calles Uruguay and 49 Este or Aquilino de la Guardia
☎269-1574
Crepes & Waffles, needless to say, serves a variety of crepes and waffles. Worth mentioning, however, is that both are tasty and inexpensive. Surprisingly, this is not your standard Belgian-Breton concept, but a Colombian chain already well established in its mother country.

The setting is impressive. Upon entering the futuristic-looking building, a streamlined room with a harmonious blend of stainless steel, brick and glass meets the eye. Daylight streams in through large French windows graced with large lateral wooden slats to subdue the bright rays of sunshine. Elegant wooden furnishings as well as a few giant posters reminiscent of the works of Botero round out the very successful interior decor. Those who prefer to eat outdoors can sit on the pleasant patio in comfortable rattan chairs sheltered from the sun beneath large parasols. The restaurant is mainly frequented by families on the weekend. A not-to-be missed restaurant, even if only to admire its decor.

Restaurante Bahia Balboa
$$$
Mon-Fri 11:30am to 10pm, Sat 5pm to 11pm, Sun 11:30am to 10pm
Avenida Balboa, between Calle 48 Este/Uruguay and Calle 49 Este/Aquilino de la Guardia
☎223-7751
Seafood and meat dishes in a sophisticated but slightly kitschy setting.

La Toja
$$$
Mon-Sat noon to 11pm
at Calle Uruguay or 48 Este and Ave. 4a A Sur
☎269-3004
The Galician owner of La Toja offers patrons excellent cuisine proudly featuring the bounties of the sea. Indeed, fish lovers should not miss out on the absolutely delicious *mero alla salsa de pimienta verde*. For those who prefer meat and poultry, the *mignon de pollo con hongos* will please the most discriminating of palates. Dishes are lavish and, for the most part, served with a refreshing

little salad. The excellent flan is a wonderful way to round off a meal. In addition to the refined furnishings and tables set in the greatest culinary tradition, the decor includes many paintings celebrating the beauty of Galicia. Flawless service. Good value.

Il Rigoletto
$$$
Calle 48 Este or Uruguay, between Ave. 5a A Sur and Ave. 5a B Sur
☎214-9632
Housed within a large villa, Il Rigoletto offers patrons an Italian menu on which pastas have pride of place. Spaghetti *carbonara*, *fettucine Alfredo, tutti quanti* and much more await. The decor is modern, even a little cool, but the Italian-style welcome soon warms things up. Unfortunately, as is too often the case in the restaurants in the *Ciudad*, it is excessively air conditioned. A patio would also be welcome.

Café Dalí
$$$
Ave. 5a B Sur or Calle 47, between Calles Uruguay and 49 Este or Aquilino de la Guardia
☎265-0182 or 214-7139
Across from Crepes & Waffles, Café Dalí bar-restaurant features a colourful, heterogeneous and fittingly Dali-esque decor of painted columns and metal sculptures with wrought-iron tables and chairs. Conversely, the menu, composed of Tex-Mex—style dishes and a few Italian offerings, is rather humdrum. Gilded youth as well as young executives congregate here. Just the place for those who wish to see and be seen.

Restaurante Yesterday
$$$
Ave. 5a B Sur or Calle 47, between Calles Uruguay and 49 Este or Aquilino de la Guardia
☎269-0994
Restaurante Yesterday features an American-influenced English-pub-style decor. In a large dining room where woodwork is omnipresent and numerous Tiffany-style lamps provide subdued lighting, diners can choose from salads, burgers, Tex-Mex dishes or pastas. To avoid the noisy televisions on the ground floor, sit upstairs on the verdant patio, attractively laid out with parasols.

El Epoca
$$$$
Mon-Sat noon to 3pm and 6pm to 10pm
Calle 53 Este, at Ave. 5a B Sur
☎265-3636
In the heart of the stylish Marbella district, next to the World Trade Centre, the Radisson Royal Panamá Hotel is, at first sight, somewhat unattractive. Once inside, however, visitors will be pleasantly surprised by the elegant El Epoca restaurant, which offers moderately priced international-style cuisine in an exquisite setting.

Madame Chang
$$$$
noon to 11pm
Ave. 5a A Sur or Calle 48, between Calles Uruguay and 49 Este or Aquilino de la Guardia
☎269-1313
☎269-9654
Although Chinese cuisine is renowned for its diversity, the same can seldom be said for the design of its restaurants, which often tend towards kitsch. Madame Chang proves that there are exceptions to the rule. The dining room boasts a modern decor accentuated by elegant columns and archways and embellished by various original Asian curios for a final touch of refinement. In this delightful setting, diners can enjoy the Chinese vegetable salad, delicious tofu with eggplant, or crispy Peking duck, while seated at a table with subdued lighting. To accompany this feast, the reasonably priced Chilean Cabernet Sauvignon is a good choice.

Finally, another pleasant surprise seldom to be found in Chinese restaurants is the good selection of desserts with which to top off an excellent meal. Try the creamy cheesecake, the enormous *cassata* or the rich chocolate *cesibón*. Of course, tea and espresso are also available. Friendly and efficient service. A fine evening to look forward to!

Gaucho's
$$$$
noon to 3pm and 6pm to 10:30pm
Ave. 5a A Sur or Calle 48, at Calle Uruguay
☎263-4469
Grilled meats, steaks, cutlets, brochettes and many other meat selections are served here in a pleasant and modern, if somewhat lukewarm Argentinian decor.

Bennigan's Grill
$$$$
Ave. Balboa, just before Punta Paitilla
☎214-7022
On the fourth floor of the new Extreme Planet building, Bennigan's Grill is an Irish-American-style pub where burgers are meant to be devoured alongside, a good helping of fries and a pint of beer. Tiffany-style lamps, opulent chairs and an overwhelmingly flowered wall-to-wall carpet make up most of the decor, not to mention televisions all over the place airing the major American channels. In short, it's the next "best" thing to being in the Unites States. There is even a large parking lot outside. When entering the building, look out for the constant stream of (big) cars!

La Cocotte
$$$$$
Mon-Sat noon to 3pm and 7pm to 10:30pm
Calle Uruguay, between Ave. Balboa and Ave. 5a B Sur
☎213-8250
For French cuisine, head to La Cocotte, where the great classics are served in a very conventional setting. Unfortunately, sampling its most noble offerings necessitates loosening one's purse strings, as the prices are sky high. To circumvent this difficulty, come by for lunch, when a full meal can be had for B/.18. Practically a bargain!

Amador

Isla Naos

La Playita
$$
Mon-Thu and Sun 9:30am to 6pm, Fri and Sat 9:30am to 10pm
Calzada Amador
☎228-0540
The modest La Playita restaurant serves regular Panamanian fare (chicken, *patacones*, *ceviche*, etc.), yet it is a rather pleasant place in which to have a refreshing drink while watching Panamanian families enjoying a day at the beach. *Horas Feliz* (happy hour) every Friday.

Isla Perico

Mi Ranchito
$$
Mon-Fri 10am to 9pm
Calzada Amador
on the Isla Flamenco-bound road
☎228-4909
Though right on the roadside and a little set back from the beach, Restaurante Mi Ranchito offers a truly pleasant setting. Whether beneath its large straw roof or one of its charming *palapas*, savour a refreshing *ceviche de corvina* as a starter, followed by an excellent dish of *gambas* or meat while seated at one of the lovely little tables, with a little Panamanian music thrown in!

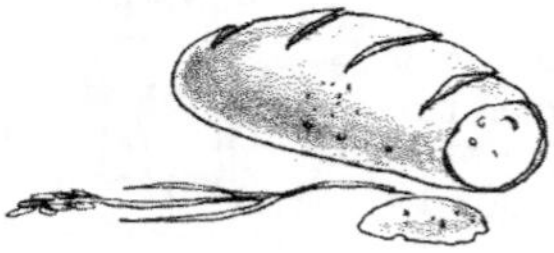

Ancón

Mi Pueblito
$$$
Tue-Sun 10am to 10pm
El Pueblito (see p84)
☎228-7714 or 228-2124
While visiting Cerro Ancón, make sure to go to Mi Pueblito, in the small, reconstructed rural village of the same name. Here, many different Panamanian specialities can be sampled, including *lombo machado* (ground beef) and excellent *pargo* fish. Makes for a pleasant break from sightseeing.

Panamá Viejo

El Trapiche
$$$
Tue-Fri 11:30am to 11pm, Sat and Sun 8:30am to 11pm
in the Merdado Artesanal, near the ruins of the cathedral of Panamá Viejo, Vía Cincuentenario
☎221-5241
Right next to the Puerto Viejo Museum, El Trapiche offers typical Panamanian and international cuisine as well as seafood at reasonable prices. This is also a good place for some refreshment after touring the nearby ruins and to enjoy the patio on the bay. Very popular with Panamanians.

Fonda Antioqueña
$$$
Vía Cincuentenario, on the left, shortly after the ruins of Panamá Viejo
☎271-0534 or 271-0519
This authentic Colombian restaurant serves specialties like *chorizos Antioqueños con arepa de*

maiz blanco (wild pig with white corn) or *lechon asado al carbon con yuca jancocada* (char-broiled pork served with yucca). The daily *ejecutivo* menu, available from 11am to 3:30pm, is a real bargain for as little as B/.5. Besides a giant television showing Colombian programs, you will find a warm, colourful decor. The place also has a nightclub, which makes for a lively atmosphere on weekends (see p 113). Since the Fonda Antioqueña is located outside the city in an area that is not very safe at night, it is best to get here by taxi *(B/.3.5)*.

Cerro Azul

La Posada de Ferhisse
$$
9am to 10pm
Calle Principal Domingo Diaz
☎***297-0197***
Located on a hill, La Posada de Ferhisse is a wonderful place to eat surrounded by exotic countryside and a beautiful panorama. The very charming owner, Mr. Ferhisse Jabbour, has family in many countries and enjoys chatting with interested patrons at their table. He is well acquainted with the region and can provide information about the richness of the surrounding flora and fauna. The menu itself features a variety of dishes, including wonderful little stuffed crabs, curry chicken, *brandade* (a purée of salt cod, garlic, oil and cream), and a dish of combined rice prepared as it is in Cuba, Mrs Jabbour's native land. What's more, there is a lovely swimming pool *(B/.2)* below the patio for those who wish to take a refreshing dip.

Entertainment

Panamá has an active nightlife; many areas have a good selection of bars and nightclubs. In general, large hotels have their own clubs (busiest nights are Wednesday to Saturday—traditionally, Sundays are for family visits and resting). Some of the more expensive hotels even have a casino.

Nightclubs in Panamá occasionally charge a cover and may refuse people wearing jeans. In Panamá City, certain restaurants double as bars or clubs. In some, shows are presented. The following are a few good places to end the day.

Casco Viejo

Café Asis
at Calle 3a Este
In the very heart of Casco Viejo, facing delightful Parque Bolívar, Café Asis is a successful initiative in the revitalization of the capital's historic district. In a small space decorated with contrasting colours, patrons can sip one of the many drinks available while seated at a candlelit table. In the evening, several tables are set out by the adjacent square, offering patrons a theatre-like setting.

The beautiful facade of the Instituto Simón Bolívar, on one side, and the square planted with trees and surrounded by a few grand houses on the other, offer a romantic atmosphere. Although the neighbouring streets are rather unsafe at night (getting around by taxi is a wise idea), this magnificent café is perfectly safe. In fact, it would be a real shame to miss out on such an opportunity. Very busy on the weekend. An absolute must!

El Cangrejo

Aleph Café
Vía Argentina, on the left-hand side when heading toward Ave. España, a little before said avenue
With its original little candlesticks on the tables, colourful decorative hammocks suspended from the ceiling, metal sculptures and scores of paintings, the Aleph Café is worth a visit for its imaginative and tasteful decor alone. Moreover, several musicians perform here on a regular basis, offering music for all tastes. For those feeling a little peckish, a good choice of both savoury and sweet crepes is offered on the menu. Young, hip clientele.

Hotel El Panamá
Vía España and Calle 49B Oeste
☎***269-5000 or 269-5421***
The Hotel El Panamá has a casino, a bar (the **Coco Club**, *happy hour 4pm to 6pm*) and a rooftop club with a view of the city.

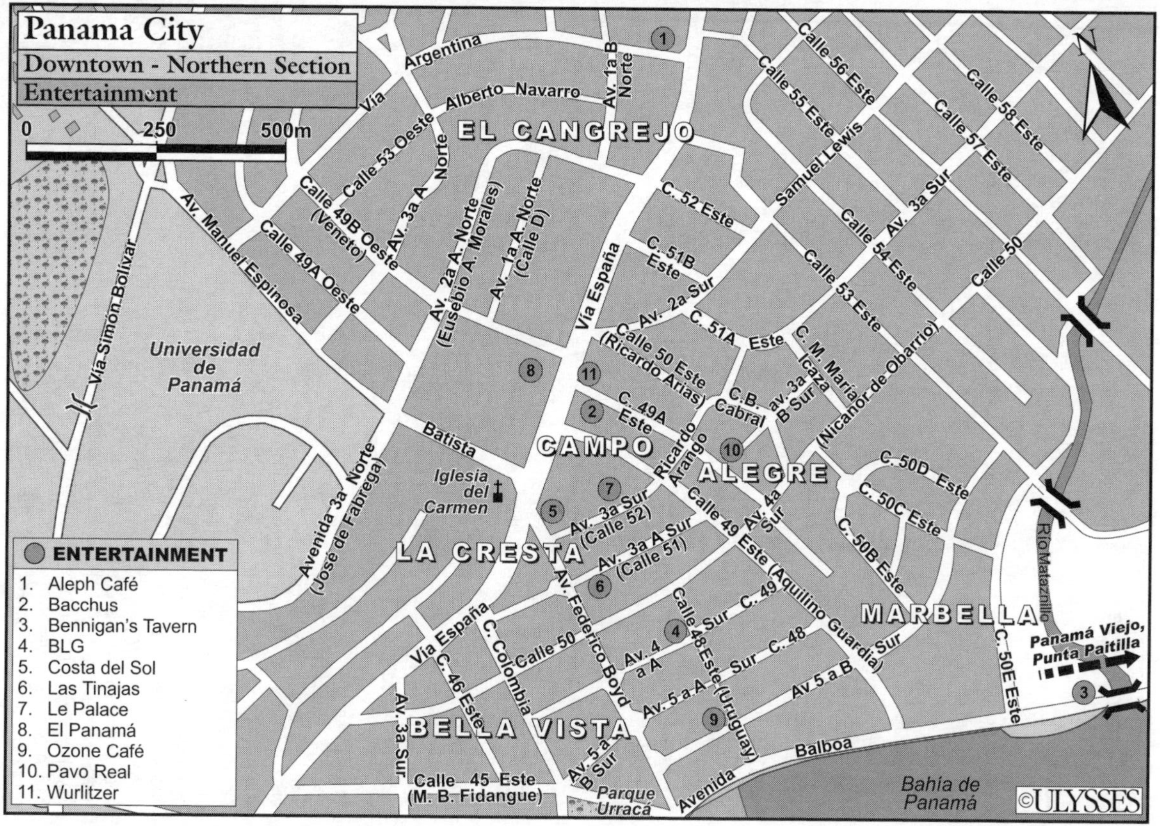
Panama City
Downtown - Northern Section
Entertainment
0
250
500m
N
EL CANGREJO
CAMPO ALEGRE
LA CRESTA
MARBELLA
BELLA VISTA
Universidad de Panamá
Iglesia del Carmen
Bahía de Panamá
Parque Urracá
Río Mataznillo
Panamá Viejo, Punta Paitilla
Argentina
Vía Argentina
Alberto Navarro
Av. 1a B Norte
Calle 53 Oeste
Av. 3a A Norte
Calle 49B Oeste (Veneto)
Calle 49A Oeste
Av. Manuel Espinosa
Vía Simón Bolívar
Av. 2a A. Norte (Eusebio A. Morales)
Av. 1a A. Norte (Calle D)
Vía España
Batista
Avenida 3a Norte (José de Fabrega)
C. 52 Este
C. 51B Este
Av. 2a Sur
C. 51A Este
Calle 50 Este (Ricardo Arias)
C. 49A Este
C. M. María Icaza
C.B. Cabral
av. 3a B Sur
Ricardo Arango
(Nicanor de Obarrio)
Calle 56 Este
Calle 55 Este
Samuel Lewis
Calle 58 Este
Calle 57 Este
Av. 3a Sur
Calle 54 Este
Calle 53 Este
Calle 50
C. 50D Este
C. 50C Este
C. 50B Este
Av. 3a Sur (Calle 52)
Av. 3a A Sur (Calle 51)
Calle 49 Este (Aquilino Guardia)
Av. 4a Sur
Av. Federico Boyd
C. 49
Sur
Calle 48 Este (Uruguay)
C. 48
Av. 4 a A
Av. 5 a A
Av. 5 a B
Av. 5 a B Sur
C. 50E Este
Balboa
Avenida Balboa
Vía España
C. Colombia
Calle 50
C. 46 Este
Av. 3a Sur
Calle 45 Este (M. B. Fidangue)
ENTERTAINMENT
1. Aleph Café
2. Bacchus
3. Bennigan's Tavern
4. BLG
5. Costa del Sol
6. Las Tinajas
7. Le Palace
8. El Panamá
9. Ozone Café
10. Pavo Real
11. Wurlitzer
©ULYSSES

There is also a café that is open 24 hours a day.

Campo Alegre

Bacchus
cover charge
Calle 49a Este, near Ave. 3a Sur or Ricardo Arango
Among the most popular nightclubs in town, Bacchus welcomes a youngish clientele (25 to 35 years old) to the varied sounds of salsa, merengue, rock, disco, etc. Wednesday is karaoke night.

Las Tinajas
22 Avenida 3a A Sur/Calle 51
☎263-7890 or 269-3840
This is a restaurant that has traditional Panamanian dancing several nights a week with beautiful Panamanian costumes, including the famous *pollera* (see box "*La Pollera,*" in The Central Provinces and the Azuero Peninsula). Shows are presented every Tuesday, Thursday, Friday and Saturday starting at 7pm. Reservations are strongly recommended.

Sunset Bar
corner of Avenida Frederico Boyd and Avenida 3a A Sur Calle 52
☎206-3333
To enjoy a lovely panoramic view of the capital by night while sipping an excellent, reasonably priced cocktail (*happy hour 6pm to 8pm*), head to the Sunset Bar at the Apart-Hotel Costa del Sol, which has an elegant rooftop bar with a patio. People also come here to dance on Friday nights.

Pavo Real
B/.3
Mon-Sat
Avenida 3a B Sur, left on Calle 51 A Este, after Ave. Nicanor de Obarrio
This small, British-style pub is frequented mainly by English-speakers between the ages of 25 and 45, along with a few Panamanians, including the capital's gilded youth. The place serves British beer, as well as meals for about B/.20. The atmosphere is relaxed, and live music is presented every Wednesday evening and occasionally on weekends, too. Happy hour from 3pm to 7pm.

Wurlitzer Bar
Calle 50 Este/Ricardo Arias, near Vía España
Whether it be for drinks or to listen to the rare Wurlitzer organ (a pipe organ designed specifically for theatres), the Wurlitzer Bar in the Riande Continental hotel is quite a pleasant spot. Happy hour from 6pm to 8pm. The clientele consists mainly of business people.

Le Palace
corner of Avenida 3a Sur/Ricardo Arango and Calle 49 Este/Aquilino de la Guardia
☎269-1844
Le Palace is a bar popular for its dance shows where the dancers' costumes range from simple to sophisticated. Parisian strip tease performed at 10:30pm every Wednesday and Saturday. Minimum purchase required.

Marbella

Ozone Café
Calle Uruguay or 48 Este, between Ave. 5a A Sur and Ave. 5a B Sur, on the right-hand side of the street when heading toward Avenida Balboa
☎214-9616
Located behind a home-decor and antique shop, the Ozone Café serves excellent fresh-ground coffee, cocktails and various little nibbles. The decor is worth a visit in itself as, oddly enough, you can see right into the shop through its back windows. Assorted antiques thus seem to be part of the setting, treating patrons to an amusing and somewhat bizarre view. Unfortunately, as is too often the case, a television set tends to spoil the muted ambiance. Hip crowd of night owls.

Bennigan's Tavern
Ave. Balboa, just before Punta Paitilla
Those in search of an establishment with an "Irish-American pub" ambiance need look no further than Bennigan's Tavern and Bennigan's Grill (see p 109), located on the fourth floor of the Extreme Planet building. You can knock back several pints of blond or amber beer while enjoying a game of pool. The music is distinctly non-local— in fact Panamá feels like a distant memory here! Watch out for the endless stream of (big) cars on their way to the parking lot near the entrance.

In Panamá, some buses are works of art on wheels!
– *courtesy of IPAT*

The ruins of Panamá Viejo testify to well-preserved history.
– *courtesy of IPAT*

In Kuna Yala (land of the Kunas), smiles and exotic scenery await you.
– *courtesy of IPAT*

The only way to explore the islands of the Comarca de San Blas accompanied by Kunas is by boat.
– *courtesy of IPAT*

Amador

Balboa Yacht Club
at the entrance to the Calzada Amador, also known simply as "The Causeway"
☎*228-5794*
Although the Balboa Yacht Club is both a restaurant and a nightclub, the patio beside the bar is the main attraction—patrons can enjoy a beautiful view of the canal and the Puente de Las Américas while sipping drinks. This is the place to watch sailors waiting to cross the canal or to find a job as a crew member aboard a ship.

Panamá Viejo

Fonda Antioqueña
Fri and Sat
Vía Cincuentenario, on the left, shortly after the ruins of Panamá Viejo
☎*271-0534*
This authentic Colombian bar/restaurant has a large nightclub, where you can kick up your heels to Latin American tunes every weekend until 6am. Guaranteed ambiance. Because this place is located outside of the city in a neighbourhood that is not very safe at night, we recommend taking a cab here (*B/.2*).

Gay Bars and Nightclubs

BOX
Avenida Ricardo J. Alfaro, aka Túmba Muerto
This new dance club, run by the owner of the former Boys Bar, welcomes a good crowd of all ages. English-language music is played. Given that the club is located outside the city centre and is reached via badly lit streets, it is safest by far to get here by taxi (at a cost of about B/.4).

Belonging to the same owner as the BOX dance club, the bars known as **Space** *(Calle 70, across from the Baron's shop, in the Obarrio area)* and **Gil's** *(Calle 51, Suite 33, across from Las Tinjas)* are also patronized by the capital's gay community.

Club BLG
cover charge with open bar
at Calles Uruguay and 4a A Sur
The latest trendy gay bar/nightclub is none other than Club BLG. While a hip mixed crowd clusters around the oversized central bar to order drinks, dance-floor divas gather on one of two dance floors (one on the mezzanine and the other in the basement). Guaranteed ambiance from 1am o'clock on.

Shopping

Casco Viejo

Second-hand Goods

Festival de Antiguedades
Sat and Sun 10am to 5pm
Parque Simón Bolívar
Right next to the Café Asis, the somewhat pompously named Festival de Antiquedades (Festival of Antiques) has a few second-hand goods of no great value on display in a modest space. The place is nevertheless fun to visit and with a little digging, you may yet find a little gem. Good luck!

Santa Ana

Food

Mercado de Mariscos
Avenida Balboa, before Ave Eloy Alfaro
If you are staying in the capital for a while and have access to a kitchen, you can go to the Mercado de Mariscos, a brand new fish market inside a modern building run by the City of Panamá. Open to the general public, it offers a wide selection of fish at reasonable prices.

Handicrafts

Mercado de Buhonería y Artesanía
every day 7am to 7pm
Plaza 5 de Mayo
The Mercado de Buhonería y Artesanía, located behind the Reina Torres de Araúz archeological museum, has a number of little stalls containing a variety of crafts from all over the country (*molas*, pottery, wooden sculptures, the famous Panamá hats, etc.), as well as all sorts of junk ranging from lighters and pens to watches, all at very attractive prices. Bargaining is standard here. Of course, in a crowded place such as this, you should be very wary of thieves.

Miscellaneous

Avenida Central
between Plaza 5 de Mayo and Parque de Santa Ana
Avenida Central is the main shopping street in

Casco Viejo, with stores for just about anything (clothes, shoes, jewellery, electronic equipment...). Prices are negotiable. Pay at least 20% to 30% less than what is asked for.

Bella Vista

Food

Supermercado Rey
open 24 hours a day
Vía España, on the right side as you head north, near the footbridge overhanging the street
Visitors who want to do their own cooking can shop at the Supermercado Rey, where they'll find everything they need at inexpensive prices. This place is like any other big North American supermarket.

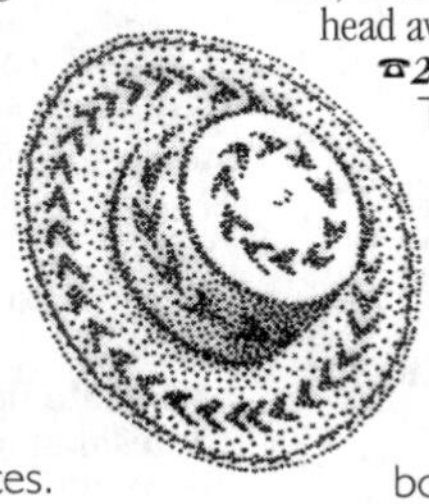

Campo Alegre

Jewellery

Reprosa
at the corner of Avenida 2a Sur/Samuel Lewis and Calle 54
☎**269-0457**
Reprosa is a store specializing in reproductions of antique (pre-Columbian) jewellery.

Souvenirs

Gran Morrison
Vía España, near Calle 50 Este, across from the Banco Nacional
☎**269-2211**
Gran Morrison is a large store with a good choice of Panamanian arts and crafts and souvenirs of every kind. They also sell records, books and clothing. The traditional crafts sold here are more expensive than outside the city, but here you can find everything under one roof.

El Cangrejo

Bookstore

Librería Argosy
at the beginning of Vía Argentina, on the right side as you head away from Vía España
☎**223-5344**
This general bookstore, run by a friendly woman named Luz Maria, sells a good choice of Spanish- and English-language books, as well as a few books in French. A very pleasant place to pore over books at your leisure.

Exedra Books
Mon-Fri 11:30am to 9pm
Sat 10:30am to 8pm
Sun noon to 7pm
corner of Vía España and Vía Brasil
☎**264-4252**
This large, modern bookshop offers a plethora of books in both Spanish and English, and boasts a cyber café as well as a children's playroom. Temporary exhibitions are also featured here.

El Hombre de la Mancha
Mon-Thu 10am to 7pm
Fri-Sat 10am to 9pm
corner of Calle 52 Oeste and Avenida Frederico Boyd
Edificio Bolívar
☎**263-6218**

Ancón

Handicrafts

In the heart of the little village of **Mi Pueblito Cerro Ancón** (see p 84) you will find a number of craft shops with products mainly from the central provinces and the Azuero peninsula. The setting is extraordinary and the selection, vast; however, the prices are considerably higher here than elsewhere.

Panamá Viejo

Handicrafts

Mercado Nacional de Artesanias
every day 9am to 6pm
near the ruins of the cathedral bell tower, beside the Museo Panamá La Viejo
Located right beside the ruins of the former capital, the Mercado National de Artesanias has two floors of handcrafted objects, including pottery, carved wood and a number of articles (*chaquiras* necklaces worn by Guaymies, Kuna *molas*) reflecting the richness of Panamanian culture.

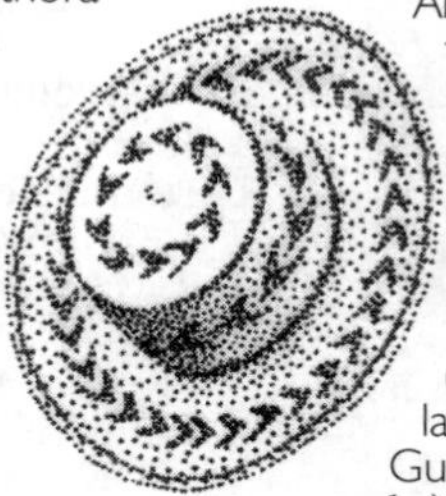

The Panama Canal

The story of the canal zone is directly linked to the creation and development of the Republic of Panamá.

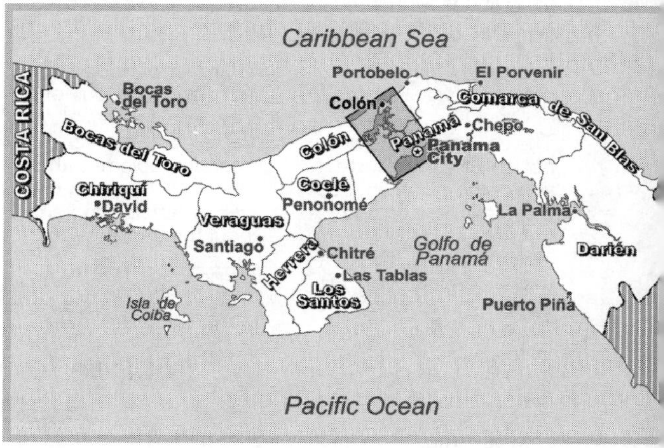

The idea of finding a passage across the isthmus from one ocean to the other is ancient. In 1534, Emperor Charles V asked his scientists to devise a trans-isthmus seaway, but plans never progressed beyond the stage of a few sketches. Much later, during the second half of the 19th century, it was the Americans who began toying with the idea of a direct passage between the two oceans. This was of particular to interest to them as a means of reaching the west since there were no road or rail links at the time. In the 1870s the U.S. Navy mounted an expedition across the isthmus in order to evaluate the possibilities of dredging a canal through Darién. Of the 27 men who took part in this expedition, only a few survived the rigours of the jungle.

It is clear that this territory had long been pegged as the site of one of the largest-ever human undertakings. Though it is understandable that some Panamanians might be tired of hearing about the canal (after all, Panamá is much more than a canal!), travellers making their way through the country should not miss an opportunity to marvel at this feat of technology. In fact, the canal zone merits a visit in its own right, as it is full of interesting sights.

A Brief History of the Panama Canal

The Panama Canal adventure began with the construction of a railroad (see box "The Panama Railroad Company," in Province of Colón) between Colón, on the Caribbean Coast, and Panama City, on the Pacific Coast. Originally intended to allow the rapid transport of goods between the two oceans, the line was destined to carry a great many adventurers heading off to settle in the American West.

Soon there was such a flood of people going west

that the United States government began to consider once again the creation of a seaway. The location was still undetermined; Nicaragua was being considered as well as the isthmus. Meanwhile, heady from the success of the Suez Canal, the French took advantage of the delay and procured the approval of the Colombian government for the construction of a maritime passageway.

The concession allowed not only for the construction of the canal, but also the administration and transfer of 5km of land on either side of it. The contract extended over 100 years. In 1875, the Société Civile du Canal Interocéanique du Darién was established in Paris. Its principal mandate was to collect funds in order to complete the construction of the canal.

The president of this company was Viscount **Ferdinand de Lesseps**, already well known as the author of the Suez Canal. In 1879, he had the final plans for the Panamá project approved. The canal would follow the course of the Río Grande and the Río Chagres, running from the Bahía de Limón to the Bahía de Panamá, thus linking Colón and Balboa. The work, which would take an estimated eight years to complete, would begin in 1880, supervised by the Compagnie Universelle du Canal Interocéanique (which had bought the Société Civile).

Nine years after work began, disaster struck. The partnership was in financial difficulties and declared bankrupt by the French government. Following this failure, the press attacked the founders of the project; several of the company's directors, along with some politicians, were called before the French courts.

A number of reasons for the failure were put forth: unexpected technical difficulties, corruption, financial problems—the list went on. One thing, however, is certain: ignorance about the transmission of malaria led to a veritable plague breaking out among workers. The legs of hospital beds were placed in containers of water to keep crawling insects away. Unfortunately, the doctors and nurses did not realize that the mosquitoes that carried the disease were breeding in these very pots. In 1885, conditions were so bad in Colón that over 5,000 people died of yellow fever and malaria.

Looking back at the limited technical means of the time, we cannot help but feel great respect for the many workers who died

Philippe Jean Bunau-Varilla (1859-1940)

This Parisian engineer worked on the canal until 1888, when the project was finally abandoned by the French. Bunau-Varilla, unable to accept defeat, tried to strike up a partnership with the Russians. The project was finally picked up by the Americans, who entrusted him to reach an agreement with Colombia on their behalf, so that they would be granted the concession. While Bunau-Varilla was a skilled negotiator, his project did not meet with success. Determined not to give up, he sought help by stirring things up among Panamá's merchant class, a revolt that ultimately lead to the country's independence. Later, as Panamá's first ambassador to the United States, he led the negotiations that would later result in the famous Hay-Bunau-Varilla Treaty. After the canal opened, he returned to France, where he took part in the First World War.

during the massive project. Consider what they were up against: moving some 259-million cubic metres of earth through hilly countryside blanketed by a dense, insect-ridden jungle, and all of this in humid tropical heat. In addition to the victims of illness, a number of workers died in landslides. As many as 22,000 in all are thought to have perished while the French were building the canal.

Meanwhile, in France, an attempt was made to revive the project with the creation of the Compagnie Nouvelle du Canal de Panamá. The people of France, however, had lost all confidence. There was insufficient interest in the canal, and the company had to abandon the project once and for all.

In the wake of the French failure, the Americans reappeared in the scene. The *Compagnie Nouvelle* offered to sell its concessions to the United States for $40 million. In the meantime, the Americans had concluded that Nicaragua was too risky a canal site because of earthquakes, so they bought the concession and signed an agreement with Colombia (at the time Gran Colombia) in 1903. That same year, however, Colombia did an about-face and criticized the treaty as being too favourable to the Americans. This marked a new turning-point in the history of the region. The Panamanian merchant class felt removed from power and wanted to see the region develop. They reacted by provoking a revolt against the central government, resulting in the proclamation of the Republic of Panamá on November 3, 1903.

The young republic, eager to maintain its newly acquired independence, quickly proposed new negotiations with the Americans, and the Hay-Bunau-Varilla treaty (named after the principal negotiators) was signed on November 18, 1903. The negotiations leading up to the signing of this treaty had been swift and, according to some, partisan: Panamá granted the Americans the right to build and administer the canal, as well as a zone stretching five miles (8km) on either side of it. These rights were granted in perpetuity! Furthermore, the United States would be able to act as owner of the land, thus opening the door to possible intervention in Panamá's internal affairs. In exchange, the Americans agreed to guarantee Panamá's independence from Colombia, which had plans to recover its former territory. The compensation package included a $10 million indemnity and an annuity of $250,000 to take effect 10 years after ratification of the treaty.

In 1904, work resumed under the leadership of Colonel George Washington Goethals, chief engineer. The project included the construction of three groups of locks and the creation of an artificial lake (Lago Gatún). The work was executed much more effectively than it had been under the French, largely because the means of transmission of yellow fever had been discovered (by Carlos Finley, a Cuban). The task of wiping out yellow fever and malaria from the region fell upon Colonel William C. Gorgas. With the help of local authorities and by spraying great quantities of chemicals all along the region of the future canal, Gorgas was able to complete the mission.

The railroad was another major reason for the success of the project. Huge "shovels" were ingeniously built and used to excavate tons of earth, which were deposited directly into gigantic hopper-cars. An incredible 259-million cubic metres of soil were displaced in this way, truly a tremendous feat!

Nevertheless, the success of the undertaking required the support of a large workforce. During the French phase of the canal many workers arrived from Barbados, as well as some from Trinidad and the French Antilles. Their European co-workers came mainly from France, Spain and Italy. As of 1906, there were 24,000 people (mostly men) involved in the construction of the canal.

When the American company bought out the French company's rights it inherited dilapidated workers' housing. For this reason, the immigration of families was discouraged at first and a call was sent out for Chinese labourers,

The Panamá Canal: A Few Facts

The canal is 80km long and has three series of locks: the Miraflores locks, the Pedro Miguel locks and the Gatún locks. The Miraflores locks are the highest because the tides are higher in the Pacific.

For 11 months out of the year, the water levels of the two oceans differ because of tides and climatic conditions; only in February are they about the same. While the Pacific tides are very high (up to 7m), those in the Atlantic are quite low.

Since the canal opened on August 15, 1914, over 725,000 ships have passed through it. Traffic is continuous, and since 1966, the canal has been lit up at night to ensure greater safety. Lago Gatún's surface area (425km^2) makes it the second-largest artificial lake in the world.

In the Gatún locks, ships are lifted 26.52m above sea level, and the lock doors weigh 750 tons.

In the Miraflores locks, a ship can be raised 9m in 15 minutes. Over 100,000 tons of fresh water from Lago Gatún are needed to fill the locks for this purpose. Thus, each time a boat passes, more than 100 million litres of fresh water spill into the ocean.

Small trains, or *mulas* (mules), as the Panamanians commonly call them, tow ships through the locks. They each weigh 47 tons and their function is to stabilize the ships on their way into the locks. On average, ships take 24 hours to pass through the canal. About half this time is spent waiting to enter the canal. The longest boat to go through the canal was the 299m *San Juan Prospector*.

The highest passage fee ever levied was $141,088, paid by the *Regal Princess* in October 1992. The lowest was paid by Richard Halliburton, who shelled out 36 cents to swim through the canal. The fees are determined according to the vessel's weight and size, and ships flying the Panamanian flag are charged a special rate.

hired only for the duration of the project. In fact the expense of the long trip made it almost impossible for labourers to send for their families. In response to protest movements mounted by the discontented workers, the company reversed its policy and authorised the installation of entire families. Consequently, many social and administrative services were put into place, creating a veritable microcosm of American society.

The work was terminated in 1914, and on August 15 of that year, the canal was inaugurated on the deck of the *Ancón* by the President of Panamá, Belisario Porras, and a contingent of American officials.

In February 1919, legislators from the Dakotas brought forth a congressional bill that would have renamed the canal after former President

Theodore Roosevelt. After several demonstrations in the isthmus and protest by the legislature of Panamá, the motion was rejected.

Oddly enough, it was not until 1931 that ferries linked the east and west sides of the artificially divided area. They could transport up to 30 cars at a time and made the crossing every half-hour at no charge. This service stayed in effect until 1942 when a rotating bridge was constructed over the Miraflores locks. On October 12, 1962 the impressive bridge Puente de las Américas was finally inaugurated, reestablishing a definitive link between the two parts of the isthmus.

As soon as the canal was opened, traffic began pouring into it, and the region started to thrive. The statutes governing the zone were later amended several times. The most important modification came with the Torrijos-Carter agreement, under which Panamanian sovereignty over the canal zone was re-established (see p 25).

The Canal Today

With the Torrijos-Carter agreement of 1977, the canal zone was abolished and its territory restored to Panamá. The new treaty also provided for joint Panamanian–U.S. administration of the various military zones along the canal. The land immediately beside the canal was administered by the Panama Canal Commission. This commission, whose mandate would run for 20 years, was made up of nine members, five American and four Panamanian. A president and a vice-president were also named, the two positions to alternate after 10 years.

Until December 31, 1989, the president was American and the vice-president Panamanian. Once the Commission's mandate expired—on December 31, 1999—administration of all canal installations was completely transferred to the republic of Panamá, which staged a public celebration that coincided with the dawn of the new millennium.

In accordance with agreements signed in 1979, the number of American employees of the Panama Canal Commission has declined steadily. By 1990, they numbered fewer than 900. Today, all of the jobs on the canal are reserved for Panamanian nationals.

As far as the American armed forces are concerned, they left the country by the same date, except for a few soldiers mandated to insure military co-operation between the two governments.

Revenue linked directly to the activity of the canal now represents 10% of Panamá's GNP.

Finding Your Way Around

By Car

There are two ways to get to the **Miraflores locks** from Panama City: the first is by Avenida Gaillard from the Calidonia sector, the second is by Calle Balboa, south of the Cerro Ancón (not to be confused with Avenida Balboa), which later becomes Calle Diablo and then joins Avenida Gaillard (also called Carretera Gaillard). In both cases, head north. The road to the locks lies to the left of the Carretera Gaillard. After passing a small bridge that crosses the Río Cárdenas, a small sign on the left side of the road, facing Fort Clayton, provides directions to the locks.

The **Pedro Miguel locks** are on the same road as the Miraflores, a little more to the north. On the way, a pleasant lookout on the left side of the road provides a view of ships coming out of the locks. A little farther north along the same main road, past the locks and on the left, is the modest **French cemetery**. Most of the men who died while working on the first phase of the canal's construction are buried here.

To get to the **Parque Nacional Soberanía** , follow the directions to the Miraflores and Pedro Miguel locks (see above)

Puente de Las Américas

and after passing them, continue on the main road. The entrance to the park is indicated on the left side of this road, and is at the first main intersection after the **French cemetery**. Drive 1.2km beyond the intersection to get to the entrance to the **Jardín Botanico summit** located on the right. If you keep going along this road you will arrive at **Gamboa**.

Back on the main road to Colón, 4.5km beyond the intersection leading to the gardens, there is a pleasant rest area with a picnic table and waterfall. The **Camino de Cruces** trail lies on the left side of the road, 1.4km farther on.

To get to **Canopy Tower**, take the same Gamboa-bound road leading to the Jardín Botanico summit and after passing it, take the second road on your right. Continue straight on along the main road, which climbs toward the old radar station.

To reach **Cerro Contratista Mirador** (Contractor's Hill) take the Puente de Las Américas. After the bridge turn right at the signs for Camp Cocolí and Rousseau, in the direction of Coco Solo village. There is a checkpoint 4km ahead. State your destination and you will be issued a visitor's permit which you will have to hand in when you leave. Keep going on the main road for 11.9km, then turn right. The Cerro Contratista Mirador (*daily 9-5*) is 0.5km farther on.

You can reach **Isla Barro Colorado** and the Smithsonian Scientific Institute from the harbour at the village of Gamboa. To visit the island, you need authorization from the Smithsonian (see p125), which must be requested in advance.

By Bus

To get to any point in the **canal zone** (including the locks) from Panama City, go to Plaza 5 de Mayo in front of the Reina Torres de Araúz museum, the departure point for numerous buses. The destinations are indicated (although not always legibly) on the windshields of the vehicles and the cost is between B/.1 and B/.3, depending on the destination. All buses to Gamboa pass close to the locks. Be aware that when going to the Miraflores locks, the bus stop is on the main road and there is a walk of 1km to reach the site. The same holds true for the **Summit Botanical Garden**.

Since there is no bus service to **Canopy Tower**, contact the establishment's staff who will pick you up at the Summit Botanical Garden (see above), which is just a few kilometres away from it.

By Taxi

In the downtown capital there is no problem finding a taxi to go to the locks, the Summit Botanical Garden or any other place in the canal zone. The cost is between B/.20 and B/.30, depending on the destination.

By Train

Since July 2001, travellers looking to cross the isthmus by train can board at the Corozal station (located northwest of Panama City). The train travels to Colón in about 50min.. Unfortunately, both the Corozal and Colón stations are located outside the city centre, so you'll have to get there by car or taxi *(around B/.3)*. Moreover, the train fare is not altogether affordable (B/.35 return and B/.20 one way).

For more information:

Panama Canal Railway Company
☎317-6070
⇌317-6061

Just one departure a day from Panama City and Colón:

Departure from Panama City at 7am, arrival in Colón at 8am.

Departure from Colón at 5:15pm, arrival in Corozal at 8pm.

Exploring

★

Puente de Las Américas

This elegant 118m-high cantilever bridge (a bridge with no cables that extends horizontally well beyond its vertical supports), was built by the Americans at a cost of $20 million between 1958 and 1962. It affords a magnificent view over the Bahía de Panamá, but you can only visit the bridge by car, and the swift traffic doesn't leave much time for admiring the sights. Finally, there is a parking area with no facilities but a good view of the bay just past the bridge on the right as you head west out of the city (follow the signs for *mirador*).

★★★

Miraflores Locks

Of the three groups of locks in the canal zone, the Miraflores locks are the most interesting. A special area has been developed above the locks, from which visitors have an unobstructed view of the operations (*every day 9am to 5pm*). As the ships pass, commentaries can be heard from the loudspeakers in Spanish and in English. You will learn, for example, that a ship might contain 4,000 cars from Sweden, oil from Venezuela, or a great variety of other cargo. You can also take in a 15min audiovisual presentation on the operation of the canal in the **little lock museum** (*every day 9am to 5pm*). The sight of a huge ship moving a few metres away is truly impressive. Electric locomotives move alongside ships that dwarf them, guiding and stabilizing vessels by means of steel cables. What power!

Operations are carried out with the utmost precision, and once a ship has passed through, the locks empty then fill back up at an astonishing speed—a process that involves several million litres of water.

The Phantom Fleet

You may have noticed the many vessels flying the Panamanian flag. In fact, the Panamanian fleet is the biggest in the world after Liberia's. Don't be fooled, however, because few of these ships actually belong to Panamanian companies. Rather, Panamá, like Liberia, offers foreign companies licenses to operate their vessels on advantageous terms. For example, Panamá charges vessels flying the Panamanian flag less to pass through the canal. Some say it is a flag of convenience, in reference to the lax restrictions imposed by both Panamá and Liberia. This phantom fleet generates more than $120 million US per year for Panamá, equivalent to 3% of the GNP.

This fleet may expand considerably in the coming years since the regulation restricting American vessels from registering anywhere but in the United States is about to be lifted.

For technical reasons, this water is fresh, and comes from Lago Gatún (saltwater could jam the machinery of the locks). The extent of these operations is even more impressive when you take into account that the locks were built over 70 years ago! Those interested in actually passing through the locks and sailing on the canal should contact one of the many travel agencies in the capital. Here are two of our choices:

Tropic Tours
☎269-3147

Argo Tours
☎228-6069 or 228-4348

Argo Tours is the tourist agency offering the widest choice of excursions. There are two interesting possibilities to mention. Those with limited time can choose a half-day cruise *(B/.90 buffet-meal and drinks included; Sat 7:30am to12:30pm or as late as 4:30pm, depending on the traffic in the canal zone)* that passes through the Miraflores locks and goes down to the Bahía de Panamá in the region of Calzada Amador, passing under the impressive Puente de las Américas. Alternatively, you might devote a full day to a complete cruise through the three canal locks *(B/.135, buffet-meal and drinks included; one departure monthly, 7:30am to 5:30pm)* to the city of Colón with return to the capital by bus.

All departures are made from Pier 18 at the port of Balboa, where Argo Tours has a reception office, which is unfortunately in a sorry state and could definitely use some serious refurbishment. Moreover, foodies should be forewarned that the meals and drinks served on board are more akin to fast food than to a real buffet.

★★★

Cerro Contratista (Contractor's Hill)

The passage made through the mountain to allow the canal to pass can be seen from Cerro del Contratista, a 115m hill overlooking Gaillard Cut (Corte de Gaillard or Corte Culebra), which was named for the engineer who supervised the work.

Opposite, you can see how the hill (Cerro de Oro) was levelled: it was reduced in size to minimise the risk of landslides into the canal. Literally over-hanging the canal, this spot offers an impressive view of the passing ships from 199m above sea level. The sight of vessels navigating between the mountains is testimony to the ingenuity of the engineers and the colossal task that had to be accomplished. The road to the observation point is in good shape and picnic tables and an observation deck have been set up on the site (*Mon-Sun from 9am to 5pm*).

★★

Summit Botanical Gardens

In this fine garden *(B/.25; every day 8am to 4pm; Sat and Sun and summer until 6pm)* laid out in the Parque Nacionál Soberanía, there are more than 15,000 species of trees and plants. Summit Garden was built by the Americans in 1923 and handed over to Panamá in 1979. A number of trails have been cleared, and the various trees and shrubs are identified. It is tempting to stay here for hours looking at all the tropical species. A section of the garden (near the entrance to the park) is occupied by a small zoo and contains most of the wild animal and bird species that live in Parque Soberanía. A map showing the various routes for walking can usually be obtained at the entrance to the park, though copies are not always available.

Gamboa

The main attraction here is the small marina on the Río Chagres—a good spot to begin an enjoyable boat ride. The marina is 8.4 km from the highway intersection at the entrance to Parque Soberanía. A little farther on the same road, you will come to a narrow bridge with an interesting view of Lago Gatún and the ships in the canal.

A few years ago, an imposing resort was built near the mouth of the Río

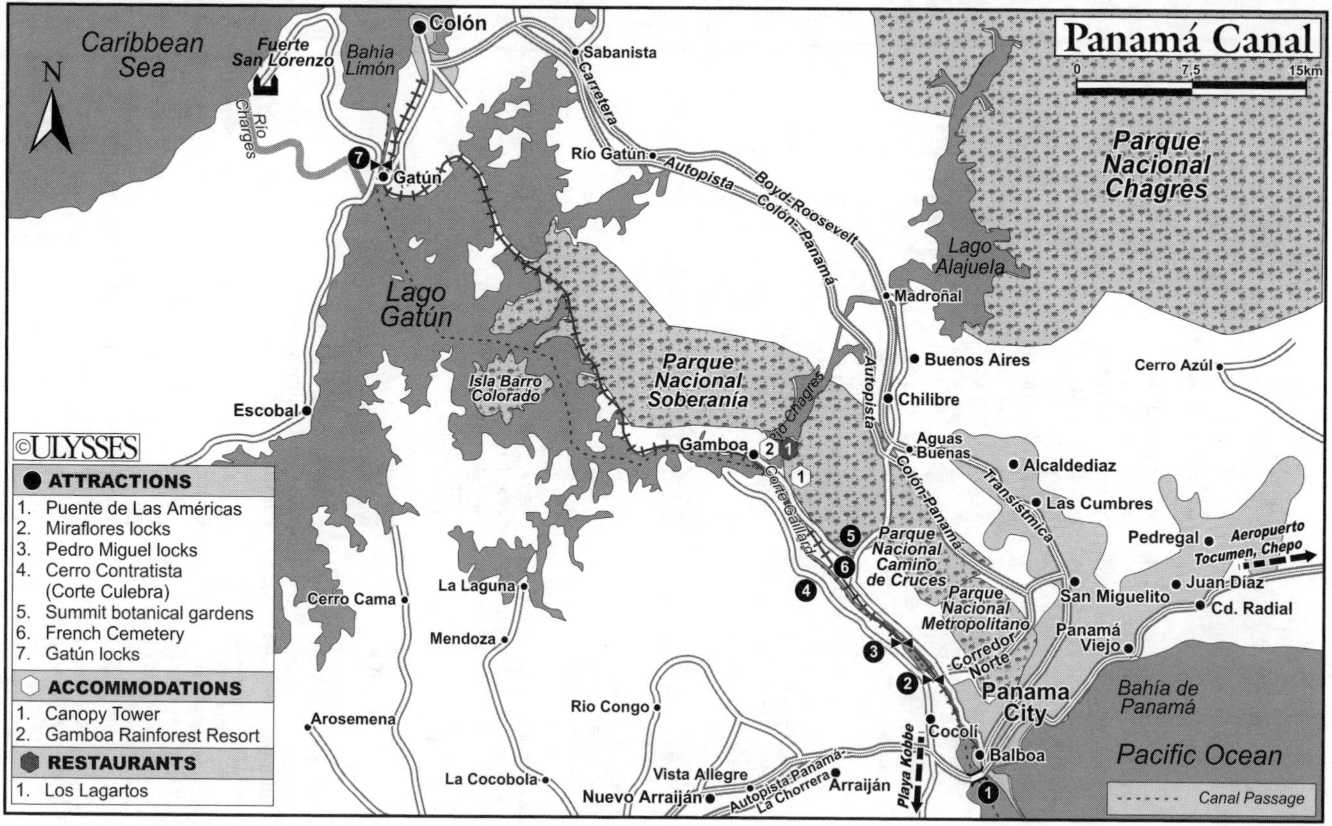

Panamá Canal
0
7,5
15km
Caribbean Sea
N
Fuerte San Lorenzo
Bahía Limón
Colón
Río Charges
Sabanista
Carretera
Río Gatún
Autopista
Boyd-Roosevelt
Colón-Panamá
Gatún
Lago Gatún
Isla Barro Colorado
Parque Nacional Soberanía
Parque Nacional Chagres
Lago Alajuela
Madroñal
Buenos Aires
Cerro Azúl
Chilibre
Aguas Buenas
Alcaldediaz
Las Cumbres
Transístmica
Escobal
Gamboa
Río Chagres
Corte Gaillard
Parque Nacional Camino de Cruces
Parque Nacional Metropolitano
Corredor Norte
Pedregal
Aeropuerto Tocumen, Chepo
San Miguelito
Juan Díaz
Cd. Radial
Panamá Viejo
Panama City
Bahía de Panamá
Pacific Ocean
Cocolí
Balboa
Playa Kobbe
Cerro Cama
La Laguna
Mendoza
Rio Congo
Arosemena
Vista Allegre
Arraiján
Nuevo Arraiján
Autopista Panamá-La Chorrera
La Cocobola
Canal Passage
©ULYSSES
ATTRACTIONS
1. Puente de Las Américas
2. Miraflores locks
3. Pedro Miguel locks
4. Cerro Contratista (Corte Culebra)
5. Summit botanical gardens
6. French Cemetery
7. Gatún locks
ACCOMMODATIONS
1. Canopy Tower
2. Gamboa Rainforest Resort
RESTAURANTS
1. Los Lagartos

Life as a Zonian

Hired for the most part in the United States, employees in the Canal Zone have state-run stores selling goods that are imported directly from the U.S. at subsidised prices. Curiously, it is mainly the Chinese who supply fresh produce. Hired for the duration of construction, they subsequently settled with their families and became the "market gardeners of the canal" by cultivating fruits and vegetables. In terms of accommodation, housing was erected by the administration of the Zone, so residents were unable to purchase their own houses. Thus, over the course of 75 years of American management, schools, churches, social clubs, golf courses and public swimming pools have created a veritable microcosm of the United States, completely separate from the host country and its citizens. For Americans born in the Canal Zone and those who have spent most of their lives there, returning to the United States entails a serious culture shock, not unlike that experienced by colonists repatriated back to Europe during the 1960s.

Chagres, in wooden buildings once held by the canal zone administration. Located here is a restaurant with a patio where you can have something to eat while watching boats navigating the canal in the distance.

Balboa

At the foot of Cerro Ancón, the imposing **Administratión del Canal** building *(Mon-Fri 9am to 4pm)* is flanked by a monumental staircase that lends it an air of formality. Inside, an equally impressive 100m² painting depicts four scenes in the important stages of the canal's construction.

On the initiative of engineer George W. Goethals, American painter William B. Van Ingen, already well known for his paintings of the Library of Congress in Washington, was commissioned for this work. The canvas was painted on several panels in New York and later reassembled here by the artist himself in 1915. The work was restored in 1993.

Since July 2001, the **Panama Canal Railway Company** has been offering passenger service on a trans-isthmus line from the Corozal station, located northwest of Panama City, to the city of Colón. The trip takes about 50min and follows the Panama Canal, offering many interesting views along the way. Moreover, the sightseeing trip takes place aboard Edwardian-style wood-panelled carriages. It makes for a pleasant little excursion, of particular interest to those without transportation who want to get an overview of the canal zone. Nonetheless, note that given the remoteness of both the Corozal and Colón stations, you'll have to take a taxi (around B/.3) to get there. Another drawback is the restricted schedule (only one departure per day), particularly since the seedy city of Colón is not a safe place to spend your time. Finally, note that at B/.35 A/R, the fare is not particularly affordable.

For more information:

☎317-6070
www.trainweb.org/panama

Parks

★★★

Parque Nacional Soberanía and the Parque Nacional Camino de Cruzes

The **Parque Nacional Soberanía** covers an area of 220km^2 and consists primarily of an impressive rain forest containing an extremely rich plant life. This forest is also home to a great variety of birds. Bird-watchers will be interested to know that the Panamá Audubon Society spotted over 525 different species between December 1992 and January 1993! Not only are the Summit Botanical Gardens (see p 122) located here, but part of Parque Soberanía is crossed by Camino de Cruces. This well-known route, in use since colonial times, is now part of the **Parque Nacional Camino de Cruzes**, created in 1993. Covering an area of almost 4,500ha, it links the Parque Soberanía to the Parque Metropolitano.

Today the path is no longer entirely accessible, as part of it was submerged when the canal was built. The section of the trail that crosses Parque Soberanía, which used to be paved, is excellent for walking. Along it, outdoor enthusiasts can admire the richness and variety of the Panamanian flora. However, for safety reasons (tourists having been robbed in the park over the past few years), we strongly advise you not to venture here without a guide.

Further information can be obtained from ANAM:

Parque Nacional en Gamboa
☎232-4291

★★

Isla Barro Colorado

This island was created in **Lago Gatún** when the valley was flooded. Some years later it became an exceptionally rich natural reserve. During the flooding, many animals took refuge here—so many that the island was classified a protected area. Because of this abundance and the island's small size (54km^2), the Smithsonian Institute built a research centre here to study the evolution of the island's animal and plant species.

The island has an impressive number of plants and shrubs, as well as different types of forests, some of which contain trees over 200 years old. As many as 1,300 different species of plants have been catalogued on these 1,500ha. In fact, 300 different species of trees have been identified in a space of less than 26ha. There are many trails (a total of some 40km), including a 2.5km-long path called the Nature Trail for people with little time and or little hiking experience. It is recommended that you wear long, light clothing as protection against the many insects (see p 50). **However, Barro Colorado is accessible only with authorization from the Smithsonian Institute** or as part of a guided tour organized by the various ecotourism operators (see p 61). There is accommodation on the island, but it is reserved for the scientific staff.

While many tour operators organize visits to the island, it's a better idea to contact the following:

The Smithsonian Institute
☎212-8026
www.stri.org

The only inconvenience is that space is limited, and all sorts of conditions apply. Group tours are Tuesdays, Wednesdays and Fridays *(B/.70 per person; from Gamboa; one departure at 7:15am)*, Saturdays and Sundays *(B/.70 per person; from Gamboa; one departure at 8am)*. The tour includes the boat trip (*Gamboa-Barro Colorado, return*), the services of a guide and a meal at the island's cafeteria. Count on a 4 to 6hr visit, depending on the availability of the guides. Payment must be made two weeks before your visit. It is also strongly recommended to reserve well in advance. Reservations and payment can be made by mail. Children must be at least 12 years of age.

Parque Nacional Chagres

Panamá boasts some 140 endemic species, no fewer than 80 of which have been seen in the Chagres National Park alone. Created in 1984, the park covers close to 1,290km² and encompasses countless waterways, which now supply almost 50% of the fresh water necessary to the functioning of the canal. Salt water is unsuitable as it leaves deposits that would eventually block the mechanism of the locks. Moreover, these waterways provide drinking water for the capital, only 52km away. The famous Río Chagres has its source in the park. A dam was built on this river in 1935, creating an enormous reservoir known as Lago Alajuela, which serves as a reserve for the operations of the canal.

Thanks to its rather limited accessibility, the park has managed to protect very rare species to which it remains home, such as the jaguar, a species of tapir and the harpy eagle. The animal and plant life here is so diverse that scientists find additional species every year.

The closest entrance to the park from Panama City is Cerro Azul, where there are various trails. However, due to the presence of dangerous animals and few marked trails, it is best to go with a guide. Also, remember that authorization is required to enter the park (see p 64).

Outdoor Activities

Hiking

Parque Nacional Soberanía

Among the short hikes that can be undertaken without a guide is the nature interpretation trail **El Charco** *(3.8km from the entrance to the Summit Botanical Garden, on the right side of the road going towards Gamboa)*. Along the pleasant 2km loop walk, there are interpretive panels denoting the origins of the trees and plants. Do not forget your insect repellent, as the mosquitoes are very much at home here.

Canopy Tower
by appointment only Semaphore Hill Road
☎264-5720
www.canopytower.com

For the uninitiated, even those with a great deal of patience, observing animals in the wild is not always easy and often requires the services of an experienced guide. The proprietor of the Canopy Tower and his team offer a number of original and instructive tours (in Spanish and English) of this extraordinary sight. Some of these excursions are described below. Prices are provisional and excursions are subject to change due to diverse conditions. They include admission to the Parque Nacional Soberanía, a light meal as well as access to the Canopy Tower and the use of telescopes for bird-watching.

"The Awakening of the Forest" *(B/.55/pers.; departure 6am, return 10am)*, is the name of the almost 4hr hike suggested for very early risers. This morning excursion allows one to discover the animals of the park during the peak of their daily activities. Rates include entry to the park, a meal, access to the summit of the old radar tower and use of a telescope. The **"night version"** of this hike *(B/.65/pers.; departure 5am, return 1am)* provides the unique experience of discovering the park's nocturnal animals, set to the music of screaming monkeys, chorusing frogs and all sorts of strange sounds that the guides are happy to explain. Guaranteed thrills!

Those "early to bed and *late* to rise" types can take a 2hr guided tour along the **Semaphore Hill Road**, which, although paved, is surrounded by dense vegetation. The guide will point out a surprising number of animals. The road slopes downhill all the way, but rest assured: a little electric car will bring you back to the starting point!

Rafting

Parque Nacional Chagres

For some time now, the Aventuras company has been organizing rafting expeditions down the **Río Chagres**, in the park of the same name. Needless to say, this activity is for very fit people with rafting experience (level 2 or 3). It is a one-of-a-kind experience, as it goes through the very heart of the park where a variety of animals and particularily lush vegetation can be observed. There are four stages to this activity: first, a drive in an all-terrain vehicle to reach a camp located north of Cerro Azul, then a 2hr walk through uneven terrain to reach the river, followed by a 6hr descent of the river to the artificial lake called Lago Alajuela. Finally, the last leg of the trip consists of a 30-minute lake crossing by motorboat to reach the road, where a car awaits to drive weary adventurers back to their hotel. Expect to pay about B/.205 per person for a party of four. Though rafting is possible all year round, the best time to go is from September to December.

For more information:

Aventuras Panamá
Apdo 9869, Panamá 4
☎260-0044
www.aventuraspanama.com

Fishing

Gamboa

The little marina is the perfect spot for people who like to fish in calm water. Boats and tackle may be rented there.

Accommodations

Parque Nacional Soberanía

Canopy Tower
$$$$$ all incl
pb/sb, hw, ⊗
Semaphore Hill Road
☎264-5720
⇄263-2784
www.canopytower.com
Enthralled by nature, fascinated by ornithology or simply keen on peace and quiet? Opt for a stay at the Canopy Tower for a taste of paradise! Located at the summit of a 900m hill, this old radar tower has been cleverly transformed into a small hotel by the proprietor, Paúl Arias de Para. Long before it was possible to buy it back from the U.S. army, he had taken note of the tower's unique site.

Indeed, isolated at the heart of Parque Nacional Soberanía and completely surrounded by lush vegetation, this spot provides an exceptional lookout for those enthralled by virgin forest. At the moment, however, the industrial appearance of the entrance is somewhat disappointing. There are plans to create a museum here. After several years of intense restoration, the old radar tower has six comfortable rooms in a rotunda on the second floor. All are charmingly decorated and are enhanced by windows looking out over the forest.

The third floor has a large circular room, entirely glassed-in, where guests can admire the dense vegetation. There is a pleasant living room corner and a library filled with books on birds and other animals of the isthmus.

Finally, on the top floor, paradise awaits! There is an oval terrace at treetop-level surrounding the old radar dome. From here the 360-degree view of the park is simply extraordinary. Besides a wide view of the park one can see in the distance the immense ships navigating the canal. From this vantage point they appear to be gliding across the forest; this is truly an astonishing spectacle!

Guests can relax, sit comfortably and observe through binoculars the innumerable birds that live in the canopy. Dusk and dawn are among the noisier moments of the day; at dawn the birds are at the peak of activity and at dusk the screaming monkeys exercise their tenor and baritone voices.

Unfortunately, dreams have a price. The "all-inclusive" plan *(from B/.115/pers. to B/.185, three meals and drinks)*, includes two hikes per day with a guide, the use of a telescope and binoculars and entrance to the national park. The less affluent need not despair, as the proprietor has different excursions at more affordable prices.

Gamboa Rainforest Resort
$$$$$
pb, hw, ≡, ≈, tv, ℜ, ⊙
Apartado 7338, Zona 5
☎214-1690 or 276-6812
⇄214-1694 or 276-6810
www.gamboaresort.com
This large resort is made up of some 40 units with living rooms occupying wooden villas built in the 1930s as residences for Panama Canal administrators and their families. Also on site are other, recently built structures that house the reception area and various facilities, as well as about 100 rooms. The units are tastefully decorated and the resort's location, near the Parque Nacional Soberanía, at the very mouth of the Río Chagres and right on the Panama Canal, is altogether exceptional. Guests can enjoy amenities worthy of the biggest luxury hotels (including tennis court, bar and dance club) while luxuriating in a perfectly exotic environment.

Several small theme parks have been laid out in the gardens, including a replica of a traditional Emberá village (one of the indigenous communities that populate the Republic of Panama), an orchid garden, a small reserve that is home to exotic frogs and snakes, as well as an aquarium encompassing various indigenous marine species. For those who appreciate the great outdoors, many guided excursions are offered, while a marina with fishing club, kayaks and pedal boats will delight water-sports enthusiasts. Guests looking for a more relaxing adventure can opt for the resort's tour of the rainforest canopy aboard an "aerial tram," offering a lovely panoramic view and the opportunity to observe the local flora and fauna at their leisure. Finally, those seeking a quieter, more relaxing vacation can partake of the tai-chi and meditation classes offered by the hotel.

Access to this little slice of paradise will cost you the princely sum of B/.220 to B/.470/day (not including meals, drinks or excursions). To benefit from more "reasonable" rates, it is advisable to opt for an all-inclusive package offered by a travel agency.

Restaurants

Miraflores Locks

Pizza Hut
on the left side of the main road leading to the locks
There are almost no restaurants near the Miraflores locks. If you feel peckish, your only choice is the Pizza Hut. Try the Taco Pizza, with *frijoles* (beans) and cheese.

Parque Nacional Soberanía

Los Lagartos
$$$$$
Gamboa
☎214-1690
☎276-6812
Housed within the Gamboa Rainforest Resort (see above), a large luxury resort near the very mouth of the Río Chagres and right on the Panama Canal, Los Lagartos boasts an altogether exceptional location. You can enjoy a meal on its pleasant patio while watching the huge ships that navigate the canal in the distance through the heart of the tropical forest. Food-wise, diners are offered not only typical Panamanian dishes, but international cuisine as well. Although the food served here can hardly be considered haute cuisine, meals are decent and the service courteous. Besides, the place alone is worth the trip for its unique, exotic environment.

Shopping

At the Miraflores locks you will find a few vendors selling T-shirts *(B/.10)*, straw hats and many other small souvenirs of the canal. A little bargaining is in order.

The Islands and Beaches of the Province of Panamá

The many islands and beaches of Panamá's Pacific coast are, like its rich flora and fauna, too often overlooked by travellers.

Isolated and not readily accessible, the islands of the Archipiélago de las Perlas are the largest group. Among these, the best-known is undoubtedly Isla Contadora. It is the only island with an international-class hotel and enough rooms to accommodate large numbers of travellers. It is also the only island in the archipelago with several daily flights to the capital.

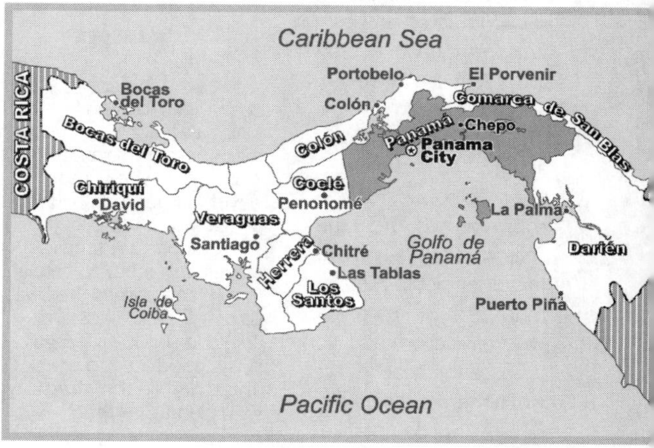

Although less frequented and wilder than Contadora, Isla San José is also home to a recently built luxury resort that will delight fishing enthusiasts and those in search of tranquility. To get there, you'll have to go through the hotel agency, which will take care of your travel arrangements—unless you have your own boat, of course.

Aside from the islands of the Las Perlas group, Isla Taboga is very popular with Panamanians. Barely an hour's boat road away from Panama City, it is literally invaded on weekends by families who come to enjoy the sand and sun and get away from the city. There is a detailed description of these three islands in this chapter.

The many beaches along the Bay of Panamá from Punta Chame to Playa Santa Clara are more accessible, located less than a 100km from downtown. Each of the 10 has its own personality and is worth visiting. Despite their beauty, the huge international hotel chains have not yet moved in, as these beaches remain somewhat off the beaten path. Though throngs of people on weekends (from Friday to Sunday afternoon), and entire families on statutory holidays, travel to the beaches, there are limited services available. The few restaurants fill up quickly and accommodation is difficult to come by. As a general rule, all you can expect is average comfort, and not necessarily the best value for your money. Most accommodations are set up for large families who bring along their own food, so it can be very advantageous to rent by the week or several days, at which point the price will drop considerably. A room can cost B/.50 the first night, but only B/.35 the other nights. Also, it is much easier to bargain for weekday accommodation because the beaches are virtually empty then. The rates below do not take these reductions into account and refer to a single night's accommodation.

El Valle de Antón, less than an hour away from the beaches, is a bit cooler and greener and offers a wide variety of restaurants and hotels, as well as a craft market. Finally, also at less than an hour's drive from the coast, there is the Parque Nacional Altos de Campana for lovers of the great outdoors.

Finding Your Way Around

Note: the following schedules and rates are provided for reference only and are subject to change.

By Boat

Isla Taboga

To reach Isla Taboga, head to pier 18, located in the Balboa area. Ferries depart from here twice a day during the week, and several times a day on weekends and holidays. Since departure times have a tendency to change often (sometimes the boat simply leaves when it is full) and service is irregular, it is a good idea to check the schedule the same day you plan to leave.

Two maritime shuttles serve Isla Taboga: the ***Expreso del Pacífico*** and the ***Calypso Queen***. While the first, a hovercraft, travels to the capital in barely 20min, the other, a conventional ship, makes the crossing in 1hr to 1.5hrs. Below are the low-season timetables. Crossings are more frequent in the high season, depending on the number of passengers.

On weekends, the best way to make sure you get on the boat is to reserve a spot, since Panamanians by the boat-loads will also be heading to the island. The best way to reach the port is by taxi since there is no guarded parking lot and the area can be unsafe. An army of taxis will be waiting for your return, which gives you the advantage of being able to negotiate a price. From the pier to Bella Vista, for example, should cost B/.5 for one person and B/.8 for two.

Timetables and fares:

Espreso del Pacífico
☎261-0350 or 229-1639

Departures from Panama City:
Mon-Fri: 8:30am and 3pm
Sat-Sun: 8:30am, 10:15am, 3pm and 5pm

Departures from Isla Taboga:
Mon-Fri: 10am and 3:45pm
Sat-Sun: 10am, 2pm, 4pm and 6pm
Fare: B/.4 one way

Calypso Queen
☎232-5736

Departures from Panama City:
Tue-Fri: 8am
Sat-Sun: 7:45am and 10:30am

Departures from Isla Taboga:
Tue-Fri: 3:30pm
Sat-Sun: 3pm and 5:30pm
Fare: B/.8

By Plane

Isla Contadora

Aeroperlas is currently the only airline offering daily flights to the island.
Travel Time: 20min
Fare: B/.52.50

Panama City to Contadora Departures:
Mon-Fri: 8am and 5pm
Sat: 8am, 8:50am, 9:45am and 5pm
Sun: 8:50am, 3:50pm, 4:40pm and 5:30pm

Contadora to Panama City Departure:
Mon-Fri: 8:25am and 5:25pm
Sat: 8:25am, 9:15am and 5:25pm
Sun: 9:15am, 4:15pm, 5:05pm and 5:55pm

There are also flights from **Colón**, **David**, **Chitré** and **Bocas del Toro**.

For information:

Contadora Airport
☎250-4022 or 250-4192

Aviatur also offers daily air service to the island, but schedules vary with the seasons.

From Panama City to Isla Contadora:
May to Nov: Mon-Sat departures at 8:30am and 4pm; Sun 4pm;
Dec to Apr: Mon-Sun departures at 8:30am and 4:30pm

From Isla Contadora to Panama City:
May to Nov: Mon-Fri departures at 11am and 4:30pm; Sun 4:30pm;
Dec to Apr: Mon-Sat departures at 11am and 5pm; Sun 9am and 5pm

By Car

To reach the interior (the area to the west of the capital) of the country, take the Puente de las Américas, and continue straight on the main highway. From Arraiján, a toll highway *(toll booth is 26km from the bridge; B/.2)* leads to La Chorrera. Shortly after La Chorrera, the highway merges onto the Interamericana. Keep left here, since there are actually two roads, and no sign to tell you how to join the Interamericana.

To reach **Playa Chame**, take the Interamericana from the capital to the village of Bejuco and follow the signs for Punta Chame at the entrance to the village, on the left. Keep going for about 25km.

For **Playas Gorgona**, **Coronado**, **San Carlos**, **Río Mar**, **Santa Clara** and **Corona**: these beaches are all easily accessible from the left side of the Interamericana as you drive from Panama City.

To reach **Parque Altos de Campana**, turn right off the Interamericana 5km after Capira when coming from Ciudad de Panama City. The road is in very bad shape and is only passable in the dry season. Though you can reach the park in a small rental car, it is advisable to have a four-wheel-drive vehicle.

To get to **El Valle de Antón** from Panama City, take the Interamericana westward. The exit for El Valle is on the right side of the Interamericana, 2.3km west of the turnoff for Playa Río Mar. The road to the village has been recently redone and passes a number of attractions. At 14.8km, you will see a small lake in an old crater. Farther on, at 22.7km, an interesting observation point has been laid out. Farther still, at 27km, there is another observation point with a sign showing the altitude of Cerro Gaital (1,185m).

By Bus

To get to **El Valle de Antón** and the **beaches** to the west of the capital, go to the bus station, *Terminal Nacional de Transporte (☎314-6171 or 314-6167)*, located near the M. Gelabert (Albrook) airport, on Calle Curundú (also known as Vía La Amistad or Calle Ascañio Villalaz) in the Curundú district. Because of its distance from downtown, it is best to take a taxi.

Unfortunately, other than the one going to El Valle, most buses will let you off on the Interamericana as they continue their route west. To get to the beach, you must then take a taxi or walk. To go to **Punta Chame**, take a bus as far as Bejuco, where there are many daily departures for this destination. Keep in mind, however, that buses stop at the Punta Chame Motel, at the beginning of the peninsula.

Exploring

★★

Isla Taboga

In the early days of the colony, this island, located about an hour from the capital, was a major port of call and many ships anchored here, including pirate vessels. From here Francisco Pizarro also set forth to discover new South American territories.

The village of Taboga was established around 1549 and was quickly populated by freed slaves cultivating pineapples and Chinese people, most of whom were involved in commerce.

Early in 1885, during the Lesseps canal construction period, the French built a sanatorium and the island became a place for convalescence. In 1904, shortly after the Americans took over work on the canal, the centre was enlarged and most of the island's income came from the sanatorium's patients. When work on the canal was completed, the government transformed the sanatorium into the Aspinwall Hotel, which was privatized in 1921.

After a brief prosperous period during which sumptuous receptions were organized by Panamanian high society, the island's fortunes slumped. With the coming of World War II and the installation of a military base, the "Island of Flowers" enjoyed a brief period of vitality. After the war the island returned to its peaceful origins until it was reawakened by tourism.

The "Island of Flowers" and Gauguin

The island's exoticism has inspired many artists over the years, particularly the Panamánian painter Roberto Lewis and the famous Paul Gauguin. The latter, who visited the island many times in 1887 while nursing his malaria, even considered building a house there. However, his meagre salary as a canal construction worker was not enough to buy land. Disappointed at not being able to buy "a piece of paradise," Gauguin left for the French Antilles before eventually ending up in Polynesia.

The trip to Taboga is a journey of discovery in itself, even today. The boat that sails the canal passes under the Puente de las Américas, which offers good views of the bridge and the Bahía de Panamá. You will also see all the boats waiting to get into the canal. Cars are forbidden on the island, and the quiet is conducive to relaxing walks. This island is blessed with a stunning array of flowers. Colourful bougainvillea, orchids and hibiscuses etc. are just a few of the types that grow here, making it no wonder the Panamanians call Taboga the "island of flowers." Taboga is also known for its beautiful white-sand beaches, dotted with palm trees and littered with pink and brown seashells. Unfortunately, these idyllic beaches fill up rapidly on the weekends. Come midweek if you are searching for serenity.

The village, with its whitewashed houses and narrow streets, extends from the harbour to the slope of the mountain and is a pleasant place to stroll. Among the buildings of interest is the small **church on the central plaza**, the architecture of the **Chu hotel** and a bit farther west, the house known as the ***La Concha***, decorated with shells (the owner sells them).

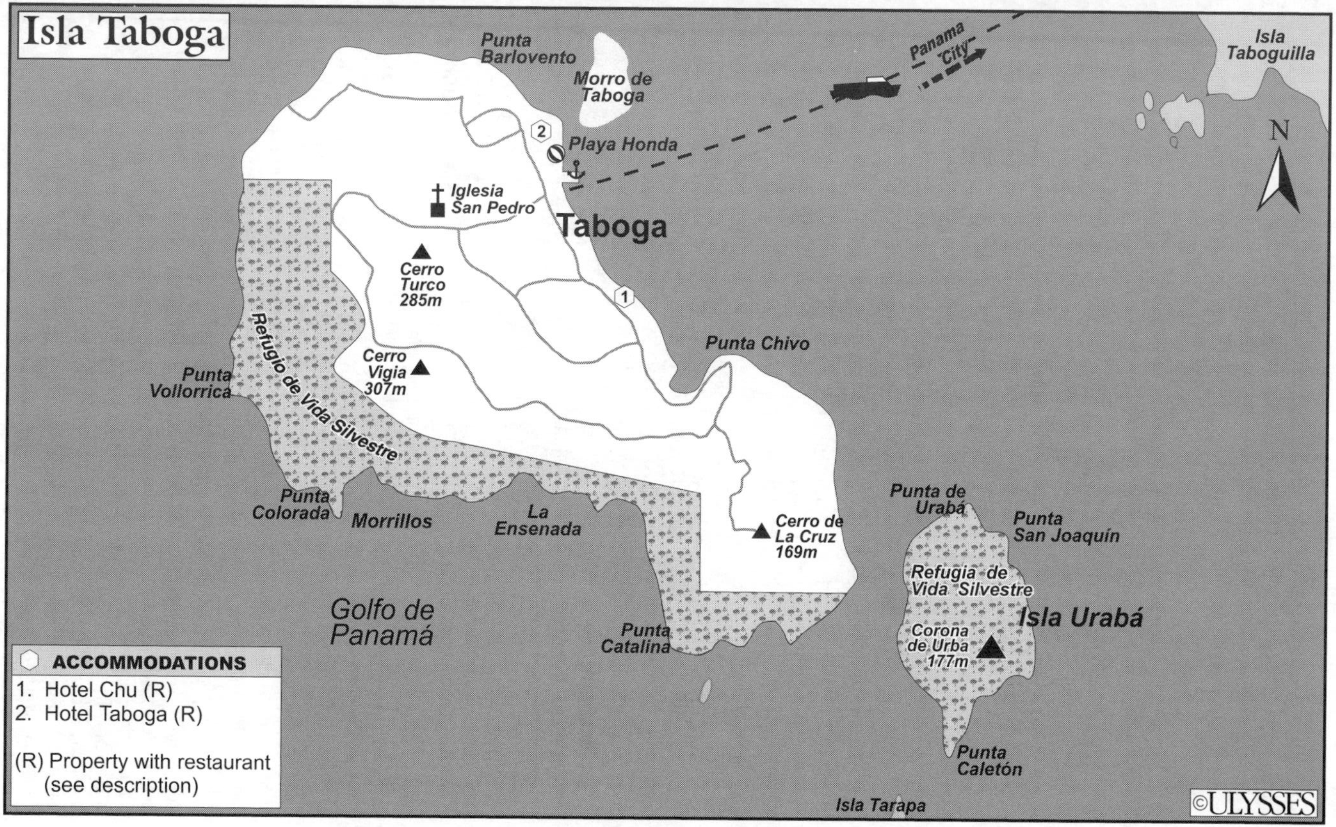
Isla Taboga
Punta Barlovento
Morro de Taboga
Playa Honda
Panama City
Isla Taboguilla
N
Iglesia San Pedro
Taboga
Cerro Turco 285m
Cerro Vigia 307m
Refugio de Vida Silvestre
Punta Vollorrica
Punta Chivo
Punta Colorada
Morrillos
La Ensenada
Cerro de La Cruz 169m
Punta de Urabá
Punta San Joaquín
Refugia de Vida Silvestre
Isla Urabá
Corona de Urba 177m
Golfo de Panamá
Punta Catalina
Punta Caletón
Isla Tarapa
ACCOMMODATIONS
1. Hotel Chu (R)
2. Hotel Taboga (R)
(R) Property with restaurant (see description)
©ULYSSES

On the other side of the island from the village is a nature reserve that harbours many species of animals, among them iguanas and a colony of pelicans. You can visit the reserve but you must first obtain authorization from INRENARE (see p 66), which will assign you a guide. The institute has a local office (often closed, unfortunately) on the road to the Taboga Hotel where you can obtain general information on the reserve. There are pleasant hikes off the reserve; two of the most interesting are described below (see p 142). If you prefer the beach, the Taboga Hotel offers an interesting package. Its water is excellent for snorkelling; unlike other beaches on the island, this one has almost no waves.

Archipélago de las Perlas

Isla Contadora is part of the Archipiélago de las Perlas (archipelago of pearls), which is made up of more than 220 islands and islets. The largest of the islands, Isla del Rey, has a surface area of close to 240km^2 and a population of approximately 2,500 people. Its capital, San Miguel, was established in 1607.

Although the archipelago was discovered by Vasco Núñez de Balboa in 1513, it was only in 1515 that his successors Francisco Pizarro and Gaspar de Morales invaded the island. After subduing "King Toe," the Spaniards exploited the island's indigenous peoples in order to harvest pearls from the surrounding oyster beds. The indigenous population very quickly died off and became extinct as early as 1518. Black slaves were then imported to make up for their loss. It was during this period that the slaves rebelled; many of them escaped and made their way towards Darién in 1546. These *cimarrones* formed bands of looters who, with the help of French and English pirates, would trouble colonial powers on numerous occasions.

When the oyster beds were exhausted, colonial powers lost interest in the archipelago and abandoned it to the pirates. Today, Isla del Rey's main industry is the production of shrimp, which are exported internationally. Only two of the islands are accessible by plane, Isla del Rey and Isla Contadora, and the accommodation possibilities in the archipelago are minimal. Touring the other islands, therefore, is only possible for travellers with a boat. Those who do will enjoy a multitude of virtually deserted islands and islets, each ringed by spectacular beaches. Not to mention that rich underwater fauna makes this a prime area for scuba diving and deep-sea fishing. Au such, those partial to this kind of activity will want to visit Isla San José, where a luxury resort, the Hacienda del Mar, offers fishing and scuba-diving packages.

La Peregrina

La Peregrina is the name given to the largest pearl ever discovered. Shaped like a droplet or, according to some, a teardrop, La Peregrina was found in the Archipiélago de las Perlas and sold by the wife of the then-governor to the wife of Charles Quint, Doña Isabel. After passing through the hands of several English royals, a French emperor, numerous nobles and business people, it is today owned by famous American actress Elizabeth Taylor.

★

Isla Contadora

Isla Contadora is the most easily accessible of the islands. While small, (only 1.2km^2) it is the most developed, and a regular connection to the mainland (see p 131) is guaranteed several times a day. The presence of a large resort makes it the most popular island in the archipelago. This popularity is due mainly to the beauty of its white-sand beaches, low cliffs, calm sea perfect for swimming and of course its crystal-clear waters.

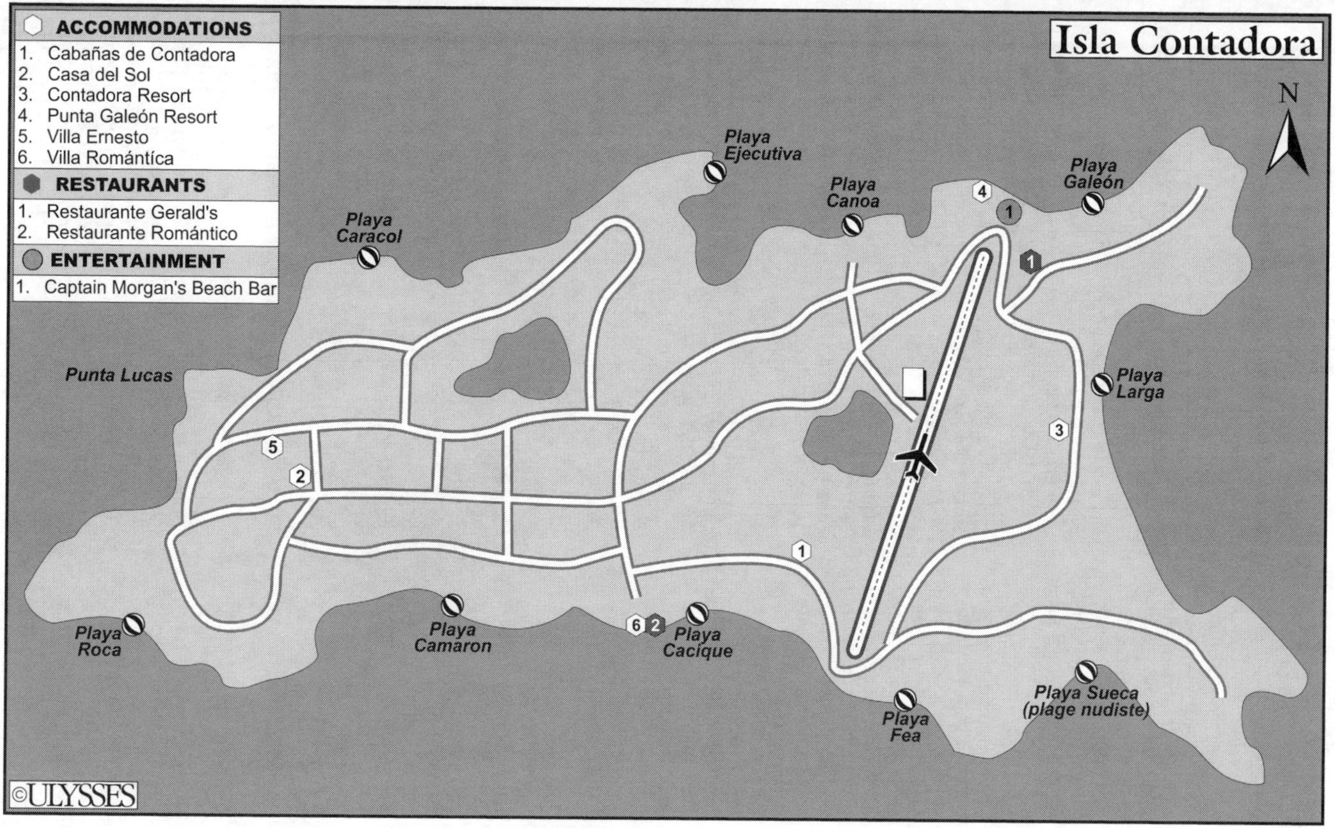
Isla Contadora
N
ACCOMMODATIONS
1. Cabañas de Contadora
2. Casa del Sol
3. Contadora Resort
4. Punta Galeón Resort
5. Villa Ernesto
6. Villa Romántica
RESTAURANTS
1. Restaurante Gerald's
2. Restaurante Romántico
ENTERTAINMENT
1. Captain Morgan's Beach Bar
Playa Ejecutiva
Playa Canoa
Playa Galeón
Playa Caracol
Punta Lucas
Playa Larga
Playa Roca
Playa Camaron
Playa Cacique
Playa Fea
Playa Sueca (plage nudiste)
©ULYSSES

In the 1970s, notable personalities, like the former Shah of Iran, chose to exile themselves on this island. Its name was established once and for all in 1983, when the presidents of Mexico, Venezuela, Colombia and Panamá met to restart negotiations for peace in Central America.

Among the best beaches on the island, **Playa Cacique** is particularly beautiful and virtually deserted, even in the high season. For a swim in calm, safe waters, **Playa Larga,** facing the Contadora Resort, is a better choice. The latter is, however, busier. Nudists tend to congregate on **Playa Sueca**, south of the resort. Wildlife abounds on the island, and it is not unheard of to see hummingbirds near the beach, or even deer bounding by farther inland.

The same is not true of the vegetation, and during the dry season, what little exuberance it has essentially dries up. Contadora is an exceptional site for those in search of beaches and limpid waters and nothing else. If catching some rays isn't really your thing, you might consider limiting your stay to one day —plenty of time to explore the island. If you want to rest, or play water sports, this is the place.

But if funds are in short supply, think again.

★

Isla San José

Isla San José is second only in size to Contadora in the Las Perlas archipelago. Its 44km^2 harbour is an abundance of flora and fauna, two-thirds of its surface area being covered in tropical rain forest teeming with wildlife. Today, a major part of the island is privately owned by the Hacienda del Mar resort, made up of about 10 wooden cabins distributed throughout various settings, each more exotic than the last. The only way of reaching the island is by private boat or by using the air service made available to the hotel's guests. Because the Hacienda del Mar is the only commercial enterprise on the island, visitors must rely on it for all transportation, food and excursion services, which cost a rather pretty penny.

The island harbours some 30 magnificent white-sand beaches with spectacular ocean beds populated by coral, exotic fish and crustaceans. A stay on Isla San José thus mainly caters to beach bunnies, those in search of peace and quiet, and fishing and diving enthusiasts with deep pockets.

★★

El Valle de Antón

This little village, located 600m above sea level in a resort area frequented by wealthy inhabitants of the capital, is renowned not only for its fresher climate and its greenery but also for its little local market. On Sundays, peasants come from neighbouring regions to sell all kinds of things, many from Andean countries like Ecuador and Peru. There are bargains on carpets, sweaters, handbags, pottery and sculptures and the products are of high quality. Panamanians also flock to the El Valle market for the exotic plants and flowers, like the celebrated flower of Panamá, the white orchid known as *espíritu santo*.

Ranas doradas (golden frogs) can also be found in this region. These strange and impressive-looking creatures are orange with black spots. Their long, thin feet and slightly wrinkled skin make them appear undernourished. However, although they may seem weak and fragile, they are able to jump or climb on any surface. Unfortunately, they are not easy to find, particularly as they are threatened with extinction. They are on display, however, at the El Nispero Zoo or the Hotel Club Campestre (see p 149) where you will discover another curiosity, *arboles*

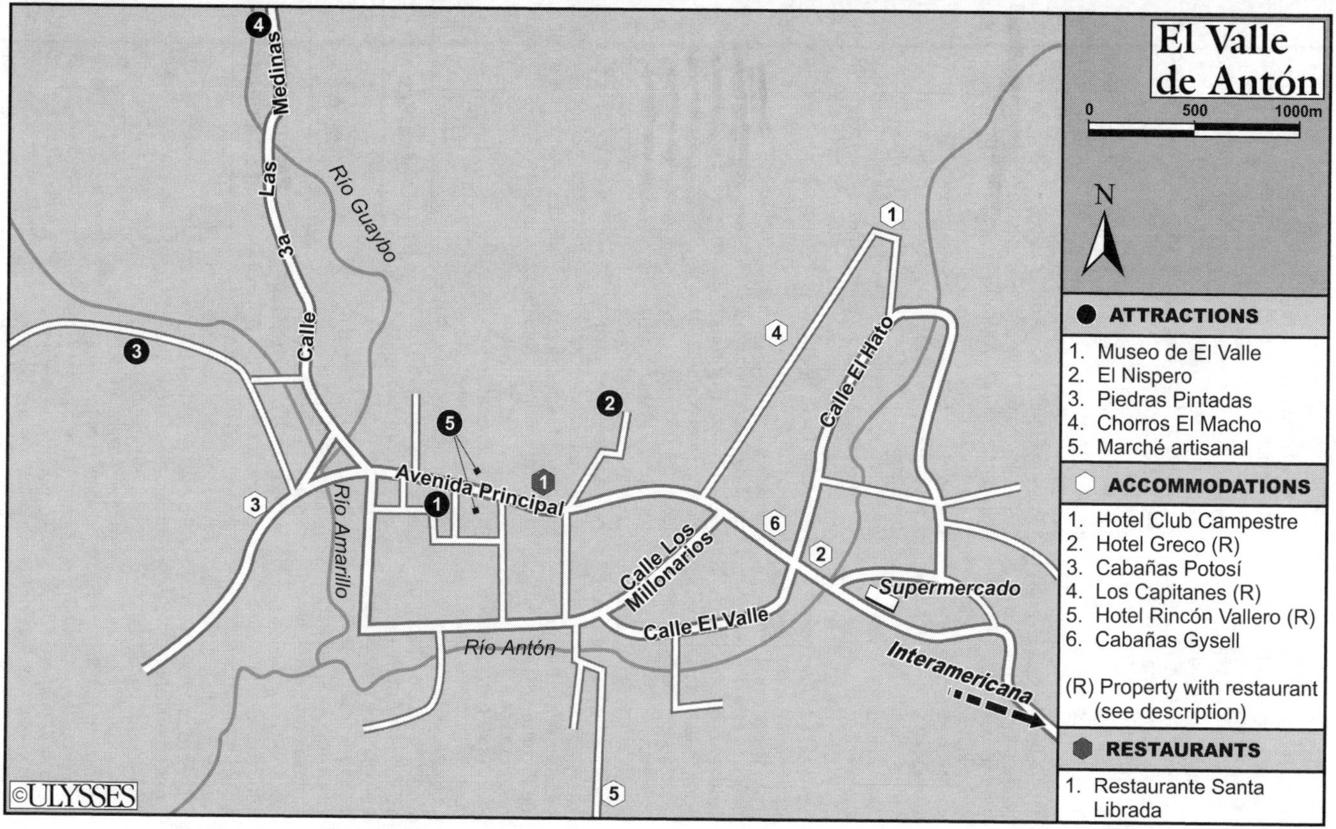
El Valle de Antón
0
500
1000m
N
ATTRACTIONS
1. Museo de El Valle
2. El Nispero
3. Piedras Pintadas
4. Chorros El Macho
5. Marché artisanal
ACCOMMODATIONS
1. Hotel Club Campestre
2. Hotel Greco (R)
3. Cabañas Potosí
4. Los Capitanes (R)
5. Hotel Rincón Vallero (R)
6. Cabañas Gysell
(R) Property with restaurant (see description)
RESTAURANTS
1. Restaurante Santa Librada
Calle 3a Las Medinas
Río Guaybo
Avenida Principal
Río Amarillo
Río Antón
Calle Los Millonarios
Calle El Valle
Calle El Hato
Supermercado
Interamericana
©ULYSSES

quadradas, trees with square trunks that grow behind the hotel (access through the building, payment required), and do not seem all that square in reality. According to hotel advertisements, this is the only place where such trees can be seen.

The little village of El Valle is beautifully decorated with flowers and the road there leads through lush green countryside. As an added attraction, people sell handicrafts (especially baskets and pottery) along the road.

Several hikes and horseback rides are possible from the town. El Valle thus makes for a particularly refreshing trip, and is easily reached from the beaches on the Golfode of Panamá.

For those who want to know a little more about village history, the **Museo de El Valle** *(B/.0,25; Sun 10am to 2pm; Av. Principal, beside the Iglesia San José, in the center of the village)* has five rooms devoted to the history of El Valle de Antón and the surrounding area. There are very small collections of petroglyphs, pre-Colombian urns and folk costumes on display. Although the exhibits are very simply presented, a visit would be worthwhile, if only to provide much-needed encouragement to Panamá's museums.

No visit to El Valle would be complete without at stop at **El Nispero** *(B/.2; 8am to 6pm; when coming from San Carlos, turn right at the Intel and right again at the police station)*, a private hacienda that is both a zoo and a botanical garden. As well as "golden frogs", monkeys, tapirs, pheasants and exotic birds, there is a pond full of many different species of fish. El Nispero is also famous for its orchids.

Crossing El Valle village on the main road in the direction of the church, you will end up at a little bridge over the Río Amarilla. Continue on the main road and turn left at the intersection and right at the next street. Keep walking straight until you reach a sign for **Piedras Pintadas** (the petroglyphs). Once there, you must follow a small dirt path through a wooded area that runs along a river for a bit. This little hike takes barely five minutes. If you are concerned about getting lost or want to have a chat with the locals, accept one of the many offers from the local children to guide you. B/.2 will get you many appreciative looks, bursts of laughter and explanations of all kinds—not very scientific, perhaps, but always entertaining!

Although there are many waterfalls in the area, **Chorros El Macho** *(entrance fee, B/.2; every day 8am to 4pm)* are the best-known and most accessible to the general public. To get there, first follow the same directions as for the petroglyphs but continue straight ahead in the direction of the village of La Mesa at the first intersection. There will be a sign on the left pointing out the 35m falls, which are surrounded by lush vegetation and fall into a basin in which some visitors swim *(B/.2)*. There are a variety of other outdoor activities offered on-site (see p 143).

As you continue westward, do not be surprised to discover a landing strip along the Interamericana, between Playa Santa Clara and Penonomé. This was built by the Americans during the Second World War. Ironically, nearby, on the left side of the road, there are a number of old military buildings used in the days of Noriega. Quotations from the former dictator can still be read on the walls. This area is slated for major development in the near future. Plans include the construction of resorts on the beach, while the airport may be renovated and upgraded to an international airport for charter flights—sort of Panamanian Cancún.

Parks

★★

Parque Altos de Campana

The Parque Altos de Campana was Panamá's first national park (1966) and has an area of more than 4,800ha. Although human activities have greatly affected the park's flora and vast areas have undergone extensive deforestation, today there are still at least 20 native species. The average annual temperature of 24°C is conducive to the growth of epiphytic, bromeliaceous and orchidaceous plants. In addition to the numerous species of rare birds, various kinds of sloths and innumerable small mammals, you will also find the country's most amazing frog, the *rana dorada* or "golden frog," in an area close to the village of El Valle de Antón. Seeing it in the wild requires a great deal of luck as well as an experienced guide. Once in the park, you are guaranteed magnificent views of the coast, with the Punta Chame peninsula visible in the distance. For access to the park, see (see p 131).

Beaches

★★

Punta Chame

This peninsula, jutting like a finger into the sea, has immense, white-sand beaches. The road leading to it is a delight, with pleasant views of the neighbouring mountains.

If you are lucky, you will see dolphins from the beaches on the inside coast of Bahía de Chame. Also, the beach on this side slopes gently toward the ocean, whereas on the Bahía de Panamá side, the waters get deep quickly and the resulting stronger currents make swimming risky. The latter beach is not as nice, and a favourite spot of pelicans. To get to either beach, take any road perpendicular to the main road. Just 100km from Panama City, this place is ideal for swimming and sunbathing. Be careful, however, as swimming at low tide is highly discouraged because of the strong undertow and the presence of stingrays. Before diving in, check if there are other people swimming or ask some locals.

Playa Gorgona

Extremely busy on weekends, Playa Gorgona has a nice, though narrow, beach of white and black sand. This place is particularly ideal for travellers who thrive on throngs of people or who want to hang out with suited Panamanians and their families. Music, crying, laughing kids and lots of activity are the general rule on weekends. Two small resorts with pools, showers, bars and various other services are located on site (see p 147). The beach fronting the Gorgona complex is less appealing because of the horrible barbed wire which was installed to stop intruders from entering the complex.

★★

Playa Coronado

This resort area, which lies along an interesting beach where black and white sand intermingle, is the site of many second homes belonging to wealthy Panamanians from the capital. Pretty villas surrounded by vibrant gardens overflowing with vegetation and exotic flowers line the road from the Interamericana and all the way to the beach. A "Halt, who goes there" attitude seems to prevail, though, as just a few kilometres beyond the Interamericana you will come upon a security gate. You will have to state your name and the reason for your visit. However, since all beaches in Panamá are public, after this checkpoint you may continue on your way.

A luxury hotel with a golf course, the Coronado Club Suites Resort (see p 148) opened several years ago just a few kilometres from the beach. It is a pleasant place for a drink or breakfast.

Unfortunately, the numerous villas that have been built bordering the beach have gradually made access to the beach difficult. Visitors must therefore look for an access path between two houses, which is not easy because most private lots are contiguous. One of the paths that is still accessible is near the Club Gaviota. Follow directions to the club and an IPAT sign just before it will indicate the way from there. For those who wish to quench their thirst by the sea, the friendly Club Gaviota (see p 148) offers a popular pub and pool at the western end of the beach. Although this is supposed to be a private members-only club, a small entry charge will get you in and even give you access to the swimming pool. Be aware, though, that the club closes at 5pm on weekdays and 7pm on weekends.

★

Playa San Carlos

Along with Playa Gorgona, this is probably the most popular beach along this part of the coast. After driving through the picturesque village of San Carlos, a tiny road leads to the shore where there is a restaurant run by IPAT (see p 39). A handful of palm trees line the waterfront beside a ribbon of beautiful white sand. Beachgoers have a lot of room on this wide beach, despite the crowds. Plus, just off the Interamericana, numerous little shops have everything you need for a picnic on the beach.

★★

Playa Río Mar

The waterfront on Playa Río Mar is not as wide, but the surrounding landscape of jagged cliffs and palm trees more than compensates. The sloping beach is blanketed with white sand with a few rocks and streams of black sand. A little river empties into the sea right next to the beach, making the setting particular charming. Though you may see a few people swimming, remember that it is not a good idea to swim in untreated freshwater because of the risk of infection from schistosomiasis (bilharziasis) bacteria. A resort on site has a few facilities, including a good restaurant with a view of the sea, *cabañas*, as well as a lovely patio and swimming pool (see p 148).

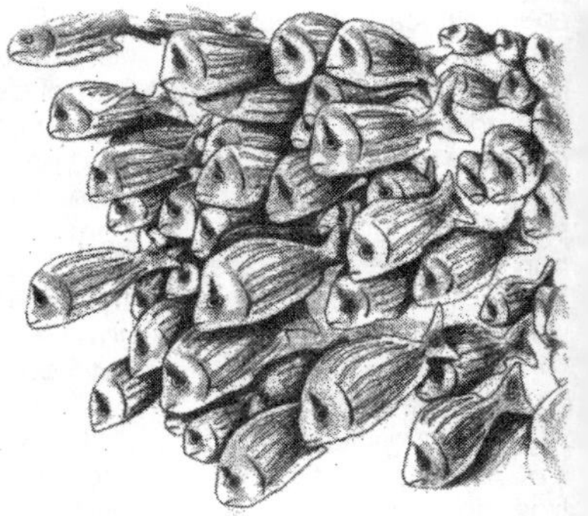

★

Playa Corona

Beyond Río Mar, there is endless white sand, framed by low cliffs and palm trees. However, the difficult access and the lack of services there are inconvenient. To reach the coast you have to go through the Playa Corona Hotel, since this whole section of the coast is lined with private homes which block access to the beach. By way of compensation, the hotel is surrounded by lush vegetation and a nice little restaurant (see p 151) and bar where you can enjoy fresh fruit juice or an inexpensive meal. A series of stairs leads right to the beach from the hotel's cliff top location.

★★★

Playa Santa Clara

Along with neighbouring Playa Farallón, Playa Santa Clara is probably the most delightful beach along this part of the coast. Lined with lovely homes, blossoming gardens and a small hotel complex with *cabañas*, the fine white sandy beach extends for several kilometres. Tourists in search of tranquility and a change of scenery will spend hours wandering along the coast in this idyllic spot far from the weekend vacationers. A wonderful place to rest and catch up on some reading.

★★

Playa Blanca

Following Playa Santa Clara, Playa Blanca is aptly named indeed, made up as it is of beautiful white sand. Like that of its neighbour, its beach is particularly extensive and the ideal spot for long walks. A huge resort, the Royal Decameron, has materialized here and the once-deserted beach is now popular with tourists. There are now various services as well as several lifeguards stationed on the beach, making swimming safer than in the past.

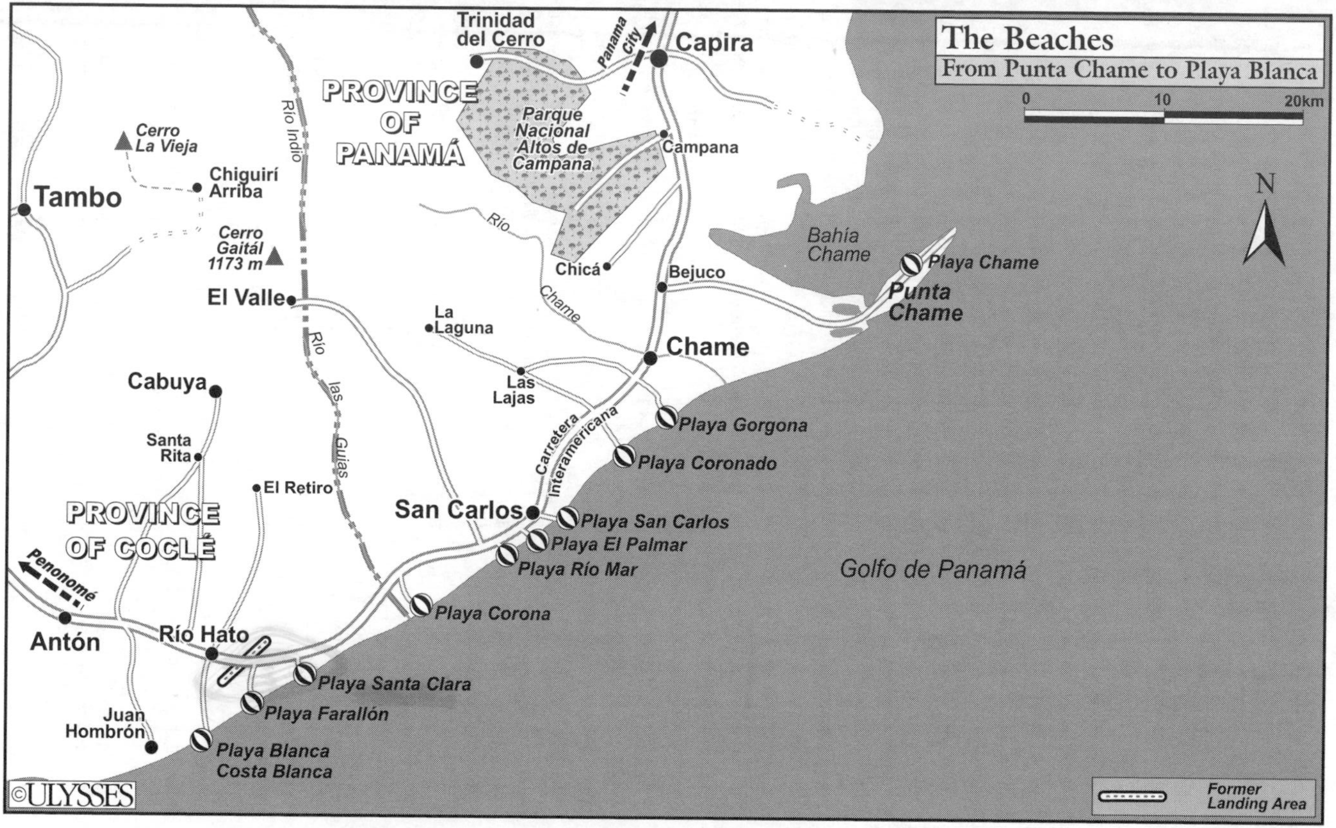
The Beaches
From Punta Chame to Playa Blanca
0
10
20km
N
Trinidad del Cerro
Panama City
Capira
PROVINCE OF PANAMÁ
Parque Nacional Altos de Campana
Campana
Cerro La Vieja
Chiguirí Arriba
Tambo
Cerro Gaitál 1173 m
Río Indio
Río Chame
Chicá
Bejuco
Bahía Chame
Playa Chame
Punta Chame
El Valle
La Laguna
Chame
Las Lajas
Río las Guias
Cabuya
Santa Rita
El Retiro
Carretera Interamericana
Playa Gorgona
Playa Coronado
San Carlos
Playa San Carlos
Playa El Palmar
Playa Río Mar
Golfo de Panamá
PROVINCE OF COCLÉ
Penonomé
Antón
Río Hato
Playa Corona
Playa Santa Clara
Playa Farallón
Juan Hombrón
Playa Blanca
Costa Blanca
©ULYSSES
Former Landing Area

Outdoor Activities

Hiking

★★★
Isla Taboga

Of the many hikes possible, we have chosen two which will allow you to see most of the island. But first a few tips:

• wear insect repellent: the mosquitoes can be bothersome in the undergrowth.

• do not forget bottled water, sunglasses and a hat.

• this island is home to many lizards, frogs and iguanas, many kinds of birds, and two types of snakes: the first is small, thin and slender, and almost looks like a dead branch, the second, the boa, can grow to an impressive size. Neither of these snakes is poisonous. In fact, they are rather cowardly, which means you probably won't even see one.

• avoid this island during the weekend, when it is literally overtaken by city residents and the beaches are strewn with litter.

Hike No. 1

This hike leads to the highest point on the island, Cerro Vigia (307 m), and offers splendid views of the island and Panama City in the distance. While the climb is not difficult, some effort is required. Allow a maximum of one hour to reach the summit. For this hike, begin at the central plaza, in the middle of the village. Take the street to the left of the church (going toward the centre of the square) and start climbing. You must first take some small village streets to get to the trail. Keep going up and away from the Hotel Taboga. The villagers can show you the way (ask for "*el sendero por el Cerro Vigia*").

Once you reach the base of the trail, walk to the old reservoir on your left (just past an overhanging house) then turn right. Keep going upwards to the next house and just in front of it climb the "steps" on the right. Keep following the main trail to the top. Hiking boots that cover the ankles are recommended for this hike.

Hike No. 2

Easier than the first hike, this one takes you along the coast. Begin facing the entrance to the Hotel Taboga and take the road to the left. After 50m, take the concrete road to the right. A few metres beyond this you will notice a bunker on the left (barely visible under leaves) and then shortly after a second bunker, also on the left. These bunkers were built by the Americans during the Second World War (don't forget the strategic importance of the canal!). Turn right, and take the dirt path facing the bunker, where there is a water pump that serves the Hotel Taboga.

The trail continues past a house and then opens onto a lovely, isolated beach. To return, retrace your steps to the second bunker and take the small trail opposite it, to the left of the trail. This trail, steep at the beginning (a rope makes the climb easier), leads through some dense vegetation. A short distance farther on, you will come to some rocks; with a little patience, where you can spot dozens of little black frogs with bright green spots. They are not poisonous, and you can even try to touch one. Don't forget, however, that they are a protected species and that it is strictly prohibited to take one with you.

The trail then reaches the main road to the hotel. Allow less than an hour to complete the tour.

★★
Parque Altos de Campana

This magnificent park, located 58km from the capital (see p 139), offers some excellent hiking opportunities.

Two lovely hikes can be organized: those who are prepared for a long hike can head off from the Interamericana and hike up to the park warden's office (at 6.1km); those who prefer shorter hikes can drive directly to the warden's office (the road is in very bad shape, strewn with potholes and rocks) and then hike to the summit from there (about 4.4km). Several unmarked trails depart from the summit. A four-wheel-drive vehicle is preferable for reaching the warden's office. Once there, ask for a map of the trails (unfortunately not always available). Hiking boots that cover your ankles are a good idea because there are venomous snakes in the park. Both hikes provide the opportunity to enjoy some terrific scenery, mostly made up of steep mountains. A vibrant palette of colour unfolds on these verdant slopes, dotted here and there by darker green trees and shrubs. Adding to the scenery are occasional glimpses of the Pacific Ocean. Don't forget that you need authorisation from ANAM *(☎244-0092)* to enter the park; otherwise, you can leave the modest sum of B/.3 at the guard post when it's open.

El Valle de Antón

El Valle is an ideal base for travellers looking to do some hiking. What better way to discover the wonders of the tropical forest, and keep fit at the same time? Be careful though, as the trails are rarely marked. Also, it is a good idea to enlist the services of a guide who can provide all sorts of information on the flora and fauna of the region... and also give you a chance to practise your Spanish! The locals are very friendly, and it's easy to find a guide.

Among the region's particularly educational hikes is the one to **El Macho Falls**. For a fee of B/.10, naturalist guides will bring you to the top of the falls on a path that passes many types of vegetation and where, with a bit of patience, you will be able to see a variety birds. The hike lasts approximately two hours and the path is quite easy for most people to follow.

Swimming

El Valle de Antón

Pozos de Aguas Termales
B/.1
every day 9am to 5pm
Who would have believed that a hot bath in these climes could be pleasant? For a change from the climactic "rigours" of El Valle, a little dip in the Pozos de Aguas Termales will do you a world of good. The little pools of hot water (40°C) are fed by a volcanic spring a stone's throw from the Río Antón. According to locals, the murky waters possess curative powers. Say goodbye to arthritis, rheumatism and other joint disorders—the important thing is to believe!

To get to these miraculous waters, follow the main road through El Valle, heading towards the church and take the first left just after the supermercado at the entrance to the village. Continuing straight ahead, there will be signs leading the way to the waters.

Snorkelling, Scuba Diving and Cruises

Isla Taboga

Hotel Taboga
about 300m to the right of the pier
☎250-2122 or 264-6096
☎264-1748
Scuba gear can be rented for a reasonable price on this lovely, white-sand beach. On site you can safely explore the shores and rich marine wildlife of tiny Isla de Morro de Taboga. And for about B/.5 you can also use the hotel's facilities (shower, beach shacks, etc.) and get an item from the menu (drink or dish) equal to the fee. Unfortunately the island's beaches are packed on weekends and the cleanliness of the area suffers accordingly.

Isla Contadora

Punta Galeón Resort
☎214-3719 or 214-3720
Beyond the airstrip you will find the Punta Galeón Resort, where you will find everything you need for a host of aquatic activities. Besides renting the necessary equipment for scuba diving (wetsuit, tank, mask, weights, flippers, etc.), the resort offers various excursions with or without a guide.

Las Perlas Sailing Corp.
near the Contadora Resorts hotel
☎**250-4214**
The owner of the Cabañas de Contadora (see p 145) offers various water sports at reasonable rates. Among the packages offered, sports enthusiasts will particularly appreciate the 4hr ocean excursion, with two snorkelling stops to discover the marine flora (B/.35/pers), and adventurers can treat themselves to a cruise exploring seven of the archipelago's islands (B/.35/pers).

Golf

Playa Coronado

Coronado Club Suites Resort
Playa Coronado, on the main road leading to the beach, after the guardhouse and just before the"bombeiros" station, turn left at Avenida P. Prieta and continue for 1km
☎***240-4444 or 264-3164***
USA and Canada
☎***800-267-6465***
Close to the beautiful beach at Coronado, this 18-hole course is a golf lover's dream. It is a part of the hotel and therefore normally reserved for the use of clients or club members, nevertheless the manager may allow access to outsiders for a fee.

Motorcycling

Isla Contadora

Right next to the airfield, near the pier, is a small counter where you can rent motorcycles and scooters *(expect to pay B/.20 for two hours or B/.45 for 24 hours).* This is a great way to explore the back roads of the island and check out all the beaches.

Personal Watercraft

Isla Contadora

Mar y Diversión
Playa Larga, close to the Contadora Resort Hotel
If you are a personal watercraft enthusiast and not on a tight budget, do not pass up an opportunity to go to Mar y Diversión where there are beach buggies as well as Sea-doos for B/.60 per hour.

Las Perlas Sailing Corp.
near the Contadora Resorts hotel
☎***250-4214***
For all scuba-diving rentals or a ride in a personal watercraft, contact the owner of the Cabañas de Contadora hotel (see p 145). Count on spending B/.60/ per hour or B/.35/ for 30min per person. For those looking to explore part of the archipelago by personal watercraft with a guide, that can be arranged for B/.35 per person (two passengers per watercraft).

Fishing

Around Panama City

Cafetería Parque El Lago
every day 10am to 9pm
Located 40minutes from the Panama City and 1.8 km west of the small village of Capira, near the Interamericana
Cafetería Parque El Lago offers the bounty of a large artificial lake full of fish. You can fish *(B/.0.50 per pound)* along with other Panamanian fishing enthusiasts. You can also rent a boat for B/.5 per half-hour. A good restaurant with a large patio adjoins this neat little spot.

Isla Contadora

Las Perlas Sailing Corp.
near the Contadora Resorts hotel
☎***250-4214***
Fans of this sport should contact Henry, the owner of the Cabañas de Contadora hotel (see p 145), who offers half-day and full-day fishing packages at reasonable rates. Count on spending B/.400 per day for a maximum of five people or half that sum for a half-day. Taking part in this excursion as a spectator will cost you B/.20.

Canopy Tours

El Valle de Antón

Canopy Adventures
B/.40
every day 8am to 10am and 1pm to 3pm
☎983-6547 or 264-5720
www.canopytower.com/adventure
If you are a budding Tarzan and not afraid of heights, you may be be tempted by an excursion to the El Macho Falls, the only trip of its kind in Panamá. Here, you can swing between tree tops, secured by a harness and pulley system. You must first hoist yourself up to a platform perched on a tree top, then glide along a set of cables from one tree to another, all the while watching the vegetation whizzing by beneath your feet. Clearly, this adventure is for people in good physical shape and demands suitable footwear (running or walking shoes). Those subject to vertigo should stay away. To get to the falls, (see p 138).

Horseback Riding

Sr Victor Muñoz
☎993-6360
El Valle is a wonderful spot for riding. This pretty, garden-filled town is set in a valley framed by mountains and enjoys warm temperatures year-round. Here, you can rent horses for B/.5 per hour. You can also hire a guide for B/.10 for 2hrs. In four hours you can see the Chorro del Macho, Las Mosas and Las Piedras Pintadas (petroglyphs painted by indigenous peoples.) (see p 138).

Accommodations

Isla Taboga

Hotel Chu
$
ℜ
on the main street , 200m to the left of the pier, take the road going up
☎250-2035 or 263-6933
Hotel Chu is a charming old colonial-style hotel, made completely of wood. Rudimentary comfort (badly soundproofed, no private baths or screens), although each room has a small balcony with a fine view.

Hotel Taboga
$$$
pb, hw, ≡, ℜ, *tv,* #
about 300m to the right of the pier, Taboga, Apdo 55-0357
☎269-1187 or 264-6096
☎264-1748
⇄223-0116 or 223-5739
A fine hotel on a beautiful private beach facing the small island of Morro de Taboga. The rooms are only adequately comfortable, but tastefully decorated. People not staying at the hotel may use the beach for B/.5, which includes a shower, changing room, and a drink or snack worth the same price as the entrance fee. Snorkelling equipment for rent.

Isla Contadora

Villa Ernesto
$$ *bkfst incl* .
Apartado 55-0398, Pantilla
☎250-4112
⇄250-4029
A charming German couple runs the Villa Ernesto near Playa Caracol. Eduard and Marie Ernst rent out two pleasant and well-maintained rooms to tourists passing through. Besides a warm welcome, guests enjoy an excellent German breakfast, a real treat! There are also lounge chairs in the small flower garden. Besides German of course, the owners speak English and Spanish.

Cabañas de Contadora
$$ bkfst incl.
pb, hw, ⊗, *tv, K*
☎/⇄250-4214
www.cabanasdecontadora.com
The Cabañas de Contadora, are only a few minutes' walking distance from the beach are the Cabañas de Contadora. A couple of French expats rent four small studios with a functional, yet comfortable layout. The only drawback is the lack of space, though admittedly compensated by rates that are very reasonable for Contadora. At press time, two furnished apartments with two double rooms and mezzanine were under construction and should therefore be available in 2003. Free transportation is provided to the *cabañas*. Bicycles and snorkelling gear are also

available to guests at no extra charge. What's more, Henry, the owner, organizes various nautical activities, from cruises to scuba diving (see Las Perlas Sailing Corp., p 144).

Casa del Sol
$$ bkfst incl.
pb, hw
☎250-4212
www.panama-isla-contadora.com/index.html
The young owners of this small bed and breakfast, set in a lovely ochre villa surrounded by a pleasant garden, offer a single, attractively decorated room. Bicycles are made available to guests at no extra charge and various water-sports packages are offered as well.

Villa Romantica
$$$-$$$$
pb, hw, ≡, ℜ
☎250-4067
⇄250-4078
www.contadora-villa-romantica.com
Located near a beautiful white-sand beach, Villa Romantica hotel offers four guestrooms housed in a private villa. While two of them have an ocean view, the remaining two look out on a pleasant garden. The decor is modern, but more kitsch than "romantic." Nevertheless, they are perfectly comfortable and the beauty of the surroundings quickly banishes such trifles from your mind. For large families, a fully equipped guesthouse is available. It is somewhat set back from the beach and can accommodate up to 10 people. The owners rent out equipment for both water- and land-based activities (bicycles and all-terrain vehicles).

Contadora Resort
$$$$ all incl.
pb, hw, ≡, ≈, ⊙, ℜ, *tv*
Apdo 9728, Zona 4
☎264-1510 or 264-1498
⇄264-1178
www.hotelcontadora.com
The Contadora Resort overlooks the most beautiful beach on the island is the Contadora Resort. Its 354 rooms are housed in several buildings surrounded by gardens. Though all the rooms are comfortable, some stand out for their lovely decor. Furthermore, because of the extreme dryness which dominates the island periodically, the hotel seems to have difficulty providing a steady supply of running water and its purification system is not up to par. There are four restaurants, a nightclub, a casino, a gym, two pools (one with a bar) and showers close by.

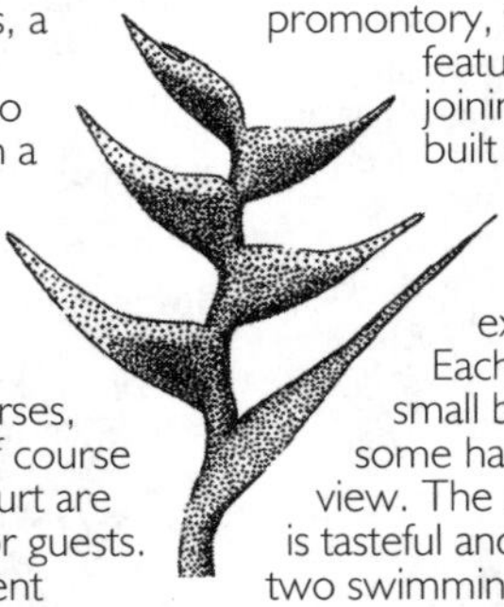

In addition to aquafitness courses, a nine-hole golf course and a tennis court are also available for guests. The management seems to prefer the all-inclusive formula offered by travel agents. Travellers without reservations can nevertheless get a weekend pass *(B/.180 per person; two nights)* including meals, accommodation, and a variety of services.

All packages provide guests with unlimited access to snorkelling, badminton, volleyball, pedal-boats and kayaking equipment. Those in search of peace and quiet should avoid the rooms around the pool, since the music that accompanies the aquafitness classes is loud and the pool bar stays busy well into the night. Note that a small beach at the other end of the hotel is reserved for nudists. Finally, there is a doctor at the hotel to tend to your health concerns. This hotel will delight those in search of entertainment, beach action and fun evenings.

Punta Galéon Resort
$$$$-$$$$$ all incl.
pb, hw, ≡, ≈, ℜ, *tv*
☎214-3719 or 214-3720
☎250-4134
⇄214-3721 or 250-4135
www.puntagaleon.com
Located near the airstrip, at the top of a small, rocky promontory, this hotel features 48 adjoining concrete-built units, topped with straw roofs for a touch of exoticism. Each room has a small balcony and some have an ocean view. The units' decor is tasteful and includes two swimming pools, which are surrounded by lovely gardens. Overhanging the rocks, a large wooden patio dotted with tables and chairs allows guests to gaze out at the ocean and the beach while admiring the sunset. On the small beach below the hotel, a bar and several deck chairs are also at guests' disposal.

Isla San José

Iacienda del Mar
$$$$
b, hw, ≡, ⊗, ≈, ℜ, ℝ, #, ⌂,
269-6613
264-1787
The Hacienda del Mar esort is made up of about 0 wooden cottages listributed throughout 'arious settings, each nore exotic than the ›ther. All *cabañas* feature balcony and a view of he ocean and the tropical ainforest. The rooms are lecorated with care and comfort in mind. The most uxurious among them are ir conditioned. In the ›uilding housing the recep- ion area, an attractively lecorated lounge with bar nd pool table provides a elaxing haven. For those vho wish to work out, a auna and small gym are lso on site, as is a fabulous wimming pool with an ›cean view. Finally, a estaurant specializing in ish and seafood, all of vhich is freshly culled from he surrounding waters, ounds out the resort. Access to this little corner of paradise will cost you a ninimum of B/.250 to 3/.300/day, not including neals.

Because the Hacienda del Mar is the only commer- ial enterprise on the sland, visitors must rely on for all transportation, ood or water-sports ervices. Moreover, given he particularly high prices ere, the most "economi- al" solution is an all-inclu- ive package purchased hrough a travel agency.

Punta Chame to Playa Blanca

Cabañas Playa Gorgona
$$-$$$ Mon-Fri
$$$-$$$$ Sat, Sun and holidays
≈, K
Playa Gorgona, 2.2km from the Interamericana, to the right of the road when heading to the beach
☎269-2558 or 269-2433
⇄223-1218
www.propanama.com/gorgona
Despite their modern appearance, these *cabañas*, rented out by the El Prado restaurant, are not particularly comfortable and are poorly soundproofed. Music, laughing, yelling and loud children are guaranteed, but a friendly and charming Panamanian family atmosphere more than makes up for it. By opting to stay here during the week and outside public or school holidays, you'll enjoy quieter surroundings. Unfortunately, the atrocious wire fence separating the small resort from the beach sometimes makes it more akin to an army camp than a holiday centre. Guests have the use of a private parking lot.

Hotel Gorgona Jayes Resorts
$$ Mon to Fri
$$$ bkfst incl. Sat Sun and holidays
ℜ, ≈, ≡, hw, tv
Playa Gorgona, 2km from the Interamericana via an unpaved road
☎223-7775 or 240-6095
⇄264-3487
This small, simple hotel complex offers 44 equipped rooms set around a charming interior garden. Their decor is a bit old and could use some sprucing up. Athletes will enjoy the tennis and volleyball courts and the mast for *pelota basca*, while party types will delight in the nightclub and the *bohío* with its bar and large terrace. Part of the facilities, including the pool and showers, are located next to the beach, about a 10min walk from the hotel. The staff is particularly attentive.

Hotel Playa Corona
$$-$$$
pb, hw, ≡, *ℜ, K, tv*
Playa Corona, 2km from the Interamericana
☎240-8037
Set in a particularly pleasant location, this hotel overlooks the beach and offers several types of accommodation, from small rooms with two beds to apartments with two or three rooms. There are also suites and trailers for those on a tighter budget, all of which are surrounded by verdant grounds.

Cabañas La Veraneras
$$-$$$
sb, ⊗, *K,* ℝ, *ℜ, tv*
Playa Santa Clara
☎993-3313 or 230-1415
⇄993-3313
The Cabañas La Veraneras are little houses perched on a hilltop that can accommodate two to six people. The kitchenette and living room are on the ground floor while the bedrooms are on the second floor. The *cabañas* offer peace and quiet, and a small terrace with a view of the sea in the distance.

Hammocks are also available. Good price/quality ratio.

Club Gaviota
$$-$$$$
pb, hw, ≡, ≈, *tv*
Playa Coronado, from the main road leading to the beach, turn right after the chapel, then follow the signs for the Club; Apdo 5929, Panamá 2
☎227-4929
⇄227-4969
In addition to renting eight pleasantly decorated *cabañas*, comfortably fitted out and located a stone's throw from the ocean, Club Gaviota also rents out second homes in the area. There are many fully equipped homes available in a particularly quiet and lush setting. Although this is a rather expensive option, it may appeal to those travelling in a group. All of the club's equipment and services are available to clients.

Hotel Playa Río Mar
$$$
pb, hw, ≈, ≡, ℜ, #
Playa Río Mar, 3km from the Interamericana
☎223-0192 or 240-8027
⇄264-2270
Located in a particularly pleasant setting on the top of a small cliff near the beach, Hotel Playa Río Mar rents out simple and comfortable semi-detached *cabañas*. Some are poorly soundproofed, so ask for a *cabaña* away from the restaurant and the noise. For a fee of B/.5 per family, visitors can use the showers as well as the locker room; pool access costs B/.2 per adult.

Motel Punta Chame
$$$
pb, ≡, ℜ, #
on the left, at the end of the road leading to the point
☎264-4036 or 223-1747
☎264-7560
Here all kinds of lodging is available, including small, basic cabins *(B/.60)*, small houses with living rooms and kitchenettes *(B/.70-75)*, and a villa for four people with a private pool *(B/.80)*. Some are along the beach and offer a lovely view of the bay.

Apartamentos Río Lajas
$$$
pb, ℝ, *K,* #, ≡, *tv*
head towards Playa Coronada, then follow the signs to Club Gaviota
☎220-1863 or 220-2447
Fully equipped studios overlooking the beach lie in a particularly calm, verdant setting. Ideal for those in search of rest and relaxation. The beach is accessible through a pretty flower garden, and the staff is friendly.

Cabañas Las Sirenas
$$$ for five people
$$$$ for seven people
based on a two night minimum
pb, ≡, *tv, K*
Playa Santa Clara, 3km from the Interamericana
in Panama City
☎263-8771
⇄263-7860
in Santa Clara
☎993-3235
This small hotel complex with 11 semi-detached units is located in a beautiful flowery setting, next to the beach. The decor in the small houses is tasteful and the landscaping is particularly well done. The kitchenettes are well equipped but there is no hot water. For the setting and facilities, this is a good deal. There is no restaurant on site, but there are two supermarkets (*supermercados*) close by so you can stock up for a reasonable price. The first one is located at the intersection of the Interamericana and the main road leading to the beach; the second is in Río Hato, about 8km west on the Interamericana.

Coronado Club Suites Resorts
$$$$
$$$$$ all incl.
pb, hw, ≡, ≈, *tv,* ℜ, ⊙
Playa Coronado, on the main road leading to the beach, past the guard post and before the bombeiros station, turn left on Avenida P. Prieta for 1km, Apartado 4381, Panamá 5
☎240-4444 or 264-3164
from North America
☎800-267-6465
⇄223-8513 or 240-4380
www.coronadoresort.com
Coronado Club Suites is a resort with 76 suites, all furnished with a large living room with sofa and dining table. The bedroom is cleverly separated from the rest of the suite by a series of shutters, and even has a safe. The combination of modern and bamboo furniture makes for a harmonious and pleasant decor. Though a large window overlooks the garden, the room could use a terrace. The bathroom is well equipped but the harsh fluorescent lighting and noisy fan are bothersome. While the all-inclusive plan is offered at a seemingly attractive price, it is not particularly worthwhile because too many extras are added to it.

Among the various facilities available are two large pools, an exercise room with trainer, a spa, a tennis court and a golf course. Also, small whirlpool baths scattered throughout the blossoming gardens provide private relaxation. A casino will delight gaming enthusiasts, and shows are regularly presented for those who like to stay out late. These occasionally showcase well-known folklore performances.

Since the hotel is quite far from the beach, a shuttle transports guests along a bumpy road to the El Fogón bar *(Mon to Thu 9:30am to 5:30pm, Fri to Sun until 6pm)*. This charming *bohío* is right by the beach and has a restaurant (with a limited selection of dishes) and a small pool. Even if you aren't staying at the Coronado Club Suites Resort, check out this great spot, and enjoy a good meal (see p 152) or a refreshing drink on the poolside terrace.

The Shangri La
$$$$$
pb, hw, ≡, ≈, *tv*
Playa Coronado, Apdo 8357, Panamá 7
Mon to Fri
☎223-8597 or 223-0895
Sat
☎264-6317
⇄269-0633
The Shangri La is an interesting form of lodging for families or small groups. Overlooking the beach and framed by greenery, the four villas have large glass windows looking out onto the gardens and the sea. Each villa features two storeys and has three bedrooms, two bathrooms, direct beach access and a shoreside terrace. There is also a small pool available for those who prefer not to swim in the sea. In order to benefit from reduced rates, go during the week, when prices can drop by as much as 50%.

Royal Hotel Decameron
$$$$$ all incl.
pb, hw, ≡, ≈, ℜ
☎214-3535
⇄264-3539
www.decameron.com
This large resort houses over 500 rooms distributed throughout several buildings, right on the Playa Blanca beach. The rooms, though simply furnished, feature a pleasant decor, and most have a balcony with a lovely ocean view. Ask for a room in a building right by the beach as the resort is spread out over more than 1 km and some buildings are slightly set back from the coast. Guests can take part in various activities such as dance and aerobics classes, and use the establishment's sports equipment, including snorkelling gear, kayaks and bicycles. Children's recreational activities are also offered. Seven swimming pools, eight bars, a dance club and no fewer than six restaurants round out this mega-resort. Here, you can sample everything from Panamanian, Thai or Japanese food to seafood dishes and simple grilled meats. With shows held nightly, it goes without saying that this place will primarily suit those with a liking for both daytime and night-time entertainment. Various excursion packages are also available to guests.

El Valle de Antón

Hotel Greco
$
pb, hw, ≡, ℜ, #, ≈
in El Valle on the right side of the main road at the entrance to the village
☎983-6149
Small *cabañas* in a pretty, natural setting. A simple but clean hotel.

Cabañas Potosí
$$
pb
☎983-6181
These small, simple cabins are located in a lovely setting, and are ideal for travellers on a tight budget.

Hotel Club Campestre
$$-$$$
pb, hw, ⊗, ♯, *tv*, ℜ
Calle El Hato, at the entrance to the village, on the right side; shortly after passing the *supermercado*, take the second road to your right
☎983-6146
☎/⇄983-6460
The somewhat passé Club Campestre has rooms with various levels of comfort. While those in the main building are dark, inadequately soundproofed and less expensive, those in the new building are comfortable, well-lit and have a rather pleasant decor. Unfortunately, the bathrooms are too small and lack privacy because their windows look out directly onto the passageway leading to the rooms. Although the hotel claims to have a pool, during our visit it had been neglected and looked

more like a swamp... Also, the old-fashioned restaurant with its outdated style was reminiscent of a large school cafeteria and not conducive to convivial dining. Despite these inconveniences, the hotel is acceptable thanks its lush green environment and impressive mountains nearby. Speaking of impressive, you can also have a look at the *ranas doradas,* or "golden frogs," for which the area is famous, in a (too) small cage to the right of the hotel entrance.

The Cabañas Gysell
$$-$$$
sb, hw, ⊗
at the entrance to the village, on the right side after the *supermercado,* corner Calle El Hato and Av. Principal
☎983-6507 or 232-6604
Located at the entrance to the village, the Cabañas Gysell offers a few rooms that can accommodate two to six people. It is clean, relatively comfortable and quiet, despite its proximity to the main road. The Deco is adequate but very basic.

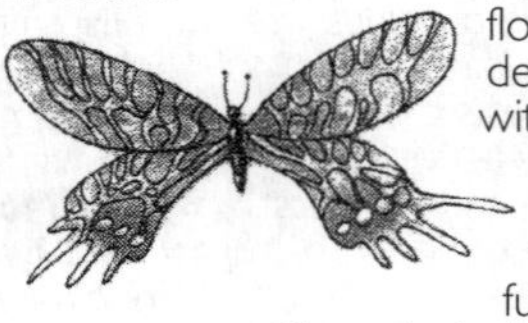

Los Capitanes
$$$-$$$$
sb, hw, tv, ⊗, ℜ
Calle de la Cooperativa, Apdo 87-4381, Panamá 7
☎983-6080
⇄983-6505
www.panama.com/loscapitanes
Whether in the main circular building or one of the outbuildings, this hotel's bedrooms will charm you. There are many types of accommodations offered here, from rooms for two people to apartments for four with a separate day room. The main building, which also houses a restaurant features rooms with small but pleasant balconies. Regardless of where you stay, expect tastefully decorated and comfortable rooms. In addition to the tranquility, visitors can enjoy the view of the beautiful, well-maintained gardens with the mountains in the background.

Hotel Rincón Vallero
$$$-$$$$ bkfst incl
sb, hw, ⊗, *tv,* ♯, ℜ, ≈
at the entrance to the village, just after the *supermercado*
☎983-6175 or 226-7554
⇄226-6567
Bearing a curious resemblance to a *hacienda*, the Hotel Rincón Vallero consists of several lodgings within a small flowered garden, complete with a small fish pond where ducks and fish peacefully cohabit. Charmingly decorated rooms can accommodate two to four people. Unfortunately, they are somewhat poorly soundproofed and their proximity to one another as well as to the restaurant and pool, does not help. In addition, the mattresses are not very comfortable. These little inconveniences detract from the comfort of this establishment, but its country charm compensates for them. The hotel is at least worth a look.

Restaurants

Around Capira

Cafeteria Parque El Lago
$$$
every day 10am to 9pm
located on the Interamericana, 1.8km west of Capira
The Cafeteria Parque El Lago is a popular meeting place for fishermen who frequent the artificial lake. Inside a quaint, gabled building decorated with pretty tables and wood and leather chairs, the cafeteria has a distinctly country atmosphere. Tasty meat dishes and *ceviche* or *corvina* for B/.10 each await at the counter. For a quick snack, try the delicious *bollo de maiz* (corn mousse, enveloped in a banana leaf) or a plate of fried *platanos* for as little as B/.5. For those who wish to sample some of the lake's offerings (duck, oysters and fish), a pretty terrace with a view of the lake provides a wonderful setting. The staff is very courteous and friendly.

Isla Taboga

Restaurant Chu
$
on the main street of the village 200m to the left of the pier, head up the road
☎250-2035 or 263-6933
This small restaurant is located in the hotel of the same name, overlooking the beach. In a lovely old-fashioned colonial setting, you can enjoy traditional fish and chicken dishes on

the pleasant terrace. Good fruit juices too!

Restaurant Hotel Taboga
$
300m to the right of the pier
☎250-2122 or 264-6096
☎264-1748
In addition to the hotel's restaurant, which serves a selection of Panamanian and international dishes, the hotel has a cafeteria where you can order simpler meals.

Isla Contadora

Restaurante Romantico
$$$
☎250-4067
Housed in a villa, Restaurante Romantico offers classic yet conventional international and Panamanian fare. Its main asset is its patio, which, though simply furnished is surrounded by wonderful vegetation and offers a pleasant view of the golden beach and the ocean.

Restaurante Gerald's
$$$$
☎250-4061
near the Las Perlas Sailing Corp. and the golf club
If you're looking for more elaborate cuisine, head to Restaurante Gerald's, where a German-born chef whips up delicious fish- and seafood-based dishes. Grilled scampi in white-wine sauce, garlic lobster or Panamanian-style fish of the day are just a few examples of the dishes offered on the menu. And those who prefer meat or poultry can indulge in the chicken fillet in curry sauce, beef fillet with pepper sauce or grilled pork chops with mushroom-and-onion sauce. In short, there's something for everyone! While this is not exactly fine cuisine, the selections are good and the place is particularly appealing, set beneath a *bohío* surrounded by a pleasant garden.

Punta Chame to Playa Blanca

Restaurante Hotel Playa Corona
$
Playa Corona, 2km from the Interamericana
☎240-8037
This small beachfront restaurant in the hotel, with its kitschy decor, serves simple, classic Panamanian cuisine in a particularly lush and leafy setting.

Los Camisones
$$
every day 10am to 10pm
4.8km west of the turnoff for Playa Corona, turn right off the Interamericana on an unpaved road
Located on a hill, away from the Interamericana, Los Camisones serves Panamanian cuisine under a pleasant *bohío* decorated with plants and flowers.

Bar Restaurante Punta Chame
$$
On the left at the end of the road leading to the point
This is a small restaurant in an enchanting setting, with palm trees, a good view and a covered terrace. The interior of the restaurant is charming, with orchids on every table. The *langostinos al ajillo* or *a la Parilla (B/.10)* is good, as is the steak *(B/.6)* and *pollo al horno (barely B/.5)*. For die-hard fast food lovers a *queso hamburguesa* is available for B/.3.50. Finally, enjoy a good *flan de la casa* to finish up a meal that is not quite gourmet, but certainly filling.

Gorgona Jayes Resort
$$
2km from the Interamericana on an unpaved road
☎223-7775 or 240-6095
The restaurant at the Gorgona Jayes Resort serves basic Panamanian cuisine, and it is essentially for the pretty terrace adjoining a small flower garden that people come here. The staff is courteous and friendly.

Los Ches
$
to the right on the Interamericana going west, just before the turnoff for Playa Coronado
This small, charming, well-decorated restaurant has tables set on a covered terrace. It serves simple cuisine (grilled chicken, spaghetti, etc.) In generous portions.

Parrillada Malibu
$$
Thu-Tue 8am to 11pm
at the intersection of the Interamericana and the turnoff for Playa Coronado
Located on the left side of the main road leading to Playa Coronado, the small restaurant has a large terrace covered with tiles and surrounded by trees and flowering plants. Among the various meals on the menu, you can try *corvina* (served with many

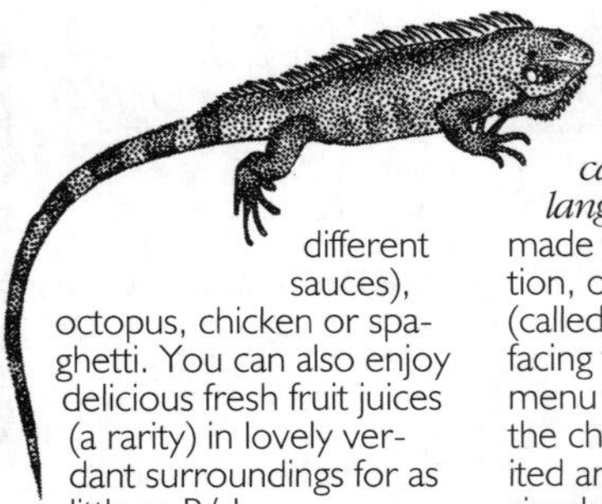

different sauces), octopus, chicken or spaghetti. You can also enjoy delicious fresh fruit juices (a rarity) in lovely verdant surroundings for as little as B/.1.

Club Gaviota
$$
Playa Coronado, on the main road leading to the beach, turn right at the chapel and follow the signs for the club; Apartado 5929, Panamá 2
☎225-1559 or 227-4969
This private club with attractive pool is a lovely place to enjoy a meal or just a drink. It offers simple but delicious chicken, fish and seafood dishes. The restaurant is tastefully furnished and the bar is located under a traditional *bohío*. The setting, overlooking the beach, offers unending, spectacular views of the coast, much to the delight of photographers. Since access is reserved for members of the club, an admission fee of B/.5 is charged. Here courteous and friendly staff do their best to put you at ease.

Río Mar
$$
every day, 9am to 11pm
Playa Río Mar, 3km from the Interamericana
☎223-0192 or 240-8027
With a solid reputation among Panamanians for its seafood, the Río Mar offers a variety of dishes served with rice in a lovely setting. Savour the *camarones* or *langostinos* that have made this place's reputation, on the large terrace (called the Rancho Bar), facing the sea. Though the menu seems extensive, the choice is actually limited and the dishes are simply prepared.

Las Veraneras
$$
every day 8am to 7pm
Playa Santa Clara
☎993-3313
The pleasant Las Veraneras restaurant welcomes its guests beneath a giant beachside *palapa* reached from the hotel (see p 147) by a series of stairs and a long footbridge. Although there is nothing fancy on the menu (mostly fish and seafood), the view of the ocean from the lovely beach makes dining here very pleasant.

Restaurante Don Jacobo
$$$
every day 8am to 10pm
turn left off the Interamericana at the *Centro Turistico Salud y Felicidad* sign shortly after the turnoff for Playa Santa Clara
☎993-3536
For travellers who crave the sea's bounty, the Restaurante Don Jacobo, also a fish and seafood wholesaler, has the distinct advantage of stocking exceptionally fresh goods and a wide selection of dishes. The restaurant has a lovely covered terrace with finely crafted leather chairs. This is a good address to remember for a meal and a drink, and is close to the Interamericana.

The Club and La Terraza
$$$$
Tue-Sun 6pm to 10pm
Playa Coronado, on the main road leading to the beach, past the guards station and before the bombeiros station, turn left on Avenida P. Prieta over 1km
☎240-4444 or 264-3164
Set in a residential neighbourhood in the heart of the Coronado Club Suites Resort complex, the Club restaurant serves elaborate cuisine. *Yuca sanchoco, calamares a la romana, ceviche, rollitos de pato a la naranja, corvina en salsa de coco, lenguado a la champaña, medallones de langosta en finas herbas* or *centallo gratinado* are just some of the possibilities.

A half-moon shaped window offers a view of the gardens from the enjoyably decorated dining room. Service is professional and attentive.

For those who prefer a lighter meal, **La Terraza** *(every day 6am to 10pm)* is another restaurant in the Coronado Club Suites that serves international and Panamanian cuisine. This is also an interesting place for breakfast. Besides the fact that both restaurants are set in particularly luxurious setting, they might be considered the best restaurants of the region.

El Valle de Antón

Restaurante Hotel Greco
$
on the right side of the main street, at the entrance to the village
☎983-6149
This small, unpretentious restaurant offers a daily menu of local cuisine. The choice is limited (only three or four dishes), so it is better to arrive early.

Restaurante Santa Librada
$
to the right when coming from San Carlos, between the Intel and the post office
The Restaurante Santa Librada boasts a good reputation for its Panamanian cuisine and its friendly service.

Los Capitanes
$$
Calle de la Cooperativa
☎983-6080
Set in a circular, open-air room, the Los Capitanes hotel's restaurant is worth the detour. For less than B/.10, guests can enjoy a meal including soup, main dish and dessert. In addition to typical Panamánian foods, the restaurant also serves German specialities, as the owner is of German descent. Good home-style cooking. After dining, you can relax in the garden and admire the majestic mountains encircling the valley in the distance.

Rincón Vallero
$$$
at the entrance to the village; past the *supermercado*
☎983-6175
Facing a garden with a fish pond, the Rincón Vallero hotel's restaurant features classic Panamánian dishes. There are no surprises and the prices are a bit high, but the country-style decor is quite pleasant.

Entertainment

Isla Contadora

Captain Morgan's Beach Bar
Mon and Tue, Thu-Sat 3pm to 3am, happy hour from 9pm to 10pm
For a beer and a great beach-side location, head to Captain Morgan's Beach Bar where, besides a guaranteed good time in the evening, you can see the planes taking off. The bar is actually located just down from the end of the airfield. Lots of fun!

El Galeón
$$$
every day 3pm to 10pm
on the Paseo de los Guaymie, to the northwest of the airport runway
The small El Galeón restaurant has a pool table as well as a small terrace with a view of the sea.

Shopping

Isla Contadora

Playa Canoa
every day 9am to noon and 3pm to 4pm
Playa Canoa
Shell collectors won't want to miss the Playa Canoa shop, where for about B/.10 you can pick up some fine pieces. Very pretty sculptures created by the Guaymie people are on sale, though they are pricey.

El Valle de Antón

If you are passing through El Valle on a Sunday, don't miss the opportunity to go to the **Mercado Artesanal** *(Sun 7am to 5pm)*. Here, people, mostly Indigenous, from the surrounding countryside come to sell soapstone sculptures, rugs, sweaters, pottery, hats, leather items, baskets and many other crafts. There is also a wide selection of orchids. This market will appeal to those who want to bring back a few souvenirs without spending too much.

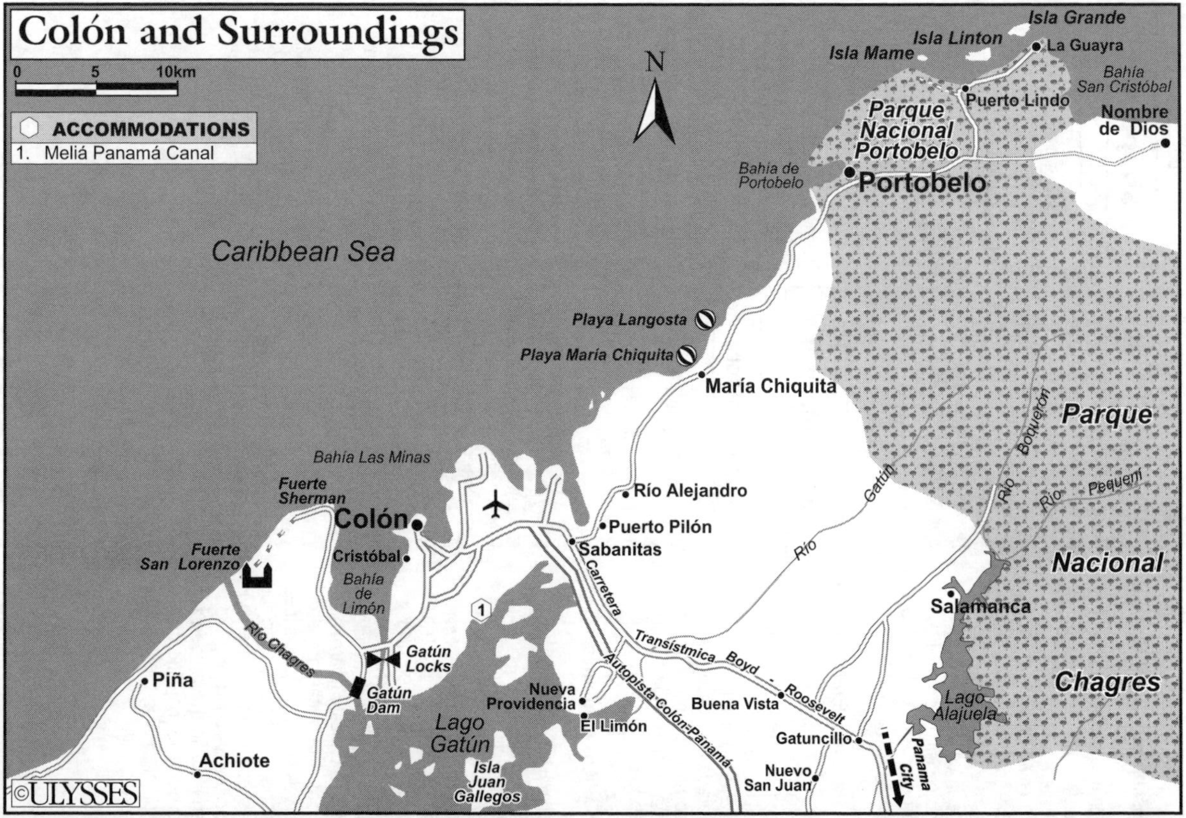
Colón and Surroundings
0
5
10km
ACCOMMODATIONS
1. Meliá Panamá Canal
N
Caribbean Sea
Isla Grande
Isla Linton
Isla Mame
La Guayra
Bahía San Cristóbal
Puerto Lindo
Nombre de Dios
Parque Nacional Portobelo
Bahía de Portobelo
Portobelo
Playa Langosta
Playa María Chiquita
María Chiquita
Parque Nacional Chagres
Río Boquerón
Río Pequení
Río Gatún
Bahía Las Minas
Fuerte Sherman
Colón
Río Alejandro
Puerto Pilón
Sabanitas
Fuerte San Lorenzo
Cristóbal
Bahía de Limón
Carretera Transístmica Boyd - Roosevelt
Autopista Colón-Panamá
Salamanca
Río Chagres
Gatún Locks
Gatún Dam
Piña
Nueva Providencia
El Limón
Buena Vista
Lago Gatún
Lago Alajuela
Gatuncillo
Panama City
Isla Juan Gallegos
Achiote
Nuevo San Juan
©ULYSSES

Province of Colón

The Province of Colón (pop. 168,000) has a glorious past, for the Central American isthmus was "discovered" here.

It was also the site of the first colonial settlements in Central America: Nombre de Dios and Portobelo on the Atlantic coast. Because these two towns were linked to the Pacific coast by overland trails, significant trade developed with the mother country, Spain.

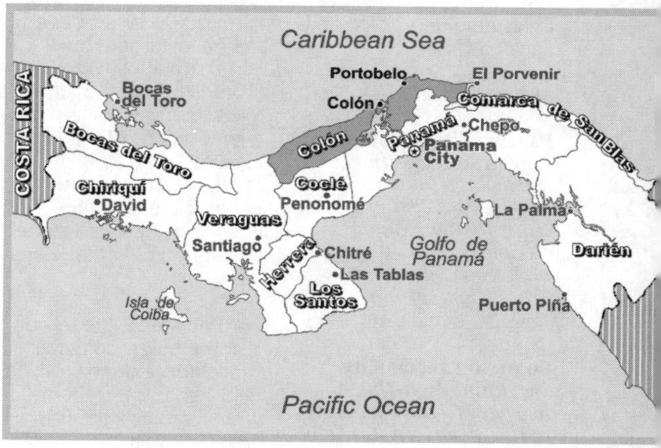

The new colony was ideally located along the trade route between South America and Europe, and riches from Perú and Ecuador passed through it. However, due to piracy and other troubles in Europe, Spain abandoned this route for good in 1746 and the area began to decline. It was not until the mid-19th century that the province of Colón became important again, first with the creation of a railway line linking the two oceans, then with the titanic excavation work of the Panamá canal.

Today, the province's main economic activity is still linked to the canal and Colón's Zona Libre, one of the largest free zones in the world. Moreover, the province's tourist industry has been experiencing significant growth over the last few years. More and more people are visiting Portobelo, a World Heritage Site, and Isla Grande. Unfortunately, Colón, the province's capital, is still the country's most crime-ridden city, curbing the attractiveness of a region that is still worth visiting. Much like Bocas del Toro, the region is characterized by its population, largely composed of descendants of African slaves and Afro-Caribbean immigrants hired for the construction of the canal.

During festivities such as the carnival, you can admire a one-of-a-kind folk dance, the *Congo*, whose rhythm and instruments recall the population's African origins.

Finding Your Way Around

By Plane

One airline offers direct flights between Colón and Panama City:

Aeroperlas

Panama City to Colón
Departure: Mon-Thu two flights a day (8:45am and 5:25pm); Fri two flights a day (8:45am and 5:05pm).
no weekend flights
Travel Time: 15min
Cost: B/.36 one way

Colón to Panama City
Departure: Mon-Thu two flights a day (9:10am and 5:35pm); Fri two flights a day (9:10am and 5:15pm).
no weekend flights

Colón Airport
☎430-1038

By Car

There are two roads that reach **Colón** from the capital. The faster way is to take the Corredor toll highway north from Albrook Airport or from Avenida Simón Bolívar in the La Cresta district. It will lead you straight to the toll highway.

The longer route is on a beautiful road that travels through the countryside and Parque Nacional Soberanía. From Panama City, take the Carretera Gaillard and keep heading north toward the Miraflores and Pedro Miguel locks. This highway runs past the Soberanía park entrance. About 10km past the intersection for the entrance to the park, turn left before the overpass, then, at the top of the hill, turn left again on the main road. Here the road becomes busier, less beautiful and more commercial. Nineteen kilometres past the turnoff for the park, you will pass over a branch of the Río Chagres, then at 40km, the Río Gatún. Upon entering the city, keep going straight ahead at the sign announcing the "Zona Libre."

For **Portobelo**, the turnoff is about 66km along the Transístmica on the right-hand side of the road when coming from Panama City, at the village of Sabanista. Keep a sharp eye out, for the road is not very well posted. Once past a footbridge overhanging the Transístmica, you will notice the Supermercado Rey; make a right turn.

Proceed along the main road that runs through the village for close to 3km, then turn right toward Maria Chiquita, then Portobelo. The road is in excellent condition.

For **Fuerte San Lorenzo**, at the exit for Colón, drive toward the Gatún locks and follow the main road, always keeping to your right. You will later see an intersection with signs to the fort. Just before you get to the locks, some 3km from the sign, you will see a control post with a gate. Tell the people at the post where you are going, and you will be asked to cross a small bridge right at the foot of the gates. The drive over this bridge is most impressive, especially when you consider that those turn-of-the-century gates are holding back thousands of tons of water. Continue for over 14km to the checkpoint, then cross the town of Fort Sherman. Turn left at the end of the street (14.6km), and then left again after 200m. The asphalt soon gives way to dirt and gravel. At a turnoff 22km farther on, you have a choice: to the right, the road leads directly to Fuerte San Lorenzo (22.4km); to the left, it leads to the seaside, where you can enjoy a fine view of the fort.

To get to **Isla Grande**, take the road leading to the village of Portobelo (see above) and, past the village, continue over 9km along the main road to the turnoff for Nombre de Dios. Once there, turn left at the turnoff, which leads to the village of Puerto Lindo, the village of La Guayra; from here, a small boat goes to the island. The crossing, which costs B/.1, takes a little over 5min. The road from Portobelo to Isla Grande is in dismal condition and impassable with a touring car after heavy rain. The trip takes at least 45min.

The Panama Railroad Company

The French were the first to draw up plans for a railway that would cross the Central American isthmus, but in 1848, after presenting the project to the government of New Grenada (which was made up of the Republic of Colombia and Panamá), they abandoned the project because of the enormous expense it entailed. At the same time, gold was discovered in California, and many adventurers in the eastern United States began to move west to seek their fortunes. Back the, the fastest way to reach the western United States was through Panamá. In order to develop the West more quickly, Congress commissioned George Law and William H. Aspinwall to create two private steamship routes. The first route was to run between New York, New Orleans and the Bay of Chagres, and the second from Panamá City to the west coast of the United States. However, because crossing the isthmus overland was long and difficult, Aspinwall and his associates decided to build the railroad right across it, creating the first transoceanic railroad in the world. After the government of New Granada granted Aspinwall and his associates ownership of the railroad for 49 years in 1850, the Panama Railroad Company was born.

Work quickly began on the Atlantic coast, on the island of Manzanillo, in the Bay of Limon, just metres away from the mainland. With the arrival of many workers, the site soon grew into a small town called Colón. Although an agreement was reached with the government of Granada stipulating that the railway be completed within six years, the workers had to overcome enormous obstacles: rugged terrain, extreme heat and humidity, and jungle-like vegetation. Despite these troubles, the railroad was finished one year ahead of schedule. On January 28, 1855, the first train crossed the isthmus, and the transoceanic railroad was a success.

Despite its rapid success, the Panama Railroad Company began to see its profits decline in the 1880s and was bought by the French Compagnie Universelle du Canal in 1887. One of the reasons for its decline was the heavy transportation taxes levied by the government of New Grenada in 1863, after extending the Panama Railroad Company's concession from 49 to 99 years. But the main reason for the company's downfall was the competition from new railway lines in the United States. Under the French, the transoceanic railway ceased to be a passenger train and was instead used to help build the canal. In 1889, history repeated itself, and the Compagnie Universelle du Canal went bankrupt, losing control of the canal and the railway. The Americans took over once again by buying the canal from the French in 1904 and continued to use the railway to build the canal. Shortly before the canal's completion, the railway was relocated to a higher level of the canal, where it can still be seen today.

By Bus

To get to **Colón** from Panama City, go to the bus stop at the **Terminal Nacional de Transporte** *(☎314-6171 or 314-6167)*, located on Calle Curundú, near the M. A. Gelabart airport. All buses to the province of Colón depart from the new bus station.

Depending on the type of bus (regular or express), the trip takes 1 to 1.5hrs and costs between B/.3 and B/.3.50.

There are two ways to get to **Portobelo**. The first is to take a bus from Colón (*B/.2.50; every day, Ave. del Frente; Travel Time: about 1hr*), which stops in Sabanista. The second is to take a bus from Panama City to Sabanista, and from there to take the bus from Colón to Portobelo.

To get to **Isla Grande** you first have to go to the little village of La Guayra, where one of several ferrymen can take you to the island for B/.1 per person. Though there is bus service to La Guayra from the cities of Colón, Sabanista and Portobelo, bear in mind that it is irregular and depends on weather conditions, among other things. An alternative way is to go to Portobelo and take a taxi to La Guayra. Because the roads are not paved east of Portobelo, they can become impassable after a few days of heavy rainfall; it is best to get there in a four-wheel-drive vehicle.

William H. Aspinwall

In 1850, a wealthy New York merchant, William H. Aspinwall, along with various associates, created the Panama Railroad Company to build a railway line linking the Atlantic to the Pacific coast of Panamá. With a million-dollar budget, the entrepreneurs likely did not expect the bill to reach just under a whopping $9 million before the exceedingly difficult and downright deadly work was completed! Fortunately, the operating permit was valid for a period of 99 years. A one-way train ticket was priced at $25 in first class and $10 in second class—the most expensive train fare on the planet for such a short distance (about 50km)! The railway turned out to be a success, however: between 1850 and 1869 no less than 600,000 travellers a year took this line and a record 1,200,000 passengers was reached in 1889.

Exploring

Colón

The present-day town of Colón was founded in 1850. It owes its origins to the Trans-isthmian Panamá Railroad, on which work started in Limón Bay, just a few metres offshore on a small island then known as Manzanillo. With the arrival of scores of workers, the place quickly turned into an actual town and many shops opened for business. The island was soon joined to the mainland by a jetty and transformed into a peninsula.

The town was named Colón, while a port was built and named Cristóbal. The first train to cross the isthmus from coast to coast did so on January 28, 1855. To commemorate the event, the U.S.-based Panamá Railroad Company asked permission to rename the town Aspinwall City, after the initiator of the project, American William H. Aspinwall, a wealthy businessman from New York City (see box). But the request was denied and the city's name remained unchanged.

The city slowly expanded, but really started to develop thanks to the construction of the canal, which was begun by the French in 1880. Thousands of people of all backgrounds worked on the canal, contributing to the development and prosperity of Colón. With its busy port, the city prospered and developed a reputation as a city full of shops and restaurants, with an exciting nightlife. Beautiful neo-colonial homes were built, giving Colón the appearance of a Louisiana city.

In the 1980s, various factors (economic crisis, fewer cruiseships) resulted in the city's gradual financial decline. This was accentuated by a series of economic and social factors, such as the establishment of financial centres in the capital, by-laws discouraging effective urban management, and an increase in unemployment. The situation was further aggravated by a significant migration to the nearby capital of Panama City.

Today, Colón is still Panamá's second-most populated city (pop. 140,000), but it is in a state of decay. Poverty, social hardship and unemployment (almost 46%) are increasing in alarming proportions. Nevertheless, the city has its fair share of attractions, such as its historical buildings with their old-world charm, the Zona Libre (free zone), where activity is beginning to pick up, shops with unbeatable prices, and its view of the Caribbean and its crystalline waters. Given all this, if a serious social and urban renewal policy were implemented, Colón could become a very appealing city. The new owners of the beautiful Washington Hotel have demonstrated this, and a number of other buildings could be used as examples that the city is worth renewing. For the moment, however, a visit to Colón might make some visitors feel uneasy at the sight of such poverty-stricken neighbourhoods.

In recent years, with the help of local authorities and merchants' associations, various people have decided to take the future of the city into their own hands realizing that the city could greatly benefit from its Zona Libre. A first step was taken with respect to legislation that prohibits the service sector, such as banks, insurance and security companies, from conducting business in the Zona Libre. These companies, by necessity, must be located near the zone and should contribute greatly to an economic renewal. The existing Zona Libre is truly isolated from the city, and with global trade on the rise, it is undergoing unprecedented commercial development.

There is every reason to believe that this new measure, once adopted, along with the opening up of world markets, can only benefit Colón and restore its past prosperity. Many people already see a brighter future for Colón, and its said that numerous houses and properties have been bought by people from all over the world. New apartment buildings have also cropped up in certain neighbourhoods.

Some guides advise against visiting this city for safety reasons. While safety is indeed a real concern that should not be ignored, we feel that as long as certain guidelines are respected (see p 53), a brief visit to this city is a must. In addition to visiting the Hotel Washington, you will get the opportunity to shop at extraordinarily low prices.

It is also worth mentioning that the city prides itself on having spawned nine world boxing champions, a sport that has always been popular here. It was also in Colón that Isabel Perón, a cabaret singer, met the Argentinian dictator who was here in exile.

The **Hotel Washington** ★★ *(at the end of the Avenida del Frente)* is a very handsome, Churrigueresque building of pink and white. Its architecture alone makes it worth a visit. The lobby is of interest not only for its luxurious decor, but also for its sheer size. Outside, at the back of the building, you can enjoy a fine view of the ships in the distance, waiting to enter the canal. Even if you are not staying here, take the time to enjoy a drink on the terrace and admire this magnificent building, where Perón, Argentina's former dictator, once lived in exile. On the left side of the hotel is the house where Ferdinand de Lesseps lived while he supervised the building of the canal.

El Catedral *(Calle 5, near Avenida Amador Guerrero)* is worth a visit for its lovely pediment. The harmonious interior is adorned with an attractive altar.

At the corner of Avenida Bolívar and Calle 6 is another fine building, graced with handsome wrought-iron columns. Although it has not been restored, it shows that the city still has significant architectural potential.

The **Zona Libre** *(Mon-Fri 8am to 5pm, closed Sat and Sun; entrance on Avenida Roosevelt)* is in fact a giant distribution centre. Vast quantities of goods arrive here from the countries where they are produced (Japan, for example), and are then combined with other incoming goods and shipped out to a multitude of countries. Essentially, the Zona Libre functions as follows:

First, a freighter from Japan arrives full of fax machines; a freighter from Taiwan arrives full of colour televisions; a freighter from Korea arrives full of cars; a freighter from Australia arrives full of aluminum ingots.

Then, some of the fax machines, colour televisions, cars and aluminum ingots are loaded onto five freighters heading to Brazil, Argentina, the east coast of the United States, Chile and Morocco.

Since the merchandise can be imported here without duty as long as it is immediately re-exported, this place is a huge international zone where companies can redistribute goods and even package them.

For this reason, a number of companies take advantage of this transshipment to put the appropriate instruction manuals with the appliances depending on where they are being shipped. In our example, instruction manuals in English, Spanish, Brazilian, and Arabic were included with the fax machines and colour televisions before the merchandise was shipped out. The Zona Libre is also a huge warehouse. Merchandise is shipped to the zone from the country where it is manufactured and is stored here until orders come in, at which point it is redistributed to customers.

Due to the proximity of the Panama Canal, through which all freighters shipping goods between the east coast of the Americas, Asia and even Europe must pass, the Zona Libre is ideally located. Of course, Panamá's inexpensive labour and the quality of its financial and administrative services also play a role in the phenomenal development of this zone.

Surrounded by walls, the Zona Libre was created in 1948, now employs 13,000 people and covers 300 ha. With over 1,600 firms, it is the second-largest free zone in the world after Hong Kong in size and volume of business, generating $4 billion a year. Because it is a duty-free zone, it attracts numerous wholesale and retail buyers from around the world. The Zona Libre was initially restricted to one district of Colón, but now encompasses another area on the outskirts of town, near the France Field Airport; the two zones are linked by a bridge. Given the ever-growing demand, the government is already contemplating extending the free zone to other areas.

While the offer may seem tempting, there are a number of hurdles to overcome before and while shopping. First, you must show your passport at the entrance. The guards may seem a trifle picky, but this formality should not be too bothersome. Second, you cannot take your purchases with you; the next time you see them will be on the day you leave, at the airport. This of course is to avoid fraud and the entry of tax-free goods into the country.

Given these difficulties, if you are shopping for minor purchases, it is much better to head to downtown Colón, where prices can be just as good – provided, of course, that you haggle! In some cases you may even get 60% of the advertised price. Despite these major discounts, however, note that in most cases,

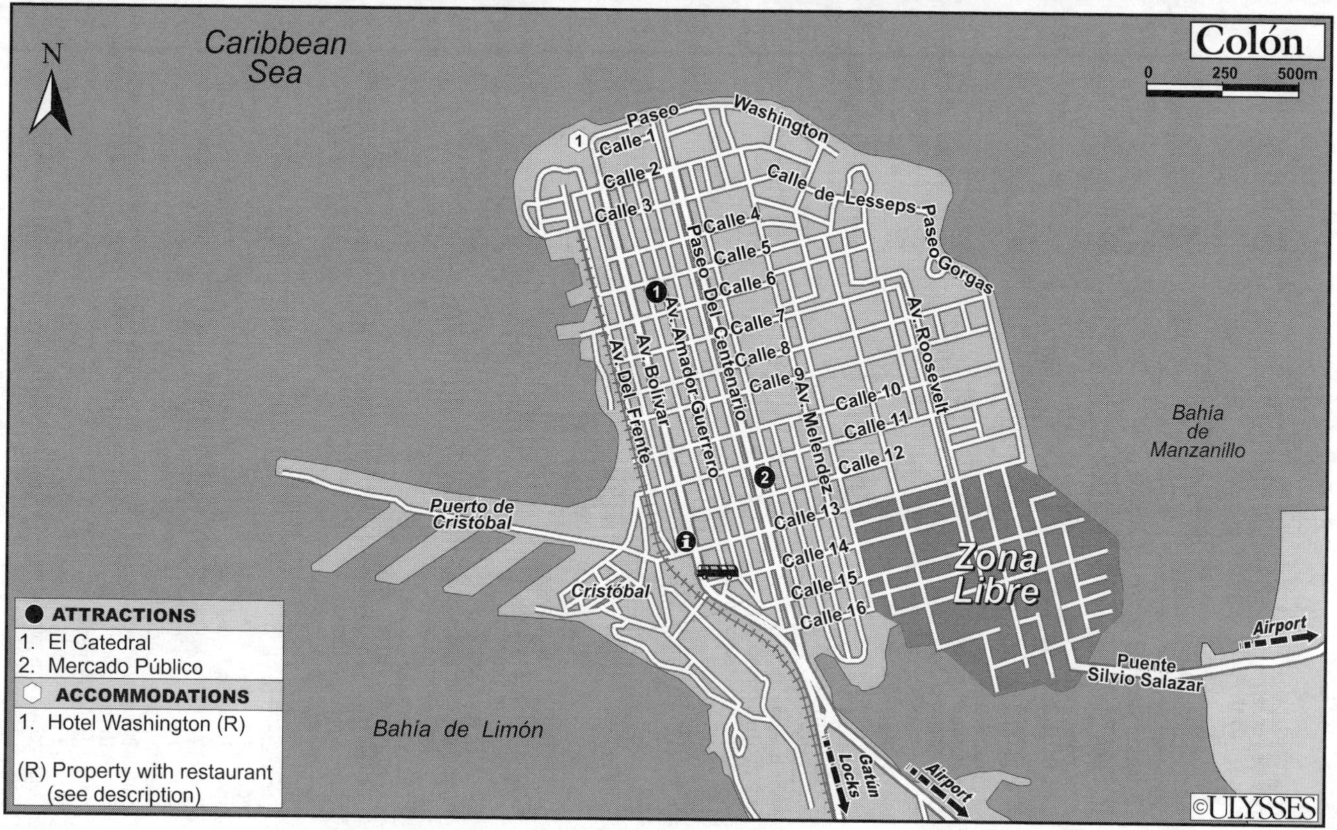
Colón
0
250
500m
N
Caribbean Sea
Paseo Washington
Calle 1
Calle 2
Calle 3
Calle 4
Calle 5
Calle 6
Calle 7
Calle 8
Calle 9
Calle 10
Calle 11
Calle 12
Calle 13
Calle 14
Calle 15
Calle 16
Calle de Lesseps
Paseo Gorgas
Av. Roosevelt
Av. Melendez
Paseo Del Centenario
Av. Amador Guerrero
Av. Bolívar
Av. Del Frente
Puerto de Cristóbal
Cristóbal
Zona Libre
Bahía de Manzanillo
Bahía de Limón
Puente Silvio Salazar
Airport
Airport
Gatún Locks
ATTRACTIONS
1. El Catedral
2. Mercado Público
ACCOMMODATIONS
1. Hotel Washington (R)
(R) Property with restaurant (see description)
©ULYSSES

electronics bought here may be more expensive than in North America.

★★

Fuerte San Lorenzo

Set amidst magnificent surroundings, Fuerte San Lorenzo was erected at the mouth of the Río Chagres in the 16th century, during the reign of King Philip II of Spain. At the time, the Río Chagres was a major maritime route used by the Spanish to transport precious goods from Ecuador and Perú to the Atlantic coast. After having reached the fort of San Lorenzo, the merchandise was shipped to Portobelo and Cartagena, where other goods were loaded onto the ships and sent to Spain.

Despite being virtually impregnable, the fortress was attacked in January 1671 and occupied by pirate Joseph Bradley, the right-hand man of sinister filibuster Henry Morgan. Bradley died during the siege and Morgan decided to settle here for a while to strengthen his army. His goal was to attack Panama City by way of the river. In February of 1671, equipped with a fleet of about 30 ships, he set out to conquer the capital and, after an arduous journey upstream and a short-lived battle, Morgan seized the city. After several days of pillaging, Morgan and his crew returned to Fort San Lorenzo, where, after a brief rest, they headed for Jamaica. Morgan lived up to his notorious reputation and set fire to the fortress upon his departure, leaving nothing but ruins and desolation in his wake.

After having been fully rebuilt by the Spanish during a period of relative calm, the fort was stormed once again in 1740, this time by Sir Edward Vernon. Commissioned by Great Britain following the outbreak of the Anglo-Spanish war in 1739, Vernon was assigned to seize the enemy's colonial fortresses, among which were Portobelo and Fort San Lorenzo. After being destroyed by the English, the Spanish abandoned Fuerte San Lorenzo for good.

Today, besides an old gunpowder factory and supply rooms, you can see several old canons on site, some of which are still inscribed with the effigy of the Spanish crown. After enjoying the unobstructed view of the sea and the river, take a tour to the trenches where, four centuries ago, soldiers were sent to defend the colony. There, they suffered from isolation and were surrounded by alien and hostile flora and fauna, at a time when people still believed in devils and demons. Both the fortress and the town of Portobelo were listed as a UNESCO World Heritage Site in 1980.

Sensitivas

While strolling through the site of Fuerte San Lorenzo, you may notice interesting plants on the ground. These are a kind of mimosa, called *sensitivas* in Panamá. Touch them gently and see how quickly their leaves retract and even, if you persist, one of their branches coiling up the stem! Out of respect for nature, do not pick the plants or take back home with you, because they have a great deal of trouble adapting to other climates.

★★★

Portobelo

Portobelo owes its existence to pirates. Indeed, it was after the destruction of the village of Nombre de Dios in 1596 by pirate Francis Drake that the Spanish built the Castillo San Felipe farther west, in a bay named Portobelo, in 1597. That same year, several other forts, as well as a port and a church were built, marking the official foundation of the village of Portobelo. Because of the deep waters surrounding it, Portobelo became a major port of trade; ships with provision from Spain came to unloa their cargo, while others stocked with goods from South America would sail off for the mother country

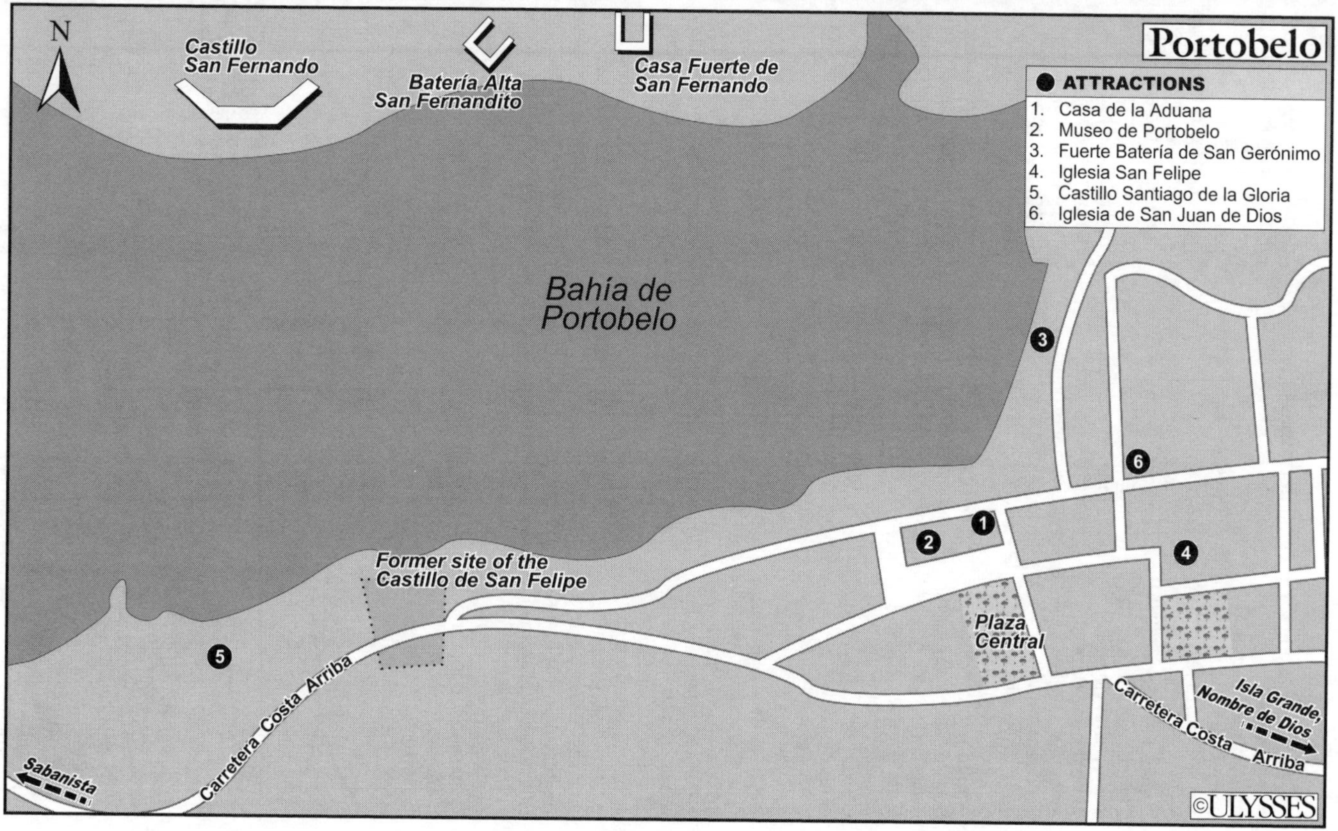

Portobelo
ATTRACTIONS
1. Casa de la Aduana
2. Museo de Portobelo
3. Fuerte Batería de San Gerónimo
4. Iglesia San Felipe
5. Castillo Santiago de la Gloria
6. Iglesia de San Juan de Dios
N
Castillo San Fernando
Batería Alta San Fernandito
Casa Fuerte de San Fernando
Bahía de Portobelo
Former site of the Castillo de San Felipe
Plaza Central
Carretera Costa Arriba
Carretera Costa Arriba
Isla Grande, Nombre de Dios
Sabanista
©ULYSSES

The port soon made the village prosper and, by 1668, no less than 400 families had settled permanently in Portobelo. Moreover, during the unloading of ships from Spain, which sometimes lasted several months, the village became the site of great *ferias* (fairs) and was literally overrun by swarms of merchants, officials and other distinguished people who temporarily settled here in makeshift lodgings (tents and wooden cabins). During these periods, the population of Portobelo could reach 8,000. Precious metals were exchanged at these fairs, generating a great deal of trade for the town. A customs house was built in 1630 so that the authorities could collect royal duties on imports and exports. This influx of riches attracted marauding pirates of all nationalities and acts of piracy quickly multiplied. In 1668, the "invincible" Castillo San Felipe was stormed by pirate Henry Morgan, who destroyed the fort and plundered the village. Determined to defend the town, the authorities built four fortresses to fend off various attacks.

At the start of the Anglo-Spanish war (1739-1748), Portobelo was captured by Englishman Admiral Edward Vernon, and was returned to the Spanish after the war. Later on, renewed acts of piracy and, above all, the losses suffered during the war, led Spain to abandon Portobelo as a transhipment point for merchandise, and the village fell into decline.

Today, Portobelo is a simple, quiet village with such a rich past that UNESCO listed it as a World Heritage Site in 1980. Its ruins make it a must to visit, and if you have the opportunity to go in the fall, do not miss the *Cristo Negro* festival, which takes place on the week of October 21. The event features a parade of people dressed as Christ and is very colourful indeed!

Among the ruins worth checking out are the remarkable remnants of the **Castillo Santiago de la Gloria ★★★**, located on the left-hand side of the road just before the last bend leading to the village. This fortress was the last one built in the area, between 1753 and 1760. Today, these fortified ramparts are just charming, with 17 perfectly aligned canons pointing out to sea, and bear precious testimony to Spain's colonial power. This fort replaced the imposing Castillo San Felipe, which was originally located a few metres away and was supposed to be impregnable. Unfortunately, nothing is left of the Castillo San Felipe; the road to Portobelo was built over part of it.

Once in the heart of the village, you can't miss the **Casa de la Aduana ★★**, also known as the *Contaduría*, which once housed the royal tax offices. Taxes were imposed on all the goods that passed through the village. Built in 1630, damaged many times and entirely destroyed in 1744, the Casa de la Aduana was later rebuilt, then destroyed once again by an earthquake in 1882. It has

Castillo Santiago de la Gloria

now been remarkably restored and cuts a fine figure with its great archways facing the small central plaza. The *casa* also houses the **Museo de Portobelo** *(Tue-Sun 9am to 5pm)* with displays on the region's history, including one on Spanish colonial military fortifications throughout the world.

While passing through the Casa de la Aduana's archways and reaching the other side of the building, you can see the vaulted entrance to the **Fuerte Batería de San Gerónimo** ★★★ on the right. Above it is a beautiful carved-stone coat of arms. On top of the fort, you will see several rather decrepit canons and a beautiful view of the bay. Erected in 1659, this fort was expanded between 1753 and 1758.

East of the central plaza is the **Iglesia San Felipe** ★. Built in 1814, its bell tower was added in 1945. Inside is the famous wooden statue known as *El Cristo Negro*, or the Black Christ. Legend has it that each time someone attempted to take the statue out of the village, the sea became turbulent, thus preventing any ship from sailing away with it. Many miracles have been attributed to the statue, and among the best known is one related to the cholera epidemic that ravaged the region in 1821. The inhabitants of Portobelo prayed to the Black Cross to spare them from this terrible ill, and their prayers are said to have been answered. Each year on October 21, a great procession is organized to commemorate this event and is attended by scores of pilgrims from across the country.

Behind the church of San Felipe lie the ruins of the oldest church in the area, the **Iglesia de San Juan de Dios**, built in 1599, just a year after the official foundation of Portobelo. It also served as a hospital for victims of yellow fever.

Finally, there are also several ruins on the other side of the bay, notably the **Castillo de San Fernando**, the **Batería Alta San Fernandito** and the **Casa Fuerte de San Fernando**. However, because they are hard to reach and of limited interest, those with little time to spare need not bother visiting them.

Nombre de Dios

Although its name is steeped in history, Nombre de Dios has no ruins and little to offer travellers, except for a little peace and quiet. Moreover, it has no hotels or restaurants worth mentioning, and the road leading here is in very bad condition, even virtually impassable on days with heavy rainfall.

Beaches

While there are many beaches in the province of Colón, most provide no services, are not supervised and are mostly located on private land. With the exception of those on Isla Grande, the only pleasant, easily accessible beach on the way to Portobelo is **Playa Langosta**, a fine beach with many services. Very popular on weekends and school holidays, the beach is located 17km from Sabanitas, on the way to Portobelo.

★

Isla Grande

Located just off the mainland, Isla Grande boasts beautiful white-sand beaches, as well as wild and dense wilderness at the heart of the island. The island can be reached from the small village of La Guayra (see p 156), where you can park your car for B/.1 a day while staying on the island. The 5min crossing also costs B/.1. The island's main activites are tourism, fishing and growing coconuts—the best in country, according to the locals. Despite the presence of several hotels and restaurants, most of which are lined up along the only existing "road," these establishments offer a rather low level of comfort.

As elsewhere on the Atlantic coast, mosquitos are numerous and it is advised to bring plenty of insect repellent. The island's southwest headland has larger beaches, some of which slope gently down to the sea. The northern part of Isla Grande, a short 15min

Province of Colón

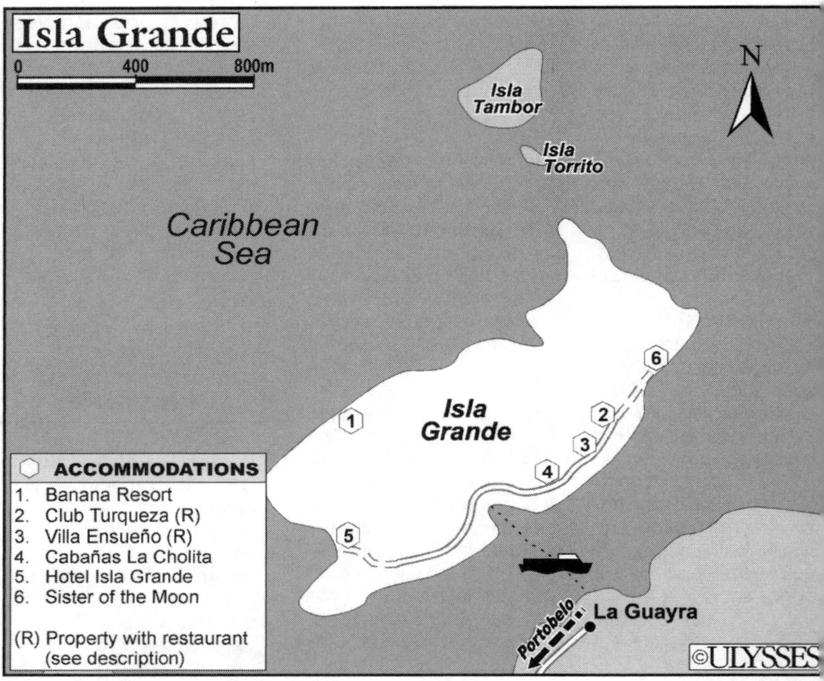

boat ride away, is sparsely populated and has no tourist facilities beyond a high-priced hotel complex. Moreover, the boat crossing, though pleasant, is rather pricey at B/.10 for the return trip (from the south to the north of the island).

During carnival time, Isla Grande attracts scores of visitors for its folklore and *Congo* (see p 35), famous lively and colourful dances. The island is also busy on weekends when it is literally overrun with locals, making it somewhat overcrowded and noisy. To really enjoy this spot, visit it during the week. Isla Grande will mostly please beach-goers.

Outdoor Activities

Diving

Portobelo

Scuba Portobelo
5km before Portobelo
on the left side of the road
☎*261-3841*
Owned by the Scubapanama travel agency, which specializes in scuba-diving lessons, this small scuba-diving club offers scuba lessons with PADI certification. Count on spending B/.100/day for the diving lesson and equipment rental and B/.20 for snorkelling gear.

Isla Grande

Diving School
on the main road running through the village, a little past the church when heading east
The affable owner of the Diving School offers an introductory diving course for B/.40 (2hrs) as well as a three day package for B/.140, which includes 20 hrs of theory classes and three ocean dives.

Accommodations

Colón

Hotel Washington
$$$
pb, hw, ≡ ℜ, ≈, *tv*
at the end of Av. del Frente
☎441-7133
⇄441-7397
This beautiful hotel with somewhat faded charm offers all the services one would expect from a major hotel. Take the time to admire its monumental entrance and beautiful lobby.

Meliá Panamá Canal
$$$$$
hw, pb, ≡, ≈, ℜ, ⊙, *tv*
Residencial Espinar
☎470-1100
⇄470-1200
www.solmelia.com
Set within a huge building that once housed an American school, this hotel with 300-plus rooms offers all the comforts desired for a stay in the lap of luxury. Located right on Lago Gatún and just 15min from the city of Colón, it features spacious, tastefully fitted out rooms, most of which offer a beautiful view of the lake and the tropical rainforest. Various excursions on the lake as well as to the canal locks are offered. Among the hotel's many amenities, the swimming pool deserves particular mention for its size, as does the casino, which provides night-time entertainment. The Meliá Panamá Canal will suit both business people who must go to the Canal Zone every day and travellers seeking tranquility and luxury.

Portobelo

Scuba Portobelo
$$ Mon-Fri
$$$ Sat, Sun and holidays
pb, ≡
5km before Portobelo
on the left side of the road
☎261-3841
Owned by the Scubapanama travel agency, which specializes in scuba-diving lessons, this unassuming hotel is made up of six rather humble *cabañas* equipped with cold-water showers and air conditioning. A small, private beach is also available to guests. Basic but suitable for those determined to stay near Portobelo.

Isla Grande

Sister of the Moon
$ dormitory
$$$
pb, ⊗, ≈, ℜ
on the southeastern tip of the island
☎226-2257 or 448-2182
www.hotel-sistermoon.com
Off a small, muddy and hard-to-reach road, the Sister of the Moon hotel sets guests up in wooden cliffside cabins. Despite being decorated with attractive colours and bamboo furnishings, the rooms lack comfort. Moreover, both the swimming pool and adjacent bar-restaurant are too small. Overall, this hotel seems to suffer from a lack of maintenance, which is all the more unfortunate as the place has undeniable charm and offers beautiful views of the coast. The hotel offers budget travellers dorm-room accommodations at B/.15 a night per person.

Cabañas La Cholita
$$
pb, ≡, #
☎232-4561
A small hotel composed of very rudimentary *cabañas* devoid of any particular charm.

Villa Ensueño
$$
pb, hw, ⊗/≡, ℜ
west of the free clinic
☎269-5819
⇄235-9917
A favourite with Panamanian families, the Villa Ensueño hotel is quite a lively place. The rooms are in cottages surrounded by a lovely flowered garden, the whole located behind a large seafront restaurant. Though the rooms are air-conditioned, they provide rather rudimentary comfort, are poorly lit and lack privacy. Moreover, its concrete seafront facing the *Cristo del Mar* is rather unappealing. This place is ideal if you have children because the beach here is shallow and therefore safe for the young ones to swim in.

Club Turqueza
$$-$$$
ps, hw, ≈, ⊗, ℜ
west along the road skirting the coast and just past the Villa Ensueño
☎265-5044 ext. 10833
☎639-2230 (Tuesday)
Club Turqueza is second only to the Banana Resort. French owner Jean-Yves Ricard, who has been living on the island for

quite some time, has recently built several motel-style units around a large swimming pool on a former palm grove.

The rooms are comfortable, well kept and sport a simple decor with white walls. For greater comfort, each bed has mosquito netting. Each unit has a small porch with a hammock, and there is an excellent restaurant (see p 169) nearby. Though the hotel is not right on the coast, the beaches are only a few hundred metres away and within easy walking distance. Various excursions are also available, including one on horseback around the Bay of Manzanillo. For the best deals, stay here on weekdays.

Hotel Isla Grande
$$$
pb, ⊗, ≡, hw
☎225-6722 (for reservations in Panama City)
This hotel complex, which was being expanded during our visit, offers shabby *cabañas* by a lovely beach well away from the village. There are also several modest concrete buildings that house ordinary rooms distributed over several floors, as well as a restaurant that serves typical Panamanian fare, a bar, a ping-pong room and a pool room, which are all located in an old, less-than-engaging building.

Banana Resort
$$$$$
ps, hw, ≡, ≈, ℜ
Av. Frederico Boyd, Edificio Parque Urrucá, PB, Apdo 6-7519, El Dorado, Panamá
☎263-9510 or 263-9766
⇄264-7556
Set up by a lovely little beach, in the northwestern part of the island, the Banana Resort has 16 large rooms in small cliffside cabins. The cabins' bright, white-and-yellow colour scheme contrasts marvelously with the many surrounding palm trees, banana trees and other vegetation. All the rooms have king-size beds and a large balcony with an ocean view. The decor, though refined, is relatively simple and even a tad kitsch. The restaurant is located in a circular beachside building that has a large swimming pool outside. All this is surrounded by a beautifully landscaped garden, which is delightful to relax in.

The price of a room *(B/.75 to B/.90 per person)* includes transportation from La Guayra, excursions to other beaches on the island, beach equipment (for games, etc.), breakfast and lunch or dinner. This isn't as great a deal as it sounds, as it only covers up to B/.10 on meals, and most à-la-carte dishes are more expensive. Despite this, the Banana Resort is unquestionably the most appealing and comfortable hotel on the island.

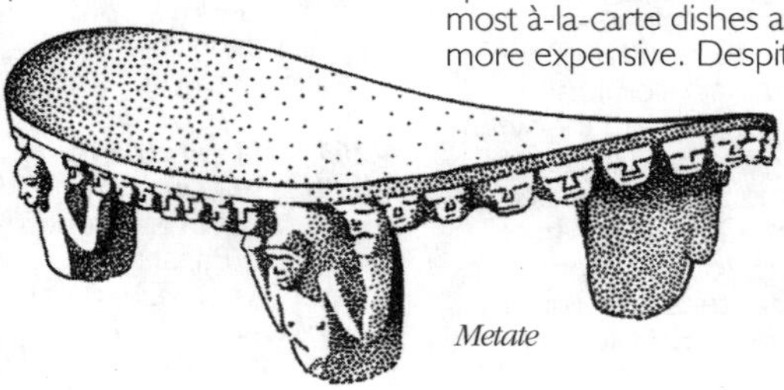

Metate

Restaurants

Colón

Hotel Washington
$-$$
in the hotel of the same name, at the end of Avenida del Frente
☎441-7133
Here you have two options: a classic restaurant serving fine French cuisine in a welcoming atmosphere, or an unpretentious cafeteria where the fare is simple but good. Whatever your choice, you will be served with a smile. In addition to the restaurant, there is a bar and a gorgeous terrace with a pool facing the ocean.

Portobelo

La Torre
$$$
Tue to Fri 11am to 6pm, Sat and Sun 8am to 9pm
3km from Portobelo
☎448-2039
On the right-hand side of the main road to Portobelo, La Torre is aptly named indeed (*torre* means tower in Spanish). Located on the second floor of a modest bar and a little set back from the road, the restaurant, with its large palm-roofed dining room open on all four sides, does somewhat resemble a *mirador*. Enjoy Creole-style rice and

With its astonishing fauna and amazing flora, Panamá is a paradise for naturalists. – *courtesy of IPAT*

A pensive white-faced capuchin monkey. – *courtesy of IPAT*

Isla Contadora boasts several beaches for snorkelling or simply relaxing – *courtesy of IPAT*

Pointed toward the sea, the cannons of Portobelo are a reminder of the tumultuous history of New World colonies. – *courtesy of IPAT*

beans or Colombian-style *empanadas* while seated hidden between the trees at one of the large wooden tables draped with tablecloths. Warm welcome in a Robin Hood-like setting!

Los Canoñes
$$$
on the left-hand side of the Portobelo-bound road
Los Canoñes is renowned for its fish and seafood specialties—such as octopus, *corvina*, shrimp and crab—which you can sample on its large terrace overlooking the bay.

Isla Grande

Villa Ensueño
$$
west of the free clinic
☎269-5819
Facing a concrete seafront and *Cristo del Mar* in the distance, the restaurant of the Villa Ensueño will please those who primarily enjoy socializing and non-stop bustle.

Whether seated in the shade on its large covered terrace or at one of the small seashell-encrusted concrete tables, the various simple and affordable Panamanian dishes are a real treat. Several vegetarian dishes are available on request every day. The restaurant also makes delicious tropical-fruit juices. After your meal, take a stroll through the establishment's flowered garden, which is home to numerous butterflies.

Club Turqueza
$$$
west along the road skirting the coast and just past the Villa Ensueño
☎448-2990
The restaurant at Club Turqueza is the best on the island and an absolute must. Jean-Yves Ricard, a Frenchman who has been calling Isla Grande home for some years now, serves a refreshing *mozzarella en carozza* (tomato-and-mozzarella salad with basil leaves) as a starter, followed by a delicious seafood crepe. Also featured on the menu are various fish selections as well as a good coq au vin and, to accompany your meal, affordable Californian or Argentinian wines.

The dining room, a large covered terrace on a wooden dock, is most pleasant and offers a lovely view of the mainland. The owner has succeeded in giving the place an original style with hammocks suspended here and there, and swings used as seats around the bar. Fabulous!

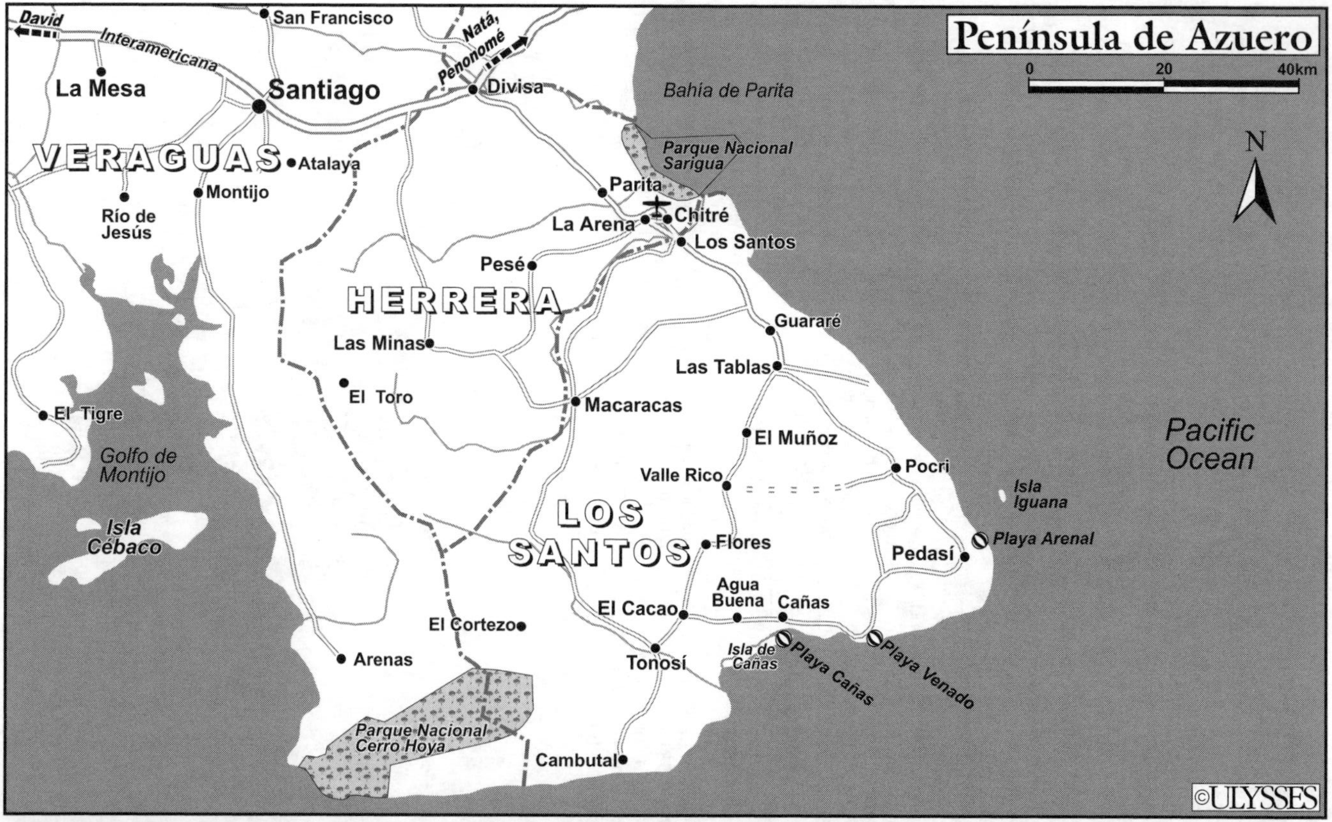
Península de Azuero
0
20
40km
N
David
Interamericana
San Francisco
Natá, Penonomé
La Mesa
Santiago
Divisa
Bahía de Parita
VERAGUAS
Atalaya
Parque Nacional Sarigua
Montijo
Parita
Río de Jesús
Chitré
La Arena
Los Santos
Pesé
HERRERA
Guararé
Las Minas
Las Tablas
El Toro
Macaracas
El Tigre
El Muñoz
Pacific Ocean
Golfo de Montijo
Pocri
Valle Rico
Isla Iguana
LOS SANTOS
Isla Cébaco
Flores
Playa Arenal
Pedasí
Agua Buena
Cañas
El Cacao
El Cortezo
Arenas
Tonosí
Isla de Cañas
Playa Cañas
Playa Venado
Parque Nacional Cerro Hoya
Cambutal
©ULYSSES

The Central Provinces and the Azuero Peninsula

This region has a population of 547,000 and includes the provinces of Coclé, Herrera, Los Santos and Veraguas.

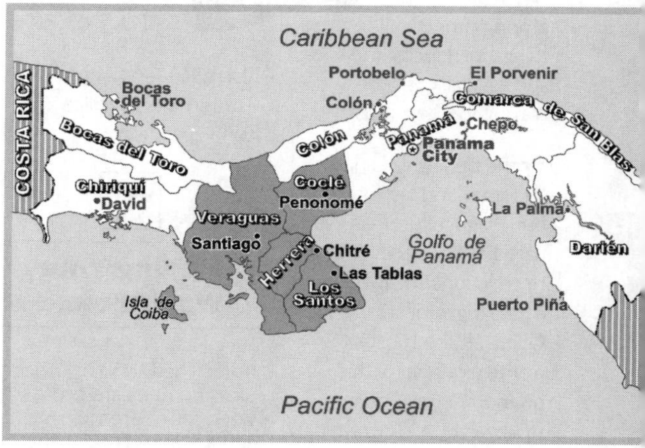

The pre-Columbian era saw significant development of this region, when it was under the control of indigenous chiefs, some of them (Natá, Urracá and Paris) went on to gain notoriety after the arrival of the Spanish because of their desperate resistance to the invaders. The provinces have a significant cultural heritage, both pre-Columbian and colonial. Each province possesses its own historical sites and its own sense of regionalism: Coclé with its unfortunately ill-maintained El Caño archeological site, Herrera with its noteworthy museum, Los Santos with its uniform museum at Guararé, and Veraguas with its fine Iglesia de San Francisco. What's more, regionalist sentiment is strong here, and even the attitudes of the inhabitants differ from one province to another.

The Azuero Peninsula is the veritable guardian of traditions dating from the Hispanic era, and in keeping with this, carnival celebrations are quite traditional here. The carnival lasts four days, from Saturday to Shrove Tuesday (*martes de carnaval*), at which time all hotels are full and businesses are closed. In some cities, an equally festive *carnavalito* is held the week before. Note that hotel prices can quadruple during carnival time!

Careful preparations for the festival begin early, as the most prominent clothing designers create stunning costumes, always very respectful of tradition.

The Las Tablas carnival is the most celebrated carnival in Panamá, and is the setting of a friendly competition between the Calle Arriba and Calle Abajo (High Road and Low Road). Each one names a queen and tries to outdo the other by, among other things, producing the most spectacular costume and playing the best music.

The peninsula is now semi-arid, as "slash and burn" agriculture has eliminated every trace of its once luxuriant vegetation. The Sarigua desert, near Chitré, is the most extreme example of this phenomenon. Today, stock farming is increasingly replacing crop farming, which is virtually disappearing. In fact, because of the impoverishment of the land, many farmers have left the area in recent years for the province of Darién, thus accelerating the depopulation of the central provinces. If the state of Panamá does not intervene to prevent these farmers from using the same methods in their new environment, there is a definite risk that a part of Darién will suffer a similar fate in the near future.

This region is also quite mountainous and is only just being discovered by travellers. A visit to the verdant little village of Chiguirí Arriba is a must. Visitors can now enjoy this magical spot while staying in the Posada Cerro la Vieja, amidst extraordinary wildlife and lush vegetation.

Finding Your Way Around

Note: The following schedules and rates are provided for reference only and are subject to change.

By Plane

As this guide goes to press, **Aeroperlas** is the only company that flies to these provinces and only the city of **Chitré** is served.

Chitré

Panama City to Chitré
Departure: Mon-Fri 6:40am and 4:15pm;
Sat-Sun 4:15pm
Travel Time: 35min
Cost: B/.31.50 one way

Chitré to Panama City
Departure: Mon-Fri 8:25am and 5pm; Sun 5pm
Travel Time: 35min
Cost: B/.31.50 one way

Chitré
☎996-4021

Panama City
☎315-7500

By Car

The Interamericana runs through most of this region. The Azuero peninsula can be reached by heading south from Divisa.

To get to **Penonomé** from Panama City, take the Interamericana westward. Penonomé is located 149km from the capital, to the right of the intersection with the Interamericana. To reach **Natá**, head west until the next major intersection. The village is 31km from Penonomé. When you get to the intersection, turn left (near the Véda restaurant) and continue straight ahead.

El Caño lies between Penonomé and Natá. To reach it from Penonomé, travel west on the Interamericana and take the turn-off to the left at the sign for the Parque Archeologico El Caño. This sign is 1.4km past the bridge over Río Salobre. After the turn-off, continue over 2.5km, then turn left and follow the signs. The 4km road is only paved for 1km; the rest is dirt and gravel, with many potholes, so watch out for the undercarriage of you car.

For the town of **Chitré**, take the Interamericana westward. Turn left at the Divisa intersection (34km from Natá), then follow the main highway for 37km as its runs through the villages of **Parita** and **La Arena**.

To get to the **Parque Nacional Sarigua**, go through the small village of Parita to the intersection where a sign indicates the park, then take the road to the left. Continue over several kilometres and, at the next intersection, turn left and drive for 1km to the park entrance where the INRENARE station is located.

The villages of **Los Santos**, **Guararé** and **Las Tablas** lie on the main road heading south from Divisa. They are located 47km, 69km and 75km, respectively, from Divisa.

Santiago is located 69km west of Natá. To get downtown, turn left on the Interamericana at the main intersection and go straight ahead to the end of the road. Then turn right, and continue to the central plaza, where you will find the church.

For **San Francisco**, turn left on theInteramaricana at the Santiago intersection, and keep going on the main road over 18km.

To reach **Chiguirí Arriba** *(Posada Cerro la Vieja)*, go to Penonomé first. From there, turn right on the road after the Hotel Dos Continentes, towards Churuquita. A 20km drive through a lovely tropical landscape will take you to Sofres, after which point the road is no longer paved and is in poor condition for the remaining 9km to the Posada Cerro la Vieja.

By Bus

Buses to the central provinces and the Azuero peninsula depart from the **Terminal Nacional de Transporte** *(☎314-6171 or 314-6167)*, located on Calle Curundú, near the M. A. Gelabert airport.

To get to Chiguirí Arriba from the capital, you have to go to **Penonomé** first. Departures take place every 30min *(approximately B/.4; Travel Time: between 2 and 3 hrs)*. Get off at the Penonomé bus stop on the Interamericana. From there, it is a 10min walk to the bus stop next to the Mercado Municipal in the centre of town *(B/.2; Travel Time: between 1.5 and 2hrs)*. The bus to Chiguirí Arriba departs from there.

To get to **Natá** from the capital, take any bus (except an express bus) leaving for Chitré or Santiago and tell the driver where you are going. No bus goes directly to the village centre, so to get there you must take a taxi from the bus stop on the Interamericana. This is also the case for the **El Cano** archaeological site.

Many buses go to **Chitré** *(about B/.8)* by way of **Parita** and **La Arena**. Buses for **Los Santos**, **Guararé** and **Las Tablas**, as well as other destinations on the peninsula, leave from the Terminal de Transportes de Herrera, situated on the Via Circunvalación (sometimes called Roberto Ramírez de Diego or Calle 19 de Octubre).

There are several daily departures for the town of **Santiago** *(about B/.8; Travel Time: 4hrs)*. To get to the small village of **San Francisco**, go to Santiago, then take a bus (30min ride) to the centre of town.

Practical Information

Telecommunications

Chitré
Calle Belardino Urriola

Santiago
Calle 8, two streets west of the intersection with the Interamericana

Tourist Information

Santiago

IPAT:
Avenida Central, Plaza Palermo

David

IPAT:
Central Plaza;
left of the church, below the Pazin store;
first floor of the Galerma building, suite 4

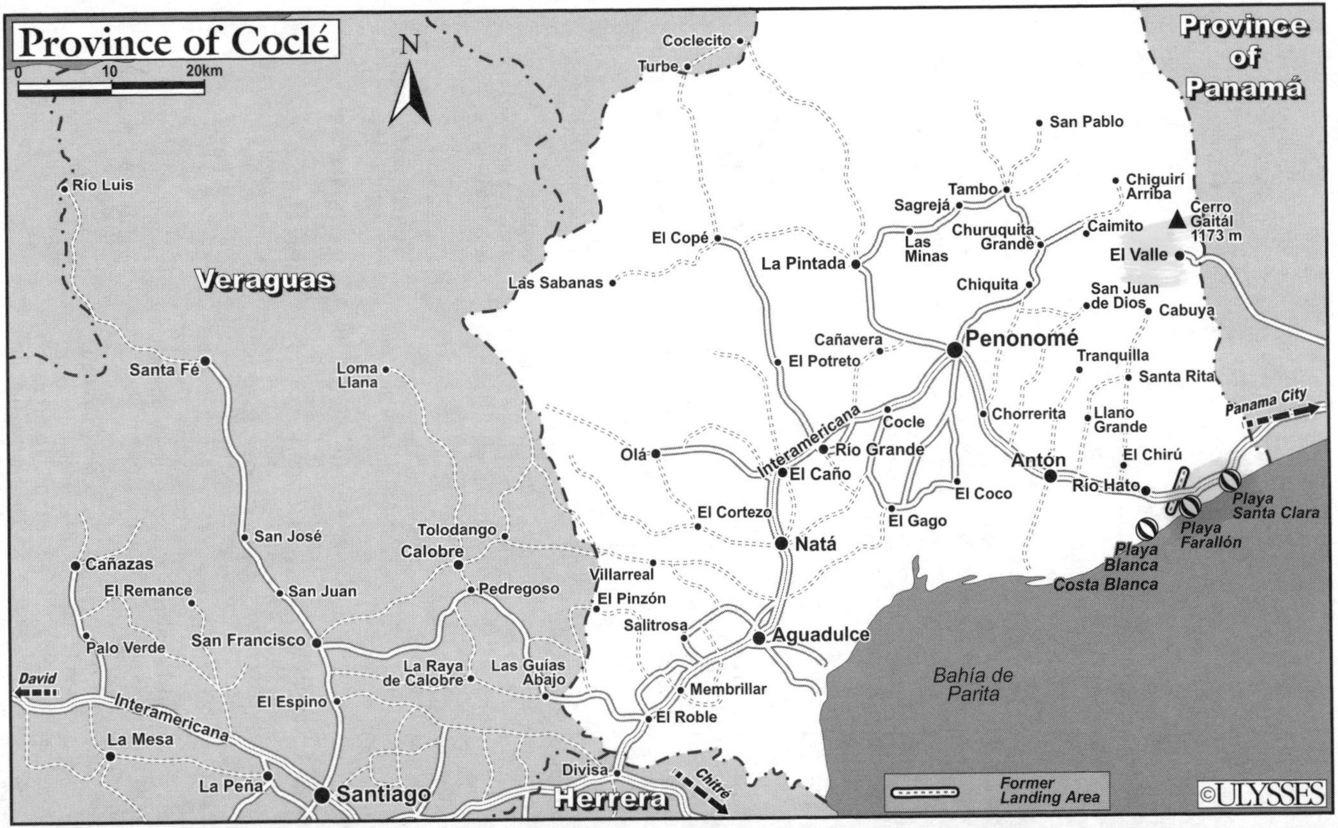
Province of Coclé
0
10
20km
N
Province of Panamá
Veraguas
Herrera
Coclecito
Turbe
Río Luis
San Pablo
Tambo
Sagrejá
Chiguirí Arriba
Cerro Gaitál 1173 m
Caimito
Churuquita Grande
Las Minas
El Copé
La Pintada
El Valle
Las Sabanas
Chiquita
San Juan de Dios
Cabuya
Cañavera
Penonomé
El Potreto
Tranquilla
Santa Rita
Santa Fé
Loma Llana
Chorrerita
Llano Grande
Panama City
Cocle
Interamericana
Río Grande
Olá
El Caño
Antón
El Chirú
Río Hato
El Coco
Playa Santa Clara
Playa Farallón
Playa Blanca
Costa Blanca
El Cortezo
El Gago
San José
Tolodango
Calobre
Natá
Cañazas
Villarreal
El Remance
San Juan
Pedregoso
El Pinzón
Salitrosa
Aguadulce
Palo Verde
San Francisco
La Raya de Calobre
Las Guías Abajo
Membrillar
Bahía de Parita
David
El Espino
El Roble
La Mesa
Divisa
Chitré
La Peña
Santiago
Former Landing Area
©ULYSSES

Exploring

Province of Coclé

This was one of the first regions to be colonized after the capital. Many of the area's indigenous people were assimilated by the colonists, while others chose to flee to the western provinces.

Today, in these mountainous regions, there are still small, isolated indigenous communities. The province of Coclé is also the largest agricultural area nearest the capital, producing rice, corn, sugar cane and citrus fruit.

Coclé is also famous for its crafts, such as the famous Panamá hat or *montuno*, a hat made from palm fronds. (see box The Panamá Hat or "Montuno" in this chapter) Because it is sometimes available in two colours (straw and black), it is commonly called *sombrero pintado*, or black and white hat.

Penonomé

With over 60,000 inhabitants, this pleasant commercial town is worth a short visit, as much for the charm of its small central plaza and its church as for its lively shopping streets. Take a walk in the little park facing the church, where you will find a handsome statue of Simón Bolívar. In addition to its colonial facade, the church has a lovely pulpit made of carved wood.

The town was founded in 1581 and, according to legend, was named after an indigenous man called Nomé who, having been expelled from his land by the Spaniards, died of homesickness (*peno* means "sadness").

The city is known as a marketing centre for arts and crafts. On the left side of the west-bound Interamericana highway, a little before the turn-off for Penonomé, is where you will find the **Mercado de Artesanías**.

The market, set up in little cottages with pretty tile roofs, displays a great variety of interesting objects made in the region.

The **Museo de la Historia y de la Tradición Penonomeña** *(B/.0.50; Tue-Sat 9am to 12:30pm and 1:30pm to 4pm, Sun 9:30am to 12pm; Calle Simón Quiroz near Parque Rubén Darío Carles, ☎997-8494)* offers visitors an opportunity to familiarize themselves with the region's history. Located in a house built at the beginning of the 20th-century, the exhibit features artefacts from different periods, ranging from 10,000 BCE to AD 1520. Notice how the objectss became much more complex over time, and learn about the evolution of ceramic painting in the years leading up to the arrival of the Spanish. A lovely chandelier made of hammered and embossed silver, depicting a unicorn, can also be seen, as well as a beautiful silver collection, both testimony to the colonial presence. Several of the objects come from the Iglesia San Juan Bautista in Penonomé.

★ Chiguirí Arriba

The mountainous region north of Penonomé is a pleasant area to explore. The higher altitude means cooler temperatures and fewer mosquitoes, and there are extraordinary landscapes to behold. The fauna and flora are as fascinating as the culture and traditions of the villagers.

Here, all sorts of curiosities await: coffee beans, still in their shells drying in the sun; oriole (*oropéndolas*) nests hanging from trees; unripened, flat guavas... everything to astound any urban dweller! Small, thatched-roof houses scattered about in the forest are a reminder of the presence of local peasants, who, by "cultivating" this forest, are able to support themselves without harming the environment. This region is actually very sparsely populated. Their thatched roofs last about five years, and are made of wood and vines (*bejucos*) to attach the palms.

If you decide to stay in Chiguirí Arriba, you will most probably lodge at the Posada Cerro la Vieja (see p 188), situated 450m below sea level and some 30km from Penonomé. Here the staff can suggest various excursions on foot or on horseback, guided

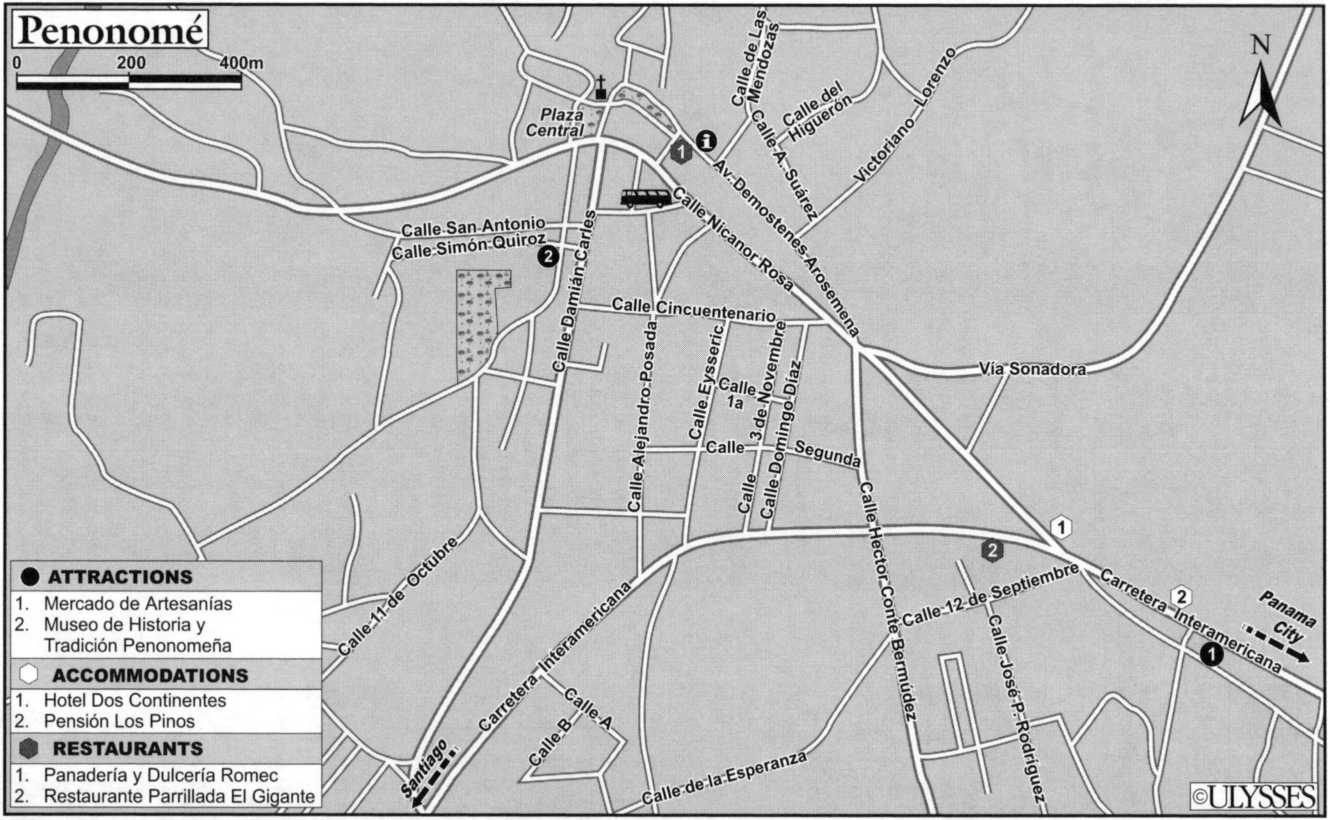

Penonomé
0
200
400m
N
Plaza Central
Calle de Las Mendozas
Calle del Higuerón
Victoriano Lorenzo
Calle A. Suárez
Av. Demostenes Arosemena
Calle Nicanor Rosa
Calle San Antonio
Calle Simón Quiroz
Calle Damián Carles
Calle Cincuentenario
Calle Alejandro Posada
Calle Eysseric
Calle 1a
Calle 3 de Novembre
Calle Domingo Díaz
Calle Segunda
Vía Sonadora
Calle Hector Conte Bermúdez
Calle 12 de Septiembre
Calle José P. Rodríguez
Carretera Interamericana
Calle 11 de Octubre
Calle A
Calle B
Calle de la Esperanza
Santiago
Panama City
ATTRACTIONS
1. Mercado de Artesanías
2. Museo de Historia y Tradición Penonomeña
ACCOMMODATIONS
1. Hotel Dos Continentes
2. Pensión Los Pinos
RESTAURANTS
1. Panadería y Dulcería Romec
2. Restaurante Parrillada El Gigante
©ULYSSES

by residents of the neighbouring village of Tabridal. Do not miss this opportunity, as the locals are the only ones who can truly reveal the richness of the Chiguirí Arriba's plants and wildlife. Guide services are included in the packages offered at the Posada, but it is nonetheless customary to tip *(about B/.5 for a 3hr tour for one or two people).*

Among the different possibilities for excursions in the area, we especially recommend a trip to **El Valle** (see p 136) or **El Congal**. On clear days, both oceans are visible from the latter. There are also lovely waterfalls here, named in honour of **Chorro Antolino**, an indigenous chief, and you can also swim. There are also **petroglyphs** (drawings or carvings on rock) nearby but getting to them requires good walking shoes and long trousers, as there are many thistles on the path.

El Caño

El Caño *(B/.1; Tue-Sat 9am to noon and 12:30pm to 4pm, Sun 9am to 1pm)* is one of the few pre-Colombian archeological sites in Panamá. Here, admire stone steles pointing towards the sky. Little is known about this ancient construction, but certain historians believe it to have been some sort of game. On a mound a little farther, a deep hole has been dug into the ground, where a tomb contains the remains of a *cacique* (indigenous chief) and his family. The tomb also contains pottery, as well as assorted objects that once belonged to the *cacique.* According to archaeologists, the remains, and the pottery and the other objects are about 1,500 years old.

Despite the rarity of this kind of site in Panamá, authorities have not invested much effort into promoting such a heritage site and protecting the ruins. In fact, because the tomb is merely sheltered by a simple straw roof and left to the vagaries of nature, it may well deteriorate rapidly in the years to come. However, a small museum adjoining the site displays some of the items found here.

★ Natá

For a long time, Natá, along with Panamá Viejo, was one of the main towns in the country. The village was named after the indigenous chief who controlled the region before the Spanish arrived.

In 1515, Gaspar de Espinosa began settling these territories by establishing a military station in the region. lin 1522, governor Pedro Arias Dávila officially founded the village of Natá de los Caballeros. Many merchants were soon attracted by the garrison; they settled here and made the town prosperous.

Now a peaceful little village, Natá is home to the oldest **colonial church** ★ still in use in the country. The building, which was promoted to the rank of a basilica and classified as a historical monument in 1941, has a fine colonial facade and remarkable interior. The altar of the Virgin, on the right, is especially interesting because of its two columns with sculpted fruit, leaves and two feathered serpents. This unusual decoration clearly shows the influence of indigenous culture. Another curiosity is the painting of the Holy Trinity. Located to the right of the altar to the Virgin, this painting was created in 1758 by the Ecuadorian artist José Samaniego. For a long time it could not be displayed because it was deemed inconsistent with Church dogma. Indeed,

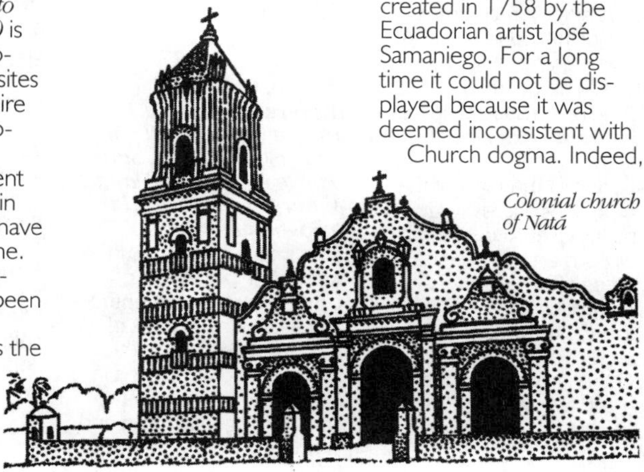

Colonial church of Natá

Central Provinces and the Azuero Peninsula

the representation of the Trinity as three persons who all look like Christ was contrary to Church canons. The fine interior of the church has recently been renovated and is complemented nicely by the carved wooden pulpit and wooden pillars.

The village of Natá also features a number of well-preserved colonial houses.

Province of Herrera

Parita

The **Iglesia de Santo Domingo de Guzmán ★★**, in the centre of the village of Parita, is worth a visit. While its exterior appears relatively simple, it boasts magnificent altars and an interestingly decorated pulpit. The interior, made of wood, is richly and harmoniously decorated and the three wooden altars date from the 18th century. The central altar, supported by two serpents, reflects the indigenous influence. The side altars stand on columns with plant motifs, such as leaves, grapes and other fruits. The beautiful, Churrigueresque pulpit is also worth examining.

A door to the right of the choir gives access to a small museum of colonial religious art, where fine pieces of silver are displayed. If the church is closed, the village *padre* can let you in; his office is on the right side of the street, facing the church.

La Arena

This village is known above all for its many craft shops. Among the items offered at very good prices: a vast selection of pottery, highly decorative papier-mâché masks (used during festivities and religious processions), fabric decorated with traditional motifs and much more. Most of the shops are located along the main street.

★ Chitré

This pleasant town features a lovely church and a very interesting museum that is worth a visit. Besides its many bargain-filled stores, it has a small central plaza, which is a good place to unwind at the end of the day. Chitré is certainly worth your while.

The **Iglesia de Chitré** *(beside the central plaza or Parque unión)* doesn't look like much from the outside, but it is worth a peak inside for its rich and harmonious wooden decor. Take a look at its gilded altar and mahogany vault.

The Museo de Herrera ★★★ *(B/.1; Tue-Sat 9am to 12:30pm and 1:30pm to 4pm, Sun 9am to noon; Calle Manuel Maria Correa y Avenida Julio Arjona, ☎996-0077).* is an interesting museum located in the centre of Chitré. It traces the entire archaeological history of the central region of the isthmus, and is installed in a stylish house that was first a bourgeois home and later a post office. Starting at the entrance, explanatory panels (only in Spanish but highly visual) guide visitors through the exhibition. Prior to the arrival of the Spanish, three distinct types of art developed on different part of the isthmus. You can admire various objects dating from prehistory until the 17th century, found at archaeological sites located in the central region of the country. In addition to arrow tips from 8,000 to 10,000 BCE, vases and ancient pieces of pottery, the museum also displays some fine reproductions of pre-Columbian gold jewellery, called *huacas*. The original pieces are exhibited in the capital (see Museo Antropológico Reina Torres de Araúz, p 82). The final item in the first exhibition hall is a life-sized reproduction of the grave of an indigenous chief, with a text containing notes jotted by Gaspar de Espinosa at the time of the burial, in 1519.

The second hall, one floor up, covers the history of the province since its creation. Part of the exhibition is dedicated to the founders of the region, while another contains traditional costumes and lace.

To take another route back to the Interamericana from Chitré, use the road that goes through Las Minas.

A mixture of mountain roads and plains, this route offers lovely views but no cultural sights, and will appeal mostly to those who appreciate the countryside. It is important to note, however, that this

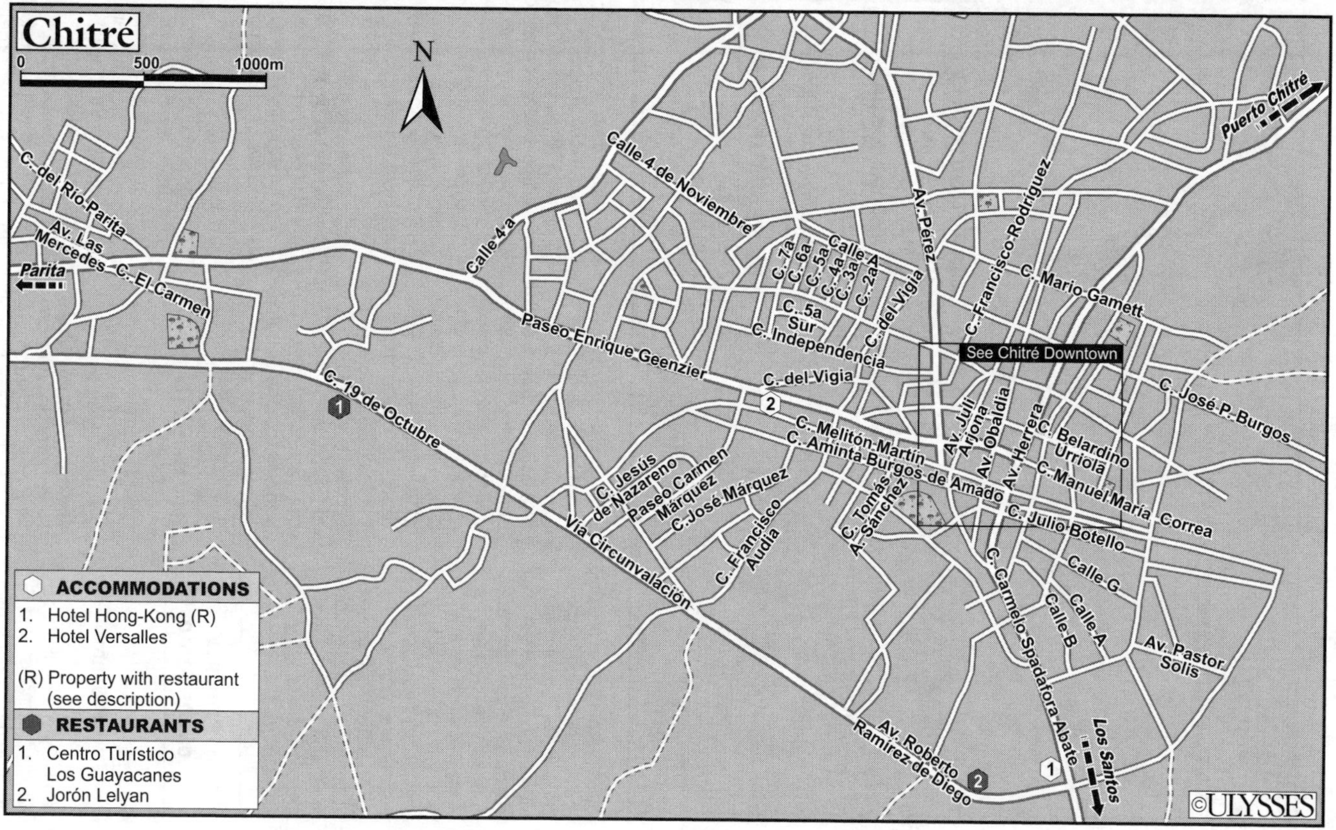
Chitré
0
500
1000m
N
Puerto Chitré
Parita
Los Santos
C. del Río Parita
Av. Las Mercedes
C. El Carmen
Calle 4a
Calle 4 de Noviembre
Paseo Enrique Geenzier
C. 19 de Octubre
Vía Circunvalación
Av. Roberto Ramírez de Diego
C. 7a
C. 6a
C. 5a
C. 4a
C. 3a
C. 2a
Calle A
C. 5a Sur
C. Independencia
C. del Vigia
C. del Vigia
Av. Pérez
C. Francisco Rodríguez
C. Mario Gamett
See Chitré Downtown
C. José P. Burgos
Av. Juli Arjona
Av. Obaldia
Av. Herrera
C. Belardino Urriola
C. Manuel María Correa
C. Julio Botello
C. Melitón Martín
C. Aminta Burgos de Amado
C. Jesús de Nazareno
Paseo Carmen Márquez
C. José Márquez
C. Francisco Audia
C. Tomás A. Sánchez
C. Carmelo Spadafora Abate
Calle G
Calle A
Calle B
Av. Pastor Solís
ACCOMMODATIONS
1. Hotel Hong-Kong (R)
2. Hotel Versalles
(R) Property with restaurant (see description)
RESTAURANTS
1. Centro Turístico Los Guayacanes
2. Jorón Lelyan
©ULYSSES

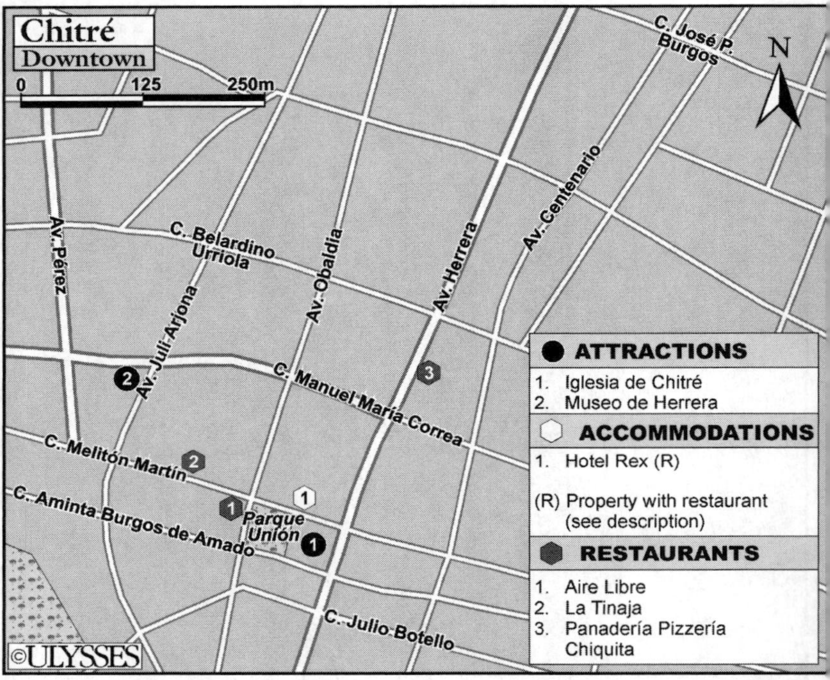

alternative route is about 47km longer and because the road is winding, it is slower. To get to this road, drive toward Pesé. Once there, past the police station (on your left), you will come to a stop sign. Turn right, then immediately left to get back on the road to Los Pozos. Once there, continue to Las Minas and then on to the Interamericana.

Province of Los Santos

★ Los Santos

A lovely group of old gabled houses clustered around the village's main park and on the road leading to it can be admired in this quiet little town founded in 1557. The colonial **church of San Atanacio** ★ is also worth seeing for its lovely rococo reredos of red and gold (take a look at the centre of the vault as well). Los Santos can also boast that the call to arms against the Spaniards, called the "Cry of Los Santos", which culminated in the independence of the country, was sent out from here. The Museo de la Nacionalidad explains the various stages of independence.

Los Santos is also known for its celebration of the **festival of Corpus Christi**, when a religious procession is held, featuring a struggle between the *diablico sucio* (dirty devil) and the *diablico blanco* (white devil), symbolic of the struggle between good and evil. The feathers stuck on some of the papier-mâché masks reflect an indigenous influence. The procession is held every year in June.

The **Museo de la Nacionalidad** ★★ *(B/.1; Tue-Sat 9am to noon and 1pm to 4pm; Sun 9am to 1pm; Calle José Vallarino, near the church, ☎996-8192)* displays various objects and documents, and traces the history of the region from colonial days to independence and its attachment to New Granada. Among other things, there is a map illustrating the conquest of the country, a war order

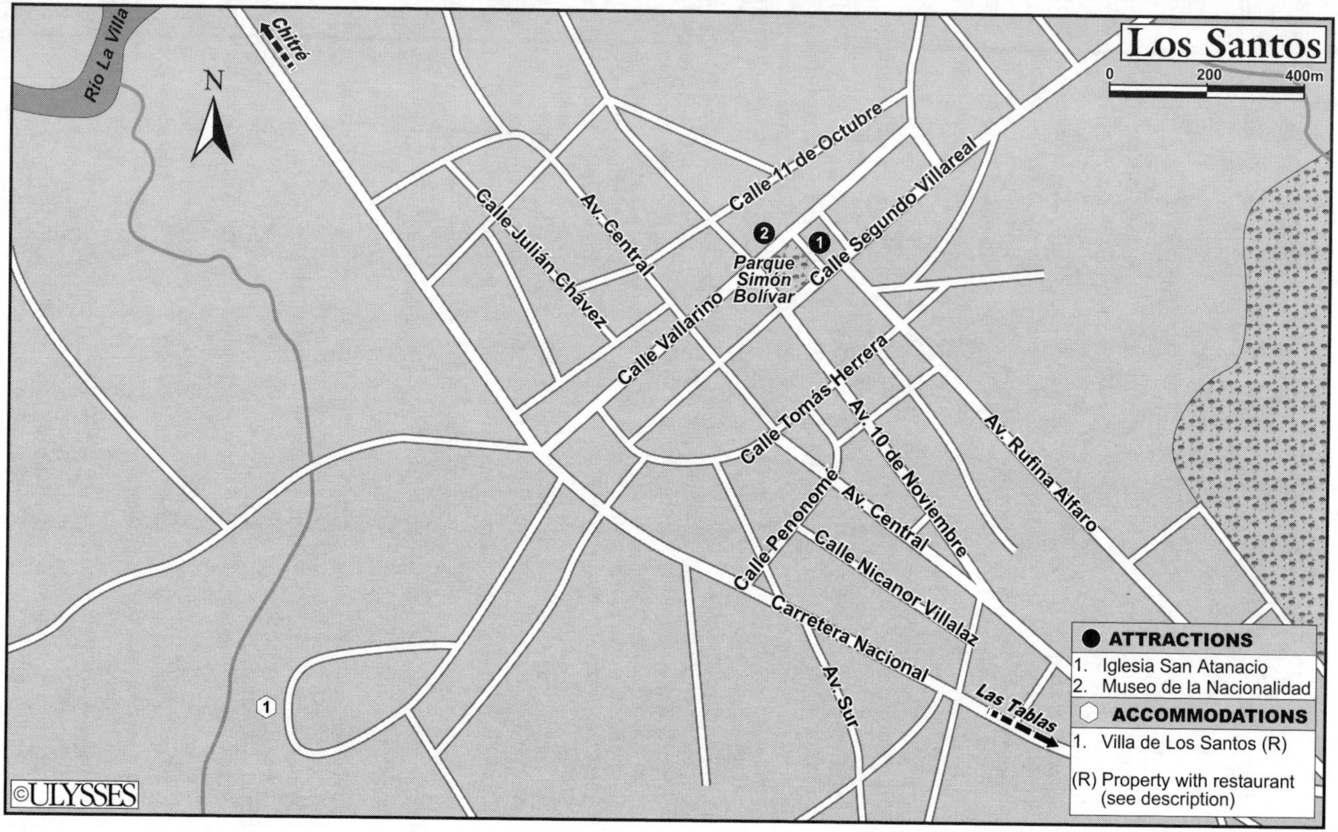

Los Santos
0
200
400m
N
Río La Villa
Chitré
Calle 11-de-Octubre
Calle Segundo Villareal
Calle Julián Chávez
Av. Central
Parque
Simón
Bolívar
Calle Vallarino
Calle Tomás Herrera
Av. 10 de Noviembre
Av. Rufina Alfaro
Calle Penonomé
Av. Central
Calle Nicanor Villalaz
Carretera Nacional
Av. Sur
Las Tablas
ATTRACTIONS
1. Iglesia San Atanacio
2. Museo de la Nacionalidad
ACCOMMODATIONS
1. Villa de Los Santos (R)
(R) Property with restaurant (see description)
©ULYSSES

La *Pollera*

This traditional costume is worn by women during major festivities or during the annual festival that takes place in September in the village of Guararé. It consists of a blouse and a long skirt, both fringed. Generally, they are white with colourful embroidery. A number of accessories complete the costume. The hair is decorated with golden combs, *tembleques* (tremblers), and several *cadenas* (golden or gilded chains) engraved with the national emblem, the fish. The *tembleques* are finely crafted and are made of many pearls, beads and even fish scales, among other things. Some of the pearls are hooked on very thin supports, so that they tremble when the *empollerada* begins to dance—hence the name *tembleques*. A number of hair clips are placed in the hair, creating the effect of a lovely bouquet. Often, these clips are shaped like flowers or insects. Indeed, Panamanian flora and fauna are always represented on national costumes or crafts. This is not surprising considering the rich natural beauty to which inhabitants of the isthmus are constantly exposed. Panamanians take genuine pride in the beauty and many details that go into the design of the *pollera*, and consider it a veritable national costume. In contrast, the men escorting the *empolleradas* dress very simply: trousers, a linen shirt and the famous straw hat, a symbol of virility.

There are doubts as to the origin of the *pollera*; some claim that it began with the gypsies. The dress was originally much simpler and was apparently worn by the maids who accompanied affluent ladies settling in the new colony. Later, merchant-class women began to wear the dresses themselves, having first embellished them with all sorts of decorations (see illustration).

against the Spaniards signed by Simón Bolívar himself, items that belonged to the conquistadors, and a copy of the Declaration of Independence.

The museum is set up in a house built in the style of a Spanish hacienda, and is decorated with period furniture. To the left of the entrance is a reconstruction of the Council Chamber, where the Declaration of Independence was signed. The beautiful chandelier hanging there comes from the colonial church at Cañazas, in Veraguas. Behind the museum is a lovely garden that offers an pleasant view of the house and the church's bell tower.

Guararé

Guararé is known mainly for its costume museum. This charming village is so quiet that it has an otherworldly feel to it.

Every September 24, however, the village comes out of its isolation and quietude to celebrate the Festival Nacional de la Mejorana, where the best singers in the province are chosen and a parade of decorated, oxen-drawn chariots makes its way through the village. On the floats, Panamanian girls wearing their best *polleras* sit enthroned, vying for the title of the most beautiful *empollerada* in the parade. A variety of folk dances are executed as well. Besides the *pollera* dress is also the *montuna* for women and the *montuno* for men. These less ornate costumes originated in Los Santos, but are worn all over the peninsula. They are usually worn by the less privileged, as alternatives to the *pollera*, which is very expensive (a simple *pollera*, without accessories, can cost up to B/.4,000). The *montuna/o* are not without their charms, however. The composition of the costume can vary greatly from one region to another, and even from village to village. In the village of Ocú, for instance, women wear hats. Sometimes a *montuna* is worn with a long frilly shawl. Generally, though, the *montuna* consists of two pieces of clothing: a gathered blouse and long skirt in warm colours. There are variations of the *montuno* as well. This costume consists of a shirt made of coarse linen and simply embroidered, leather sandals with laces (called *cutarras*), a small matching pouch carried over the shoulder, and the indispensable hat. Although traditional *montunos* include knee-length shorts, long pants are worn in some regions. These clothes were originally worn every day, but have become rarer and are now can only be seen at traditional festivals or in small, isolated country villages.

Casa Museo Manuel F. Zárate ★★★ *(B/.1; Tue-Sat 8am to noon and 1pm to 4pm, Sun 8am to noon).* This museum is devoted to folk costumes and contains an impressive collection of masks (representing heads of animals or demons), dresses, ornaments, musical instruments, and, of course, the famous *pollera*, the Panamanian national costume, and its accessories. There is also the famous costume of the *diablico sucio* (see p 180) used in various religious festivals.

Las Tablas

The town of Las Tablas is famous for its exceptionally lively carnival. It is also here, that the finest *polleras* in the country are

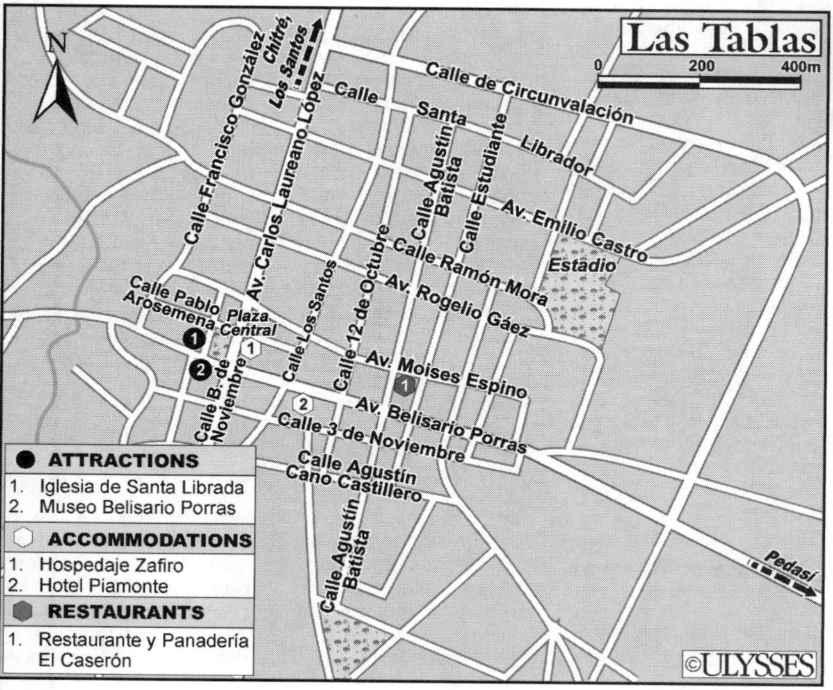

made, as well as the jewels and decorations worn with this dress. The town church, the **Iglesia de Santa Librada ★**, dates from 1789, and its gilded reredos is worth a look. It is decorated with angel heads, some of which, curiously enough, have moustaches! Another strange item—a crucified virgin —is located to the right of the entrance. The village also features a history museum.

Museo Belisario Porras *(B/.0.75, Tue-Sat 9am to 12:30 and 2pm to 4pm; Sun 9am to noon; Avenida Belisario Porras, across from the Parque Central; ☎994-6326)*. This museum is dedicated to Belisario Porras, the three-time president of the republic (1912-1924) who was born in Las Tablas. Porras studied in Colombia and Belgium, and during his career served as ambassador to the United States, France, Great Britain and Italy. During his terms, he contributed to the creation of a law school in Panama City (the ancestor of the present university) and instituted the state register. He also faced a short territorial war with Costa Rica in 1921. The many decorations awarded him by foreign countries such as France and Belgium are on display. Unfortunately, the museum does not provide enough historical background on the objects exhibited.

Province of Veraguas

Veraguas is the only province in the country with access to both coasts, hence its name: *ver-aguas* means "to see the waters." This province consists predominantly of large-scale farming operations and pastures, but there are also a few old gold mines and saltworks. Outside of San Francisco, Veraguas has little in the way of attractions or services for travellers. For most, it is simply a place to pass through on the way to the province of Chiriquí. A journey across this province via the Interamericana will be especially appreciated by people who enjoy dry, hilly landscapes.

Santiago

While Santiago is the capital of the province, it is not a very pleasant or interesting place to visit, particularly as many of its hotels and motels are located on the Interamericana rather than in the centre of the city. Indeed, Santiago is more of a city to pass through. However, if you do choose to pass here, you should not miss an opportunity to visit the Escuela Normal Juan Demóstenes Arosemena ★ to admire the facade of the main building, of Baroque style. This school was founded in 1938 by the President of the Republic. It was for some time one of the most important schools in the country, and many Panamánians completed a portion of their studies here. In addition, Santiago is situated about halfway between David and Panama City, making it a convenient place to rest a while or even stay the night.

★ San Francisco

This small village has a magnificent church and lovely waterfall tumbling into a natural pool. The road to the village is a pleasant one; some 12km from the Interamericana, a narrow suspension bridge built in 1925 adds a little bit of adventure to the trip.

The **Iglesia de San Francisco de la Montaña ★★★** probably has one of the most beautiful and harmonious interiors in the country. The altar is made mostly of wood, and is a veritable jewel of the colonial period. With many details that show an indigenous influence, the altar has some remarkable decorations. Study the fruit and vegetable motifs (incorporating pineapples, grapes, corn and other items) on the columns and the rich decoration of the reredos, where the dominant colours are red and gold. Beautiful silver *adornos* (ornaments) on either side of the altar embellish the overall arrangement. The unusual base of the altar rests on a creature that is half animal, half human.

The two side altars are admirably crafted, containing a multitude of small details, and blend in perfectly with the high altar. The pulpit is also worth a close look; the figure supporting it bears pronounced indigenous traits. The baptismal fonts at the right of the main entrance

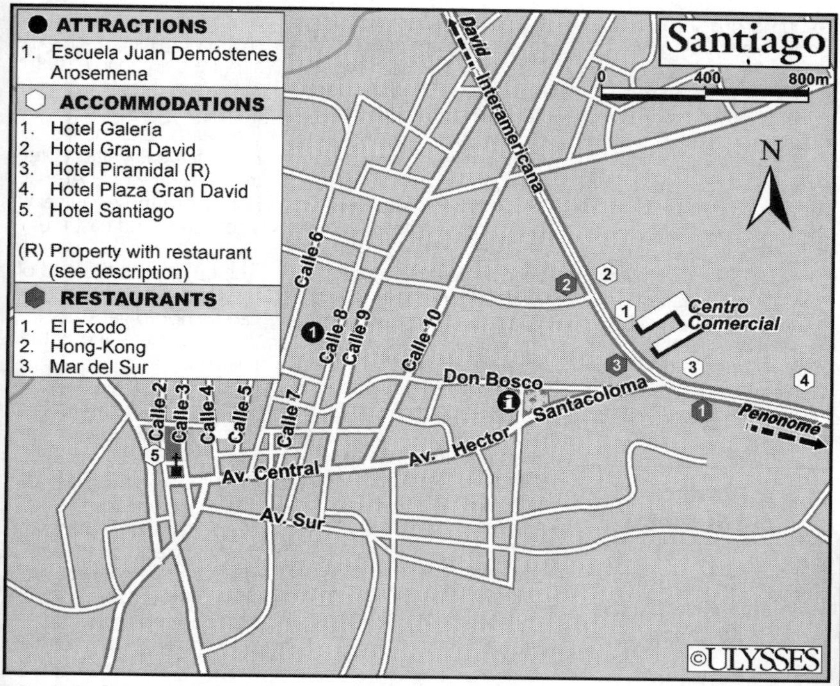

date from 1727, when the church was built. The bell tower is also accessible, and not only is there a fine view from the top, but visitors can also admire three old bells from the colonial period, each of which has a different tone. The outside walls of the church are made of a mixture of brick and stone, and the tower serves as an entrance which is quite rare in Panamá.

The **Balneario El Salto**, a small, natural fresh-water basin, is formed by a waterfall. People actually bathe here since the water is reputed to have curative powers. You can reach it by turning right after the church, then taking an immediate left. Go down the hill and turn right after the baseball diamond.

Parks

Province of Herrera

Parque Nacional Sarigua

Visitors will certainly be surprised to discover this park, where the word "arid" is no exaggeration. This veritable desert is the result of intensive deforestation practised by farmers during the first half of the 20th century, which destroyed a once luxuriant flora. More than 8,000ha were transformed into an arid zone where only a few scrawny bushes grow, and no less than 4,500ha are now a semi-desert. Scientists estimate the desert's progression to be one metre per year. Even though the average temperature in the park zone is about 27°C, readings of 41°C are not infrequent. Also, during the dry period (January to May) violent winds, sometimes reaching up to 100km/h, sweep up great quantities of sand, shifting millions of cubic metres per year.

In the 1940s, the discovery of human bones led to the conclusion that the region, some 11,000 years ago, was inhabited by a sizeable fishing community. To date, this is the earliest proof of human presence in the country. In addition to numerous shards of pottery, several tombs containing precious objects have been discovered here, the most impressive number of pre-Colombian objects ever found in Panamá. A small portion of these has been brought to the Museo Antropológico Reina Torres de Araúz (see p 82). Unfortunately, only a few of the less important pieces of pottery are exhibited at the ANAM station *(☎966-8216)*. No visible trace of this ancient community exists on the site.

Province of Los Santos

Refugio de Vida Silvestre Isla de Cañas

The Refugio de Vida Silvestre Isla de Cañas has been classified by the ANAM as a protected area since 1947. Located at the tip of the Azuero peninsula, this island reserve, about 14km long and partially covered by mangroves, is one of the favourite spawning grounds of marine turtles. There are eight different kinds of marine turtles in the world, four of which can be observed here (see box "Sea Turtle," in Province of Bocas del Toro).

Although there is neither electricity nor running water on the island, the **Cooperativa Isleños** Unidos does have very basic cabins *(B/.10; don't forget a mosquito net and a good insect repellent)* and offers a simple snack-bar service to visitors. This is a well-known attraction for those who are interested in turtles. To reach the island from Playa Venado, head west towards El Cacao. After the village of Cañas, a few kilometres west, a sign on the right side of the highway indicates the small road to Isla de Cañas. This unpaved road, accessible by car, leads to the coast, where you must take a boat to the island. However, before departing, check the availability of transportation and lodging by reserving your cabin in advance at the **Comunidad de la Isla de Cañas** *(☎995-8002)* or at **ANAM** *(☎994-7313)*. Guides will welcome you here, and in their company you will be able to observe the night work of the marine turtles during spawning season.

Beaches

Province of Los Santos

The beaches described below are all located in a loop running from Las Tablas to El Cacao through El Arenal, then back to Las Tablas through the mountains.

The road from Las Tablas to Playa El Arenal runs through fairly dry countryside with small hills, and is in quite good shape. The main activity in this region is stock breeding. Past the village of Pocri, on the right side of the road, is a small cemetery where tombstones are built in the shape of miniature chapels and are painted in pastel colours such as sky blue and candy pink. To get to the beach, take the first road to the left after entering the village of El Arenal, just before the Accel service station and past the Hotel Residencial Pedasí. The beach is at the end of the road, 3km farther (be careful not to get stuck in the sand at the end of the road).

★ Playa El Arenal

Playa El Arenal is a large white-sand beach that seems to stretch out endlessly. Except for a few crabs wandering here and there, it is empty. Since there are no trees, the only shady place is a small open cabin at the edge of the beach. In the distance, you can see the Isla Iguana wildlife reserve. There are no services on the beach, but supplies may be purchased from the village grocer, on the main road through El Arenal. There are also two small restaurants. The beach is not supervised, so swimmers are advised to be cautious.

Playa Venado

For those who enjoy surfing and big waves, Playa Venado is a dream spot, and thrill-seekers will not be disappointed. The beach is not supervised, however, so be careful, and do not venture too far out. The less adventurous can enjoy long walks on the vast sandy beaches, or just soak up the sun.

To get to Playa Venado from Pedasí, follow the same main road west, which gradually becomes greener and more winding. The countryside is characterized by small hills that are often topped by palm trees. Along the road, you will likely come across many people on horseback sporting the omnipresent straw hat. The stretch of road from Pedasí to Playa Venado is not in good condition, and the many potholes will limit your speed to 40km/h.

Playa Cañas

Playa Cañas is not really a beach for swimming, but rather a lagoon in whose waters grow many trees and shrubs, giving it a certain charm. This spot is part of a nature reserve, and if you enjoy ornithology, you will simply love it. Many birds, mostly waders, can be observed here.

To reach Playa Cañas, get back to the main road leading to Tonosí. On the road, 4.5km past Playa Venado and on the way down, is a very fine view of Isla Cañas. Once you have entered the village of Cañas, turn left at the main intersection, and continue over some 1.5km, at which point you will see the beach on your left.

El Cacao to Las Tablas

The road from Playa Cañas to El Cacao is quite bad, riddled with potholes. Along the side of the road, you might encounter several birds, including raptors. At El Cacao the main road divides: to the right is the road to Las Tablas, and to the left the road to Tonosí. The road from El Cacao to Las Tablas is good, but from Flores to El Munio, it is particularly winding. It passes through some beautiful mountainous regions, however making for a lovely drive.

There is another way to drive up the peninsula to Los Santos: at El Cacao, head toward Tonosí and then to Macaracas.

Those in need of sustenance before heading north may want to stop for a drink or a snack (though the choice is very limited) at Tonosí's Restaurante Linda.

Outdoor Activities

Hiking

Chiguirí Arriba is an ideal base for travellers looking to enjoy a bit of hiking. What better way to discover the wonders of the tropical forest and keep fit at the same time? Be careful, however, as the trails are rarely marked. Also, unless you plan on heading far from the villages, it is a good idea to enlist the services of a guide who will provide all sorts of information on the flora and fauna of the region... and will give you a chance to practise your Spanish. As a general rule, the guides are from Tabidal, a small neighbouring village, and they will probably take you to a waterfall called Salto el Chorro Antolino, which is fed by the Río Tabidal. From there, another excursion along the *río* to admire the petroglyphs will be suggested. For the latter excursion, however, be sure to wear good walking shoes and long trousers, as there are many thistles along the path.

Horseback Riding

If you are staying at the Posada Cerro la Vieja (see p 188), in **Chiguirí Arriba**, the staff can suggest various guided trail rides. It is possible to get to **El Valle** by horse, but you'll have to get up early and prepare yourself for a full day of riding. The horse will cost about B/.24 for 3hrs. Note that the trip takes the same amount of time on foot and horseback. Guide services are included in the packages offered by the Posada, but it is customary to give the guide a small tip (usually about B/.5 for 3hrs for one or two people).

Accommodations

Province of Coclé

Penonomé

Los Pinos
$
pb, hw, ≡, ⊗
on the right side of the Interamericana, just before Penonomé when coming from Panama City
☎997-9518
This small hotel offers 11 very basic rooms.

Dos Continentes
$$
pb, hw, ≡, ≈, ℜ
at the entrance to town when coming from Ciudad de Panama City, Apdo 54
☎997-9325
⇄997-9390
This simple, non-descript hotel is advantageously located at the entrance to town.

Chiguirí Arriba

Posada Cerro la Vieja
$$$-$$$$
pb, hw, ⊗, ℜ
Apartado 543-9A, Calle 51, Casa 24, local 4
☎983-8900 in Panama City
☎223-4553
⇄264-4960
Considering its isolation, the packages at the Posada Cerro la Vieja are a good idea: B/.70 per person for one night's lodging and three meals or B/.140 per person for two nights and six meals.

This establishment is certainly one of the most interesting additions to the Panamanian tourist industry in recent years. You'll feel a million miles away, amidst an extraordinary landscape, surrounded by mountains blanketed by a tropical forest.

Rooms are simple but comfortable. Groups of four to ten people may want to stay in one of the two adjoining *cabañas*, set atop a hillock and offering a beautiful view; a number of hammocks hang on its large terrasse beside the main building. One of the advantages of lodging at the Posada is that meals are eaten around large round tables, where you will surely encounter Panamanians and other travellers intrigued by the natural surroundings.

Province of Herrera

Chitré

Hotel Rex
$$
pb, hw, ≡, ℜ, *tv,* #
facing the central park
☎996-4310 or 996-2408
⇄996-4310
(we suggest you call beforehand)
This hotel is not luxurious, but offers good value for the price. It also offers the advantage of being located right downtown. The third story has a beautiful terrace with a view of the central plaza and the church. The newer back rooms are brighter and quieter and offer a pleasant although slightly kitschy decor. The staff is welcoming and helpful.

Hotel Hong Kong
$$
pb, hw, ≡, ℜ, *tv,* #
on the right side of the main road from Chitré to Los Santos, just before the intersection with Via Circunvalación
☎996-4483
⇄996-5229
This is a very pleasant hotel with an interesting Chinese-style decor. The rooms are comfortable and well maintained, and the pool makes the place even more appealing. Good value.

Hotel Versailles
$$
pb, hw, ≡, *tv,* ≈
Paseo Enrique Grensier, Apdo 298
☎996-4422 or 996-4563
⇄996-2090
With its large, lacklustre concrete facade, the Hote Versailles appears at first glance to be rather charmless. However, the interior is attractively decorated and exhibits various objects crafted by artisans, including many reproductions of pre-Columbian pottery.

The rooms are modern, clean and comfortable, anc look out onto the pool. A large garden and lawn complement the arrangement, and a parking area with attendant is available to guests. Although the hotel is located a short distance from the downtown area, it offers the best value in the city.

Province of Los Santos

Hotel La Villa de Los Santos
$
pb, hw, ≡, ≈, ℜ, *tv,* #
on the road from Chitré to Los Santos. As you leave Chitré on the way to Los Santos after passing the Río La Villa, turn right at the third intersection, just after the Delta station (where there are signs for the Restaurante Las Palmeras). Follow the main road and at the obelisk, take the road on the left. The hotel is a little farther on
☎**966-9321**
⇄**996-8201**
Although it is called a hotel, the two rows of accommodation at La Villa de Los Santos more closely resemble a motel. The rooms are dingy and not very comfortable, nor is the soundproofing the best; ask to assigned next to an unoccupied room. A more recently constructed third wing, next to the pool, is more comfortable. This hotel's major asset is its swimming pool, surrounded by palm trees and greenery. Swimming here is a real pleasure. Non-guests may also use the pool for B/.2, and the hotel also has a small bar and a restaurant.

Guararé

Residencial La Mejorana
$$
pb, hw, tv, ≡
on the Carretera Nacional, on the right side of the highway to Las Tablas
☎**994-5794**
⇄**994-5796**
On the main highway between Los Santos and Las Tablas, La Mejorana offers clean, attractive rooms. Although the building is quite modern, the owner has created a warm atmosphere by choosing tasteful wooden furniture. Unfortunately, most of the rooms, while equipped with all of the necessary comforts, are fairly small. This establishment offers good quality for the price.

Las Tablas

Hospedaje Zafiro
$
pb, hw, ≡
corner Belariso Porras
☎/⇄**994-8200**
This small guesthouse, located on the second floor of a corner building, has a dozen or so rooms that do not afford the greatest comfort, but are well maintained. Tiles form the basis of the decor and are found everywhere. The advantage of this establishment is its central location facing Parque 8 de Noviembre and the largest church in the city, the Iglesia Santa Librada. If possible, rent one of the rooms facing the rear in order to avoid the noise from the numerous businesses on the building's main floor.

Hotel Piamonte
$$
pb, hw, ≡
Avenida Belisario Porras
☎**994-6372**
Modern and without any particular charm, Hotel Piamonte offers the advantage of a central location. It is the most comfortable establishment in town.

Pedasí

Pension Moscoso
$
Av. Centrale in Pedasí, on the left side of the main road
☎**995-2203**
The Pension Moscoso is a boarding house. It is charming and clean, though the rooms lack privacy.

Hotel Residecial Pedasí
$$
pb, ≡, ℜ
at the entrance to the village on the road to Las Tablas
☎**995-2322**
Decidedly less charming than the Pensión Moscoso, the Hotel Residencial Pedasí is a good alternative if the small guest house has no vacancies.

Playa Venado

Those who wish to stay on the beach will have to settle for very basic cabins (five in all) with a corner for the shower and toilets. Lacking a sign, but known as **El Jorón** *($)*, these rooms are not equipped with air-conditioning or mosquito netting. Although a generator provides electricity, power failures are not unheard of. As the number of *cabañas* is limited and it is possible to reserve, but it is best to avoid weekends. This place is suitable only for those with an adventurous spirit!

Province of Veraguas

Downtown Santiago

Hotel Santiago
$
pb, hw, ≡
Calle 2, behind Santiago's church
☎998-4824
The Hotel Santiago is located in a pretty little house with colonial charm, made all the more attractive by a small interior courtyard. Unfortunately, the rooms are not that comfortable.

From Divisa to Santiago along the Interamericana

Gran David
$$
pb, hw, ≡, ≈, ℜ, *tv,* #
on the Interamericana before the intersection for Santiago
☎998-2622 or 998-4510
⇄998-1866
A fine, tastefully decorated establishment, the Hotel Gran David has a pleasant pool and offers good value for the price. If you are looking for a quiet atmosphere, however, avoid this hotel, since there is a constant stream of guests coming in and out. The hotel is quite large and accommodates many families. Its cafeteria ***($)*** should only be used as a last resort, as there is no set menu and only a limited choice of dishes. Furthermore, the staff is not very welcoming.

Plaza Gran David
$$
pb, hw, ≡, ≈, ℜ, *tv,* #
on the right side of the Interamericana highway heading west, just before the turn-off for Santiago
☎998-3433
⇄998-2553
This hotel-motel is recommended above all for its quiet setting and large pool. The decoration, however, is rather dubious. Note that, you can park your car next to your room.

Hotel Piramidal
$$
pb, hw, ≡, ≈, ℜ, *tv,* #
on the right side of the Interamericana heading west, shortly before the turn-off for Santiago
☎998-3123
⇄998-5411
Despite its interesting architecture and comfortable rooms, this hotel lacks charm. There is a garage in front of the entrance, and the many trucks that use it make a lot of noise.

Hotel Galería
$$
pb, hw, ≡, *tv,* ℜ
via Interamericana
☎958-7950 or 958-7951
⇄958-7954
The Hotel Galería offers rooms that are not very charming, but comfortable nevertheless. As well as being reasonably priced, this hotel has the advantage of being next to Santiago's commercial centre.

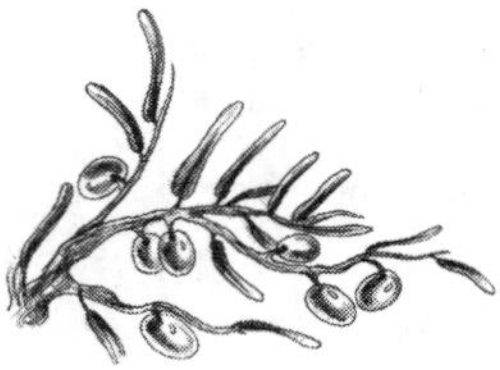

Restaurants

Province of Coclé

On the Interamericana

Rincón Los Camisones
$
on the Interamericana, 12 km past San Carlos on the right when going to Santiago
Set on a small hill overlooking the Interamericana, this quaint outdoor restaurant boasts a fine view. It serves classic Panamanian meals with no great surprises. The restaurant is not very easy to see from the road, so watch for signs advertising the place.

Penonomé

Panaderia y Dulceria Romec
$
near the central plaza, to the right of the church, facing the post office
Good pastries and coffee, fruit juice and *chicha* are available at this pleasant spot, which features a little terrace and a friendly staff.

Parrillada El Gigante
$
to the left of the road, after the turn-off to the city, from Panama City
This restaurant serves pizza, Panamanian cuisine and a few Lebanese dishes in a pleasant, traditionally decorated setting.

Chiguirí Arriba

Posada Cerro la Vieja
$$
☎997-8191 or 223-4553
The Posada Cerro la Vieja offers package deals including accommodation and dining, but you can also eat here if you are only passing through. Meals are served at round tables that can seat about a dozen people, making it easy to meet other nature-lovers, often Panamanians. The meals are served buffet-style, and when there are fewer patrons, only one dish is prepared. Salad, potatoes or rice, plantain and dessert are the usual accompaniments. Considering the out-of-the-way location, you will eat quite well.

Natá

Vega
$
on the Interamericana, to the left, at the intersection for Natá
The Vega is a small, ordinary restaurant with a simple, standard menu.

Province of Herrera

Chitré

Aire Libre
$
Av. Obaldia, across from Parque Unión
In a room with minimalist decor that opens onto the street, the Aire Libre restaurant serves various simple Panamánian-style rice dishes. This place is ideal for travellers seeking simple, inexpensive fare.

La Tinaja
$
Calle Meliton Martin, a little beyond the Rex Hotel, on the way toward the Herrera Museum
Decorated with arcades, this tiny, unpretentious restaurant has a great atmosphere, except for the omnipresent, blaring television. The staff is very friendly and welcoming. This spot opens early in the morning and in the afternoon (closed at night). Good family cooking at very reasonable prices *(main dishes with soup B/.3)*. To take advantage of this bargain, you should arrive early, as lunch in Chitré begins at 11am. After that, the choice is very limited.

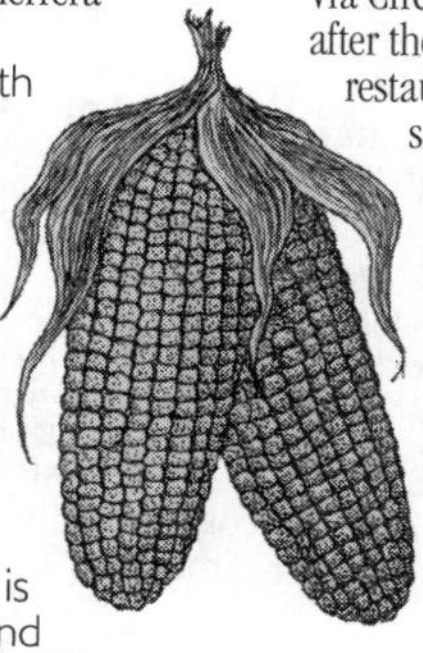

Panadería-Pizzeria Chiquita
$
Av. Herrera
If good pizza is what you crave, the place to go is the Panadería-Pizzeria Chiquita. In the large, open dining room, you can order excellent pizza with your choice of toppings, and choose from a vast assortment of desserts, such as ice cream. This establishment is very popular with young locals, and even though its only decor is the street scene outside, it is still attractive.

Jorón Lelyan
$
on the road from Chitré to Los Santos, before the intersection of Via Circunvalación. Turn right after the Hotel Hong Kong restaurant and on the right side
This open-air bar and nightclub with palm roof serves copious meals and beverages at very inexpensive prices *(B/.0.45 for a beer)*. The choice, however, is limited. This is a good place for listening to popular music. Open late afternoons only.

Hong Kong
$$
on the right of the main road from Chitré to Los Santos, just before the intersection of Via Circunvalación
☎996-4483
The Hong Kong is a beautiful, elaborately decorated Chinese hotel-restaurant. It offers a varied menu at affordable prices, and the staff is very welcoming. Breakfast served from 7am.

Centro Turístico Los Guayacanes
$$$
via de Circunvalación on the right side of the road to Los Santos
☎996-9758
Although it is outside the downtown area of Chitré, on the Via de Circunvalación, the brand-new Centro Turístico Los Guayacanes is worth the detour thanks to its beautiful surroundings. Perched on a hill, the restaurant of this mini-complex has a pleasant view of the surrounding countryside.

Guests can either choose to dine in the large open-air dining room, which is protected from the sun by a tile roof, or the indoor dining room. This room is more formal and has air-conditioning, but lacks the view. In either case, the menu offers many Panamánian dishes as well as international cuisine. For visitors seeking a refreshing dip before their meal, the swimming pool *(B/.2)*, with locker room and showers, is available in the lower part of the complex.

Restaurante El Mesón
$$$
facing Parque Unión, in the Rex Hotel
☎996-4310 or 996-2408
The Restaurante El Mesón specializes in seafood, and thanks to its friendly staff and tasteful decor, it is a pleasant spot to eat. Here, enjoy such dishes as *longorones, langostinas a la criolla o al ajilloa* (scampi with tomatoes, onions and pepper or garlic), *camarones* (shrimp) and *corvina*. Lighter meals are available at the cafeteria, facing the restaurant, where you can also enjoy fresh fruit for breakfast (a rarity in Panamá).

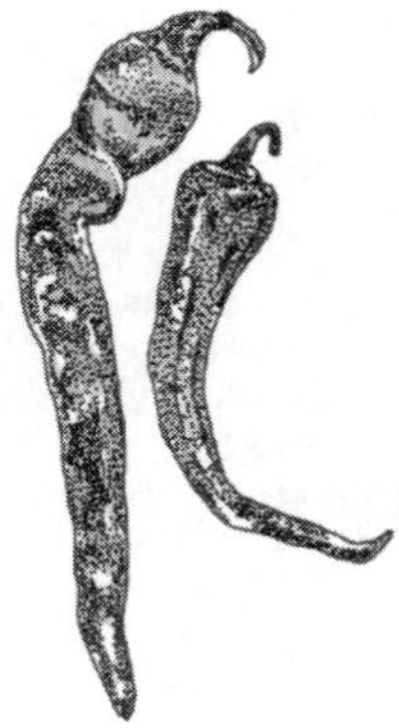

Province of Los Santos

Los Santos

Las Palmeras
$
in the Villa de Los Santos Hotel
Las Palmeras is a small, open restaurant with a view of the garden and the pool. At night, though, the interior is poorly lit. The simple cuisine is Panamanian and the choice is limited.

Las Tablas

Restaurante y Panadería El Caserón
$$
every day 8am to 9pm
corner Av. Moisés Espino and Augustin Batista
☎994-6066
With its charming terrace on the street corner of a picturesque district, the Restaurante y Panadería El Caserón is the right choice for those who like a quiet, authentic atmosphere. The extensive menu will satisfy those who appreciate the typical cuisine of the country, as well as those who prefer more classic offerings. The warm reception by the owners makes up for the particularly slow service.

Pedasí

Pedasí
$
Carretera Principal, at the entrance to the village, on the road to Las Tablas
☎995-2322
At the modest Hotel Residencia Pedasí, you will find reasonably priced food, but the choice is limited.

From Playa Arenal to Playa Venado

Shortly after crossing the Río Oria, you will see a small sign that reads *Pepsi Nancy* on your left. By heading up the little road, you will reach a house whose occupants sell drinks and pastries. Although very modest, the place makes for a pleasant little stop on this otherwise not very relaxing road. The view of the sea from here is beautiful. Welcoming staff; breakfast served starting at 7am.

Playa Venado

El Jorón
$
Right on the beach near the little cabins, El Jorón is a simple, open-air restaurant. There are no signs, but it is known as El Jorón. A few balboas *(approximately B/.2 to B/.3)* will buy a plate of fish and rice or *patacones*. Simple but nourishing!

Province of Veraguas

From Divisa to Santiago on the Interamericana

Piramidal
$
turn right on the Interamericana, head west, just before the intersection for the town
☎998-3123
Large self-service cafeteria serving a number of traditional meals: chicken, *corvina*, beef... This may not be the most attractive place, but the meals are cheap and the choice is good.

Restaurante Hong Kong
$
facing the Hotel Gran David on the Interamericana
The Hong Kong is an unpretentious place that serves a small selection of light meals. The television is always on.

Restaurante Hotel Plaza Gran David
$$
take a right on the Interamericana and head west; just before the turn off for Santiago
The restaurant in the Hotel Plaza Gran David serves traditional, family cuisine with no surprises.

Mar del Sur
$$$
☎998-6455
on the left side of the westbound Interamericana facing the shopping centre
On par with the original restaurant in David, Mar del Sur prepares authentic Peruvian dishes such as *papas a la huancaina* and *almejas a la sureña*. Excellent Chilean and Argentinean wines are available. Prices are reasonable for the quality.

Downtown Santiago

Pasteleria Abeja
$
Calle Estudiante and Avenida C, two streets west of the intersection for Santiago
This pastry shop is worth a visit for its vast choice and low prices. The brightly coloured cakes are a big part of the decor!

Entertainment

Province of Herrera

Chitré

On the Vía Circunvalación, not quite centrally located, the brand-new **Centro Turístico Los Guayacanes** *(Via de Circunvalación, on the right side of the road to Los Santos, ☎996-9758)* features two bars, a nightclub and a restaurant in a building set on a rise. If you arrive before sunset, you can enjoy a lovely view of the surrounding countryside. Great atmosphere and Panamánian music guaranteed.

Discoteca Angelina
near the church and the central plaza
This is an excellent place to buy records, tapes and CDs of local music. The owner will be pleased to introduce you to the various styles of Latin and Central American music and answer your questions about the area.

Shopping

Province of Herrera

Chitré

Downtown Chitré is an excellent place to shop. You can find almost everything you need at very reasonable prices *(pants for B/.10, jeans for B/.15, shirts for B/.10, T-shirts for B/.5)*. Be careful, however, since the quality of the clothes is not always up to par.

Province of Los Santos

Las Tablas

Talabarteria Gonzalez
downtown, on Calle Pablo Arosemena, about 100m from the central plaza, on the left
This small store sells a number of leather articles, including belts. Leather chairs are made here, as are beautiful saddles at incredibly low prices—perfect for riding fans.

On the Interamericana, toward La Peña

Mercado Artesenal Veraga La Peña
Mon-Fri 7am to 4pm, Sat 7am to noon
6.4km from the turn-off for San Francisco, on the left
Stopping by this little co-operative is a must in order to admire the fine reproductions of pre-Columbian pottery and figurines. You can also buy quality leather goods (such as sandals and belts). Stop by the workshop to observe the highly skilled, craftsmen at work and learn some of the secrets of their trade.

The Panama Hat or "Montuno"

Who is not familiar with the famous "Panama" hat? Contrary to what one might think, this hat did not originate in Panamá but rather in Ecuador, in the Montecristi region, where they are made by numerous craftspeople. The name comes from the fact that many workers wore these hats as protection from the sun and rain during the construction of the canal. Ironically, many Panamanian men, particularly in the towns of the Azuero peninsula, proudly sport two kinds of *montuno* hats, which are mostly made in the villages of Ocú and La Pintada. The most popular model is the *ocueno* (usually made in Ocú), which has only one narrow black line as decoration and a turned-up brim. The other model, called the *pintado* (made in the village of La Pintada), is decorated with black patterns and has a straight brim. Both hats are made from the white fibres of the palm tree, and the dark patterns come from the same material, dyed with a special ingredient that is a carefully guarded secret. The braided cord attached to the hat is exclusive to the little village of Ocú. This cord is either black or another colour.

Province of Coclé

Penonomé

Penonomé is famous for its crafts. There is a vast choice of beautiful items at the **Mercado de Artesanías** *(left side of the Interamericana west, just before the turn-off for Penonomé).*

Province of Veraguas

Santiago

For avid shoppers, a trip to the new **Centro Comercial** *(on the Interamericana, just before the turn-off for the road to the downtown area)* is essential. Everything is available here: footwear, clothing, electronic equipment, records, groceries, etc. However, do not expect competitive prices or original objects; this complex is basically like every other mall in the world.

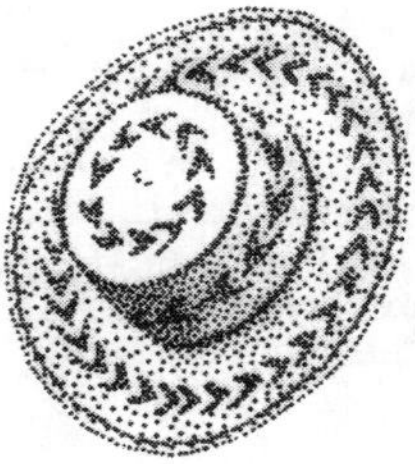

Province of Chiriquí

In the Guaymie language, Chiriquí means "Valley of the Moon."

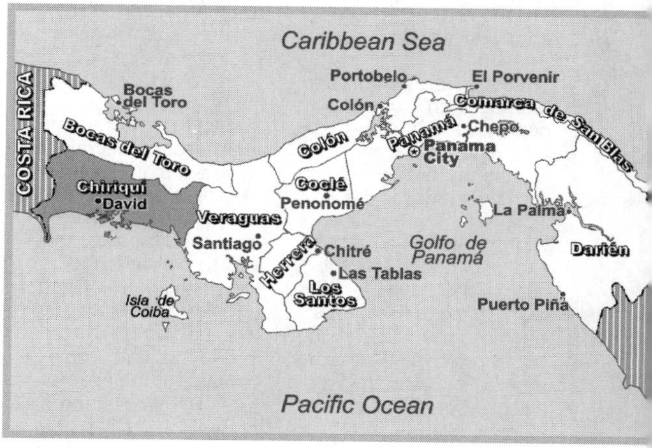

With the Volcán Barú and Parque Internacional La Amistad, this region (with more than 370,000 inhabitants) is not only the highest in the country, but also the one with the most varied landscape. Chiriquí features vistas to suit every taste, from verdant mountains and white, sandy beaches to trails bordered with wild flowers. Thanks to an amazing climate, which is usually in the 20-degree range, agriculture is a major and diverse activity. For example, at higher altitudes, you can enjoy the province's cheeses, excellent coffee and oranges (reputed to be the best in the country), while in the lower regions, banana groves and sugar cane fields offer an ideal treat for anyone craving exotic flavours. The main attraction in this province, however, is hiking, as the cool climate is perfect for it. Whether it's a climb up Volcán Barú (3,475m), an expedition in the tropical forest in search of the quetzal, or a simple walk across the flowered valleys along narrow streams, nature-lovers will find a wide selection of hiking opportunities here. Along with Bocas del Toro, the province of Chiriquí is also one of the rare regions in the western part of the country where there is a large population of natives, the Guaymies.

The Mama Chi Movement

Facing increasing expropriation of their land, the Ngobes (see p 31) began to form several opposition movements in the 1960s, most of which leant heavily towards messianism. To understand the attraction to such an idealistic defiance, one must look back to the turn of the century, a time when immigrant farmers and, more specifically, the United Fruit Company settled on land inhabited by the Ngobe people. Indeed the employment of seasonal workers by land owners and their large banana plantations greatly upset the indigenous ways of life. Traditionally, work was distributed by the elders and was performed according to community needs. The sudden apparition of personal wealth created a new, more individualistic lifestyle and focused on needs that had previously been unknown. The younger, schooled generation began to question the power of leaders and religious authorities; it no longer wanted to follow in its ancestors footsteps. It is in reaction to this upheaval that many small political groups begin advocating the refusal to work for *Latinos*, seclusion and the return to more traditional ways.

In 1960, the Chiriqui Land Company employed nearly 5,000 Ngobe-Bugle workers in its banana plantations throughout the province of Bocas del Toro. The same year, a widespread strike erupted and, after a long and difficult walkout, over 1,700 workers were fired, most of whom had little choice but to return to their community. It is in the midst of this bleak context that Mama Chi appeared. Delia Bejerano, then in her 20s, lived with her young daughter on one of the plantations owned by the company. In September 1962, she claimed that she had seen a man and a woman clad in white descend from the heavens on what appeared to be a motorcycle. As they touched the earth, the ground shook violently and two nearby hillocks noisily crumbled. At this point, she fainted.

When she awoke, the strangers were in her house. They told her that they lived in the sky and that the father of the sky had sent them down to earth for the first time to ask her for a sack of earth for God. The strangers also asked the woman to gather together the Sukias (medicine men) and Ngobes every other year to welcome God. Further commandments included banning the *clarida*, *balsería* and *chichería* customs and having the Ngobes gather regularly to pray in chapels over the next five years. Work had to be reduced to five days a week so that weekends could be dedicated to the worship of God.

Should these commandments not be heeded, it was said, that life on earth would be destroyed. Delia Bejerano was handed an encrypted message that was to be transcribed by the faithful; non-indigenous peoples were not to set eyes upon the sacred inscriptions that would be revealed in the near future. This story is the basis of the Mama Chi movement. In the language of the Ngobes, Mama Chi means "little mother," while Mama Kri means "big mother," the name given to the Virgin Mary. The number of followers has never been known, but it seems that this is one of the most significant Ngobe opposition movements ever to exist.

Mama Chi succumbed to illness on September 14, 1964 without seeing the reunification of her people. Her daughter, the Niña Chi, was to inherit the divine mission when she came of age. In the meantime, Sandalio Moreno was mandated by Mama Chi to pursue the goals of the movement. In April 1965, given his more political nature, Moreno organized a meeting of nearly 4,000 Ngobes (an indication of the size of the Mama Chi movement), at which time a vote was passed declaring a free Ngobe republic. Soon after the creation of the Ngobe Republic, Sandalio became president and a constitution and flag were adopted, based on the commandments given to Mama Chi.

However, the Panamanian government was quick to react and within the year sent troops, under Omar Torrijos Herrera. To avoid a war, the president of the short-lived republic signed a treaty with Torrijos. This significant event marked the downfall of the Mama Chi movement and its subsequent split into various factions.

Nowadays, faithful followers of the prophetic vision of Mama Chi include the Sukias, who inhabit the San Felix sector. Niña Chi is rumoured to live among them, adulated by her followers and completely isolated from non-indigenous people since it is strictly forbidden to have any contact with them. Some say that the movement, now called *Mama, Tadta y Niña Chi* (father, mother and little girl), represents nearly a quarter of the Ngobe population. Although the Mama Chi movement failed to accomplish many of its goals, it did succeed in reuniting the Ngobes and teaching them the importance of political unity in order to claim what is theirs by right, their ancestral land.

Finding Your Way Around

By Car

To drive to **Playa Las Lajas**, turn left at the intersection of the road to San Félix and the Interamericana. Stay on the main road for the next 3km, then turn left at the intersection. Keep going for 9.2km; the beach is at the end of the road.

To get to **David** from Panama City, take the Interamericana west and 438km farther, at the intersection for Boquete, take the main road on the left. This road will take you directly to the centre of town.

To reach **Boquete** from the Interamericana highway, turn right at the intersection for David. Keep going north for 14.4km until the next major intersection. Take the road to the right (there is a sign for Boquete) and again keep going north. Boquete is 35km past the Interamericana. There is also another way to reach the village: take the same road, but at 33.5km on the Interamericana, turn on the road to the right of the main road, where a sign points you to Boquete. This is the less spectacular road. It runs along the Río Caldera and ends at the village central plaza.

To reach **Caldera** from the Interamericana, take the road to Boquete for about 30km. The intersection for Caldera is on the right side of the road.

To get to the **Carta Vieja** rum distillery in Alanje from David, take the Interamericana west, and 21km farther, follow the main road on the left. The entrance to the distillery is about 4km farther, on the left of the road.

To drive to **Cerro Punta** and **Volcán**, turn right off the Interamericana at the exit for La Concepción. This turn- off is about 24.2km west of the one for Boquete and David. Now drive north along the main road until you get to Volcán. You can also follow the signs for the Bambito Hotel, which is on the same road. To get to Cerro Punta, turn left at the end of the village of Volcán and follow the signs. The road to Cerro Punta is very pleasant and at times runs along the Río Chiriquí Viejo.

Note: the following schedules and rates are provided for reference only and are subject to change.

From San José (Costa Rica)
See p 41.

By Plane

David

The **Enrique Malek airport** (see below) in David is the only airport in the province. It is situated 3km from David. To get there by car, drive south on Avenida 3 de Noviembre. As no bus service is provided between the airport and the downtown area, a taxi is the only option *(approximately B/.2)*. A small cafeteria on the second floor of the building offers a limited choice of drinks and snacks.

Mapiex-Aero and **Aeroperlas** are the only two airlines that currently service this destination from the capital.

Mapiex-Aero

Panama City to David
Departure: Mon-Fri 6:25am, 11:30am and 4pm; Sat 9:30am and 4pm Sun 8am and 4pm.
Travel Time: 1hr
Cost: B/.57 one way

David to Panama City
Departure: Mon-Fri 7:35am, 12:50pm and 5:10pm; Sat 10:35am and 5:10pm; Sun 9:15am and 5:10pm.

David
(Enrique Malek Airport)
☎721-0841 or 721-0842

Aeroperlas

Panama City to David
Departure: Mon-Fri 6:30am, 10:30am and 4:30pm; Sat 7am, 10:30am, 3:30pm; Sun 8am and 3:30pm.
Travel Time: 1hr 5min
Cost: B/.57 one way

David to Panama City
Departure: Mon-Fri 7am, 11:30am, and 5pm; Sat 8:30am and 5pm; Sun 9:30am and 5pm.

David
(Enrique Malek Airport)
☎721-1195

By Bus

David

Panama City to David (or any other westbound destination)
Departure: every hour between 7am and 6pm from the Terminal Nacional de Transporte *(☎314-6171 or 314-6167)* on Calle Curundú (also called Calle Ascanio Villalaz or Vía La Amistad) in the Curundú section of town, close to the M. Gelabert airport. Rate: B/.12 one way by regular bus; B/.15 one way by express bus.

Some buses go directly to David, while others stop frequently along the way. Depending on the bus, the length of the trip may vary between five and seven hours.

Other Destinations

Buses to **Chiriquí**, **Boquete**, **Cerro Punta**, **Playa Las Lajas**, **Puerto Armuelles** and other areas in the province leave from the terminal in David since there is no bus service from the capital. In most cases, buses to small villages are fairly old and uncomfortable, and stop frequently. This, combined with the poor state of the roads, makes even short trips seem like an eternity. For instance, getting to Boquete—only 37km away fromDavid—takes between 60 and 90min. Generally, most regional buses travel at 30km/h, and because the sun begins to set at 6:30pm in Panamá, itineraries should be planned accordingly. The following are a few examples of travel times and rates to some of the most popular destinations in the province:

David Terminal de Transporte
Paseo Estudiante

Boquete
Travel Time: 1hr to 1hr 30min
Rate: B/.2 one way

Cerro Punta
Travel Time: 2hrs 30min
Rate: B/.3 one way

Volcán
Travel Time: 2hrs
Rate: B/.2.50 one way

Puerto Armuelles
Travel Time: 2hrs 45min
Rate: B/.3.50 one way

Jaguar

San José (Costa Rica)

Tracopa
Calle 5 Este, between Calle Central and Calle A Sur
☎775-0585
Tracopa has coaches connecting David to the capital of Costa Rica, San José.
Departures: every day 8:30am
Travel Time: 8hrs
Rate: B/.13 one way

Practical Information

Post Office

David
Calle C Norte 3/4 and Avenida Bolívar

ANAM (INRENARE)

David

Via Aeropuerto
☎775-7840 or 774-6671
⇄775-3163

IPAT (Tourist Office)

David

left of the church, on the first floor of the Galherma building (office #4)
☎775-4120

Paso Canoa

next to the border station

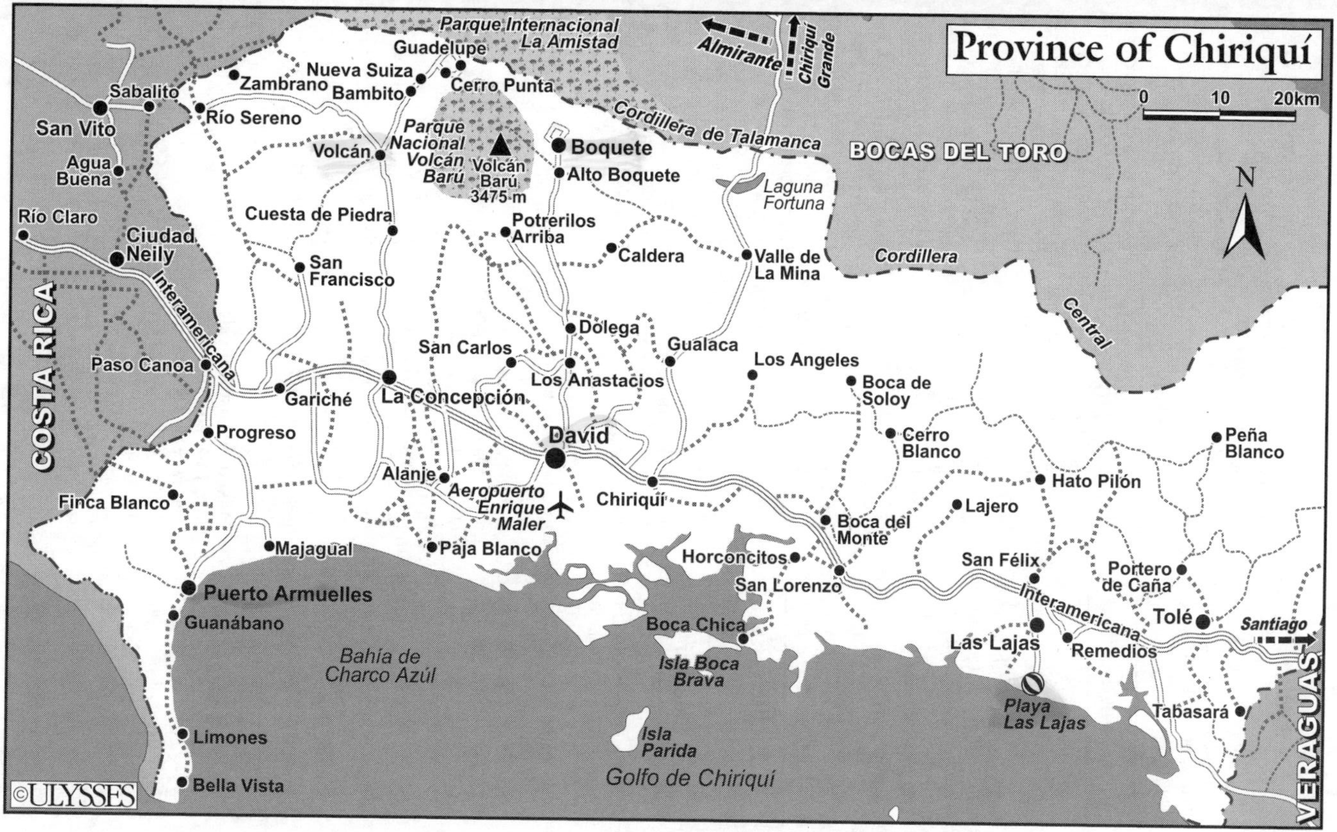

Province of Chiriquí
0
10
20km
N
Parque Internacional La Amistad
Almirante
Chiriquí Grande
Guadelupe
Nueva Suiza
Zambrano
Bambito
Cerro Punta
Sabalito
San Vito
Río Sereno
Cordillera de Talamanca
BOCAS DEL TORO
Parque Nacional Volcán Barú
Volcán Barú 3475 m
Boquete
Alto Boquete
Volcán
Agua Buena
Laguna Fortuna
Río Claro
Cuesta de Piedra
Potrerilos Arriba
Caldera
Valle de La Mina
Cordillera
Ciudad Neily
San Francisco
Interamericana
Central
COSTA RICA
Dolega
Gualaca
San Carlos
Los Angeles
Paso Canoa
Los Anastacios
Boca de Soloy
Gariché
La Concepción
Progreso
David
Cerro Blanco
Peña Blanco
Alanje
Hato Pilón
Aeropuerto Enrique Maler
Chiriquí
Lajero
Finca Blanco
Boca del Monte
Majagual
Paja Blanco
Horconcitos
San Félix
Portero de Caña
San Lorenzo
Puerto Armuelles
Interamericana
Tolé
Santiago
Guanábano
Boca Chica
Las Lajas
Remedios
Bahía de Charco Azúl
Isla Boca Brava
Playa Las Lajas
Tabasará
VERAGUAS
Isla Parida
Limones
Golfo de Chiriquí
Bella Vista
©ULYSSES

Boquete

on the right side of the road heading to Boquete, just before the descent leading to the village

Exchange Office

David

Banco Exterior, one block south of the central park (across from the church on the right side), at the corner of Avenida 4 Este The bank also accepts traveller's cheques.

Exploring

Chiriquí

The only points of interest in this small rural village, situated near to the Interamericana: the fact that it is along the way to Chiriquí Grande (in the Province of Bocas del Toro), and the fact it holds cock fights.

Upon entering the village, you will notice a green wooden building on the right with a sign reading *Club Galisticó*. This is an indication to visitors that cock fights are held here.

Guacala

This lovely village on the road to Chirquí Grande is exactly 18km from the Interamericana and features small, attractively adorned rustic houses. Adding to the country atmosphere, a number of villagers travel on horseback. Guacala is a pleasant little stop on the way to the Caribbean.

David

David (pop. 110,000) is far from being an architecturally outstanding city, and its general appearance leaves much to be desired. However, you should not miss the opportunity to visit the city's interesting history museum, as well as its many restaurants and boutiques.

This is the only large city in the province, and consequently, its lively ambiance is entertaining. Many buses leave from David, carrying passengers to Panama City or San José (Costa Rica). As well, **Parque Cervantes**, the heart of the village, is a good vantage point for observing the constant comings and goings of shopkeepers, travellers and school children, all in a typical Panamanian ambiance. David is also a good city for shopping, with reasonable prices and a good selection. Besides the usual items (clothing, music, shoes), various handicrafts, including beautiful *molas* at good prices *(B/.10 to B/.15)* are sold in Parque Cervantes.

Museo de Historia y de Arte José de Obaldía ★★★ *(B/.1; Tue to Sat 8:30am to 4:30pm; Avenida 8A Este, between Calle A Norte and Calle Central, ☎775-7839)* has been set up in a large turn-of-the-century bourgeois house, once the home of the Obaldías, a famous political family. Don José de Obaldía Orajuela was the founder of the province of Chiriquí and his son was the second president of the country.

Various objects and documents relating to the Spanish colonization can be found in the entrance hall. Note the map in the lobby, which describes the history of piracy along the isthmus. You can also see military equipment, such as stirrups and swords, which once belonged to the *conquistadores*. In many respects, however, the room on the right is more interesting, displaying pre-Columbian objects, some of which date back to 500 BCE, along with several large funeral urns. In the past, deceased people were exhumed years after they had been buried, and their bones were placed in these urns.

A glass case at the end of the hall contains some very interesting pieces of pottery. They have been well preserved and are handsomely decorated with figures of reptiles and humans. There are also jade jewels and ancient utensils on view. The room to the left of the entrance is devoted to religious art; its objects illustrate well the influence of the Spanish church during colonization days. Especially striking is the sadness depicted in the figures—a reflection of the humility and sacrifice that are considered moral virtues in the eyes of the church.

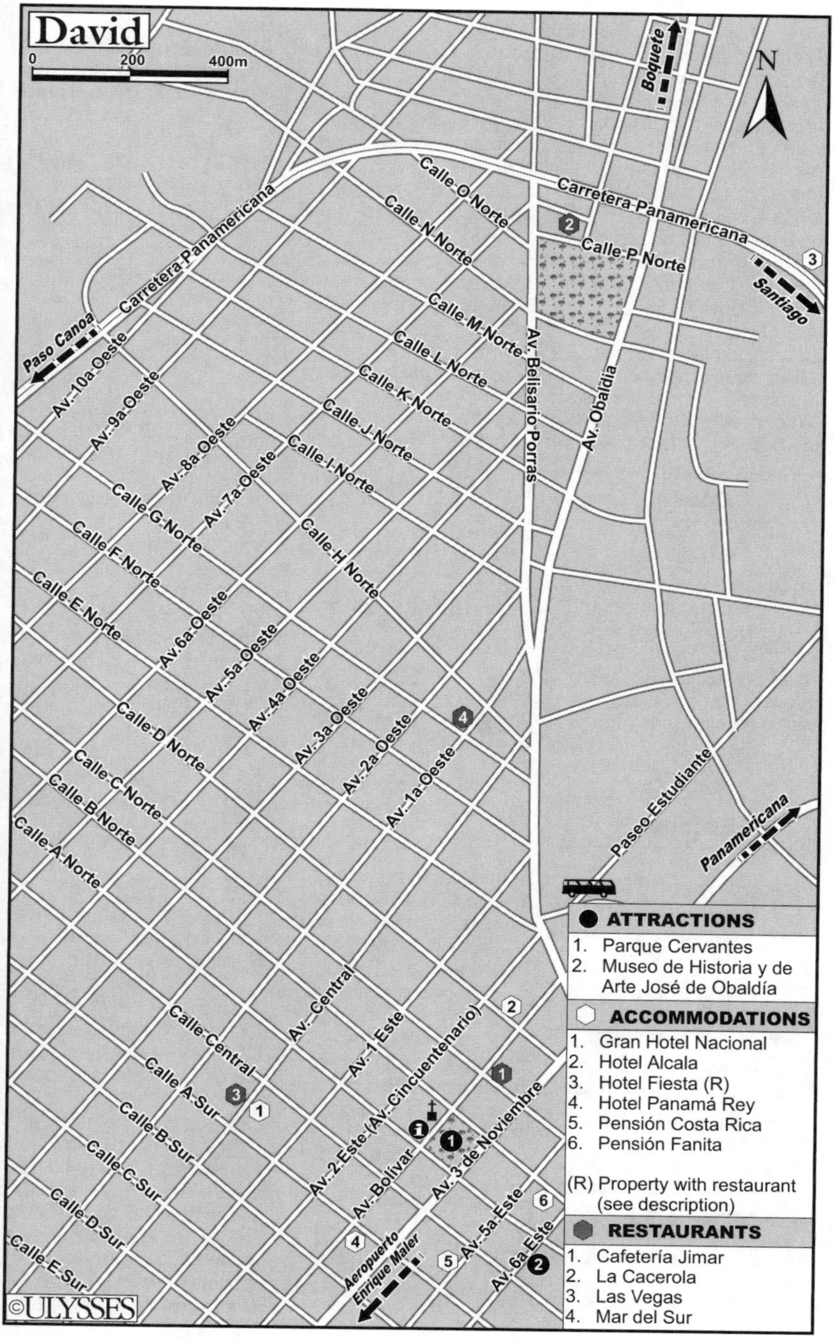
David
0
200
400m
N
Boquete
Carretera Panamericana
Calle O Norte
Calle N Norte
Calle P Norte
Calle M Norte
Calle L Norte
Calle K Norte
Calle J Norte
Calle I Norte
Calle H Norte
Calle G Norte
Calle F Norte
Calle E Norte
Calle D Norte
Calle C Norte
Calle B Norte
Calle A Norte
Calle Central
Calle A Sur
Calle B Sur
Calle C Sur
Calle D Sur
Calle E Sur
Santiago
Paso Canoa
Av. 10a Oeste
Av. 9a Oeste
Av. 8a Oeste
Av. 7a Oeste
Av. 6a Oeste
Av. 5a Oeste
Av. 4a Oeste
Av. 3a Oeste
Av. 2a Oeste
Av. 1a Oeste
Av. Central
Av. 1 Este
Av. 2 Este (Av. Cincuentenario)
Av. Bolívar
Av. 3 de Noviembre
Av. 5a Este
Av. 6a Este
Av. Belisario Porras
Av. Obaldía
Paseo Estudiante
Panamericana
Aeropuerto Enrique Maler
ATTRACTIONS
1. Parque Cervantes
2. Museo de Historia y de Arte José de Obaldía
ACCOMMODATIONS
1. Gran Hotel Nacional
2. Hotel Alcala
3. Hotel Fiesta (R)
4. Hotel Panamá Rey
5. Pensión Costa Rica
6. Pensión Fanita
(R) Property with restaurant (see description)
RESTAURANTS
1. Cafetería Jimar
2. La Cacerola
3. Las Vegas
4. Mar del Sur
©ULYSSES

There are four rooms on the second floor. The first showcases several documents about the Obaldía family and a number of papers relating to the foundation of the Republic of Panamá, including a copy of the treaty declaring the isthmus independent from Colombia. The other rooms are reconstructions of rooms in the Obaldía family residence, with period furniture and accessories. There are also old photographs depicting the building of the canal.

Dolega

Located on the road to Boquete, about 13km from the Interamericana, the village of Dolega is worth a short stop. Admire its small church, with a lovely altar in detailed wood and gold.

★★★

Boquete

Inhabited since 1880 by local peasants and immigrants from various countries such as Switzerland, Germany, the former Yugoslavia and even the United States, Boquete is undoubtedly the most pleasant area in the province and, only 40km from David, a favorite vacation spot for many Panamanians. Perched at an altitude of 1,600m and averaging ideal temperatures of 20°C throughout the year, this village features idyllic scenery composed of superb mountains, the tumultuous Río Caldera and flower-bordered roads. You will see primroses, lilies, impatiens, carnations, roses and a bounty of other species. Boquete has gained quite a reputation thanks to these flowers and they have become an important part of the local economy. Every year, during the third week of January, the **Feria de Las Flores y del Café** takes place, a competition to determine which villager has the best garden. Besides flowers, Boquete is known for its exceptional coffee. Three kinds of coffee are grown in the area, including the famous Arabica. Many Guaymies from Tolé and the nearby mountains flock to the area during the coffee-bean harvesting season for seasonal work. And last but not least, the region of Boquete is renowned as one of the best places to observe exotic birds, such as the celebrated quetzal. According to ornithologists, the optimum time to observe this rare bird is in April or May.

In the village, commonly known as Bajo Boquete, there is not much to see but a stroll on the main bridge near the Parque Central offers a lovely view of the river and the region. Every weekend, the **Parque Central** or **Parque Domingo Médica** becomes a market where Guaymies come to sell their products, stock up on supplies and socialize with friends and family. Once the day's trading is done, the evening becomes particularly festive and the women don their traditional dresses.

For an educational introduction to the coffee-making process, visit the **Finca Café Ruiz** *(Avenida Central, past the centre of the village on the right side of the road leading to Los Cabezos, ☎720-1392, www.caferuiz.com)* This small but famous enterprise reaps the fruits of the coffee tree and lovingly transforms them into aromatic coffee beans.

A tour in Spanish, English and German *(B/.10 per person; 9am to 2pm, visit takes at least 3hrs)* can be reserved by calling ahead of time (preferably a week in advance). Visit early in the morning as this is the busiest time of day, and, during the harvest period (from November to March), employees can be seen at work in the plantation. Those for whom coffee drinking is a religious experience should not miss this informative visit, which also provides an opportunity to purchase various products made on site (see p 220).

Gardeners, as well as those who merely admire gardens, will love **Mi Jardín es su Jardín** *(Avenida Central, 50m pa[st] the Finca Café Ruiz)*, located within the Gonzále[z] family's large estate. Flowers, fruit trees, a fishpond and a small chapel make up this enjoyable garden, located next to a lovely residence. Also to be see[n] here are various replicas [of] animals of all sizes, such a[s] cows, an elephant and even a dinosaur. Moreover, the site is dotted with small windmills, conferring a fun, kitschy aspe[ct] to the place. Although th[e]

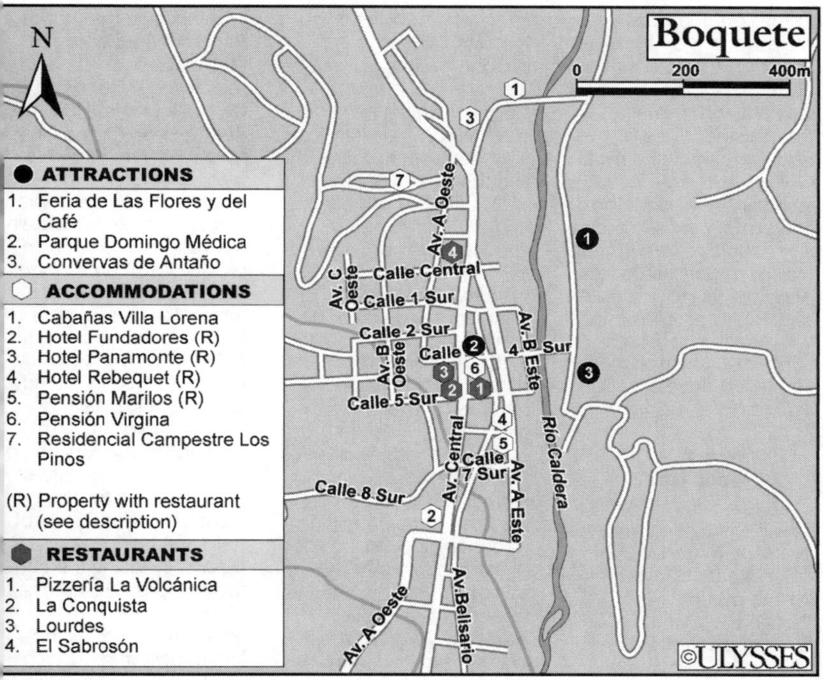

private property, the owners allow visitors on the grounds provided, of course, that they respect the environment.

The secrets of making mango jam are revealed during a tour of the **Conservas de Antaño** *(from the Parque Domingo Médica, cross the bridge and follow the road to the right for 100m ☎720-539)*. A variety of other jams simmering in large cooking pots can also be sampled.

Take a walk through the village in the evening, along narrow flowered paths, and your senses will be awakened by the smell of numerous flowers. To fully appreciate the beauty of the area, two tours are suggested below.

Alto Boquete

Those who appreciate sweeping vistas will not want to miss the panoramic view of the town of Bajo Boquete and the Río Caldera from the **Mirador de la Virgen de la Gruta** ★★ *(on the right side of the main road to Bajo Boquete, just before it curves and descends to Boquete)*. This spot is ideal for photography so have your camera ready.

★★★

Boquete and Surroundings

As you leave **Boquete**, either by car or on foot, there are two interesting loop-shaped tours you can try; both start at the Hotel Panamonte (see p 213).

★

Tour No. 1

After crossing the small bridge at the end, to the right of the road facing the Hotel Panamonte, follow the main road. Immediately after crossing the Río Palo Alto, you will notice a profusion of different flowers along the side of the road. A few kilometres further on, the road crosses the Río Alto again, and later, the Río Pianista; both rivers join the Río Caldera, which runs through the village of Boquete. Along the route, white and orange lilies, impatiens, and many other flowers join the surrounding mountains to constitute the main tourist attraction. Although this tour should present no problem, since the road is in satisfactory condition, it is strongly advised to drive only during the dry season.

★★★ Tour No. 2

This is the more spectacular of the two tours, with gorgeous vistas overlooking the mountains. Although the road is resurfaced in parts, there are still several potholes. While it is possible to enjoy the journey in a regular vehicle, if you can afford it, it is more comfortable in a four-wheel-drive vehicle. Whatever vehicle you use, make sure to take the tour only when the weather is clear, and in the dry season. Count on an average speed of 10 to 20km/h, or about 1hr to complete the circuit. On foot, it will take a full day.

Shortly after starting the tour, you will see a rare geological formation on the left of the road, a hexagonal basalt flow. Here the rock has taken a surprisingly regular shape, perpendicular to the rock. Nature is showing off its sculpting talents! These formations are visible from two places on the tour. Continue along a beautiful river, which will lead you through a village to an imposing waterfall (about 20m high), also worth a stop. Following the same road, you will zig-zag your way into a steep valley, and the many impressive vistas are all worth a stop.

A massive, almost oppressive wall of rock, covered with immense trees, stands between the road and the river. It is easy to grasp the insignificance of humans in the whole scheme of nature in a place like this. As well, along the route, you will see Guaymie dwellings. Farther along in the valley, the road turns back and climbs abruptly to the top of the rock wall. At the summit, the tour continues through *fincas* (coffee plantations) where the deep-green leaves are the crowning glory of the countryside. From December through April, Guaymies pick coffee on the plantations. With wicker baskets strapped to their waists for collecting the harvest, the average worker receives B/.1 and B/.2 for every 4kg basket of beans picked. A worker can pick between five and twenty baskets per day.

Following the road, you will come back toward Boquete along a grandiose slope.

Alanje

Located between the towns of David and La Concepción, Alanje is best known in the region for its production of rum from sugar cane, said to be one of the best in the world. Although the village is not that spectacular, do not miss the chance to visit the **Carta Vieja rum distillery** ★ *(free admission; Mon-Fri 7:30am to noon and 12:30pm to 4pm, www.roncartavieja.com)*, where a guide will explain the various steps of rum production. You can see the fermentation tanks, where the cane juice is kept, and follow the different distillation processes. Depending on its intended use, the percentage of alcohol varies: 80% to 95% for the production of gin; and 40% for regular rum, destined for use in most bars. The quality of taste is influenced by many factors, including the container (here, vats are made of white birch from Canada), as well as the length of storage, which can be en average from six to eight years. Outside the warehouses, two old stills (one of which was imported from Italy) date back to earlier times; a small room next to the offices commemorates the glorious past of the distillery (active since 1915) in a series of photographs. Count on 30 to 60min for the tour. In addition to the educational benefits of this excursion, the road leading out passes through very pleasant sugar cane fields.

From La Concepción to Volcán

Mirador AlanHer *(B/.0.25; from the Interamericana, drive 16km on the road to Volcán. The mirador is on the left side of the road)*. On the way to Volcán and

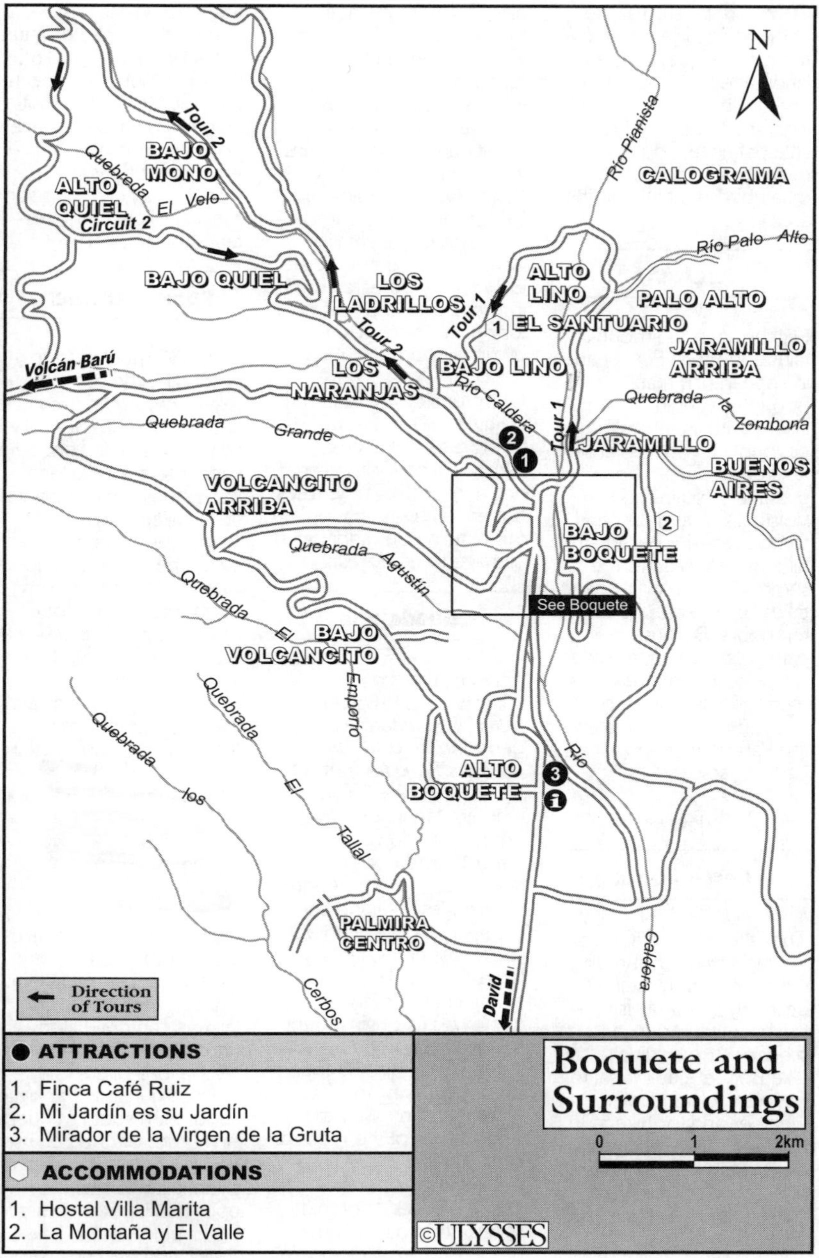

ATTRACTIONS

1. Finca Café Ruiz
2. Mi Jardín es su Jardín
3. Mirador de la Virgen de la Gruta

ACCOMMODATIONS

1. Hostal Villa Marita
2. La Montaña y El Valle

Boquete and Surroundings

0 1 2km

Cerro Punta, stop at the Mirador AlanHer to enjoy the picturesque, verdant landscape and, should the urge arise, taste one of the local specialties. With a little patience, you may even spot some of the many birds that inhabit the area.

Volcán

Higher up in the mountains and more European in appearance than Boquete, Volcán is a small village with little to offer beyond a few hotels and restaurants. From here it is possible to scale the Volcán Barú and descend to Boquete. However, the hike from Volcán to the summit is quite difficult and takes between eight and ten hours. Because the path is unmarked, a guide is essential. Volcán is thus more of a stopping point between Cerro Punta and the Parque Inter-nacional La Amistad.

★

Cerro Punta

The little village of Cerro Punta, which is not really extraordinary in itself, is definitely worth a visit for the beautiful mountain scenery surrounding it. Like Boquete, it is ideal for people seeking cooler weather and for hikers. In the area called Bella Vista, hiking trails lead over steep hills, some of which are cultivated. The growing of vegetables is a central activity in the surrounding region. If you like fresh produce, this is a good place to buy straight from the producer. Guaymies work the land in the region for farmers, some of whom immigrated from Europe long ago. As a result, families with origins in such faraway lands as Yugoslavia, Germany or Switzerland are common. The style of the small houses and the immediate environment create an impression that one is no longer in a tropical country but in Europe.

Unfortunately agriculture is taking a toll on the mountain forests of Panamá. Clearing land for farming not only destroys the trees but encourages erosion; this in turn does additional damage to the forests.

Guadelupe

This small, enjoyable town is known for its flowers *(after passing through Cerro Punta, continue straight on the main road until Guadelupe)*. Those who are fascinated by orchids should visit the **Finca Dracula** ★ *(B/.7; ☎771-2223)* where Andrés Maduro lovingly and patiently tends to over 1,200 species of orchids in a large garden. The rather strange name of the garden owes its origins to the hundred *Telipogon vampirus* orchids he found already growing on site when he purchased the land. A tour of the grounds lasts 90mins, and is conducted in groups of six or less. Biologists or orchid specialists provide comprehensive explanations in English or Spanish.

In the town itself, make a quick stop at the **Los Que zales Hotel** (see p 216), the only tourist lodging in the park. Budget permitting, this is an experience not to be missed. Those who are just passing through can enjoy a good meal in its charming restaurant (see p 219).

Puerto Armuelles

Puerto Armuelles (pop. 40,000) is the second-largest city in the provinc and has no extraordinary sites, unless you have a keen interest in banana plantations. Private planta tions called *fincas*, formerly owned in the majo ity by the Chiriquí Land Company, extend from the borders of the city beyond sight. Professing lack of profitability, the famous company closed doors in 2001, devastatin the town; today, more than half its inhabitants ar unemployed. The only attractions worth mentio ing are the immense deserted beaches that embellish the nearby coastline.

Unfortunately no service are available so food and drink must be brought in Those interested in oil tankers can drive along a unpaved road to the installations of the Petroterminal de Panam about 6km south of Puer Armuelles on the Penínsu Burica. Visitors can watch gigantic tankers as they pour their precious cargo into a pipeline that links t Pacific and Atlantic coasts

R.U.C. 313836-1-411946
D.V. 97
Tel.: 991-0508 y 991-0509

HOTEL *Las Fuentes*

Nº 5481

PANAMÁ, PENONOMÉ
Compañía GLEZ

Fecha: 09 de enero de 2005

Vendido a: George Brian Starr

CANTIDAD	DETALLE	PRECIO	TOTAL
1.	Cargo 117	18.00	18.00
		TOTAL	18.00

SEIMPRIME/997-1129/Penonomé

Hora: 6:35 am

Parks

★★

Parque Internacional La Amistad

In 1974, the first conference dedicated to the conservation of natural and cultural resources in Central America passed a resolution to create, for the very first time, a park involving two sovereign countries, Costa Rica and Panamá. The resulting Parque Internacional La Amistad was to extend along the Talamanca mountain range that borders both countries. To endorse this historical agreement, the two countries began a cooperative project in 1979 to ensure the protection of the area and, in 1982, signed a treaty in which they agreed to define the respective zones covered by previous agreements. During the same year, an area of 193,929ha was defined in Costa Rica; however, it was not until 1986 that Panamá alloted 207,000ha to this project. Soon after its creation, the Costa Rican park, along with 14 neighboring zones, was declared a UN Biosphere Reserve (248,337ha) and a year later, in 1983, a World Heritage Site. It was not until 1990 however, that UNESCO listed the Panamanian park as a World Heritage Site. It has yet to be classified as a Biosphere Reserve in this country, but there are plans in the works to add five protected zones to it, including the Volcán Barú national park, extending this zone to close to 4,000km^2. The La Amistad Biosphere Reserve would thus encompass over 10,000km^2, making it the largest protected area in Central America.

In Panamá alone, many summits exceed 3,000m, the highest being the Barú volcano, at an altitude of 3,475m. With temperatures ranging between 15°C and 24°C and annual precipitation between 2,500 and 5,000mm, this is one of the most humid regions in the country. This immense wilderness encompasses seven of the existing 13 life zones of the Panamanian isthmus. It is thus a very bountiful region, rich in flora and fauna, where vegetation changes with altitude. Among the numerous wild animals that live here are a number of endangered species, possibly the most impressive of which are the jaguar, the tapir, the white-tailed deer and the famous quetzal. Studies reveal that over 1,000 species of mammals, 60 kinds of reptiles, 100 types of amphibians and 400 varieties of birds inhabit the park. Current estimates show that the park is home to 60% of all vertebrates and invertebrates in Panamá. The sheer size of the territory allows big cats such as jaguars, pumas and ocelots to hunt and reproduce without being disturbed. Jaguars, for instance, which weigh up to 150kg, require hundreds of hectares of land to roam and hunt agoutis, peccaries and deer.

Although the park is actually located in the neighbouring province of Bocas del Toro, access to the park is easier from the province of Chiriquí. And although part of the access road can in fact be driven in a regular car, a four-wheel-drive vehicle is preferable for the few kilometres leading up to the entrance, only passable during the dry season.

Once inside the park itself, there are no driveable roads (except on the Costa Rica side) and the only way to get around is on hiking trails. To get to the entrance in the village of Cerro Punta, turn left at the main intersection of the village and keep following the signs. The entrance to the park is 6.8km farther, and the road is beautiful. As you get closer to the park, the vegetation becomes more dense, almost engulfing the road. Here, humans here seem rather insignificant and at the complete mercy of nature. This route, until the entrance of the park, is a pleasant trip for those who want to admire the extraordinary natural beauty of the park close up without actually venturing on an expedition.

The park currently does not have many marked paths or tourist facilities. Nonetheless, it is a magical place where hardy adventurers, accompanied by guides accustomed to long hikes through dense and humid tropical forests, can scale mountains and observe many animals that are hard to spot in other parts of the country. Birdwatchers will also find it an exceptional observation ground, off the beaten track, where the chances of sighting the famous quetzal are high.

To fully appreciate the park's bountiful nature, newcomers are urged to use the services of local tour agencies who work with ecologists. Furthermore, because of the park's immense territory, it is not recommended to venture out alone.

Before entering the park, you must obtain authorization from INRENARE. While there is no official system in place for keeping track of visitors, it is **strongly** recommended that you get the proper permit. To obtain authorization or further information, contact INRENARE, in the capital (see p 66) or at its local office in David (see p 198).

★★

Parque Nacional del Volcán Barú

Located next to the Parque Internacional La Amistad, the Parque Nacional del Volcán Barú covers over 14,000ha of land.

Rising to 3,475m above sea level, it is home to the highest peak in Panamá. Like its neighbour, this park fosters extremely varied vegetation, which changes with altitude. At low altitudes, there is a prevalence of species common to the tropical rain forest, which give way, with rising altitude, to much scrawnier trees. Above 1,800m, the vegetation progressively recedes and is replaced with volcanic rocks and shrubbery. Temperatures at the summit can change rapidly, often plummeting within minutes from 16°C to below 10°C when clouds move in.

To enjoy a view of the two largest oceans on the planet, the Pacific and the Atlantic, on a clear day, it is best to reach the summit at the crack of dawn. Unfortunately,because it is the highest mountain in the country, it plays an important role in telecommunications, and antennae and radars deform the landscape. Be that as it may, the park is reputed to be one of the easiest places to sight the quetzal (provided you have a good guide).

From May to December, hiking to the mountaintop is inadvisable because of the heavy rains which turn paths into mud slides.

Beaches

★

Playa Las Lajas

This immense beach lies 12.2km from the Interamericana. It is just the place for people who like long walks along quiet shorelines, as long as they avoid weekends. Those who wish to swim should be very careful as the waves are violent and sharks reputedly visit this area.The fine, white sand of Playa Las Lajas is bordered by luxuriant vegetation. There is no cozy accommodation available on site, but the **Gran Club** does provide a few rudimentary services (cabins, snacks, drinks, showers). To get something to eat before heading to the beach, stop at the cafeteria at the intersection of the road to Las Lajas, just to the right of the Interamericana. Most of the time, there is also a merchant who sells the delicious oranges grown in the region, as well as *pipas* (coconuts).

Outdoor Activities

Hiking

★★

Volcán Barú

The hike up the Volcán Barú is for people in good physical condition who mountain-climb on a regular basis. Two trails wind their way up the volcano. The first trail starts from the main road in Boquete and takes about four to ve hours. The second tarts in Cerro Punta and equires up to 8hrs of iking. As the entrance to ne park from Cerro Punta ; along the road to 'olcán, the most conveient starting point is ioquete. To get there, go orth on the main road nrough the village and urn left on the first street fter the church. After 0km or so on a fairly ood road, continue on oot or four-wheel-drive ehicle as the road starts ooking more and more ke a battlefield. Those vho choose to drive hould not do so alone as ou might get into an ccident. It is best to hire a ocal guide who is accusomed to driving on such oads.

hould you decide to limb the volcano on foot, ne following advice will elp you reach your destiation more easily.

ecause clouds move in uickly during the morng, it is best to reach the ummit at day break to get clear view of the coast r, if you're lucky, both oasts. To do so, you hould hike by night, startng at around 1am.

o save your energy for ne lengthy climb to the ummit, have a taxi drop ou off at the park enance. From this point, ne hike is a good 10km, vhich should take some our to five hours.

ring warm clothes as emperatures at the summit can be very low.

Do not hike alone at night. Bring a reliable flashlight, food and plenty to drink.

Do not forget that in order to enter the park you must have acquired authorization beforehand from INRENARE. While this formality is not always observed or supervised, it is still necessary to ensure that flora, fauna and travellers are protected. Both the authorization and additional information on the park are available in the capital (see p 66) and at the local INRENARE office at David (see p 198).

Río Monte Ecological Tours
☎720-1327 or 720-1324
www.chiriqui.com/panamonte
Another local company, Río Monte Ecological Tours, affiliated with the Hotel Panamonte, also organizes excursions to the summit of the volcano including breakfast at the hotel, transportation, a snack, binoculars as well as the services of a nature guide. B/.75 per person (price based on the participation of a minimum of three people).

From Cerro Punta to Boquete

Los Quetzales
Guadelupe, Apdo 55-0039
☎771-2182 or 771-2291
www.losquetzales.com
If a hike from Cerro Punta to Boquete sounds appealing, contact Los Quetzales. Two local guides accompany hikers beyond the Volcán Barú, where there is extraordinary flora to see. The expedition lasts between six and eight hours and is meant for people in top physical shape who are accustomed to long hikes. Expect to pay about B/.40 per person (this includes a picnic and return transportation the next day to Cerro Punta or Guadelupe). Because of the length of the hike and the return on the following day, hikers should plan to stay overnight in Boquete. A similar tour is also available on horseback.

Bird-Watching

Boquete

Río Monte Ecological Tours
☎720-1327 or 720-1324
www.chiriqui.com/panamonte
For people who are especially interested in quetzals, Río Monte Ecological Tours, affiliated with the Hotel Panamonte, offers a very interesting guided tour through the tropical rain forest of Colograma, reputed to be frequented by families of quetzals as well as toucans and other exotic birds. During the excursion, you will also have the chance to spot small mammals as well as an incredible number of plants and flowers, especially orchids. The tour lasts approximately 5 hours, and costs B/.75 (three or more people), including transportation, a naturalist guide, picnic and rental of binoculars. Although the cost might seem a little steep, the

Parots

package is a good idea because the guides are extremely knowledgable about the region and are familiar with bird-watching. With an experienced guide, you will have more of a chance to spot a quetzal, a bird that is both rare and difficult to see because of its camouflage. According to ornithologists, the best time to observe quetzals is in April and May. For people staying in the capital, various eco-tourism agencies offer packages departing from Panama City (see the "Hiking" section in that chapter, p 90).

David

Agencia de Viajes 4 Tours
Vía Belisario Porras, Apdo 12
David
☎775-1397 or 775-4282
Those staying in David who are interested in this type of excursion, should contact the Agencia de Viajes 4 Tours, which offers a variety of package deals. As tour agencies abound in the region, do not hesitate to shop around and bargain for a better price.

Parque International La Amistad

Los Quetzales
Guadelupe, Apdo 55-0039
☎771-2182 or 771-2291
www.losquetzales.com
With its evocative name, Los Quetzales is yet another specialized agency which offers numerous expeditions in Parque Internacional La Amistad, as well as very unique accommodations. Fifteen different hikes are available, ranging in length from 30min to 4hrs and priced accordingly. A Guaymie guide will point out many varieties of birds during a walk through the park. Approximately 100 different bird species have been identified by the Audubon Society and Smithsonian Institute, both of which still conduct regular surveys in the park.

Swimming

From David to Boquete

Two "refreshing" stops on the way to Boquete allow swimming enthusiasts to dive into one of the many *ríos* that irrigate the region. Swimming is free of charge at the **Balneario Majagua** *(4km from the intersection with the Interamericana),* located on the right side of the main road to Boquete. This delightful site features a small waterfall cascading into a freshwater pool. There is parking right in front of the swimming hole as well as a restaurant-bar that serves basic meals. If it is too crowded, continue a few kilometres north to the **Balneario La Cascada** *(B/.50; swimming from 9am to 5:30pm; 9km from the intersection with the Interamericana, on the right side of the road to Boquete)*, another swimming hole with a much mightier waterfall. The setting is just as enjoyable but there is a fee for most services. There is also a parking lot and a small restaurant. As both these freshwater basins are fed by rivers, it is important to follow certain hygiene precautions (see "Additional Health Care Advise, p 50).

La Concepción

'arque Recreativo
3orinquito
3/.1, children B/.0.75 11am
o 10pm
ıt the end of Av. Centenario
☎770-4625
Children and adults alike vill enjoy the olympic-ized pool and tennis :ourts at the Parque Recreativo Borinquito in Solano. Also, guides will accompany visitors free of :harge on walks along a eries of paths lined with igns.

Gariché

Nine kilometres from the :ity of Concepción, en oute to the Costa Rican oorder, the Interamericana :rosses the Río Gariché, vhich originates in the Cordillera de Talamanca. Many *Chiricano* families enjoy swimming in the iver's calm, shallow wa-ers. Right after the bridge, urn right off the main road onto a dirt road. This leads o a parking lot (free) and he **Balneario Restaurante Camino al Cielo** (see) 219) where there is a estaurant overlooking the *río* and changing rooms for visitors. Stairs lead down to the shore of the river, which is a good place for a swim. On weekends and holidays, this becomes a very popular picnicking spot for Panamanians. To avoid any unpleasant surprises, do not leave anything of value in a parked car.

Rafting

The **Río Chiriquí** originates in the Cordillera Central and, after flowing into the Lago Fortuna, which is formed by a dam, continues another 100km or so to the Pacific Ocean. Once a powerful river now controlled by human hands, the Río Chiriquí regains its original force with the Río Estí, which flows into it a few kilometres after the small village of Ricón. The harnessed flow of the Río Chiriquí makes it one of the only rivers on which whitewater rafting excursions are available all year long.

One group organizes rafting outings for beginners as well as more experienced thrill seekers:

Chiriquí River Rafting
Apdo 1686, Balboa, Ancón
☎720-1505
⇄720-1506
www.panama-rafting.com
Participants travel from the capital or David to the small town of Gualaca before reaching the Río Chiriquí, a little further on. The ride down the river lasts between two and four hours depending on the level of difficulty. Prices vary between B/.75 and B/.210 according to the chosen option (with or without accommodations) and the number of participants. Excursions include one or more meals as well as the services of guides.

Accommodations

David

Pensión Fanita
$
sb, ℜ
Corner of Calle B Norte and Avenida 5 Este, two streets southeast of the Plaza
☎775-3718
The very basic rooms at the Pensión Fanita are noisy but, for B/.6 a night, who can complain? This spot should only be considered by those whose budget is in serious need of a break.

Pensión Costa Rica
$
pb/sb, ⊗
Corner of Avenida 5 Este and Calle A Sur
☎775-1241
In the same category, the Pensión Costa Rica has a charming facade and

rooms which are a little more comfortable but rustic all the same. Prices are low and range from B/.6 to B/.12 depending on whether the bathroom is shared or private. Its proximity to a bus station makes it fairly noisy. Friendly welcome.

Hotel Panamá Rey
$
pb, hw, ≡, #
Avenida Bolívar
☎775-0253
The Panamá Rey is a large, moderately comfortable hotel with haphazard decor. The street is fairly quiet compared to others in the area, but the staff is somewhat unaccommodating.

Hotel Fiesta
$$
pb, hw, ≡, ≈, *tv,* ℜ, #
on the right side of the Interamericana heading west, at the intersection with the road to Boquete
☎775-5453
☎775-5454/55/57
⇄774-4884
Situated on the Interamericana, the motel-like Hotel Fiesta has 59 simple but tastefully decorated rooms set around a large pool and garden. Choose a room at the back so as not to be bothered by the noise of the nearby road. During the week, breakfast is served starting at 6:30am, ideal for early expeditions. On sweltering days, its pool is much appreciated. Good quality for the price.

Hotel Alcalá
$$
pb, hw, tv, ℜ
Avenida 3 Este and Calle D Norte
☎774-9018 or 774-9019
⇄774-9021
Situated close to downtown David, the Hotel Alcalá has 54 comfortable and simply decorated rooms. Its proximity to many busy commercial streets, the bus station and the *mercado público* will please travellers who enjoy lively areas. Another advantage is its private, guarded parking lot.

Gran Hotel Nacional
$$
pb, ≡, ≈
corner of Calle Central and Calle Primera, Apartado 37-B
☎775-2222
⇄775-7729
Located in the heart of a large Spanish-style villa, the Gran Hotel Nacional has 75 acceptably comfortable, well-kept rooms, but the decor is simple and lacks charm. Its location in the heart of the city, as well as its moderate prices, nevertheless make it one of the best places in the downtown area.

From David to Boquete

Cabañas La Cascada
$
pb, ℜ, #
on the right side of the road leading to Boquete, 9km from the Interamericana
☎776-0011
These small, barely comfortable *cabaña*-style rooms are situated in lovely leafy surroundings. The setting is enhanced by a waterfall plunging into a small basin. The number of *cabañas* is restricted so it is best to reserve in advance, especially on weekends. Expect to pay B/.11 per night for a double room.

Boquete

Hotel Rebequet
$
pb, hw
take the main street in the village and turn right on the second street after the Texaco station, watch for a small sign for the hotel
☎720-1365
Small family hotel, clean, and fairly comfortable. A pleasant indoor garden adds to the setting.

Pensión Marilos
$
follow the signs for the hotel Rebequet on the main street of the village; the boarding house faces the hotel
☎720-1380
This unpretentious little boarding house provides a pleasant family setting.

Pensión Virginia
$-$$
pb, hw, ℜ
on the central plaza
☎720-1260
The Pensión provides either ordinary or more luxurious rooms, depending on the price. The owner's daughter is very kind and speaks English (she lived in the U.S. for a long time). The place is well kept and the interior is enhanced by a small garden. You will be received warmly.

Hotel Fundadores
$$
pb, hw
to the left of the main road at the entrance to town
☎720-1298
This hotel offers comfortable rooms, located in a lovely setting. The rooms face a garden through which a pretty river flows, and some rooms offer views of the surrounding mountains.

Cabañas Villa Lorena
$$
pb, hw
Calle 11 de Abril
☎720-1848
A stone's throw from the Panamonte Hotel, right next to the bridge over the Río Caldera, the Cabañas Villa Lorena are three small cabins set in an attractively landscaped garden facing the Río Caldera. The cabins are connected to the owners' residence but set back slightly from each other. The small, comfortable rooms provide a peaceful stay accompanied by the sound of birds and the nearby river. Renting a cabin costs about B/.45 per day.

Residencial Campestre Los Piños
$$$
pb, hw, tv, K
Av. Central, Apdo 275, on the left side of the road heading to Los Naranjos
☎775-1521
⇄774-6536
www.members.tripod.com/lospinos/
Perched on a small hill, the Residencial Campestre Los Pinos is a new building whose modern appearance clashes somewhat with its surroundings. It includes five modern, fully furnished two-storey apartments. Each apartment contains a fully equipped kitchenette, a small dining room and living room, and guest rooms on the upper floor. The decor, although basic, is tasteful, and each apartment features a small balcony affording a "plunging" view of the village of Boquete far below. Although the site is somewhat lacking in charm, the garden and lovely country scenery will remind you that you are indeed in exotic territory. Good quality for the price for small families.

Hotel Panamonte
$$$-$$$$$
pb, hw, ℜ, #
at the edge of town, turn right at the intersection and head toward the small bridge which crosses the river
☎720-1327
⇄720-2055
www.chiriqui.com/panamonte
The Hotel Panamonte is a charming hotel composed of two pretty wooden houses facing each other. The main house, painted blue, is very tastefully decorated, with a lovely entrance hall where a collection of old objects testifying to the European roots of the owners are displayed. A spacious and elegant dining room, which also serves as a restaurant, is located to the right of the hall. In the left wing, at the back, is a lounge equipped with a bar and a pool room, making a pleasant ensemble. At the beginning of the evening, you can relax in comfortable armchairs and warm up near the fire, since the air at this altitude can get quite c... nightfall. The rooms ... very comfortable, spread out on the first floor around a magnificent garden which is home to hundreds of different plant species. At the back of the garden, small *cabañas* with porches and kitchenettes have been set up harmoniously.

The second house, just as charming as the first, has a large apartment which can house from six to eight people *(B/.165)*, as well as several individual rooms *(from B/.55)*, all decorated in the English style and complete with hardwood floors. A warm welcome tops off this enchanting spot. At the reception, guests can gather information on the region, or sign up for numerous hikes organized by the hotel (see p 209). As this spot is well-known for its beauty and the quality of service, it is highly recommended that you reserve well in advance.

Jamarillo Arriba Sector

La Montaña y El Valle
$$$$
pb, hw, K
Apdo 4-014, Jamarillo Arriba, Boquete
☎/⇄720-2211
www.coffeeestateinn.com
For those in search of peace and quiet, La Montaña y El Valle is the ideal location. It features three hillside cabins surrounded by greenery and located on a vast property where orange and coffee trees grow alongside wild vegetation. Paths allow

guests to roam about and get a full appreciation of the local flora and fauna.

Each cabin includes a large living room with a view of the mountains on the horizon, dining room, guest room with top-quality mattress, and a fully equipped kitchen complete with dishes, oven and microwave. As for the decor, the Canadian owners were inspired by local Panamanian handicrafts. Leaving nothing to chance, even a parking space has been included beside each dwelling. Furthermore, smoking is forbidden in the cabins. As for meals, the health conscious will delight in such creative dishes as the tasty country-style moussaka, prepared by Barry Robins and Jane Walker. Meat lovers, for their part, can savour the likes of tender garlic-seasoned beef filet with mustard sauce. Delicious cookies, cakes and other temptations are served at the end of the meal. It's a shame that such delicious meals are reserved for hotel guests only! Prices range from B/.6 to B/.9 per dish. For a change of pace, visit the library and pick up one of more than 1,000 English and Spanish books available to guests.

El Santuario Sector

Hostal Villa Marita
$$
pb, hw
2km north of the centre of Boquete, in the El Santuario sector, Apdo 4077, Boquete
☎720-2164 or 720-2165
Imagine a cluster of seven small *cabañas*, set in the middle of a well-kept garden, painted in bright hues of ochre and adorned, to the great pride of their owners, with French windows. Such dwellings are found at the Hostal Villa Marita. Each cabin is warmly decorated in wood and includes comfortable double guest rooms as well as a small, fully equipped kitchen in which one's favourite meals can be prepared. The far-reaching view from each cabin, with the Volcán Barú as a backdrop, serves as a reminder that the "rooftop" of Panamá is only 2,000m above.

Volcán

Cabañas Las Reinas
$
pb, hw, K, #
29.5km from the Interamericana, at the village, turn left at the sign, 400m from the main street
☎771-4338
These small, well-equipped cabins can accommodate anywhere from two to twelve guests. They are attractively decorated and surrounded by an extensive garden. This is a good place for an extended stay.

Motel California
$-$$
pb, hw
on the left side of the main street, 200m past the intersection to Cerro Punta
☎771-4272
Guests can choose from amongst 20 rooms at the Motel California. The interior is basic but clean and the owner, originally from central Europe, greets his customers with a smile. Some of the *cabañas* include several beds and are perfect for groups.

Hotel Dos Ríos
$$
pb, hw
on the left side of the main road which crosses the village, 2km past the intersection to Cerro Punta
☎771-4271
One of the more enjoyable hotels in Volcán is the Hotel Dos Ríos. Ten dwellings face a lovely garden and meandering brook framed by the surrounding mountains. Rooms are fairly comfortable, decorated simply, and kept immaculate.

From Volcán to Cerro Punta

Cabañas Kucikas
$$$
pb, hw, K
on the left of the road from Cerro Punta to Volcán, pay attention as there is no sign advertising the *cabañas* on the road
☎/⇄771-4245 or 269-0623
The Cabañas Kucikas are located 6.8km from Volcán on the shores of the picturesque Río Chiriquí Viejo, which flows in full force all year long. It is here that Anthony and Gladys Kucikas built 18 very charming cabins, some of which can accommodate up to 10 people.

All the *cabañas* are fully furnished and the decor, although outdated, is pleasant thanks to the prevalence of wood. A fully equipped kitchen and small dining room occupy the first floor of each cabin and one or more rooms make up the top floor. There is enough space between cabins for privacy and a large lawn with swing-sets allows children of all ages to play to their heart's content. This location is perfect for peaceful stays where the only sound is the soft murmur of the river. Good quality for the price.

Cabañas Fistonich
$$
pb, hw, K
a few kilometres past the Bambito Hotel and Bambito Camping Resort; on the left side of the road leading to Cerro Punta, right after a bend, there is a small sign indicating *cabañas*; at this point, cross the wooden bridge and take the road on the right which passes by a farm and leads to the owners' residence; Nueva Suiza sector
☎771-2115 or 774-8663
f staying on a farm sounds appealing, visit the Cabañas Fistonich. Each of the several small cabins contains one or more guest rooms, a fully equipped kitchen and a small living room. Since most cabins are right on the property, guests can watch the owners performing their daily farm chores. Crops can be purchased right on the arm, providing a steady upply of fresh and delicious produce for every meal. The cabins are not ery stylish and are starting o show their age but the ite has a certain charm nd is rather picturesque. or those preferring a little nore privacy, a cabin rests eyond the little ravine eparating the property om the main road. Outdoor living at a reasonable price!

Hotel Bambito
$$$$
pb, hw, ≡, ≈, ℜ, ⊙, ⌂, tv
on the right heading toward Cerro Punta, approximately 7km from the centre of Volcán, Apdo 1753, Zona 1, District Bugaba
☎771-4265
⇄771-4207
www.chiriqui.com/bambito/
Nestled against a lush-green backdrop, the Hotel Bambito is not only the most luxurious hotel in the province but also a true haven of peace. The hotel's 46 rooms face beautiful gardens and waterfalls set against the backdrop of a dense forest. Rooms are equally elegant, sometimes even featuring freshly cut flowers. The hotel prides itself on offering all that a traveller in search of comfort might require: tennis court, swimming pools, sauna, gym, bar, night club and, of course, restaurant. Guests can borrow bicycles or go horseback riding. Ecological excursions are also available. Expensive but so very comfortable.

Bambito Camping Resort
$$$$
pb, hw, tv, ≈, ℜ
on the left side of the road to Cerro Punta, a few kilometres past the Hotel Bambito and immediately after a bridge
☎771-5126 or 265-5103
⇄264-3972 or 771-5127
www.bambito-forest-resort.com
Not to be confused with the Hotel Bambito (described above), the Bambito Camping Resort is a new tourist facility composed of a large campground and a few cabins called Royal Suites and Junior Suites. During our visit, the garden around the cabins was still being landscaped and the small swimming pool seemed temporarily unusable.

Suites are spacious and feature, in addition to one or more large guest rooms, a small living room at the entrance. The wood-filled interior lends a rustic and cozy note to the ambiance. Unfortunately, due to the high price, this option would only be worthwhile for groups. As for the campground, prices seemed excessive even though breakfast and equipment rental are included. However, do not hesitate to bargain as the owners are sometimes willing to reduce prices considerably, except on weekends and holidays.

Cerro Punta

Pensíon La Primavera
$
pb, hw
0.2km from the main intersection of Cerro Punta, just past the highway
A great choice for budget travellers, this spot is clean but rudimentary and costs between B/.12 and 15 per night.

Hotel Cerro Punta
$$
pb, hw, tv, ℜ
on the left side of the main road to Cerro Punta, just before entering the village
☎/⇄771-2020
The Hotel Cerro Punta is a pleasant alpine-style restaurant (see p 219)

with a recently added 10-room wing. Although set in a row like a motel and decorated in a somewhat outdated style, the rooms are pleasant and comfortable.

Unfortunately, no windows face the front, thus hiding the exquisite view of the lush-green valley capped by magnificent mountains. Those not in need of privacy can enjoy the view by sitting out a while on the common veranda that links all the rooms. Good quality for the price and very friendly welcome.

Guadelupe

Los Quetzales
$-$$$$
pb, hw, ℜ, ⌂, ⊘
after reaching the end of Guadelupe, turn right at the intersection; the hotel is situated on the left side of the road, Apdo 55-0039
☎771-2182 or 771-2291
⇄771-2226
www.losquetzales.com
Who hasn't dreamt of staying in the middle of the jungle in total comfort? If this possibility sounds tempting, try one of the lodging options offered by Los Quetzales, located in the small town of Guadelupe. The first is a wooden, alpine-style hotel built at the entrance to the Parque Internacional La Amistad. For those on a limited budget, women and men's dorms are also available (B/.12/pers). The 10 rooms are simply furnished but comfortable, and there is also a fine restaurant as well as a bakery. Moreover, a sauna and a spa have been set up next to the river as well as a room with a ping-pong table.

A playground and animal farm keep children busy and give parents a break. For something to do on rainy days, wood sculpting classes are offered as well as cooking classes for the less artistically inclined. Those who crave news from home despite all of these activities can take advantage of an Internet service, which is available for B/.5 an hour.

The second option, **La Amistad**, is more expensive *(between B/.75 and B/.150 depending on the size of the cabin)* but extraordinary. There are four cabins for rent in the heart of Parque Internacional La Amistad, each completely secluded and nestled deep in the forest. They come with an equipped kitchen, a lounge and a bathroom with hot water. There is no electricity in the cabins and lighting is provided by kerosene lamps. Getting there involves a 30min hike with a guide from Los Quetzales, or being driven part of the way in a four-wheel-drive vehicle *(free transportation)*.

Three of the dwellings are on the mountainside and include kitchen, living room with fireplace, guest rooms and observation deck, on two floors. The hotel provides a daily catering service for those who do not want to cook *(B/.30 per day or B/.12 per meal)*. The fourth cabin is located below a river and has two separate floors, each of which can accommodate up to six people.

Each floor has two guest rooms, living room, dining room with fireplace, kitchen and bathroom. Because the cabins are located in a national park, strict rules must be followed. For example, it is forbidden to smoke, bring a radio, pick plants, capture insects or animals and all non-biodegradable waste must be carried out upon departure. Those who can afford it should not miss this unique experience especially since it also includes two guided excursions a day at no extra charge.

Restaurants

David

La Cacerola
$
corner of Avenida Francisco Clark and Calle P Norte, to the right of the shopping centre Super Baru, turn left on the main road to David, just after the intersection with the Interamericana and Boquete
☎775-0117
This restaurant-cafeteria serves various dishes (vegetables, rice with vegetables, beef tongue, chicken, etc.) at unparalleled prices. Expect to pay B/.2.5 for a meal—a real deal!

Restaurante y Cafeteria Jimar
$
Avenida Bolivar and Calle C Norte
The Restaurante y Cafeteria is a bustling place that is particularly popular with students attracted by the inexpensive prices. The large windows give the restaurant an open feeling, even when all the tables are taken. A complete lunch can be enjoyed for B/.2. While the menu is predictable for the most part (chicken, *corvina*, shrimp), a few less common dishes are available, including smoked meat with tomato and onion, and *tortas* (a kind of Spanish tortilla made with eggs, similar to an omelette). While this is a good place for travellers who are watching their pennies, the food is average.

Restaurante Hotel Fiesta
$$
at the intersection for David and Boquete, on the right of the Interamericana
☎775-5454 or 775-5453
The Restaurante Hotel Fiesta is a large restaurant with appealing colonial decor. A wide variety of dishes, both Panamanian and French, are offered at reasonable prices.

Las Vegas
$$
11am to 3pm and 6pm to 11pm, pastries from 7am
corner of Avenida Central and Calle Primera, facing the Hotel Nacional
Whether for a generous breakfast, a delicious plate of fresh pasta, a pizza or just a simple pastry and coffee, the café-restaurant Las Vegas is a very pleasant place. A small patio filled with flowers is a great complement to this unpretentious spot, whose clientele is mostly local.

Mar del Sur
$$$
every day 11am to 3pm and 6pm to 11pm
Calle H Norte and Avenida 1 Oeste, on the right side of the main road to David, behind the Supermercado La Fe de Dolequita
☎775-0856
If you wish to sample delicious South American cuisine, be sure to try the Mar del Sur, where authentic Peruvian dishes make up the menu, including *papas a la huancaina*, *almejas a la sureña* (southern-style soft-shelled clams), or *mariscos salteados* (seafood sautéed with onions, tomatoes and garlic).

For customers who prefer meat, the *filete a la pimienta verde* or *al curry* is a good choice. To go with your meal, excellent Chilean and Argentinean wines are available at reasonable prices. Finally, for a lovely finish, try the *suspiros de Lima*, the house dessert. The atmosphere is pleasant and the decor welcoming. A good price/ quality ratio.

From David to Boquete

Restaurante Bar Bonjour
$
on the left side of the road to Boquete just after it crosses the Interamericana
The Restaurante Bar Bonjour is a large open-air restaurant that offers a range of dishes (including pizza, chicken, shrimp, hamburgers and rice). While close to the road, it is in a nice area and is surrounded by tropical plants. This is also a good place to stop for a drink.

Bar y Restaurante La Cascada
$
9km from the Interamericana on the right side of the road leading to Boquete
Typical, inexpensive Panamanian fare served in an open-air restaurant under a palm-thatched roof, next to a water fountain. A plate of chicken will set you back B/.5.

Boquete

Pizzería Volcánica
$
on the right side of the road through town, just before the central plaza
☎720-1063
For a good selection of pizza, head to the tiny Pizzería Volcánica restaurant, where you will be warmly welcomed.

Restaurante El Sabrosón
$
Calle 1 Sur and Av. Central
El Sabrosón prepares typical Panamanian fare with the ubiquitous beans, rice and *platanas fritas*. No big surprises but for B/.2 a meal, what more could you ask for?

Restaurante Lourdes
$
overlooking the main street, on the left side, just before the central plaza
Restaurante Lourdes is an unpretentious, simply decorated place that

serves home-style Panamanian food. For some reason, it is renowned for its french fries.

La Conquista
$$
on the left side of the road facing the Pizzeria La Volcanita
The La Conquista restaurant prepares a variety of simple, family-style dishes for around B/.15.

Fundadores
$$
on the left, at the start of the main road going through the village
☎***720-1298***
The restaurant in the Fundadores hotel is worth mentioning for its lovely surroundings. There are two levels; the room on the first floor offers an interesting view of a pretty flowered garden and a river which, surprisingly, runs below the building. Sculptures of exotic birds made from painted car tires are another delightful and unusual detail.

Finally, the owner adds her own personal touch with fresh flowers on every table. A complete menu of Panamanian cuisine is offered for B/.15, and good breakfasts are served for as little as B/.4. For smaller appetites, spaghetti or *arroz con camarones* (rice with shrimp) at B/.4 are perfect. Friendly staff.

Panamonte
$$$
at the edge of town, turn right at the intersection and head toward the small bridge which crosses the river
☎***720-1327***
The Restaurante Hotel Panamonte is located in an attractive and charming hotel. The menu is varied and the high-quality food is very well prepared. Dishes include filet mignon, excellent corn soup, *pernil de porco* and scampi. Desserts are simple but also very good (try the homemade flan). A very tasty cocktail made with fresh orange juice is a good way to start your meal. Breakfasts are big and inexpensive, while the staff efficient and friendly. One little drawback: the selection is limited and there is no menus as such. The staff, however, will gladly describe the various dishes available and they did promise that a menu was on the way! Very good value for money.

From La Concepción to Volcán

Mirador AlanHer
$
take the road to Volcán from the Interamericana, the Mirador is 16km farther, on the left side of the road
This modest restaurant at the bottom of a *mirador* serves very good light meals. Try the *queso deretido* (cheese on the grill) or the *batidos* (a kind of *chicha*). There is also a good selection of cheese and yogurt. This is perfect place to stop on the way to Volcán.

Restaurante La Cabaña
$
open from 7am to 6pm
north of Cuesta di Piedra, 18.8km from the Interamericana toward Volcán
A pleasant little restaurant with a lovely garden and a nice view. Simple, unpretentious local dishes.

From Volcán to Cerro Punta

Bambito
$$$
turn right onto the highway on the way to Cerro Punta, about 7km from the centre of Volcán
☎***771-4265***
Very pleasant restaurant in a charming location with a view of artificial waterfalls. Varied and refined menu, composed of Panamanian and French cuisine. Good quality for the price, with amenable staff and services.

La Campagnola
$$$
to the left of the road leading to Cerro Punta, a few kilometres after the Bambito Hotel and immediately after a bridge
☎***771-5126 or 265-5103***
Part of the Bambito Camping Resort, the La Campagnola restaurant offers an extensive Italian menu featuring mostly pasta dishes. A considerable wine list is also offered but prices are prohibitive. The two wood-panelled dining rooms are cozy and offer an attractive view of the gardens. The house also prepares meat and fish dishes for those who might not be in the mood for pasta. A little expensive.

Cerro Punta

Cerro Punta
$$
on the left of the main road, at the entrance to the village
☎***771-2020***
Located in a lovely setting, with a very good view of the mountains, this restaurant serves traditional local cuisine at affordable prices. Friendly staff.

Guadelupe

Los Quetzales
$$
at the end of Guadelupe, turn right at the intersection; the hotel is situated on the left side of the road
☎***771-2182 or 771-2291***
On the second storey of the hotel of the same name, the Los Quetzales restaurant serves pizza and Panamanian dishes at low prices. However, the pride of the house is its farmed trout served with fresh vegetables, grown locally without the use of chemical fertilizers. Its large, wood-panelled dining room complete with fireplace is particularly enjoyable and warm. After a meal, the comfortable sofas in the cozy bar beside the restaurant are the perfect place to sip a *digestif*. Finally, visit the bakery on the first floor and stock up on numerous goodies for upcoming excursions. Definitely an address to remember.

Gariché

Balneario Restaurante Camino al Cielo
$
9km from the town of Concepción, en route to the Costa Rican border, the Interamericana crosses the Río Gariché which flows from the Cordillera de Talamanca
The small Balneario Restaurante Camino al Cielo overlooks the *río*. Choice is very limited, and one must not expect a gastronomical experience, but B/.4 will buy a typical Panamanian meal. To get there, soon after the bridge over the river, turn right off the main road onto a dirt road. This leads to the restaurant's parking lot (free). To avoid any unpleasant surprises, do not leave anything in a parked car.

Entertainment

From David to La Concepción

Jorón las Totumas
every day from 11am
on the right of the Interamericana, 5km past the exit for David and Boquete
Located on the edge of the Interamericana, the Jorón las Totumas is a huge restaurant-club where you can relax and have a drink under the *bohío* into the wee hours. It's a good meeting place for young people who come to dance. There's always a fun atmosphere, and you can order simple dishes at very respectable prices: For example, *arroz con camarones* (rice with shrimp) is available for B/.4. The staff is friendly, and as long as you like plenty of action, this is a great place.

Zebede Disco
Mon-Sat
on the left side of the main road leading to Boquete, 700m from the intersection with the Interamericana, also called El Jorón del Amor
Also close to the Interamericana, the Zebede Disco attracts mainly couples after 10:30pm. The dance floor is surrounded by many tables, where you can drink or order a meal *(expect to pay about B/.10)*. Latin-American music.

Shopping

Along the Interamericana

Once you have entered the province of Chiriquí on the Interamericana and passed the large intersection which leads to Tolé but is not marked, the side of the highway is dotted with small shops with palm roofs selling indigenous arts and crafts. **Jewellery**, such as *chaquiras* (necklaces), bracelets and earrings, as well as **clothing**, including colourful dresses, are available here. Most items are made by the Guaymies. A reduction of about 10% is possible if you bargain.

David

David is a pretty good place to shop do your shopping since the prices are reasonable and the selection is varied. Other than the usual purchases (clothes, music, shoes, etc.), you can find various handicrafts in the central plaza, including very beautiful *molas* which are not too expensive *(B/.12 to B/.15)*.

Boquete

Café Ruiz
Mon-Sat 7am to 6pm; Sun 12pm to 6pm
Avenida Central, past the centre of the village on the right side of the road to Alto Lino
☎720-1392
⇄720-1292
After an educational introduction to coffee making, buy some of the country's finest coffee at the Café Ruiz. Regular, amaretto, chocolate and hazelnut coffee is available.

Conservas de Antaño
from the Parque Domingo Médica, cross the bridge and drive 100m on the street to the right
☎720-1539
After having discovered (and tasted) all the secrets of jam-making at the Conservas de Antaño, it is highly unlikely that you will leave empty-handed. Pick up some mango jam for future breakfasts (providing there's some left!). Delicious

On weekends in the village of Boquete, **Place Centrale** in the centre of town is transformed into a morning market, where the Guaymies come to sell their arts and crafts.

Along the Interamericana to Volcán

Arte Cruz
on the main road leading to Volcán, the workshop is on the left side of the road going up the hill, 26km from the Interamericana
The Arte Cruz is a small studio that sells wood sculptures and engraved glass. José Cruz Gonzalez, the artist, will be happy to show you around. Some pieces are for sale and you can special order from Gonzalez, who is very proud of his work; he'll even show you an album of his nicest pieces, some of which have won him first prize in contests. José Cruz Gonzalez, who studied in Italy, has sold pieces to buyers from the United States, Europe, and South Africa. He can even engrave a beautiful landscape in glass for you on the spot. A worthwhile stop.

From Volcán to Cerro Punta

Stalls sell fresh fruit all along the road to Cerro Punta just past the Hotel Bambito. Great for a picnic.

Province of Bocas del Toro

The Province of

Bocas del Toro is aptly named the province of "green ;old."

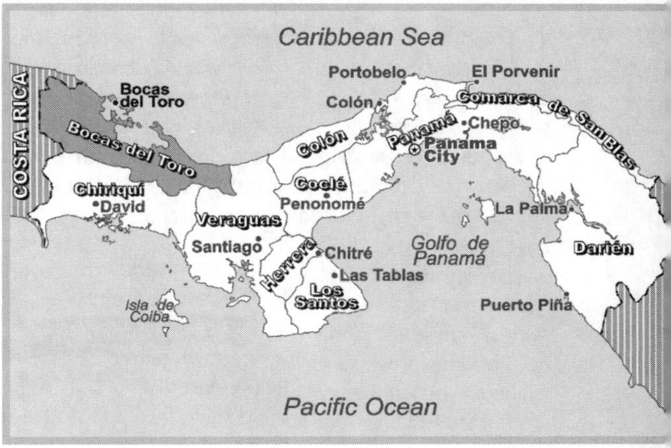

overed by exuberant vegetation, it contains 'most all of the vast arque Internacional La mistad, one of the largest rotected zones in Central merica. Although it was ne of Christopher :olombus' landing sites in 502, Spanish colonists ;nored this region be- ause of its remote loca- on, and it remained com- letely undeveloped for vo centuries.

xcept for indigenous peoples (see p 31), the nglish pirates and a small luguenot community in ıe 18th century, it was nly in the early 19th entury that the first per- nanent settlers were stablished here. As a esult, the small town of ocas del Toro was ounded in 1826. Popu- ated by landowners and ormer slaves from the lands of San Andrés and rovidencia, it started out ıore like a campsite than town. Many adventurers and merchants stopped here while hunting sea turtles, which were very much in demand at the time. With the subsequent arrival of Jamaicans, the place became a little town. Cacao cultivation, lumbering, coconut gathering and fishing were the main economic activities on the island. However, the intensive cultivation of bananas is the main reason for the development of Bocas del Toro. In 1899, the famous United Fruit Company set up its head office here and, in only a few years' time, transformed the modest city into one of the country's largest areas of available employment. In addition to indigenous populations (notably Guyamies), many former workers of the then-bankrupt canal (mainly black people from the Antilles) came here in an effort to improve their living conditions. This created significant traffic between Colón and Bocas del Toro. When the Republic of Panamá was created in 1903, this was one of its most influential regions, and the third-largest commercial district. During this era, several foreign consulates were even operating in the little city on behalf of France, Great Britain, Germany and the United States.

Unfortunately for the fledgling metropolis, prosperity was to be short-lived. During the 1920s, diseases affecting the banana crop caused the ruin of the city. United Fruit transferred its head office first to Changuinola and subsequently to Puerto Armuelles, in the neighbouring province of Chiriquí. This left the entire region destitute, and Bocas del Toro and its province have since gradually regressed to their original state of isolation.

Today, with only modest cities such as Chiriquí Grande, Changuinola, Almirante and Bocas del Toro, this large province is sparsely populated, and many of its Guyamies inhabitants are scattered through innumerable isolated communities. Since the establishment of a road between Chiriquí Grande and the Pan-American Highway, the economy has been mainly based on the transport of merchandise from neighbouring Costa Rica to the port city, Almirante.

Among other sources of revenue, an oil pipeline that runs from north to south of the country is used for transporting various products from one ocean to the other. Also, for several years now, the cultivation of bananas has resumed in the region of Changuinola, although on a more modest scale, but it still is an important economic factor.

As far as tourism is concerned, like Darién, Bocas del Toro is still among the least developed provinces, but it seems ready to take up the challenge and become fully involved with the rest of the country.

The new hotels and restaurants that have established themselves in the small town of Bocas del Toro, while few in number, indicate a trend in this direction. The island on which it is located, Isla Colón, marks the start of the Archipiélago de Bocas del Toro, which contains the only marine park in the country, at Isla Bastimentos. Well known for the beauty of its ocean floor and the richness of coral, the marine park is the principal attraction in the province. If diving an the underwater world ar particularly interesting to you, make sure to visit th area.

As for the other impor tant object of curiosit in the region, the Parque Internacional La Amistad, its main entrance is in the neighbouring province of Chiriquí, so it can be explored without passing through Bocas del Toro.

The province has enough unique ethnic aspects to be charming o its own. Since many of th inhabitants are of either Caribbean or indigenous descent, the languages spoken here are different from those in other parts of the country. English is more widespread here and, in addition to its bein spoken with strong Creo intonations, it is enriched by many Spanish and Guyamie, terms. Adding t the linguistic potpourri, in an attempt to Hispanicize the remote province, former authorities renamed or simply translate many of the place names. Don't be surprised to find two names for the same island, with *cay* transformed into *cayo*, or sometimes even *isla*.

Finding Your Way Around

Note: The following schedules and rates are provided for reference only and are subject to change.

By Car

To get to **Chiriquí Grande** when driving west on the Interamericana, turn right at the intersection, 85km past Tolé. If you are coming from David, that is, driving east, the intersection is about 10km away, on the left side of the Interamericana, just after the bridge over the Río Chiriquí. There is a service station at Chiriquí Grande, on the left at the end of the main road through the village.

To get to **Bocas del Toro** by car, the only way is to go first to Almirante, and from there to take a ferry to Isla Colón. To do so, take the Chiriqui Grande–bound road to the road leading to Almirante. Completed in 2000, the road is in good condition and it offers interesting scenery.

At Almirante, the **Expreso Taxi 25** and **Bocas Marine Tours** (see below) transportation companies will safeguard your vehicle for a modest daily rate.

To get to **Parque Internacional La Amistad** see the "Province of Chiriquí" chapter (see p 207).

Note: The following schedules and rates are provided for reference only and are subject to change.

By Plane

The best way to reach **Bocas del Toro**, the is by plane: not only is it the fastest way to get there, but also the most comfortable.

Bocas del Toro

Mapiex-Aero and **Aeroperlas** are the only companies currently serving these destinations. Flights are available from the capital or from David.

Mapiex-Aero

Panama City to Bocas del Toro
Departure: Mon-Fri 8:50am; Sat 6:30am; Sun 1:30pm.
Travel Time: 1hr
Cost: B/.50 one way

Bocas del Toro to Panama City
Departure: Mon-Fri 10am; Sat 8am; Sun 3pm.

Bocas del Toro
☎757-9841

Aeroperlas

Panama City to Bocas del Toro (stopover in Changuinola)
Departure: Mon-Fri 8:30am and 1pm; Sat 7am and 3pm; Sun 8am and 3pm.
Travel Time: between 1 and 1:5hr
Cost: B/.50 one way

David to Bocas del Toro (stopover in Changuinola)
Departure: Mon-Fri 8am
Travel Time: 50min
Cost: B/.26 one way

Bocas del Toro
☎757-9341

David
(Enrique Malek airport)
☎721-1195 or 721-1230

By Boat

Bocas del Toro

The construction of the new road linking the Interamericana to Almirante has made the city the new point of departure by boat for Bocas del Toro. Almirante is in fact much closer to Isla Colón than Chiriqui Grande. At press time, two companies provided this daily service (from 6:30am to 6pm): **Espresso Taxi 25** and **Bocas Marine Tours**. There are hourly departures. The one-way crossing costs B/.3 per person and takes 35 to 45min. Note, however, that schedules vary and are subject to a number of conditions (weather, number of passengers, condition of the craft, etc.).

Boca del Drago and the Islands of the Archipelago

Many outfitters offer transportation to the islands in the archipelago. Since almost none of the islands have hotels or restaurants, most of these excursions are round-trip. Addresses for these providers and advice about exploring the islands is found in the

"Outdoor Activities" section of this chapter.

By Bus

Chiriquí Grande

There is regular bus service between David and Chiriquí Grande; the bus stop in David is on Paseo Estudiante and the fare is about B/.6. The trip takes approximately 3hrs.

Boca del Drago

While there is bus service between Bocas del Toro and Boca del Drago, on the northeastern part of the island, it serves mainly as transportation for local workers. The trip takes about 45min *(B/.2.50 one way)* and can take you to the grotto. However, the trip back from either destination only takes place late in the day when there are sufficient passengers to make the trip worthwhile, so this mode of transportation is more adventurous than practical.

Unfortunately, aside from cycling or walking, the taxi is the only reliable way to get to Boca del Drago and costs B/.25 round trip. It is best to round up a large group of friends to split the fare, which is somewhat expensive given that the distance travelled is only 15km.

By Train

While there is a railway line between Almirante and Changuinola, and another to Guabito, they are used for transporting merchandise (mainly bananas). Since the trains offer no amenities for passengers, the owners, **Chiriquí Land Company**, are reluctant to let non-staff aboard.

To Get to Costa Rica

To get to **Sixaola (Costa Rica)** you must reach the village of Guabito, via the cities of Almirante and Changuinola. Considering, however, that these two cities offer few attractions, the most interesting solution is to spend the night at Bocas del Toro. This way, you can spend the day exploring Isla Colón before setting off for Almirante the next day.

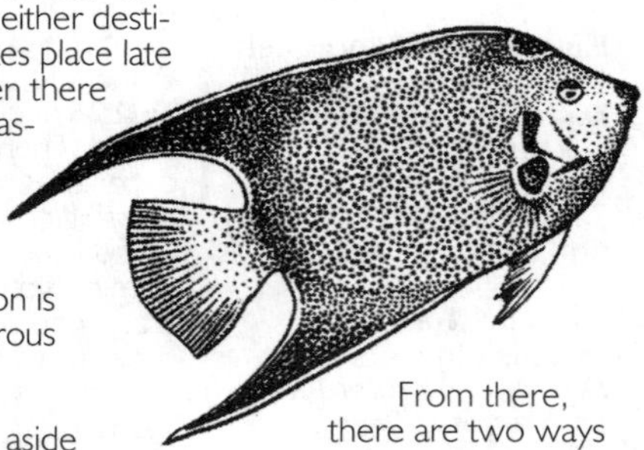

From there, there are two ways to continue your travels: by bus or by train. The bus is the more comfortable and dependable way to go. Take the bus to Changuinola and transfer to the bus for Guabito. Guabito is connected to the village of Sixaola by a bridge over the Río Sixaola (which flows along the border of Costa Rica and Panamá).

There is a one-hour time difference between Panamá and Costa Rica, so remember to set your watch back an hour when you arrive in Sixaola.

Practical Information

Bocas del Toro

IPAT Tourist Bureau

IPAT
Mon-Fri
Calle 1
☎/⇄ ***757-9642***
Located at the end of Bocas del Toro's Calle 1, in a new building that also houses the ANAM, the tourist office (IPAT) can provide you with all the information needed for a pleasant stay.

ANAM (INRENARE)

ANAM
Calle 1
☎ ***757-9244***
Vistors to the national parks, including Parque Marino de la Isla Bastimentos, must obtain authorisation from ANAM. As a general rule, local agencies do not include the cost of the permit in the excursion rate. Visitors must go to the ANAM office to obtain it.

Bank

Banco Nacional de Panamá
Avenida F, between Calle 1 and Calle 2

The magnificent facade of Casco Viejo's cathedral – a must-see!
– *courtesy of IPAT*

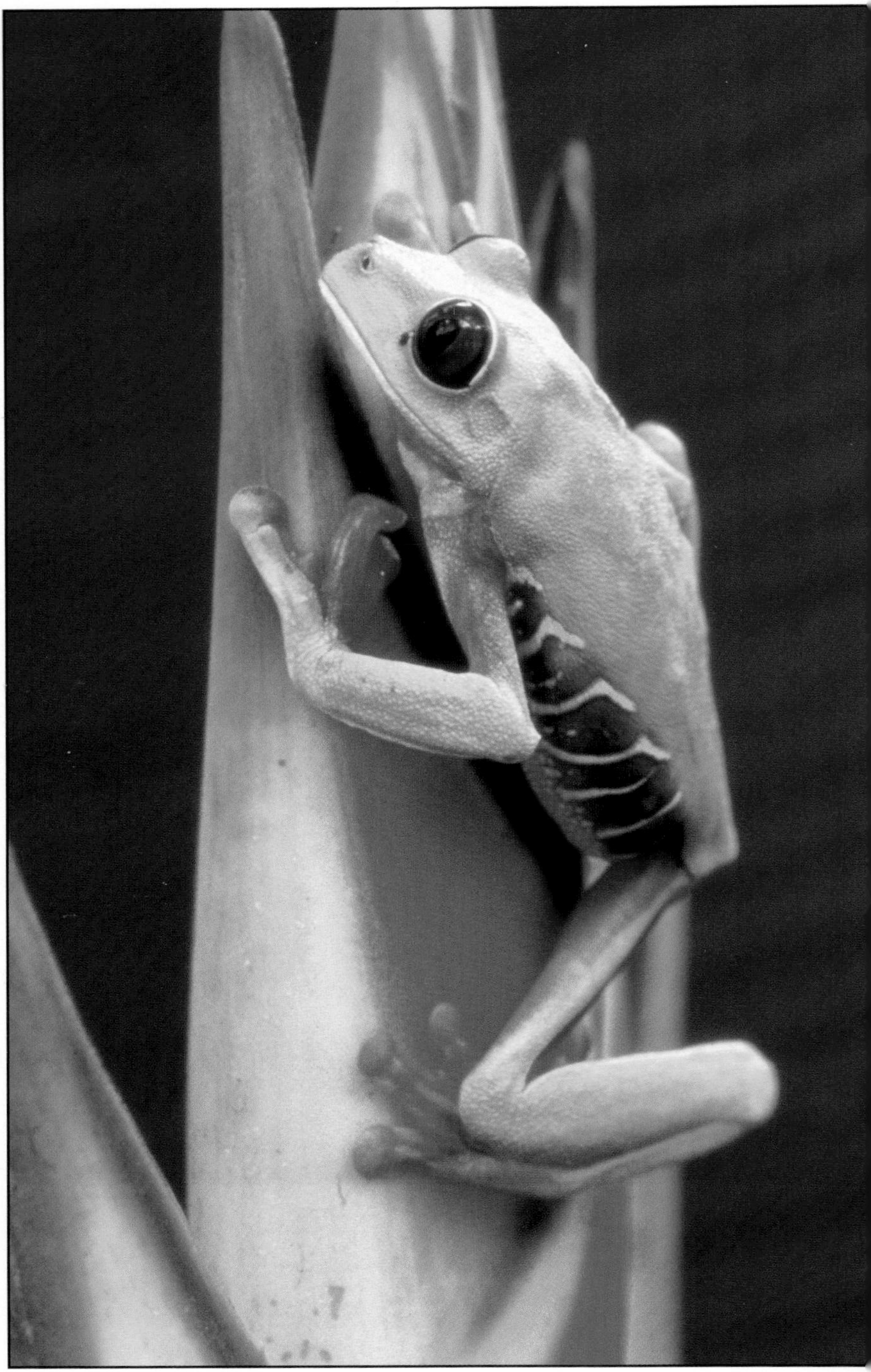

The Callidrya frog shows off its beautiful blend of colours.
– courtesy of IPAT

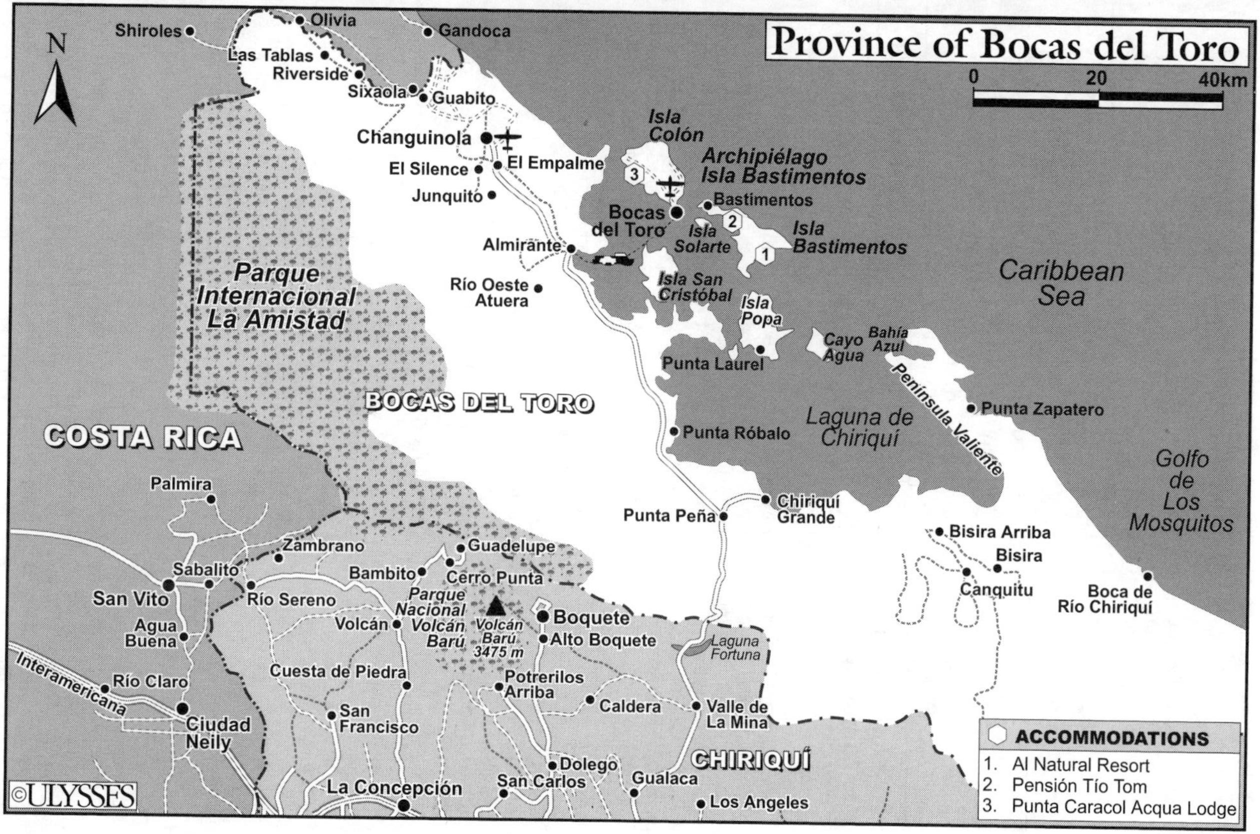
Province of Bocas del Toro
0
20
40km
N
Shiroles
Olivia
Gandoca
Las Tablas
Riverside
Sixaola
Guabito
Changuinola
El Silence
El Empalme
Junquito
Isla
Colón
Archipiélago
Isla Bastimentos
Bastimentos
Bocas
del Toro
Isla
Solarte
Isla
Bastimentos
Almirante
Río Oeste
Atuera
Isla San
Cristóbal
Isla
Popa
Caribbean
Sea
Parque
Internacional
La Amistad
Cayo
Agua
Bahía
Azul
Punta Laurel
Península Valiente
Punta Zapatero
BOCAS DEL TORO
Punta Róbalo
Laguna de
Chiriquí
COSTA RICA
Golfo
de
Los
Mosquitos
Palmira
Chiriquí
Grande
Punta Peña
Bisira Arriba
Bisira
Zambrano
Guadelupe
Sabalito
Bambito
Cerro Punta
Canquitu
Boca de
Río Chiriquí
San Vito
Río Sereno
Parque
Nacional
Volcán
Barú
Volcán
Barú
3475 m
Boquete
Alto Boquete
Agua
Buena
Volcán
Laguna
Fortuna
Interamericana
Río Claro
Cuesta de Piedra
Potrerilos
Arriba
Caldera
Valle de
La Mina
Ciudad
Neily
San
Francisco
ACCOMMODATIONS
1. Al Natural Resort
2. Pensión Tío Tom
3. Punta Caracol Acqua Lodge
Dolego
CHIRIQUÍ
Gualaca
San Carlos
La Concepción
Los Angeles
©ULYSSES

Telecommunications

There is a public telephone next to **Parque Simón Bolívar** (Parque Central) on Calle 3.

Exploring

★★

From Chiriquí to Chiriquí Grande

The road leading from the Interamericana to Chiriquí Grande makes for an especially fascinating trip. While crossing the Talamanca Cordillera, which is covered in thick jungle, the landscape is dotted with the typical dwellings of the Guaymies. As well, the landscape varies the whole way not only depending on altitude but also on which side of the road you are on. On the Pacific side, the scenery is made up of plains dotted with hills and mountains covered with either rich green vegetation scorched brown, while the Atlantic side is blanketed by a veritable jungle of tropical vegetation. The vegetation becomes particularly distinct in the Reserva Forestal La Fortuna. The entire route is attractive, and a number of dramatic views provide memorable highlights. The return trip can easily be made in a day from David or Boquete. The distances mentioned in the following descriptions correspond to distances from the Interamericana highway.

The first stop at the 30.9km marker allows you to admire a beautiful view of the plains and the hills beyond; clouds seem to have been carefully placed above to make a picture-perfect landscape.

At 32.4km and 34.5km, there are two rudimentary rest stops on the left that offer lovely views of the Pacific Ocean and, farther off in the distance, the islands of Boca Brava and Parida.

At the 45.7km marker, a small, refreshing stop is perfect for admiring a charming waterfall on the left side of the road.

At 47.9km, just after the entrance to a cemetery, the road turns left. From here, there is a good view of an artificial lake, Lago Fortuna, the by-product of a hydroelectric dam. The one-lane bridge over the lake is a great spot for beautiful vistas. A little further, on the left side of the road, a section of the oil pipeline carrying oil from Puerto Armuelles (on the Pacific coast) to the Atlantic coast is easy to spot.

At 52.8km, on the left side of the road, is another impressive waterfall (about 10 m high).

At 56km, you can stop briefly to see the continental divide for the country's water. From this point on, rivers flow toward the Atlantic. This is also the location of the border between the provinces of Chiriquí and Bocas del Toro.

There is another waterfall at 58.7km, on the right-hand side of the road. Just after it, you will see traditional Guaymie houses, balancing on high stilts. Ten kilometres ahead, the road passes through the small indigenous village of Malí.

Chiriquí Grande

A small port city that travellers and merchandise used to simply pass through, Chiriquí Grande is not really an attractive place, but is nonetheless striking and worth a brief visit. A walkway along the sea provides a good view of residential architecture typical of the region and characteristic of houses on the Caribbean coast. Turn right at the end of the main street in the village and walk to a small bridge, which you must cross to keep going straight. You will soon find yourself on a winding street past small houses on stilts. The ambiance of this place, combined with the richness of the surrounding greenery, will leave no traveller indifferent. Canoes paddled by indigenous people add to the wonder of this isolated corner of the world. Simply magical!

Unfortunately, since the opening of the new road linking the Interamericana to Almirante in late 2000, the small town has been declining and greatly suffering from the dearth of visitors, who once transited through the area to catch one of the many ferries to Bocas del Toro.

★★

Isla Colón

Aside from the airport in Changuinola on the mainland, the 60km² Isla Colón has the only airport in the province, making it the main gateway to the archipelago and the national marine park at Bastimentos Island. Almost deserted, it has a total of two roads, only one of which being partially paved. Because Bocas del Toro is the only "city" on Isla Colón, it is a required stop as far as accommodations and restaurants are concerned. With the exception of some beautiful isolated beaches (see "Beaches" section, p 231), the island's only tourist attraction is a spot called **La Gruta** (also named Sanctuario Natural de Nuestra Señora de la Gruta), located in the middle of the island. This grotto contains a statuette of the Virgin Mary that is an object of annual pilgrimages. It is also home to a colony of bats, numbering in the hundreds and very easily observable. Unless you are on the way to the beach at Boca del Drago (the road passes nearby), or wish to make a pilgrimage, the trip is not worth the 5km dirt road, which is frequently transformed into a series of mud holes after a rainfall.

Bocas del Toro

Founded in 1826 by immigrants from the islands of San Andrés and Providencia (see introduction to chapter, p 221), the little town of Bocas del Toro has certainly seen better days. Aside from being abandoned by the United Fruit Company, the town has faced several fires (1904, 1907, 1918 and 1929) and two terrible tornadoes: one in 1964, which destroyed its cathedral (built in 1897), and another in 1975. To top it all off, an earthquake damaged its landing strip and several buildings in 1991. It comes as no surprise that there are few surviving historic buildings here, just some fine examples of Caribbean-style wooden

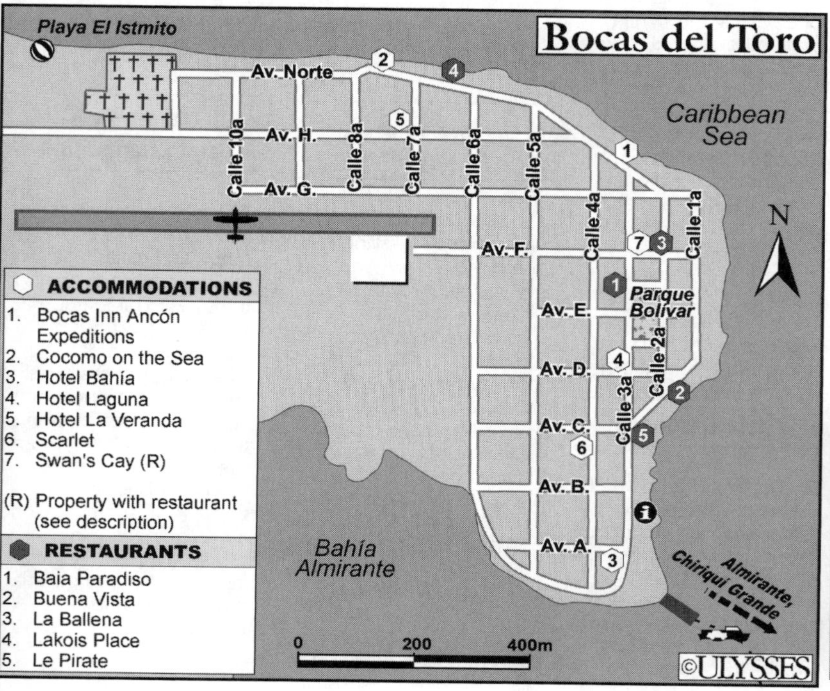

houses that too few residents seem motivated to restore. The majority of the establishments are on Calle 3, which is the town's main street and one of the rare paved roads. The park in the town centre is lovely, but badly neglected. It would also help if the information kiosk of the Caribaro Association, in the middle of the park, which seems to contain valuable information about the flora and fauna of the region, were repaired so that travellers could learn more about the area's resources.

Having a pleasant stay in Bocas del Toro is limited to visiting the islands of the archipelago or the nearby beaches, and spending the evening in one of the town's restaurants. Anyone passing through in September should make sure to catch the "Feria del Mar," a large fair with displays of crafts and local products, which is followed by enthusiastic celebrations. Finally, an amusing detail: fans of antique vehicles should stop by the firehouse (Calle 1 and Avenida G) to admire the remarkable model of a fire engine that has long been the pride and joy of the inhabitants.

Isla Carenero

Across from the town of Bocas del Toro, Isla Carenero has no specific attraction except for a few tourist-oriented restaurants. If you decide to have breakfast here, take a stroll through the neighbouring village. Just follow the shore to the left of the landing stage to the little concrete path that winds through the town. This will plunge you into the daily life of the inhabitants of Carenero and allow you to admire their houses on stilts, which are typical of the archipelago. It seems miraculous that some of them are still standing!

Isla de Los Pájaros, or Swan Cay

This tiny island, better described as a large rock, is a bird sanctuary and is mainly of interest to bird-watchers. Although landing on the island is strictly forbidden, numerous so-called "guides" will offer a little tour on the island itself. To avoid disturbing the nesting process, refuse any such offer and enjoy the beauty of the site from a boat.

Isla Solarte, or Cay Nancy

Located a mere 2km from Isla Colón, this island's history began when, hard on the heels of its establishment at Bocas del Toro, United Fruit decided to erect housing facilities for members of its staff who had caught malaria. Over the years, the 16 buildings of Hospital Point, as the company named it, became the largest hospital in the province. When the banana plantations were destroyed by disease, the company completely dismantled the hospital before leaving the area, around 1920. Although some agencies in Bocas suggest excursions to the island, there is really nothing left to see except for a few structures covered with vegetation.

Isla San Cristóbal

As is the case with many of the islands in the archipelago, the waters surrounding Isla San Cristóbal are rich with marine wildlife. The northern part of the island, with its vast stands of mangrove, is habitat for many dolphins that may be observed there. A lighthouse stands at the northernmost point of the island to guide ships on their way to Almirante, where they take on large shipments of bananas destined for America or Europe. San Cristóbal is also the name of a Guyamie village, which can be visited by some tour groups.

Almirante and Changuinola

Although these two little towns have a few modest hotels and restaurants, they are above all points of transit. Almirante is just a simple port with shabby houses, while and Changuinola is really only a centre of banana cultivation surrounded by plantations as far as the eye can see. Except for people taking the land route to Costa Rica, and those who are fascinated by the technical aspects of growing bananas, Changuinola has nothing much to offer tourists.

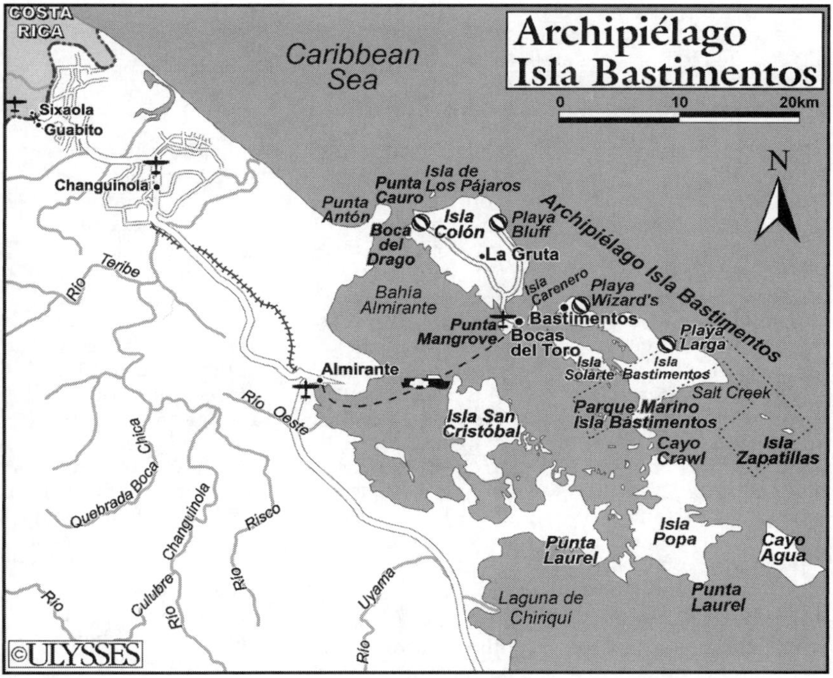

Parks

★★

Parque Marino de la Isla Bastimentos

Thanks to its rich underwater fauna and gigantic beaches that are visited by as many as four species of sea turtles, Parque Marino de la Isla Bastimentos is unique. The island section represents only one tenth of the park's 13,235ha area; the remaining 11,600ha consist of stretches of water where red and white mangroves and coral are readily observable. On the northern part of the island is **Long Beach**, or **Playa Larga**, a vast expanse of spectacular natural beauty that is difficult to reach because of the violent waves that crash against it. A large number of sea turtles (see box "Sea Turtle," in this chapter) come here each year to lay their eggs. Just a few kilometres inland from Long Beach, a vast lake serves as a refuge for freshwater turtles as well as numerous other reptiles, including crocodiles.

The park is also home to a venomous frog, *dendrobates pumilio*, whose skin secretes a toxic substance. Its skin shows a wide palette of colours ranging from vivid scarlet and bright orange to acid green. In spite of its brilliant colouring and the fact that it is present on other islands, it is rarely spotted. On the eastern side of the island, outside the park limits, is a little Guaymie village named **Salt Creek**. It is hard to get to, however, so those who wish to visit such a community should instead head to Isla Cristóbal (see above), which is more accessible. Also outside the park, this time to the west, is the fishing village of Bastimentos, which has nothing of particular note to attract visitors. The only reason to go there is the beautiful, wild **Wizard's Beach**, located 1km along a path from the village. Here, the size of the

Sea Turtles

There are eight different kinds of sea turtles that belong to seven distinct species. Sea turtles, along with land and fresh-water turtles, belong to the *chelonidae* order and are reptiles. Unfortunately, all species of sea turtles are in danger of extinction, but measures have been adopted both nationally and internationally (creation of nature reserves, protection programs, establishment of reproduction facilities, etc.) to protect them.

These unusual creatures have very limited vision when out of the water, but this is compensated by their keen sense of smell and acute hearing. Mostly carnivorous, they have no teeth so they grind up fish, shellfish and crustaceans with their powerful jaws. Their growth rate is particularly slow, and some claim that certain species can live for over 100 years. Given the limited number of species, the size and consequent weight of sea turtles varies surprisingly. Some weigh a mere 35kg, while others can weigh up to one ton. Part of the latter group, the colossal leatherback turtle is not only the largest but also the only species of turtle able to withstand water temperatures below 4°C. As a result, it is found in all of the oceans on the planet. One last fact about the leatherback: it is the only marine turtle species without a hard shell; its skin is tough and thick, but nevertheless supple.

By far the most fascinating aspect of these reptiles, however, is their method of reproduction. Indeed, they travel hundreds, perhaps even thousands of kilometres to lay their eggs on the beach where they were born. On the Pacific Coast, eggs are laid between the months of October and March, while on the Atlantic coast, egg-laying season is between April and August. Various ongoing studies are attempting to explain this strange migration. For example, as mating season approaches and both male and female sea turtles set out for the original nest site, how do they get there? To date, only a few hypotheses have been put forward. Among these, the theory that the animals can detect magnetic fields is the only one that is widely accepted by scientists. Also, why do sea turtles return to their precise place of birth and ignore other beaches with identical conditions that are sometimes right nearby? Scientists have no exact answers to these questions, arguing that is has to do with genetics. According to this theory, turtles have experienced the same ideal nest sites over centuries, and this information has been recorded in their genetic memory.

Egg laying itself is astonishing. While most of the species lay their eggs individually, two turtle species, the Atlantic ridley and the green turtle (found in the Pacific), lay their eggs in large groups. This is called the *arribada*, in which all the turtles land on the beaches at the same time, creating a surreal spectacle. In 1942, at Ranch Nuevo, Mexico, 40,000 Atlantic ridley turtles came ashore in a single night. Sadly, only 50 years later, a mere 1,500 turtles were counted there. The question is: can these animals survive without human intervention? Facing the danger of extinction sea turtles seem to have found an answer: having mated with several males, the female stores their sperm and fertilizes her eggs with the semen of the males, creating a larger gene pool.

Generally, most females lay eggs twice during egg-laying season and at two- to three-year intervals. After digging a relatively deep pit in the sand, each turtle deposits 50 to 120 eggs, depending on the species. The eggs are soft and coated with a gelatinous substance to prevent them from breaking as they fall into the pit. The temperature inside the pit determines the length of the incubation period which is usually around 60 days. At the end of the incubation period, the baby turtle uses an excrescence on its jaw to break out of its shell; this natural tool disappears shortly after birth. Like egg laying, hatching (usually in a group) also takes place at night or, occasionally, on rainy days. Once out of their shells, the young turtles face life's first challenge: they must reach the ocean before becoming dehydrated. Because they are guided to the water by the shimmering reflection of the moon on the surface of the ocean, they are sometimes misdirected by lights from houses or hotels along the beach. Many baby turtles die of exhaustion this way every year. Those who reach the ocean must manoeuvre skilfully to escape predators until they are large enough to defend themselves. Consequently, only one in 1,000 will reach adulthood—a wonderful illustration of nature's ingenuity and fragility.

waves makes swimming unsafe, so visitors are limited to romantic strolls along the shore.

An integral part of Parque Marino de Bastimentos, the **Islas Zapatillas** are entirely surrounded by coral reef and are known for the beauty of their white, sandy beaches. The two islands are lapped by shallow, crystal-clear waters, which are ideal for snorkeling (see p 233). An INRENARE research centre on the larger island is used during part of the year for the study of sea turtles.

Parque Internacional La Amistad

Although it is located almost entirely in the province of Bocas del Toro, the most convenient entrance to Parque International La Amistad is in the neighbouring province of Chiriquí. Guided tours of the region also start from there. For this reason, you will find the detailed description of this attraction in the chapter "Province of Chiriquí" (see p 207)

Beaches

As is unfortunately the case on many of the archipelago beaches, nasty insects seem to show particular delight in biting new arrivals. To take full advantage of the province's beautiful beaches, come prepared with ample supplies of insect repellent.

Isla Colón

Playa El Istmito

This popular, modest beach is not one of the most attractive, but it has the advantages of being relatively safe and of being located directly outside the town of Bocas.

Playa Bluff

Swimming is dangerous here because of the violent waves; it is best for surfing and hiking.

A 3km stretch of shoreline swept by violent waves, Playa Bluff is a great place for long, solitary walks. From June to September, many sea turtles, especially leatherbacks, come up onto the beach at night to lay their eggs. Since this is an endangered species, visitors during this season must follow certain rules. Those who wish to witness this event can do so though the auspices of INRENARE or Ancon Expeditions of Bocas del Toro, which offer guided tours here at night. If this fascinates you, make sure to visit the Biblioteca Pública de Bocas (Calle 3), where the Caribaro association can inform you about the lifestyles of these marvelous reptiles.

Boca del Drago

Opposite Bocas del Toro, on the northwest side of the island, is a bay called **Boca del Drago** and the beach of the same name. This is one of the loveliest beaches on the island. As long as a few precautionary rules are followed, beginners can safely swim in the limpid waters and sunbathe on the golden sand.

Outdoor Activities

Hiking

From Chiriquí to Chiriquí Grande

Finca La Suiza
7am to 9pm
45km from the Interamericana, entrance on the right-hand side of the road going towards Chiriquí Grande, 3.4km from Los Planes, Apdo 1152, David
☎615-3774
Herbert Brüllmann and Monika Kolher will gladly welcome you to the heart of the large **Finca La Suiza**, nestled in the heart of the mountains. They will take you on a multitude of excursions that will allow you to admire birds, butterflies and other insects, as well as waterfalls, all surrounded by exuberant vegetation. The trips are not exactly restful, but you will see magnificent scenery, including the Barú Volcano and, on a clear day, the Pacific Ocean. Good walking shoes and a lightweight raincoat are essential for this ecotourism adventure. Access to the hiking trails will set you back about B/1.8 per person.

Surfing

Playa Bluff

This long beach with brownish sand is famous for its large waves that are ideal for surfing. However, given the force of the breakers, only true experts can safely ride the waves here. Beginners should exercise utmost caution.

Cycling

Bocas del Toro

Hotel Laguna and the **La Ballena** restaurant rent bicycles by the hour or day. Expect to pay B/.3 for the first two hours and B/.1.50 for additional hours.

From Bocas del Toro to Playa Bluff

There are only two roads on the island. The first, a dirt road, travels across the island to Boca del Drago, 14km away. The other, partially paved, follows the coast to Playa Bluff. Barely 8km long, this second road offers lovely scenic views and allows visitors to admire the flora and many of the native birds. With patience and luck, you might catch a glimpse of the amusing white-faced capuchin monkeys that live in the area.

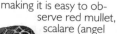

Unfortunately, midway along the road, there is an unsightly dump. Here too, an effort by local authorities to improve the environment would be appreciated. Nevertheless, the rest of the road is enjoyable. With just a few minor hills to climb and narrow streams to be forded, you will soon arrive at beautiful Playa Bluff, where signs announce the restaurant Finca Verde. The food here is very basic so a picnic lunch is in order. One last warning: sun screen and insect repellent are necessities here; but we also advise you not to wear your "best" clothing and shoes, as mud stains from Bocas seem to be indelible.

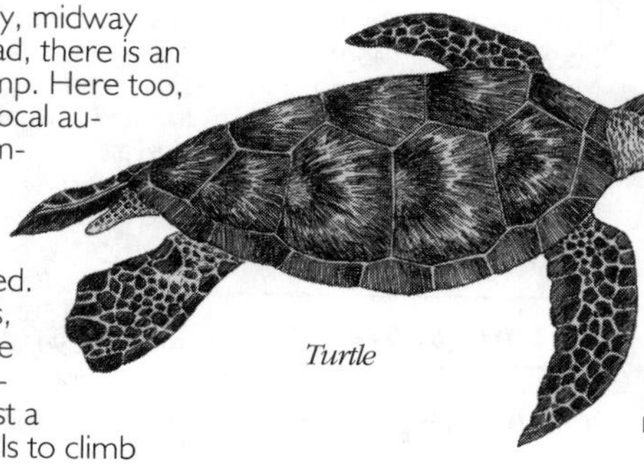

Turtle

Scuba Diving and Snorkelling

Bocas del Toro

Bocas Water Sports
Calle 3, next to the Tourist Bureau
☎***757-9541***

Transparente Tours Boats
Calle 3, at Le Pirate restaurant
☎***757-9600 or 757-9172***

All have a good selection of diving equipment for rent; everything from fins to compressed air tanks and diving masks. Prices vary according to the equipment rented and time of year.

Boca del Drago

While the beach at **Boca del Drago** is somewhat out of the way, it does offer beginner snorkellers the opportunity to observe rich marine life, provided a few safety rules are observed.

Cayo Crawl

This little island is one of the best places to snorkel. More sheltered than the Islas Zapatillas, the calm, shallow water is perfect for beginners and scuba divers will appreciate the proximity of **Bahia de Almirante**, known for its clear water and lack of waves. Although there is a modest restaurant on Cayo Crawl, we suggest you bring your own provisions along.

Islas Zapatillas

An integral part of the **Parque Marino de Bastimentos**, the **Islas Zapatillas** are famous for their crystal-clear water, ideal for snorkeling. This is a great spot for observing marine life because the islands are on a particularly rich coral plateau. A coral reef only 3 to 5m deep surrounds the islands, making it is easy to observe red mullet, scalare (angel fish), grouper, scarus (parrot fish), butterfly fish, crabs and many other species. Be careful: once outside the reef, strong currents make scuba diving problematic and too dangerous for beginners.

Cruises

Bocas Water Sports
Calle 3, next to the Tourist Bureau
☎***757-9541***

J&J Boat Tours
Calle 3, between Av. B and Av. C
☎/⇄***757-9915***

Ancón Expeditions
Av. Norte
☎***757-9226***
www.anconexpeditions.com

Transparente Tour Boats
Calle 3, at Le Pirate restaurant
☎***757-9600 or 757-9172***

All four companies offer various excursions leaving from **Bocas del Toro**. The day trip to the **Islas Zapatillas**, which stops on **Cayo Crawl**, is one of the most interesting. It provides a complete overview of the flora and fauna of the archipelago.

Those who suffer from seasickness should opt for a visit to **Carenero Island**, to **Solarte** or to the little village of **Bastimentos**: the boat rides are shorter and the waters calmer. Unfortunately for those travelling alone, the cost of these excursions is much higher for small groups. For example, an outing to the **Islas Zapatillas**, including a meal, is between B/.15 and B/.20 for groups of six or more, but can rise to B/.75 if the group is not large enough. However, competition is increasing all the time, so do not hesitate to bargain. The crossings are of significant length and the seas are not always calm, so only choose outfits with boats of a decent size, and make sure to wear a lifejacket.

Accommodations

From Chiriquí to Chiriquí Grande

Finca La Suiza
$$
pb, hw
45km from the Interamericana, entrance on the right-hand side of the road going towards Chiriquí Grande, 3.4km from Los Planes, Apdo 1152, David
☎615-3774
Herbert and Monica will welcome you to Finca La Suiza, nestled in the heights and surrounded by luxuriant vegetation. The rooms, located in a newly constructed building, are comfortable and clean, and each one has a terrace with a beautiful view of the mountains. If you like peace and quiet and are interested in birds, butterflies and insects, don't miss the chance to spend some time here. Unfortunately, the Finca La Suiza is not open year round, but only between December 1 and May 15, or July 1 and August 30. The owners, who are avid hikers, offer guests the use of several hiking paths on the property (see p 232).

Chiriquí Grande

The Hotel Emperador
$
overlooking the pier in Chiriquí Grande, to the left of the main street
☎756-9656
The Emperador is comfortable and has a large balcony with a view of comings and goings on the docks. It is fairly ordinary, but clean, and the staff is friendly.

Isla Colón

Bocas del Toro

Hotel La Veranda
$
⊗, sb
corner Avenida H and Calle 7
☎757-9211
www.laverandahotel.com
Those on a limited budget who do not mind communal-style lodgings will be welltreated by the Canadian hosts of La Veranda. On the second floor of a large wooden house, there are several rooms ranging from small with two beds to more spacious family-style rooms with several beds. Mosquito netting is available for B/.2 per night. As with most of the houses in Bocas, the rooms open onto a large gallery, in this case equipped with a stove and all the equipment necessary for those who wish to prepare their own breakfast or fix themselves a snack in the afternoon. A friendly, casual atmosphere prevails.

The Scarlet
$
pb, hw, ≡, tv
Calle 4 and Avenida C
☎757-9290
The Morales family welcomes guests to their 12-room hotel in their villa located on a corner of the main street in Bocas. Once again, the rooms extend along a lengthy corridor. Most rooms are bright, with tile floors and a modern, if conventional, decor. This establishment offers the best value in its category.

The Bahia
$$
≡, ⊗, hw, tv
Calle 3 or Calle Rev Ephraim Alphone
☎757-9626
www.panamainfo.com/hotelbahia
If you arrive by ferry, The Bahia hotel is probably the first building typical of Bocas that you will see. It has a long history, since it was the administrative seat of the famous United Fruit Company when this village was booming.

Now fully renovated, this old wooden building houses some 20 comfortable yet ordinary rooms with modern decor. While some have a view of the sea, others look right out on Bocas del Toro's main street. A good deal for those not averse to a sterile environment.

Cocomo on the Sea
$$$ bkfst incl.
⊗, sb, hw
Av. Norte
☎/⇄757-9259
www.panamainfo.com/cocomo
Built on stilts on the beach, this immaculate, white, wooden building has only four rooms, two of which face the ocean. Those seeking a restful atmosphere will be delighted by the small terrace overlooking the sea, where they can stretch out in a hammock with a book in between adventures. This charming establishment is attractive and clean beyond reproach. Ample and nourishing breakfasts are served in the owners' house next door in an equally pleasant atmosphere.

Hotel Laguna
$$$
pb, ≡, hw, tv, ℝ
corner Calle 3 and Av. D
☎757-9091
Located on the main street in Bocas, the Laguna has a dozen rooms in a Swiss-style chalet. While the rooms are dark and rather depressing, the ones upstairs display more charm and some even have a pleasant view. The hosts suggest various activities for guests (see p 232). Although sanitary facilities are adequate and the premises are immaculate, this hotel is expensive for what it offers.

Bocas Inn
Ancón Expeditions
$$$ bkfst incl.
pb, hw, ⊗
☎757-9226
⇄264-5990
This old house built on stilts offers a dozen or so clean rooms. The rooms, leading off here and there from a central hallway, are bright and simply decorated. With the exception of two rooms facing the sea, none offers an interesting view. However, there is an ocean view from the spacious open-air room on the main floor (where meals are served). The residence is charming and comfortable.

Swan's Cay
$$$-$$$$ bkfst incl.
pb, hw, ≡, tv, ℝ
corner Calle 3 and Av. F
☎757-9090 or 757-9316
www.swanscayhotel.com
Strolling down the main streets in Bocas, visitors will be surprised by the brand-new (and imposing) Swan's Cay hotel. The Treccani family's establishment testifies to the beauty inherent to Italian culture. In the main building, there are 20-odd apartments on two floors, opening onto a vast interior hall that is air conditioned and beautifully decorated. In the centre of this hall, an elegant staircase leads to a spacious gallery featuring warm tones of wood and the guest quarters. Those who prefer the view of the garden should opt for the back of the building, where 15 or so rooms on two floors surround a flowered patio. As for the deco of the rooms, Señora Treccani has demonstrated excellent taste with her beautiful selection of bedding fabrics, while lovely inlaid furniture embellishes the premises. Finally, for those who dream of spending a night in the atmosphere of the Roaring Twenties, the penthouse suite in the main building is the answer. This hotel offers excellent quality for the price.

Punta Mangrove

Mangrove Inn Eco Resort
$$$$ all incl.
1/2b, pb, ⊗
Punta Mangrove, 5min by boat from Bocas del Toro
☎/⇄757-9594
www.bocas.com/mangrove.htm
For those who enjoy scuba diving and don't mind isolation, this resort has a series of rustic cabins built on stilts at the edge of the mangroves. Packages *(B/.60 to B/.95/pers)* include lodging, meals, equipment rental and excursions in the archipelago. The only drawback, since the hotel is accessible only by boat, is that visitors are entirely dependent on the establishment for transportation.

Northwest of Isla Colón

Punta Caracol Acqua Lodge
$$$$$ ½b
hw, pb, #
☎612-1088 or 676-7186
www.puntacaracol.com
The Punta Caracol will suit environmentally minded visitors seeking quiet, secluded seaside accommodations. It comprises five luxurious wood-and-bamboo *cabañas* with palm-leaf roof, all of which stand on stilts in the middle of a small bay graced with azure waters. The owners make a point of respecting the environment to the utmost and use solar panels to supply the cabins with electricity. Moreover, the small resort's sewage

water is treated before being released into the bay so as to avoid any pollution. While each of the *cabañas'* bedrooms is upstairs, the "ground floor" is comprised of a small living room and a terrace overlooking the water from which you can admire fabulous sunsets. Although the decor is simple, the furnishings and trimmings are tasteful. What's more, guests are offered a host of excursions. Among the facilities is a pleasant, adjoining restaurant. The only drawback to this little slice of paradise is the exorbitant rates. For example, the boat ride to Bocas del Toro (20min) costs up to B/.45 per person. All that to say, in addition to packing a good book, be sure to bring your credit card.

Isla Bastimentos

Pensión Tío Tom
$-$$
pb/sb, hw
☎/⇄757-9831
Ina and Tom, a pleasant young German couple, welcome guests in a modest house built on stilts. Although the facilities are a tad rudimentary and only one of the five rooms has a private bathroom, the boarding house is spotless and cheerful. Breakfasts are top-notch and the small restaurant prepares inexpensive meals. Moreover, Tom offers various sea activities and excursions at very affordable rates. A good choice if luxury is not a priority.

Al Natural Resort
$$$$-$$$$$ all incl.
hw, pb, ⊗, #
Punta Vieja
☎623-2217 or 640-6935
www.bocas.com/alnatura.htm
If you enjoy Robinson Crusoe–style adventures, head to this magical place. Set right on the beach, the Al Natural Resort is aptly named indeed, consisting of four small *bohíos* fitted out in the most "natural" way possible. The small, round cabins are almost entirely open to the great outdoors, including the bedrooms, and look out right on the sea and the lush tropical vegetation. During your stay, you will be refreshed by the sea breeze and wake to birdsong or the sound of lapping waves. For those looking to kick back and relax, a hammock is set up on each of the cabins' small patios. Three types of huts are offered here: a standard one fitted out with a bedroom with queen-size bed and a charming bathroom built around a tree, complete with rainwater shower; two "deluxe" units, linked by a small bridge and comprising a bedroom with two beds, including a king-size model, and a bathroom with hot water and ceiling vent; and last but not least, a two-storey bungalow with two separate bedrooms, one located upstairs with a view of the bay. Although solar panels supply all cabins with electricity, only the larger ones have enough current to power a fan or small appliances. Near the bungalows is the main building, which houses the restaurant and bar. Michel, the friendly Belgian owner, offers guests a host of local excursions, including one to the nearby Islas Zapatillas. And to top it all off, good meals accompanied by wine are served for lunch and dinner, not to mention the breakfast awaiting you upon rising. The use of kayaks, sailboards and snorkelling equipment is included in the bungalow-rental rate. This "resort" will suit those looking to commune with nature and enjoy some peace and quiet.

Restaurants

Chiriquí Grande

Dally
$
to the right of the pier
The friendly owner of this restaurant prepares, at your request, freshly caught fish after 2pm; a variety of other family-style dishes are also served. This is a charming restaurant and a good place to meet local inhabitants.

Isla Colón

Bocas del Toro

Lakois Place
$
Av. Norte, between Calle 6 and 7
A small open-air terrace, a few modest tables and chairs scattered here and there and a small bar imaginatively painted—this is the decor at Lakois Place. Although very simple, this

locale is a favourite of many Bocatoreños and fine fish and seafood dishes are prepared according to local tradition. Good quality for the price.

Baia Paradiso
$
Calle 3, across from the Parque Central
As you will have guessed from its sign, the pizzeria-reposteria offers a choice of pizza (unfortunately limited and somewhat lacking in taste) as well as modest family-style dishes. While this is not the place for haute cuisine, it does offer a pleasant terrace facing the park where one can have a light snack. We might add that customers here would appreciate a welcoming smile!

Buena Vista
$$
Calle 1 and facing Calle 2
This small restaurant, managed by an American couple, has an attractive wooden terrace with a view of the ocean. A good vegetarian chilli is available as well as a choice of sandwiches, and of course the traditional hamburger. Portions are generous and English is spoken.

La Ballena
$$$
Av. F
Just beside the elegant Swan's Cay hotel, the La Ballena restaurant serves the catch of the day (unfortunately it is often pargo) accompanied with a good sauce thanks to the Italian origins of the owner. Despite a relatively attractive decor and a warm welcome, it is disappointing to note that the personnel does not seem particularly interested in providing good service. Also, the absence of espresso and tiramisu (so vaunted by the proprietor) was quite a let down.

Le Pirate
$$$
Calle 1, near the corner of Calle 3
This modest restaurant welcomes its customers to an attractive terrace on stilts facing the bay, or to a booth beside the bar. The meals served here, mostly fish and seafood, are simple and presented without frills.

Swan's Cay
$$$
corner Calle 3 and Av. F
Like the hotel where it is located, the restaurant takes us into another world, that of tables dressed in fine fabrics and set in the purest European tradition, in an elegant decor worthy of the best restaurants in the world. Even though during our visit the menu was still in the planning stages (for instance, the choice of Italian dishes was relatively limited), the meals deserved special mention for their flavour and presentation, both of which are rare in Bocas. A somewhat limited choice of fine wines is also available.

Isla Carenero

The Ocean Queen
$$
Five minutes by boat from Bocas, Isla Carenero, facing the village of Bocas, is considered by Bocatoreños to have the best location in the area. Upon our arrival, we were surprised by the large terrace on stilts. However, the only valid reason for coming here is the beautiful view of Bocas from the terrace. The meals, although good and amply portioned, are limited to seafood and the catch of the day, as well as a few other family-style dishes.

Also on stilts, right next door, the **Pargo Rogo *($)*** serves much the same fare and has the same natural "decor."

Entertainment

Isla Colón

Bocas del Toro

El Encanto
Calle 3, beside Bocas Water Sports
Near the landing dock, the bar welcomes amateurs of billiards in a small room facing the street. Just beside it, a long hallway leads to a large, open-air dance floor where exotic music reigns. For those who simply wish to relax and sip a glass of *ron con jugo de naranja (B/.0.85)* to the strains of Panamanian music, there is also a small terrace beyond the dance floor that opens out onto the bay. The establishment is somewhat dark and gloomy, but otherwise typical of the region.

Buena Vista
Calle 1 facing Calle2
Before calling it a night, sports-lovers will want to stop by this restaurant-bar, where they can watch the latest football game. In fact, the American owner has equipped the bar with a large television screen where one can catch the latest sports news direct from the U.S. And for those who like to day-dream, glass in hand, there are several tables on a pleasant terrace and American music in the background.

Bar Restaurant Las Palmitas
Av. Sur, 100m from the dock
For travellers seeking a change of pace from the bustle of Calle 3, this bar offers a modest terrace on stilts where one can sip a small glass of *ron* or a cold Panamanian beer while enjoying the soft sea breeze. Seafood and fish are on the menu.

Comarca de San Blas

Located along the northeastern coast of Panamá, in the Caribbean Sea, the Comarca de San Blas is unique in that it is the only province in the country populated exclusively by indigenous peoples—the Kunas.

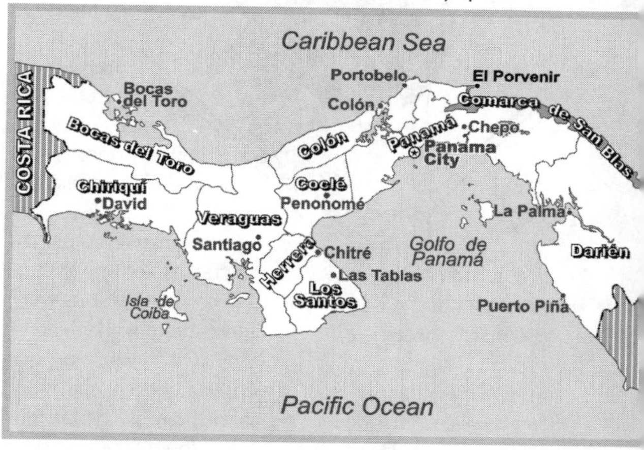

Except for matters relating to defense, it is also the only province governed exclusively by indigenous peoples. It is thus classified as a *comarca*, which means region or territory, rather than a province. Besides a long strip of land, barely 10km wide, extending along the coast to the Colombian border, the Comarca de San Blas consists of an archipelago called the Archipiélago de Las Mulatas. It is made up of some 350 islands and islets, 60 of which are inhabited. Due essentially to a lack of historical documents, little is known about the origins of the Kuna people. Certain historians believe they were originally from Colombia and emigrated to Darién, near the Atlantic coast. In any case, journals left by Spanish explorers reveal that by the 19th century, the Kunas had split into two groups: one group living inland, the other on the islands. This geographic division may have resulted from the different approaches taken by the *caciques* (chiefs) in response to the colonizers, but nothing is certain. Nevertheless, those Kunas wishing to avoid all contact with the intrusive missionaries fled deeper into the heart of the jungle, but difficult living conditions and a hostile environment, however, forced the majority of the population to settle on the coast. According to the last census taken by Panamanian authorities, there are 50,000 Kunas living on the islands and only 2,000 spread throughout Darién. About 6,000 Kunas are currently living in Panama City.

Before enjoying their autonomy, the Kunas endured a long series of humiliations. After colonization, they lived under the authority of the new Republic of Panamá when a governor for the territory was nominated in 1915. Severe restrictions on fishing and farming

Sloth

proved completely inap propriate for the Kunas, and quickly became a recurring subject of discontent. Also, in their efforts to assimilate the various minorities, the Panamanian authorities wished to abolish their traditional clothing, the *mola* (see box "The Mola," later in this chapter), and force parents to send their children to Spanish-language school.

However, it was the authorities' attempt to control the territory by deploying police and civil servants to the islands in 1923 that really angered the Kunas. After suffering brutality, namely the rape of Kuna women, *cacique* Simrol Colman, who lived on Ailigandí island at the time, declared war.

In February 1925, the Tule Republic (in the Kuna language, *Tule* refers to Kuna men in general, but also means "son of God") was proclaimed, and several police officers were killed, along with their children born of mixed marriages. Several other islands followed Ailigandí's lead, which led to widespread revolt. Panamanian officials reacted by sending in the army, but the troops were intercepted by the Americans, whose warship *Cleveland* had been dispatched to the islands. The United States forced the two sides to negotiate and resolve the conflict. Under an accord reached the same year, the Kunas withdrew their declaration of independence, and the Republic of Panamá agreed to recognize the autonomy of the Amerindians. It was not until 1930 that the accord was ratified in the Panamanian parliament, and in 1933, the Comarca was created.

Fishing, gathering coconuts and making *molas* (see box "The Mola," later in this chapter) are still the principal activities of the Kuna people. For their own needs, they regularly head to the mainland to farm small plots of land across from their islands. Tourism to the islands is constantly increasing and the sale of *molas* to travellers has become a major source of income for the Kuna. Unlike other cases, where tourism has had a negative impact on indigenous communities, the "tourist windfall" here has actually helped preserve the Kuna culture and identity. The Kuna *caciques*' opposition to the establishment of large hotel chains on their islands has undoubtedly been a wise approach.

Finding Your Way Around

Warning: Do not forget that there is a very limited choice of accommodations throughout the region, and that there is no drinking water or electricity on the islands. Furthermore, staying on an island, even an uninhabited one, without the permission of a *cacique* is prohibited. A last-minute adventure to these islands could thus be potentially dangerous and above all shows a lack of respect for the indigenous authorities. Before heading here, make sure your

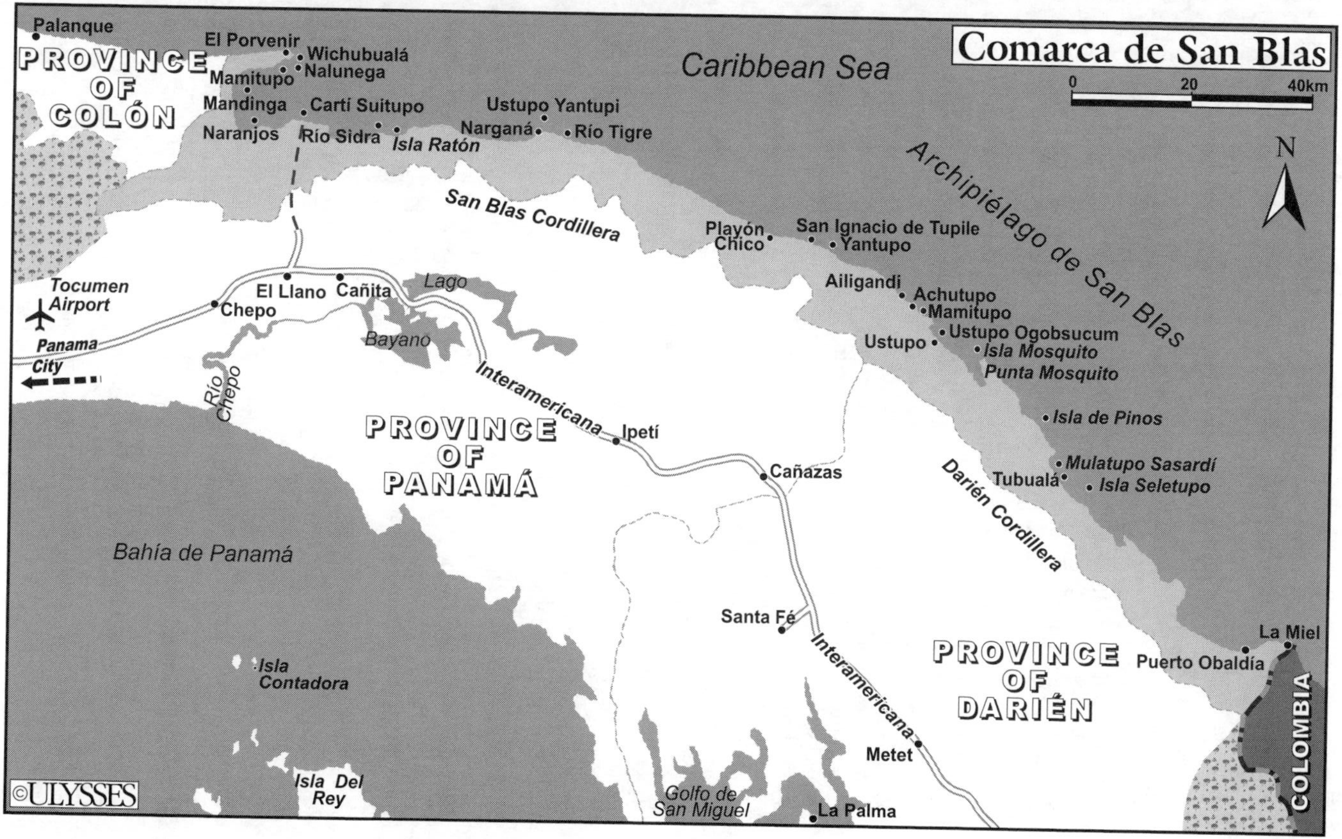
Comarca de San Blas
0
20
40km
N
Caribbean Sea
Archipiélago de San Blas
Palanque
PROVINCE OF COLÓN
El Porvenir
Wichubualá
Nalunega
Mamitupo
Mandinga
Cartí Suitupo
Naranjos
Río Sidra
Isla Ratón
Ustupo Yantupi
Narganá
Río Tigre
San Blas Cordillera
Playón Chico
San Ignacio de Tupile
Yantupo
Ailigandí
Achutupo
Mamitupo
Ustupo Ogobsucum
Ustupo
Isla Mosquito
Punta Mosquito
Isla de Pinos
Mulatupo Sasardí
Tubualá
Isla Seletupo
Darién Cordillera
La Miel
Puerto Obaldía
COLOMBIA
PROVINCE OF DARIÉN
Tocumen Airport
Panama City
El Llano
Cañita
Chepo
Lago Bayano
Río Chepo
Interamericana
Ipetí
Cañazas
PROVINCE OF PANAMÁ
Bahía de Panamá
Santa Fé
Interamericana
Metet
Isla Contadora
Isla Del Rey
Golfo de San Miguel
La Palma
©ULYSSES

Welcome to Uaguitipo

After flying over the dense Darién jungle, the tiny eight-seater begin its descent in search of a landing strip hidden somewhere along the narrow coastline. To an uninitiated traveller such as myself, the tops of the gigantic tropical trees look as if they are within arm's reach, and the wheels of the plane seem to brush against them... But where is the landing strip? For a moment, I fear it has been swallowed up by the forest, but then, suddenly in the distance, a narrow clearing appears—is it even paved? The question has barely formed itself in my mind when the plane swoops down to the ground, leaving the jungle behind. As I get off the Islander, I am greeted by the smiling face of our Kuna guide, small in stature, like most Kunas. I cannot help but stare; even though the scenery surrounding us is extraordinary, I am transfixed by her garb. Her head is covered with a bright red and yellow scarf, and she is wearing one of the stunning *molas* I have heard so much about. Her forearms and calves are adorned with tiny strands of colourful beads, a sure sign of coquetry, and a thin black line runs down the bridge of her nose. Barefoot, she leads us to a rickety boat, while smiling Kuna men bring our bags. The little motorboat shoves out to sea, where only the tops of the palm trees visible on the horizon remind us of dry land. As we approach the islands, we see clusters of bamboo huts, some of which are topped with palm roofs. Clinging to every last square inch of land, they stand harmoniously side by side. As we head toward our destination, we pass several Kuna women paddling canoes between the islands. Always a smile and a friendly wave. Their colourful clothing stands out against the turquoise blue waters, a beautiful sight in itself. All too quickly, we arrive to our island, where we are welcomed by the mother, sisters and brothers of our guide. A macaw perched on a palm tree branch watches in bewilderment. Our hut awaits... welcome to Uaguitipo!

accommodations are arranged.

By Plane

The best way to reach the **San Blas Islands** is by plane. There are regular flights to the landing strip on the coast at the edge of the jungle, and from there, small boats take visitors to the various islands. Note that because of weather conditions, all flights are scheduled early in the morning, starting at 6am. Unless you charter a flight, it is therefore impossible to return on the same day. Weekend flights are particularly busy, so if you plan on travelling at this time, get to the airport by 4am. Once there, you will need patience and perseverance to get your ticket.

One of the best ways to avoid this headache is to organize your trip through a travel agent.
In general, this will allow you to arrive at the airport later (around 5am), and a

Kuna agent will quickly hand you your ticket. Various travel agents in the capital can provide you with more details (see below).

Note: The following schedules and rates are provided for reference only and are subject to change.

At press time, only the following three companies served the Comarca:

Aero Taxi-Aeroperlas
Aeropuerto Albrook
☎***315-7500***
www.tacaregional.com/aeroperlas/index.html
The Aeroperlas-owned Aero Taxi company offers the widest selection of flights, as well as reliable schedules and reasonable rates. The carrier flies to the following destinations: Achutupu, Ailigandi, Cartí, Corazón, Porvenir, Isla Tigre, Mulatupu, Ogobsucun, Playón Chicó, Puerto Obaldía, Río Sidra, San Ignacio Tupile, Ticantiquí and Ustupu. Flights take 30 to 55min, depending on the destination. Return fares range from B/.60 to B/.90.

Ansa
Aeropuerto Albrook
☎***315-7521***
A more modest carrier that also offers regular flights throughout the Comarca, Ansa flies to the same destinations as Aero Taxi, at similar prices.

Aviatur
Aeropuerto Albrook
☎***315-0311 or 315-0309***
www.panamareservation.com/index.htm
If you fail to obtain a flight from either of the two aforementioned carriers, you can turn to Aviatur, which offers occasional flights to the Comarca.

By Car

There is a coastal road that leads to the Comarca (via El Llano) but this a long journey. Furthermore, the road is unpaved and passes no services. In short, it is not recommended. Lastly, do not forget that you need permission to enter the Comarca.

Practical Information

Among the numerous travel agencies established in the capital, some offer particularly interesting packages. Here are two worth mentioning:

Starlite Travel
Av. Roosevelt and Height Avenue, Edificio L-639, Balboa, across from the the Canal administration building Apdo 6-6200, El Dorado
☎***232-6401 or 272-2474***
www.starlitepanama.com
Among the agencies with competitive prices, Starlite Travel offers various packages including transportation, lodging, meals and excursions in the Comarca. Prices vary from B/.100 to B/.178 per person for a night at the Hotel San Blas, the Hotel Anai or the Hotel Dolphin Lodge. An agency representative will accompany you to the airport in Panama City (Albrook Airport) and a Kuna guide will welcome you when you reach your destination in San Blas. Friendly service and competent staff.

Jungle Adventures
38 Calle 50 Este/Ricardo Arias
☎***269-6047 or 269-2511***
If you are looking for adventure, but still enjoy your creature comforts, contact Jungle Adventures. For B/.180 you can spend the night on Iskardup island *(B/.280 for two nights)* in a comfortable cabin equipped with a shower and electricity produced by solar panels. The tour includes transportation, a guide, a tour of Ukupseni island, a visit to a Kuna cemetery, breakfast, a buffet lunch and a gourmet supper.

Exploring

★★★

Kuna Yula (Land of the Kunas)

Imagine more than 300 coral islands scattered across a turquoise sea and dreamy beaches of fine golden sand on an island all to yourself. Rock yourself to sleep in a hammock slung between two palm trees, to the sound of the palms rustling in the breeze. Dive into crystal-clear waters and discover a world of a million and one vivid colours. Behold the impenetrable jungle that lines the coast, forming a

The Kuna Language

The Kuna way of life and their autonomy are probably the best-preserved of all the indigenous peoples of the Americas. It follows then that they have also preserved their language. In fact, the majority of the population only speaks Kuna. Some people, mostly men who have worked at the canal, however, do speak Spanish and a bit of English. Probably less than 20% of the Kunas living in San Blas speak a second language.

This situation adds to the culture shock experienced by visitors—so much so that if a Kuna addresses you in Spanish, you will almost feel like he or she is speaking your language, because their own language is so different from anything you have probably ever heard before.

A few of the formal structures of the language illustrate the Kuna mentality. For example, to say "I want you to go swimming," you actually have to say "I want you to want to go swimming." Instead of saying "I want you to take care of yourself" you say "I want you to want to take care of yourself." Negative-sounding formulations are avoided: instead of "If you don't go this will happen," a Kuna will say "if you go this will happen."

The Kuna language is not written; it was transcribed for the first time in the 20th century. Since their language has always been maintained by an oral tradition, the Kunas had no major written works prior to 1970, when the New Testament was translated by Marvel Iglesias and a Baptist minister. The majority of Kunas still do not write their language, but for the past few years, children have been learning to do so in school. On the island of Achutupo, for example, children attend school for six years. Five percent of Kunas continue their studies in the capital, and only a small number choose to stay there after completing their schooling.

Besides the commonly spoken language, there are other forms of language used only by the chiefs during religious ceremonies or funeral rites.

stunning ribbon of emerald in the distance. In short, this region will delight dreamers in search of a lost paradise. Kuna Yala has much to offer travellers looking for a change of scenery, for it is above all the land of the Kunas, a proud and friendly people.

The main highlight of the Comarca de San Blas is the presence of the Kunas, who have preserved their unique culture over hundreds of years. Those interested in indigenous cultures can experience the Kuna way of life without too much difficulty.

The Kunas have fought long and hard to preserve their culture, and are very proud of it; it is therefore important to follow a few general rules so as not to offend the local population. Since the coming and going of foreigners is controlled by the *cacique*, each visitor is automatical assigned a guide. The guide facilitates your contact with the population and serves as an interpreter since very few Kunas speak Spanish. Plan any visits or excursions off the island with your guide. Possible activities include exploring the village and the beautiful islets with their white-sand beaches, scuba diving, visiting a Kuna cemetery or taking part in an excursion into the jungle. Avoid the rainy months of June, July and August, when the sky is almost continuously overcast.

Kuna Society Today

Contrary to mainland Kunas, who live in families and isolate themselves from one another, the Kunas of the San Blas islands live in small villages of bamboo huts built on the bare earth and topped by palm roofs. Although concrete frames and houses have been built in recent years, they are still rare (schools, hotels, clinics, etc.). In general, most of the inhabited islands are over-populated, and it is not unheard of to find islands with so many huts that virtually all trace of the coastline seems to have vanished.

The traditional single-family dwelling is simply one large room with no partitions or windows. While some Kunas sleep in beds, most sleep in hammocks. Cooking is done in the hut on an open fire. The only agricultural activity is the harvesting of coconuts which are sold to the Colombian merchants who visit the islands.

The fruits used in Kuna cuisine come from the mainland. In the early morning, the Kuna men head inland to the various plantations established by each family (in the broad sense of the word). In the afternoon, the men spend their time fishing. Fish and seafood, including the delicious conchas, accompanied by coconut, fried plantains and rice, make up the bulk of Kuna cuisine. While some islands have electricity and running water thanks to a pump, most islands do not have these services. Fresh water thus comes from rivers to the mainland, where it is collected in large barrels by the men and brought to the islands by boat. In some hotels, potable water is flown in straight from the capital.

The administrative capital of the Comarca is El Porvenir. The San Blas islands are divided into groups, each with its own administrative centre. Ailigandí, for example, is the administrative centre for Achutupo, Uaguitipo and many other islands. Like the capital, the centres offer various administrative services, such as a police station, a school and a clinic. Among the important centres, the island of Ailigandí is famous in Kuna history for being the starting point of the 1925 revolution. Several plaques commemorating the Kunas' fight for independence can be spotted at the police station. You will also see the swastika, the national symbol chosen for the flag of the short-lived Tule Republic. To reach Ailigandí, you must have your passport, and in most cases pay an admission fee of B/. 1.

Celebrations take place on February 19, 20 and 21 to commemorate the Kuna revolution, and they are particularly lively in Ailigandí. As the Kunas are very proud of their fight to defend their culture, some of them will probably ask you if there are indigenous peoples in your country, and if you answer positively, they will want to know what their rights are! In Ailigandí, you can also visit the **Instituto Nacional Cultura Ogar Yakun Nega**, an art school where the technique for making the *mola* is taught.

Customs

Supreme power resides with three chiefs elected to represent all Kunas and the interests of the Comarca. These three individuals are chosen by the village chiefs, called *Sáhila*, themselves elected and assisted by "sub-chiefs." The latter have authority over their territory and take care of various matters, like division of land, family disputes, marriages, etc. Kuna society is essentially matriarchal, and the grandmother, or *Mu*, is the center of the family. Marriages are not documented and only require a simple ceremony.

Until the 1950s, marriages were unions of convenience arranged by parents when the children were

Kuna Glossary

tule	man. Can also be collective, and is also used to designate the Kunas
ai	friend (male)
aimala	friends (male)
áia	friend (female)
áiamala	friends (female)
núedi	good day or nice, good
na	hello
deguimalo	goodbye
panemalo	see you tomorrow
an	I
nuga	name
merkey	good stranger
waga	other strangers
eye	yes
suli	no
takey	come here
mútiki	night
nega	house
kas	hammock
tupu	island
ti	water
achu	dog
úa	fish
kanil núchukua	chicken
ogop	coconut
ossi	pineapple
mas chunnat	banana
mesmalat	family
machi	son or daughter
nana	mother
paba	father
tutu	flower
sapi	tree
sapigana	trees
tommo make	to swim
múa make	to float
soul kukualet	plane
uágul	boat
mullu suli	big
pipigua	small
pannabagua	far
ittigi	close
tule poniguale	sick
ukku	hungry
ti koppíe	thirsty
kabe	sleep
ti uíet	rain
tada	sun

quite young. It was the female's family who did the choosing. Today the choice is less strict, though it must still be approved by the parents, and the husband still has to live with the wife's family. A Kuna man can change islands if he likes, but to marry a woman from another island, he must seek the permission of the island's chief. Interracial marriages are very rare amongst the Kunas and are effectively prohibited. In fact, if a Kuna marries an outsider, the couple must leave the Comarca. In the history of the isthmus, a number of unfortunate events have underlined this exclusivity; according to some, this rule is necessary to protect the Kuna culture. Between 1625 and 1725, French Huguenots settled in the region and had children with indigenous women. These mixed-blood children, along with their parents, were massacred during the indigenous rebellion against the Spanish in 1726. Another sad example took place in 1925, when Panamanian police officers and their children, born of Kuna women, were also killed. The only example of a happy union today is that of Marvel Iglesias and Lonnie Iglesias, a respected Kuna man, known for having raised the funds necessary for the construction of the hospital in Ailigandí. The couple received permission to settle in Ailigandí in 1933.

As far as religion is concerned, the Kunas believe in a God as creator of the universe, as well as in the powers of the *neles*, healers of sorts who are inspired by superior forces. Their vision of the world is that it holds two parallel universes: an invisible one harbouring spirits, and the physical life as we know it. Thus, for the Kunas, every being possesses a double personality, one visible and one hidden. The same applies to animals, plants and objects, which have two different names, one for day time and another for the night time. Only a few objects are used during religious ceremonies, including *nuchus* (wooden figures with therapeutic powers that represent particular characters), dyes, leaves and branches, and no major temples or buildings have been consecrated. Each plant, animal, object and even every part of the body has its own aura.

Young artists can gain inspiration by chanting while burning part of a *mola* that belonged to a highly creative person. Stealing, lying, murder and adultery are considered the most reprehensible acts. Among the major religious ceremonies, a girls's coming of age and a person's death are the most important. No stranger is allowed to witness these. Several other religions have influenced the Kunas. For example, although the Kunas do not have any religious holidays, Christmas is celebrated on some islands, and various Christian practices have also been adopted.

Oral tradition, village assemblies and the stories and sayings of Kuna chiefs are an important part of everyday life. All sorts of fascinating dances are also part of local customs. Some of these are performed at visitors' requests, especially on the islands of Ailigandí and Playón Chico. On Ailigandí, for example, you may have the chance to take part in an intriguing dance called the *Nogagope*, when a dozen people are carried away by lively music played on a bamboo flute and maracas.

Kuna Women

Women are very powerful in Kuna society. The woman is the one who chooses her future husband, and it is with her family that he must live. The birth of a girl is cause for great celebration since it is she who will continue the family.

Separation is accepted, and a woman simply has to put her husband's things outside the hut to let him know that she wants him to leave. The woman is then free to remarry, while the man must obtain the approval of his ex-wife or wait for her to remarry before he can take another wife. Finally, it is the wives who take care of expenses. Kuna women generally wear a long skirt with a piece of fabric rolled around their hips and a short-sleeved blouse with a *mola* sewn on it. They also wear strands of tiny, colourful beads, called *canilleras* or *wini*, on their forearms and calves. Some women wear a gold ring in their nose and have a thin black line drawn down their nose. Ethnologists say that this line is the last vestige of the painting with which they once covered the entire body. Today, it serves a purely cosmetic purpose. During certain festivities, wide necklaces and gold earrings are worn. A married woman must keep her hair short and covered with a bright red scarf with yellow designs.

The majority of Kuna woman bear between eight and twelve children. While the men spend the morning farming and the afternoon fishing, the women can spend hours sewing superb *molas*, either for themselves or to sell. It can take several weeks of steady work to make a *mola*. The *canilleras* or *wini* only last a few months and making a new one can take up to five days of work.

The woman's traditional dress is considered the most prestigious expression of the Kuna culture and is carefully safeguarded. Unfortunately, since the middle of the 20th century, there has been a breach in tradition, for some village chiefs have permitted residents to wear western clothes. Traditional dress has already disappeared from the islands of Narganá and Corazón de Jesús. Today, the islands east of the Comarca (Atchutupu, Mulatupu and Ustupu) are considered the most traditional and the *mola* is required dress for the women. The Kuna are a modest and timid people, and do not tolerate nudism. Women are also advised to wear a one-piece bathing suit rather than a bikini, which is considered provocative.

If you want to photograph a Kuna woman, children or a specific group of people, it is imperative that you ask permission first (your guide will help you). You should give a small compensation of B/.1 for"royalties." For a group photo, ask your guide how much you should give. Travellers with a video camera are obliged to obtain the permission of the chief before filming anything. You will probably be asked for a donation if your request is approved.

Accommodations

Since the cost of accommodations can double or triple depending on the season, availability or any other unpredictable eventuality, we can only provide a general price range of between B/.100 and B/.200 per person per day, including transportation, lodging and meals. Also, remember that most hotels have neither electricity nor running water.

San Blas
B/.115 per person for the first night, including meals; trips and transportation from Panama City;
B/.40 per person for each successive night including meals
Nalunega
☎262-5410
This hotel can accommodate up to 40 people and boasts a beautiful beach where fishing trips and scuba diving are organized. Very basic.

Anai
B/.125 per person for the first night, including meals; trips and transportation from Panama City; B/.65 per person for each successive night including meals
Wichub Wala
☎239-3025 or 299-9011
Ask to speak to Sr. Alberto Gonzalez
This hotel has 14 simple *cabañas*, as well as small restaurant.

Cabañas Kuahidup
B/.145 per person for the first night, including meals trips and transportation from Panama City; B/.70

per person for each successive night including meals
Río Sidra
☎227-0872
Small, rudimentary cabins located on an island of white sand and crystal-clear waters.

Iskardup
B/.180 per person for the first night, including meals; trips and transportation from Panama City; B/.180 for each successive night
Iskardup
Only through Jungle Adventure ***(see p 243)***
This hotel has 14 comfortable bamboo *cabañas* with shower and private bathroom, and electricity provided by solar panels. A buffet-lunch (meat and seafood) and a gourmet meal are served on the premises. A wonderful blend of adventure and comfort!

Hotel Dolphin Lodge
B/.165 per person per day, including meals; trips and transportation from Panama City for the first night; B/.110 per person for each successive night including meals
Uaguitupo
☎220-8898 or 263-3077
On this small island right beside Achutupu are six *cabañas*, only three of which have cement floors and private showers. Each cabin has several large beds, a table and chairs and a hammock suspended at the entrance. The shared washrooms with showers and a small washbasin are located in a separate building. Enjoy brushing your teeth while contemplating the turquoise sea behind you! There is no electricity, but at nightfall an oil lamp is brought to you. Meals are served at a large table on a bamboo terrace with a palm roof. The 270° view of the sea is like something out of Robinson Crusoe.

Shopping

The *mola* is of course the thing to buy on the islands. While exploring a village you will probably see several Kuna women (sometimes even the whole family) waiting in front of their hut, *molas* in hand, in the hopes that you will buy one on your way.

Do not, under any circumstances, be embarrassed to buy; the Kunas will not be insulted. Everyone is all smiles, often to conceal their shyness.

If you plan to buy a *mola* on your trip to Panamá, buy it here instead of in the capital, since the money goes right to the artist, and you will be contributing to the preservation of this unique art form. Expect to pay between B/.15 and B/.40 for a well-made *mola*, and between B/.20 and B/.60 for a blouse complete with both panels. You can also buy small *molas* for a few balboas each, and as of recently, much less elaborate, "imitation" *molas* for B/.5. A selection of gold jewellery (10 carats), such as bracelets and earrings, is also available. A simple chain costs about B/.30.

Mola

The *Mola*

The word "mola" once simply meant clothing in the general sense; today it applies essentially to a part of a Kuna woman's traditional dress, specifically the square piece of fabric sewn onto the blouse. The *mola* is made up of several pieces of fabric of various colours. These pieces are cut out and sewn together using the method known as appliqué; in other words, placed on top of one another to create a alternating colour motif. The *mola* is made up of two panels (one worn on the front, the other on the back) with similar patterns but with alternating colours. This use of colours demonstrates the duality of the world vision characterizing Kuna society. Certain ethnologists claim that this activity can be traced back to the paintings used by the Kunas to decorate their bodies. Why this practice was transferred to cloth remains a mystery, though some believe it can be explained by the arrival of the missionaries, who forced the Kunas to wear clothes. The Kuna elders have their own explanation for the origin of the *mola* fabric. Very long ago, an old Kuna woman succeeded in visiting the *Kalu Tiupis*, a secret place reserved exclusively for women. The *kalus* are sacred locations dedicated to different deities and hidden in the centre of one of the invisible layers (eight in all) of the earth, where all the spirits gather. After visiting the *Kalu Tiupis* where the *mola* was created, the old Kuna woman learned the technique for making the *mola*. When she returned, she was able to teach her knowledge to the village women, knowledge that is still passed on from mother to daughter. Very little is known about the *mola*, and because of the fragility of the fabric, there are few old examples to study. The oldest *mola* is on display at the Museum of Natural History in Washington and dates back to 1902. We do know, however, that older patterns were basically geometric and consisted of only a few colours, mainly red, yellow and black. Today, the colours vary as much as the designs, which usually represent characters, animals or plants. The *mola* is an impressive and creative piece of work, and is the pride of Kuna women.

Province of Darién

A dense tropical jungle covers the Darién, the most isolated and least developed province in Panamá.

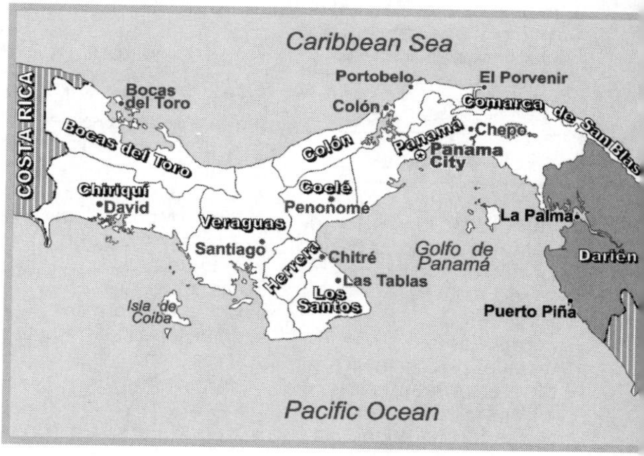

Although the Panamanian and Colombian governments have agreed to establish a ground link between the two countries by extending the Interamericana across Darién, the project has been suspended by the Panamanian government since 1995. In 1984, a route stretched from Yaviza, passing 24km from Parque National Darién. The two governments are apparently having second thoughts about the undertaking, which has been condemned by numerous environmental groups and opposed by several eminent personalities. It is becoming clearer and clearer that the new highway would have a negative impact on the biosphere, and would eventually lead to the destruction of one of humanity's greatest riches. In recognition of the area's inestimable value, UNESCO placed the Parque Nacional Darién on the prestigious list of World Heritage Sites in 1981. Faced with nature's warning signs (thinning ozone layer, vanished species, depleted soil), humans are apparently becoming aware that it is necessary to protect the environment for their own good, as well as that of future generations. Somewhat ironically, the famous Interamericana, meant to symbolise friendship between two nations, might not make it farther than Yaviza. Perhaps if it does not, Panamanian and Colombian officials will realize that their countries can also be united by a common goal—the preservation of some of the most beautiful plant and animal life in the Americas.

Finding Your Way Around

Warning: Although a few adventurous types try to cross from Darién to Colombia, it is important to note that Panamanian and Colombian officials **strongly advise** visitors not to do so. Not only is the trip physically demanding, but some regions are not policed and are known to be frequented by drug traffickers. Kidnapping is not rare, nor are outright disappearances. Furthermore, unless you have been given special authorization, crossing the border by this route is considered illegal by both countries since there is no border station. We recommend enlisting the services of a trained guide for all outings in the park. Their knowledge of the terrain and local flora and fauna will guarantee you a safe and pleasant trip.

By Plane

Note: The following schedules and rates are provided for reference only and are subject to change.

Aeroperlas (see p 43) provides regular service in this area. **Aviatur** (see p 43), for its part, also provides connections with this region, albeit with irregular departures. **Bahía Piña**, **Sambú**, **Yaviza**, **El Real**, **Garachiné**, **Jaqué** and the capital of the province, **La Palma**, are the destinations covered.

Here are a few sample schedules:

La Palma

Panama City to La Palma
Departure: Mon-Fri 9:30am; Sat 9:10am
Travel Time: 45min
Rate: B/.45 one way

Bahía Piña

Panama City to Bahía Piña
Departure: Tue, Thu and Sat 9:30am
Travel Time: about 1hr
Rate: B/.45 one way

El Real

Panama City to El Real
Depature: Mon, Wed, Fri 9:30am; Sat 9:10am (stopover in La Palma)
Travel Time: about 1hr20min.
Rate: B/.40 one way

By Car

Keep in mind that there is no road to Colombia suitable for motor vehicles, and that it is impossible to drive all the way across Darién. If, however, you would like to explore part of the province of Darién by car, take the Interamericana from Panama City toward Tocumen Airport, and keep heading straight until you reach the village of Chepo, up to which point the road is paved. From Chepo to the village of Metetí, and a short distance beyond, parts of the road are paved and other parts are covered with gravel. You can then take a dirt road to the village of Yaviza, which is as far as you can go by car. The section of road between Chepo and Yaviza is only passable during the dry season, with a four-wheel-drive vehicle.

Exploring

Darién's appeal lies mainly in its wealth of plant and animal life. Keep in mind, though, that this region is not an exotic garden where you can safely stroll around observing all sorts of birds and other animals, but rather an actual jungle, where the damp heat and teeming vegetation make it difficult to get around. Furthermore, it would be a mistake to think that the forest reveals its riches that easily. In fact, observing exotic birds and other animals requires a thorough knowledge of their behaviour and habitat. To make the most of your visit to the jungle, therefore, it is important to enlist the services of a competent guide, who can ensure your safety in a region that is not without risks. Once you have taken these precautions, you can fully enjoy this magnificent environment.

During your stay in Darién, you might be lucky enough to come across the indigenous peoples of this province. These include a small community of Kunas, who live mainly on the Atlantic coast, and the Chocoe, linguistically divided into two groups, the Emberá and the Wounaan. Like the Kunas, the Chocoe now have their own *comarcas*, or autonomous regions. There are two of them, located on the outskirts of Parque Nacional del Darién. Comarca Emberá district *Cemaco* lies to the north and Comarca Emberá district *Sambú* to the south.

Unfortunately, very little is known about Chocoe customs, which are still being researched by ethnologists. Chocoe men sometimes stain their entire body (except the top of the face) with a

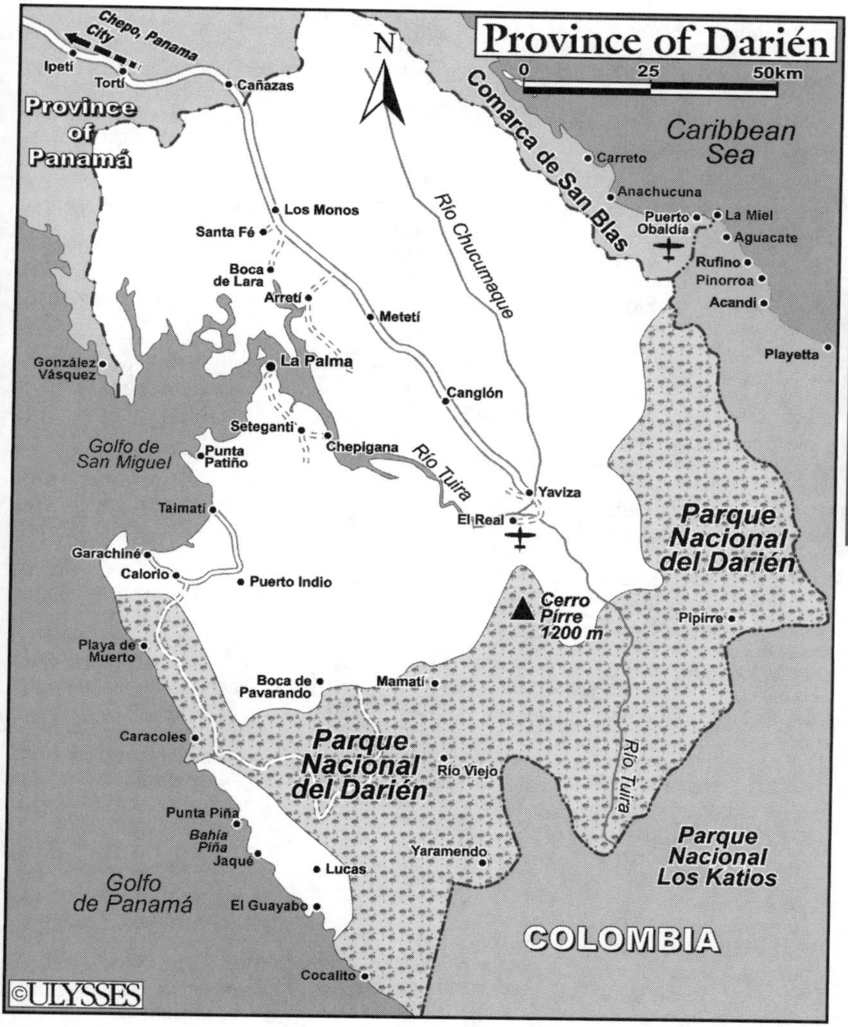

dark-coloured juice, and during certain festivities adorn themselves with animal teeth, feathers and shells. They also wear unusually wide silver bracelets, and earrings in the shape of half-moons, from which hang a series of other objects of various shapes. These earrings are held in place by two little sticks, which pierce the earlobes and are tied together with a string at the nape of the neck.

Curiously enough, the number of albinos born to Chocoe women appears to be relatively high. These children are believed to have been conceived supernaturally; born of the moon (according to Chocoe symbolism, the sun represents man and the moon woman), they are most highly venerated when they are female. Like the Kunas, the Chocoes do not mix with other groups (Kunas, Panamanians, etc.), and only unions within the tribe are accepted. They remain among the most isolated and "primitive" indigenous peoples on the planet.

In the capital, La Palma, and in sizeable villages like El Real or Yaviza, the population consists mainly of descendants of *cimarrones* (see p 134), black slaves who escaped during the Spanish colonization. Most took refuge in these areas, which were hard to reach during that era, and established themselves as farmers.

Unfortunately, as a result of continual soil impoverishment on the Azuero peninsula, many farmers have settled in this province, mostly around the huge gulf of San Miguel. Using the same cultivation methods (intensive deforestation and "slash and burn"), they are currently recreating the same conditions that forced them to move in the first place. This danger is exacerbated by the fact that large forestry multinationals, always on the lookout for high-quality wood, are pressuring the government, promising jobs and significant financial gains. If the Panamanian government is not careful, a part of Darién risks suffering the same fate as the peninsula. Aside from the indigenous villages, the Ancón-run stations of Cana and Punta Patiño, and the province's capital (La Palma), which boasts lovely surroundings, most communities in this region have no attractions as such and are of little interest to visitors.

Parks

★ Parque Nacional Darién

Parque Nacional del Darién is the largest protected park in Panamá, with a surface area of 579,000ha. Created in 1980, it was a natural addition to Parque Nacional Los Katíos (70,000ha) on the Colombian side of the border, which was established in 1973. With its coastal swamps, mountains and dense tropical forest, it is considered by experts to cover the most diverse territory of any national park in tropical America. With 2,440 plant and animal species thus far inventoried (and research continues!), this is one of the richest parks in all of Central America. There are as many as ten different types of vegetation and no less than 23 endemic animal species, including five kinds of felines (such as pumas and jaguars). Among the 400 bird species, there is the famous harpy eagle, one of the most powerful raptors on earth. Tapirs and peccaries can also be seen.

The park is home to more than 60% of the mammals found on the entire isthmus. As a result, it was declared a UNESCO Biosphere Reserve in 1983 and classified as a World Heritage Site in 1981. Mining operations have been banned in the park since the introduction of a Panamanian law in 1996. The park is also the source of the gigantic Tuira River, fed by the Río Chucumaque, on whose banks live many indigenous communities.

Since 1993, Ancón has established two large research centres in the province, one at Punta Piño bordering the gulf of San Miguel, and the other in Parque Nacional del Darién itself, at Santa Cruz de Cana. Although it primarily hosts scientists, the organization is now open to travellers, to whom it offers educational visits (see below). Due to its great diversity of birds, the Cana location is said to be one of the best spots in all of Central America for bird watching. Using the services of local guides, amateur ornithologists will have no problem spotting many exotic birds, and even, with a bit of luck, the powerful harpy eagle, symbol of Panamá.

Because of its isolation and inherent dangers (poisonous snakes, disease-carrying mosquitoes), inexperienced visitors are **strongly advised** not to venture into the park alone. Drug traffickers who frequent this region can also pose a serious threat to travellers.

The disappearance of a Canadian tourist several years ago, as well as missionary kidnappings in the region, illustrate the risks faced by those who wish to get there on their own.

Across Darién on Foot

(An account of Joëlle Jenny's trip through Darién in 1991)

How long has it been since I left the river? Three hours? Four, maybe? No point in looking at my travel clock, since it stopped working yesterday because of the humidity. I begin to worry: I passed that ridge of mountains a long time ago, and I should have reached the second river a little while after. But how can I be sure? Twice now I have confused the trail—scarcely marked—with tracks made by columns of ants. The first time, I had to go in circles for 10 minutes before getting back to the real trail. The vegetation is so thick I can hardly see the sun. I feel tiny: lost in an ocean of green.

The day is coming to an end. The long thorns covering most of the trunks scratch me whenever I carelessly lean on something. And still there is no *río*. Even walking slowly I should have reached it long ago. To continue this way would be madness. Better to retrace my steps and go back to the river I left this morning, before I run out of water: in sticky air like this, the body can become dehydrated very quickly.

Now it's night: black as ink. I hook up my hammock between two trees. My pocket flashlight has not survived the humidity any better than the clock did and in any event, I prefer not to take the risk of being spotted. Weeks can go by with no one coming this way, but still it's better to be careful. Despite fatigue, I have trouble getting to sleep. In the pitch darkness of this moonless night, I live only by my senses, fascinated by the noises around me: yelps, shrieks, the shaking of leaves. Monkeys? Pumas? Better not think about it...

With the dawn, I start off again, drained by several days of walking. Finally, at the base of a rock, a small trickle of water. What relief! Now I can wash and replenish my supplies! The cares of the night fade quickly: an animal runs by, a bird sings, a plant with blue berries stands out in this emerald universe. Everywhere there is a celebration of life. And early in the afternoon, my last fears take flight as I finally come upon the *río* I had left the day before. I roll in the water, drunk with the joy of being where I am. No more need to worry: I had been told that if I had any problems, all I needed to do was to follow the river, and after a day or two's walking I would find a native village. Then all I will have to do is find a boat...

Time to cook a little rice, then set off again.

For this reason, we have limited our descriptions to supervised accommodations that present minimal risks to travellers. Finally, keep in mind that an ANAM permit (see p 66) is required to visit the park.

Accommodations

Santa Cruz de Cana

Ancón Expeditions
Calle Elvira Méndez, in front of the Bolsa, Edificio El Dorado
☎269-9414 or 269-9415
www.anconexpeditions.com
Through its subsidiary, Ancón, Ancón Expeditions has recently started hosting travellers at its research centre in Santa Cruz de Cana, at the foot of Mount Pirre, in Parque Nacional del Darién itself. In addition to being located in the heart of one of the largest bird reserves in Central America, the centre is close to a former 19th-century gold mine. Originally worked by an Englishman, the mine rapidly fell into disuse once the stores of precious metal were exhausted.

Today, travellers can admire the small locomotive and ovens once used to extract gold, which are displayed on a grassy plot. Package tours last four days *(B/.1.327 per person, double occupancy)* and include all transportation fees, meals, guided forest hikes and a tour of the mine. There is also the option of an overnight camping trip, sleeping in tents at the summit of Cerro Pirre (1,200m). The rooms at the Ancón station are very modest (no hot water, shared washrooms) but renovations are in the works to make them more comfortable. This package will be most appealing to people willing to sacrifice some personal comfort in order to have a unique experience in the wild.

Punta Patiño

Ancón Expeditions
Calle Elvira Méndez, in front of the Bolsa, Edificio El Dorado
☎269-9414 or 269-9415
www.anconexpeditions.com
Ancón Expeditions welcomes travellers to the Ancón Research Centre in the Punta Patiño natural reserve on the gulf of San Miguel. The three-day package *(B/.550 per person, double occupancy)* includes a round-trip plane ticket from the capital to La Palma, the boat trip to the research centre, meals and several guided hikes.

Several boat excursions are also organized, including one on the Mogué River to visit an Emberá village. The rooms are located in 10 modest *cabañas*. Again, this trip will appeal primarily to those for whom the comforts of home are not a priority.

Piñas Bay

Tropic Star Lodge
B/.3,165 per week per person quadruple occupancy, including meals, transportation from the capital, and various fishing excursions
pb, ≡, ≈, hw
635 N. Rio Grande Dr., Orlando, FL 32804, U.S.A.
☎(407) 423-9931
☎800-682-3424
If you have a passion for fishing and complete isolation, the Tropic Star Lodge is the place for you. This luxurious fishing club also offers deep-sea fishing packages. A number of world records have been broken here. The place is absolutely beautiful and offers all the comforts of a grand hotel (swimming pool, air conditioning, etc.). Although it very expensive, you could be even rewarded with the sighting of a celebrity!

Glossary

Consonants

b Is pronounced **b** or sometimes a soft **v**, depending on the region or the person: *bizcocho* (biz-koh-choh or viz-koh-choh).

c As in English, *c* is pronounced as **s** before *i* and *e*: *cerro* (seh-rroh). When it is placed in front of other vowels, it is hard and pronounced as **k**: *carro* (kah-rroh). The *c* is also hard when it comes before a consonant, except before an *h* (see further below).

d Is pronounced like a soft **d**: *dar* (dahr). *D* is usually not pronounced when at the end of a word.

g As with the *c*, *g* is soft before an *i* or an *e*, and is pronounced like a soft **h**: *gente* (hente). In front of other vowels and consonants, the *g* is hard: *golf* (pronounced the same way as in English).

ch Pronounced **ch**, as in English: *leche* (le-che). Like the *ll*, this combination is considered a single letter in the Spanish alphabet, listed separately in dictionaries and telephone directories.

h Is not pronounced: *hora* (oh-ra).

j Is pronounced like a guttural **h**, as in "him".

ll Is pronounced like a hard **y**, as in "yes": *llamar* (yah-mar). In some regions, such as central Colombia, *ll* is pronounced as a soft **g**, as in "mirage" (*Medellín* is pronounced Medegin). Like the *ch*, this combination is considered a single letter in the Spanish alphabet, and is listed separately in dictionaries and telephone directories.

ñ Is pronounced like the **ni** in "onion", or the **ny** in "canyon": *señora* (seh-nyo-rah).

qu Is pronounced **k**: *aquí* (ah-kee).

r Is rolled, as the Irish or Italian pronunciation of **r**.

s Is always pronounced **s** like "sign": *casa* (cah-ssah).

v Is pronounced like a **b**: *vino* (bee-noh).

z Is pronounced like **s**: *paz* (pahss).

Vowels

a Is always pronounced **ah** as in "part", and never *ay* as in "day": *faro* (fah-roh).

e Is pronounced **eh** as in "elf," and never *ey* as in "grey or "ee" as in "key": *helado* (eh-lah-doh].

i Is always pronounced **ee**: *cine* (see-neh).

o Is always pronounced **oh** as in "cone": *copa* (koh-pah).

u Is always pronounced **oo**: *universidad* (oo-nee-ver-see-dah).

All other letters are pronounced the same as in English.

Stressing Syllables

In Spanish, syllables are differently stressed. This stress is very important, and emphasizing the right syllable might even be necessary to make yourself understood. If a vowel has an accent, this syllable is the one that should be stressed. If there is no accent, follow this rule:

Stress the second-last syllable of any word that ends with a vowel: *a***mi***go.*

Stress the last syllable of any word that ends in a consonant, except for **s** (plural of nouns and adjectives) or **n** (plural of nouns): *us***ted** (but *a***mi***gos*, **ha***blan*).

Frequently Used Words and Expressions

Greetings

Goodbye	*adiós, hasta luego*
Good afternoon and good evening	*buenas tardes*
Hi (casual)	*hola*
Good morning	*buenos días*
Good night	*buenas noches*
Thank-you	*gracias*
Please	*por favor*
You are welcome	*de nada*
Excuse me	*perdone/a*
My name is...	*mi nombre es...*
What is your name?	*¿cómo se llama usted?*
no/yes	no/*sí*
Do you speak English?	*¿habla usted inglés?*
Slower, please	*más despacio, por favor*
I am sorry, I don't speak Spanish	*Lo siento, no hablo español*
How are you?	*¿qué tal?*
I am fine	*estoy bien*
I am American (male/female)	*Soy estadounidense*
I am Australian	*Soy autraliano/a*
I am Belgian	*Soy belga*
I am British (male/female)	*Soy británico/a*
I am Canadian	*Soy canadiense*
I am German (male/female)	*Soy alemán/a*
I am Italian (male/female)	*Soy italiano/a*
I am Swiss	*Soy suizo*
I am a tourist	*Soy turista*
single (m/f)	*soltero/a*
divorced (m/f)	*divorciado/a*
married (m/f)	*casado/a*
friend (m/f)	*amigo/a*

child (m/f)	*niño/a*
husband, wife	*esposo/a*
mother, father	*madre, padre*
brother, sister	*hermano/a*
widower widow	*viudo/a*
I am hungry	*tengo hambre*
I am ill	*estoy enfermo/a*
I am thirsty	*tengo sed*

Directions

beside	*al lado de*
to the right	*a la derecha*
to the left	*a la izquierda*
here, there	*aquí, allí*
into, inside	*dentro*
outside	*fuera*
behind	*detrás*
in front of	*delante*
between	*entre*
far from	*lejos de*
Where is ... ?	*¿dónde está ... ?*
To get to ...?	*¿para ir a...?*
near	*cerca de*
straight ahead	*todo recto*

Money

money	*dinero / plata*
credit card	*tarjeta de crédito*
exchange	*cambio*
traveller's cheque	*cheque de viaje*
I don't have any money	*no tengo dinero*
The bill, please	*la cuenta, por favor*
receipt	*recibo*

Shopping

store	*tienda*
market	*mercado*
open, closed	*abierto/a, cerrado/a*
How much is this?	*¿cuánto es?*
to buy, to sell	*comprar*, vender
the customer	*el / la cliente*
salesman	*vendedor*
saleswoman	*vendedora*
I need...	*necesito...*
I would like...	*yo quisiera...*
batteries	*pilas*
blouse	*blusa*
cameras	*cámaras*
cosmetics and perfumes	*cosméticos y perfumes*
cotton	*algodón*
dress jacket	*saco*
eyeglasses	*lentes, gafas*
fabric	*tela*
film	*película*

Glossary

gifts	*regalos*
gold	*oro*
handbag	*bolsa*
hat	*sombrero*
jewellery	*joyería*
leather	*cuero, piel*
local crafts	*artesanía*
magazines	*revistas*
newpapers	*periódicos*
pants	*pantalones*
records, cassettes	*discos, casetas*
sandals	*sandalias*
shirt	*camisa*
shoes	*zapatos*
silver	*plata*
skirt	*falda*
sun screen products	*productos solares*
T-shirt	*camiseta*
watch	*reloj*
wool	*lana*

Miscellaneous

a little	*poco*
a lot	*mucho*
good (m/f)	*bueno/a*
bad (m/f)	*malo/a*
beautiful (m/f)	*hermoso/a*
pretty (m/f)	*bonito/a*
ugly	*feo*
big	*grande*
tall (m/f)	*alto/a*
small (m/f)	*pequeño/a*
short (length) (m/f)	*corto/a*
short (person) (m/f)	*bajo/a*
cold (m/f)	*frío/a*
hot	*caliente*
dark (m/f)	*oscuro/a*
light (colour)	*claro*
do not touch	*no tocar*
expensive (m/f)	*caro/a*
cheap (m/f)	*barato/a*
fat (m/f)	*gordo/a*
slim, skinny (m/f)	*delgado/a*
heavy (m/f)	*pesado/a*
light (weight) (m/f)	*ligero/a*
less	*menos*
more	*más*
narrow (m/f)	*estrecho/a*
wide (m/f)	*ancho/a*
new (m/f)	*nuevo/a*
old (m/f)	*viejo/a*
nothing	*nada*
something (m/f)	*algo/a*
quickly	*rápidamente*
slowly (m/f)	*despacio/a*
What is this?	*¿qué es esto?*

when?	*¿cuando?*
where?	*¿dónde?*

Time

in the afternoon, early evening	*por la tarde*
at night	*por la noche*
in the daytime	*por el día*
in the morning	*por la mañana*
minute	*minuto*
month	*mes*
ever	*jamás*
never	*nunca*
now	*ahora*
today	*hoy*
yesterday	*ayer*
tomorrow	*mañana*
What time is it?	*¿qué hora es?*
hour	*hora*
week	*semana*
year	*año*
Sunday	*domingo*
Monday	*lunes*
Tuesday	*martes*
Wednesday	*miércoles*
Thursday	*jueves*
Friday	*viernes*
Saturday	*sábado*
January	*enero*
February	*febrero*
March	*marzo*
April	*abril*
May	*mayo*
June	*junio*
July	*julio*
August	*agosto*
September	*septiembre*
October	*octubre*
November	*noviembre*
December	*diciembre*

Weather

It is cold	*hace frío*
It is warm	*hace calor*
It is very hot	*hace mucho calor*
sun	*sol*
It is sunny	*hace sol*
It is cloudy	*está nublado*
rain	*lluvia*
It is raining	*está lloviendo*
wind	*viento*
It is windy	*hay viento*
snow	*nieve*
damp	*húmedo*
dry	*seco*

storm	*tormenta*
hurricane	*huracán*

Communication

air mail	*correos aéreo*
collect call	*llamada por cobrar*
dial the number	*marcar el número*
area code, country code	*código*
envelope	*sobre*
long distance	*larga distancia*
post office	*correo*
rate	*tarifa*
stamps	*estampillas*
telegram	*telegrama*
telephone book	*un guia telefónica*
wait for the tone	*esperar la señal*

Activities

beach	*playa*
museum or gallery	*museo*
scuba diving	*buceo*
to swim	*bañarse*
to walk around	*pasear*
hiking	*caminata*
trail	*pista, sendero*
cycling	*ciclismo*
fishing	*pesca*

Transportation

arrival, departure	*llegada, salida*
on time	*a tiempo*
cancelled (m/f)	*anulado/a*
one way ticket	*ida*
return	*regreso*
round trip	*ida y vuelta*
schedule	*horario*
baggage	*equipajes*
north, south	*norte, sur*
east, west	*este, oeste*
avenue	*avenida*
street	*calle*
highway	*carretera*
expressway	*autopista*
airplane	*avión*
airport	*aeropuerto*
bicycle	*bicicleta*
boat	*barco*
bus	*bus*
bus stop	*parada*
bus terminal	*terminal*
train	*tren*
train crossing	*crucero ferrocarril*
station	*estación*
neighbourhood	*barrio*

collective taxi	*colectivo*
corner	*esquina*
express	*rápido*
safe	*seguro/a*
be careful	*cuidado*
car	*coche, carro*
To rent a car	*alquilar un auto*
gas	*gasolina*
gas station	*gasolinera*
no parking	*no estacionar*
no passing	*no adelantar*
parking	*parqueo*
pedestrian	*peaton*
road closed, no through traffic	*no hay paso*
slow down	*reduzca velocidad*
speed limit	*velocidad permitida*
stop	*alto*
stop! (an order)	*pare*
traffic light	*semáforo*

Accommodation

cabin, bungalow	*cabaña*
accommodation	*alojamiento*
double, for two people	*doble*
single, for one person	*sencillo*
high season	*temporada alta*
low season	*temporada baja*
bed	*cama*
floor (first, second...)	*piso*
main floor	*planta baja*
manager	*gerente, jefe*
double bed	*cama matrimonial*
cot	*camita*
bathroom	*baños*
with private bathroom	*con baño privado*
hot water	*agua caliente*
breakfast	*desayuno*
elevator	*ascensor*
air conditioning	*aire acondicionado*
fan	*ventilador, abanico*
pool	*piscina, alberca*
room	*habitación*

Numbers

1	*uno*	12	*doce*
2	*dos*	13	*trece*
3	*tres*	14	*catorce*
4	*cuatro*	15	*quince*
5	*cinco*	16	*dieciséis*
6	*seis*	17	*diecisiete*
7	*siete*	18	*dieciocho*
8	*ocho*	19	*diecinueve*
9	*nueve*	20	*veinte*
10	*diez*	21	*veintiuno*
11	*once*	22	*veintidós*

23	*veintitrés*
24	*veinticuatro*
25	*veinticinco*
26	*veintiséis*
27	*veintisiete*
28	*veintiocho*
29	*veintinueve*
30	*treinta*
31	*treinta y uno*
32	*treinta y dos*
40	*cuarenta*
50	*cincuenta*
60	*sesenta*
70	*setenta*
80	*ochenta*
90	*noventa*
100	*cien*
101	*ciento uno*
102	*ciento dos*
200	*doscientos*
300	*trescientos*
400	*quatrocientoa*
500	*quinientos*
600	*seiscientos*
700	*sietecientos*
800	*ochocientos*
900	*novecientos*
1,000	*mil*
1,100	*mil cien*
1,200	*mil doscientos*
2000	*dos mil*
3000	*tres mil*
10,000	*diez mil*
100,000	*cien mil*
1,000,000	*un millón*

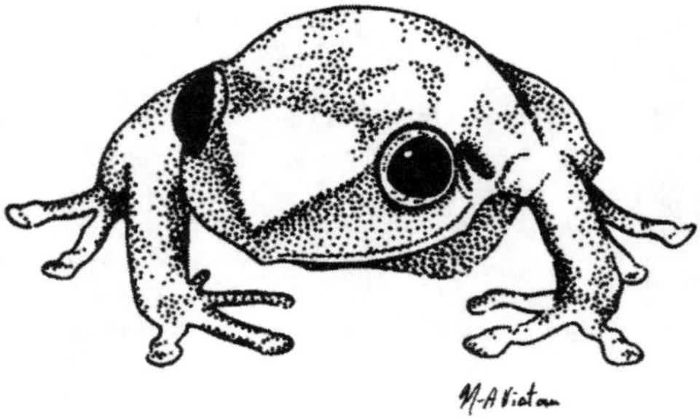

Index

Index